MODER

Also available from Lyceum Books, Inc.

3RD EDITION

Modern Social Work Theory

Malcolm Payne

LYCEUM

BOOKS, INC.

5758 S. Blackstone Ave.
Chicago, Illinois 60637

For Susan

Published by

LYCEUM BOOKS, INC.
5758 S. Blackstone Ave.
Chicago, Illinois 60637

Tel: 773 643–1902
Fax: 773 643–1903

Library of Congress Cataloging-in-Publication Data
Payne, Malcolm, 1947–
  Modern social work theory / Malcolm Payne ; foreword by Stephen Anderson.—3rd ed.
    p. cm.
  Includes bibliographical references and index.
  ISBN 0–925065–83–8 (alk. paper)
  1. Social service—Philosophy. I. Title.
HV40.P33 2005
361.3'01—dc22   2004030918

Printed in Great Britain

Foreword

Since it was first published in 1991, *Modern Social Work Theory* has become one of the major social work education texts. It provides one of the more thorough and complete reviews of contemporary social work practice theories. A key strength of the text is that it presents a range of social work theories that reflect social work practice from an international perspective. Thus, the text provides the reader with perspectives not only from other Western countries, but also from other divergent spiritual and cultural views. Further, it is a text that provides an examination of the construction, use, and assessment of social work theory for practice. The text continues to be one of the most intellectually stimulating treatments of contemporary social work theory available today.

The third edition of the text continues to provide its users with an updated bibliography while retaining the classic references for the different theoretical perspectives. In addition, the text has become more helpful in a number of ways. First, the author has moved the chapter on assessing social work theories from the end to the front of the text. Thus, there is a logical progression from the construction of social work theory and the use of theory in practice to the assessment of theory. The remaining chapters focus on the presentation of the various theories. Each chapter includes an introduction to the chapter, a summary of the major points of the theory, and the practice issues and concepts introduced by each theory. In addition, each chapter contains a case study with questions to stimulate critical thinking and a comparison with other theoretical perspectives. The number of tables and illustrations presenting theories in visual form has also increased.

The content of the text has been updated to reflect current debates about differing ways of viewing theory today. The chapter on psychodynamic perspectives has been expanded to include coverage on attachment theory. The chapter on social psychology pulls it together with a discussion of social construction and the chapter on humanism and existentialism now includes a thorough discussion of spirituality. Feminist perspectives are now presented as a separate chapter. The revisions to this edition are substantive and serve to reflect the current state of social work theory for practice.

I remain as enthusiastic about this text today as I did when I first reviewed the manuscript of the first edition over 13 years ago. It is a rich text for either undergraduate or graduate-level students to learn about and differentiate divergent social work theories. A significant strength of this text over others has always been the inclusion of social development, feminist and radical theories that are not often covered in texts written in the United States. Yet, these theories are often at the forefront of practice in other parts of the world. With the current emphasis on globalism and the preparation of practitioners to practice in a global context, this text stands out above all others. Over time, the text has only become richer and once again, Malcolm Payne has provided a stimulating contribution to our profession.

DR. STEPHEN C. ANDERSON, LISW
DIRECTOR AND PROFESSOR
School of Social Work
New Mexico State University

Contents

List of Figures

List of Tables

Preface to the Third Edition

Since the first edition of this book in 1991, many people have helped me in my understanding about social work theory. They are now too numerous to mention, so I have stopped listing them in these acknowledgements. Please accept my grateful thanks for the personal support and many corrections. I have often failed to respond to advice and comments (sometimes because they were conflicting). I am frequently told that this book is too difficult (to which I reply that it is difficult to understand and work with theory) or that it is too simple (to which I reply that any abbreviated general review can only form an introduction to the complexities and full glories of the real thing).

This new edition contains substantial changes throughout. None of the example texts used in the first edition now remains, and many used in the second edition have also been replaced. The discussion in Chapters 1, 2 and 3 (in the second edition, 1, 2 and 13) about the social construction of theory, its use in practice and its evaluation have been totally recast yet again to reflect my changing views, debate within social work and the increased availability of insightful literature. The chapters on humanism and existentialism and on social psychology have been substantially changed to include spirituality and construction theory respectively. New example texts appear in Chapters 4: two new texts; 5: one new text; 6: new edition; 8: one new text; 11: new edition and new text; 12: one new text; 13: one new text; 14: one new text. The material concerning radical/critical practice (11–14) has been extensively renewed and recast into four chapters, from three, feminism attaining its own chapter. This has led to a substantial reassessment of these aspects of social work theory. The separation is somewhat artificial, as the amount of cross-referencing between these chapters shows, but I believe it makes the different strands of thought clearer and gives feminist ideas their theoretical importance, even though I believe there is not yet a comprehensive account of their application to social work generically, but rather detailed work on feminist priorities and extensive evidence of its influence on critical theory. I have continued to update the bibliography and there are nearly 300 new references, while some older citations have been dropped. Nevertheless, I hope the book still remains a useful bibliographic resource, with over 1200 citations to the literature, about a third of them post-1995, representing a balance between the up to date with the classics of social work theory and useful older material.

The book's structure

The book is now in two parts. The first three chapters, which comprise Part I, present general discussion about social work practice theory – what we mean by this, what it consists of, and how broadly we can use it to become better social work practitioners. Part II (Chapters 4–14) reviews groups of theories in terms of their main themes and applications, making an assessment of their value. The chapters of this section follow a set structure, briefly outlined below. An asterisk indicates sections that are new to the third edition.

- *What this chapter is about*, a brief introduction to its contents
- *Main points*, a summary of the major points made in the chapter
- *Practice issues and concepts* introduced by each theory are then noted
- *Wider theoretical perspectives*, indicating some sources of ideas from outside social work
- *Connections*, discussing the relationships between the theory and other social work ideas
- *The politics of the theory*, discussing debates about its nature and content
- *Major statements*, noting briefly major works that have influenced the contemporary use of the theory
- *Example texts* showing how one or two writers use the theoretical ideas reviewed in the chapter to present a generic application of it to social work practice
- *Critical practice focuses* in each chapter. These contain a brief account of a case situation relevant to the chapter and questions to encourage critical thinking about the application of the main ideas of that chapter and alternative theories that might criticise the approach of the theories dealt with in that chapter
- *Commentary*, a discussion and evaluation of the theory, basically a for and against discussion
- *An overview of the theory* as a contributor to social work.
- *Further reading*, including reference to journals and internet sites.

I have also extended two features of previous editions in chapters where I think I can achieve a helpful result: a diagram showing aspects of a particular theory, and a table setting out the main points of the practice guidance given by the major writers reviewed. I hope that these will be useful to those who prefer a visual or structured presentation, rather than a narrative account.

I am grateful for the support and stimulation of my colleagues at the Department of Applied Community Studies, Manchester Metropolitan University and the Swedish School of Social Science and Department of Social Policy, University of Helsinki, where I have been privileged to work over the past few years.

I have continued to restrain the size of the volume, so that it remains accessible. This reduces the breadth of coverage, and means that to any expert in a particular theory my account of it is only a beginning. Judgements about what to put in and take out and my, at times heavy, condensation are disputable and disputed. However, my aim is to give access to a range of ideas useful to those who would know social work more fully. I can only repeat, below with emphasis, the final paragraph of the acknowledgements in the first edition.

Clearly, any writer of a review of social work theory relies on the ideas of other writers, and I commend any reader to progress from this introduction to the comprehensive accounts to be found in the books and articles referred to. I have found them stimulating and full of ideas for practice and understanding. I am sure you will do so, too.

MALCOLM PAYNE
Sutton, Surrey

Acknowledgements

The publishers and author wish to thank the following for permission to reproduce copyright material:

Colin Whittington and Ray Holland (1985) 'A Framework for Theory in Social Work', *Issues in Social Work Education*, **5**(1), published by the Association for Teachers in Social Work Education, and David Howe (1987) *An Introduction to Social Work Theory*, published by Wildwood House, for Figure 3.1.

Every effort has been made to trace all the copyright holders, but if any have been inadvertently overlooked the publishers will be pleased to make the necessary arrangements at the first opportunity.

A Note on Terminology

'Clients' and other words for the people we work with

There are problems with putting people into categories. Many social workers dislike giving the people they work with category names like 'client', 'patient', 'resident' and 'user'. It sometimes leads to them being called 'the clients' or 'the users' in a disrespectful way, and all these terms are unacceptable to some of the people to whom they are applied.

Different countries have varying preferences. Since this book has an international circulation, I have often used the term 'client' as the most inclusive and generally understandable term for its wide range of readers. I use other terms where the circumstances are appropriate, for example 'patients' when referring to health care situations, 'residents' when referring to residential care and 'users' when referring to people who are receiving packages of services or referring to services to people with learning disabilities, where this term has the widest currency.

PART I

Thinking about social work theory

CHAPTER I

The Construction of Social Work Theory

What this chapter is about

How do social workers know what to do when they do social work?

At this moment, somewhere in the world, 'clients' are struggling into an office to meet with a 'social worker'. Perhaps the worker is visiting the client's home, or works with clients in groups, in residential or day care, or in community work. In most societies, this something called 'social work' goes on. It is widely enough spread for international associations of social workers and a shared language and literature of social work to exist, so people must assume that these social workers are doing something useful. Their agencies are tasked with the realities of life: with crisis and disaster and everyday human problems.

What they do emerges from expectations taken up from that society. In particular, people form or construct social work and its agencies by their demands and expectations, and therefore social workers and their agencies are influenced to change by their experiences with the people they serve. Clients and their experiences are the realities that social work has to deal with; they make social work what it is. Workers, clients and agencies contribute to some extent to any society's expectations and its political and social processes by their own thinking and doing. That is a process of social construction in which people who do things together and as part of the same social organisations come to share common views of the world that they see as a social reality. It is a circular process, with each element – agency, client, social worker – influencing each other and all in the context of the social expectations that come from their wider social relations and the practical realities they all face. I explain more about social construction in Chapters 3 and 7.

This book is about the social work practice theory that claims to guide social workers in what to do when the social construction 'social work' interacts with the realities of life. The first part, Chapters 1–3, provides a general introduction to debates about theory in social work. Theory is a contested idea, that is, people argue about what a theory is or ought to be. This first chapter, therefore, examines practice theories, the focus of this book, and distinguishes them from other types of theory about social work. Among those theories are ideas about what social work is, because how we practise inevitably depends on what we think our aims are. So Chapter 1 goes on to discuss how social work is constructed as social workers, agencies and clients interact with the reality of the world around them.

Chapter 2 focuses on how theory may be used in a practical activity such as social work. Chapter 3 on 'issues in social work theory' identifies the range of social work practice theories and goes on to look at debate about how we assess them. Chapters 4–14 each discuss a group of theories that are current in social work at the time of writing. These show how particular theories are used in practice.

MAIN POINTS

> ▶ The main aim of the book is to review social work practice theories.

> ▶ All practice is influenced by formal and informal theories of what social work is, how to do social work and the client world.

> ▶ Practice theories participate in a politics, in which groups within the profession contend to gain influence over practice by achieving influence for particular theories.

> ▶ The discourse between three perspectives of social work (reflexive-therapeutic, socialist-collectivist and individualist-reformist) form the context in which social work theories are constructed as part of the politics.

> ▶ Social work is the product of modernist social organisation, in which the democratic state replaced the churches in providing welfare, and modernist assumptions about knowledge, in which science plays an important part.

> ▶ Practice theories are ways in which knowledge affects social work practice.

> ▶ Social work is socially constructed in three main arenas of debate and practice theories in the arena of relationships between clients, workers and social agencies.

Practice and practice theories

It is possible to think about social work in practical terms, for example as a sequence starting with assessment, moving on to intervention and then termination. To practice, you would follow practical guidelines perhaps based on research about effective ways to behave while carrying out activities of each kind, how to communicate for example. Defining social work through such processes can be mechanical (Morén, 1994). It takes for granted both our ideology about the aims of social work and also the practice theories that tell us what things it is important to assess, what we should intervene in and how, and when and how we should end the process. Even if guidelines tell you how best to interview someone, how would you know what to assess or how to intervene? If someone says: 'this is an effective way to interview', the next logical question is: 'effective for what purposes?' Simple 'do this, then that' guidelines conceal the theory and knowledge that underlies them. Social work practice is a process of deciding action from a variety of alternative positions (Berglind, 1992). We always have a theory that helps us decide why and how to choose between the alternatives, even if we hide it from ourselves (Howe, 1987).

Therefore, social workers need to have ideas that try to *explain* why and how we should make our practice decisions. I have three aims in this book in exploring these theories:

- To contribute to understanding how these theories and the distinctions between them may be used in practice.
- To identify different groups of theories and what they offer practitioners, making them more accessible for use in their practice.
- To contribute to understanding how theories are used in the discourse of social work practice and professional debate.

This book is a *review* of practice theories, not an attempt to construct a new theory. Therefore, I reflect what is available rather than extending it further. My focus is on *social work* and its *practice theories*, which try to explain, describe or justify what social workers do. I do not deal extensively with the wider social and psychological theories that connect to practice theories, but point to connections for you to explore.

Practice and other theory

A theory is an organised statement of ideas about the world. Fook (2002) argues that even putting names to things helps to provide explanation and understanding in practice. Many different ideas and ways of expressing them are relevant to practice. In Chapter 2, I suggest that using reflection and reflexivity as a consistent way of working through ideas as part of our work allows us to take ideas and apply them where they seem relevant. In social work, the term 'theory' covers three different possibilities:

- *Models* describe what happens during practice in a general way, in a wide range of situations and in a structured form, so that they extract certain principles and patterns of activity which give practice consistency. Models help you to structure and organise how you approach a complicated situation. A good example is task-centred practice (Chapter 5).
- *Perspectives* express values or views of the world which allow participants to order their minds sufficiently to be able to manage themselves while participating. Perspectives help you to think about what is happening in an organised way. Applying different perspectives can help you see situations from different points of view. Examples of perspectives are feminist (Chapter 12) or systems theories (Chapter 7).
- *Explanatory theory* accounts for why an action results in or causes particular consequences and identifies the circumstances in which it does so. Some writers reserve the word 'theory' to ideas that offer this causal explanation. To them, theories have to tell you 'what works'. Cognitive-behavioural theory (Chapter 6) is an example of explanatory theory.

Perspective, theory and model are all necessary in a theory that is to be useful in practice. Because social work is practical action in a complex world, a theory or perspective must offer a model of explicit guidance. Failure to do so often leads to criticism (as with early radical theory) or its rejection in daily practice (as with early cognitive theory). Yet action is not entirely pragmatic, it must be based on evidence about what is valid and effective, so a model should be backed by explanatory theory. Model and explanatory theory can only gain consistency over a wide range of social work and offer general usefulness if they offer a view of the world which allows us to transfer ideas between one situation and another and order a pattern of work, so they also need to have a perspective.

Sibeon (1990) distinguishes between formal and informal theory, as shown in Table 1.1. Formal theory is written down and debated within the profession and academic work. Informal theory consists of wider theories and values that exist in society and constructions from practical experience; those everyday practices that I mentioned at the outset of this chapter. This may include ideas from formal theory.

You may need an explanation of the mention of informal theories 'inductively derived'. *Induction* means generalising from particular examples, *deduction* means arriving at conclusions about the particular instance from a general theory. For example, perhaps you have worked with several dying people who get angry, then depressed then accepting about their approaching death. It is induction if you conclude from that experience that most people will go through this sequence. Your induction gives you an informal model of the progression of emotional reactions to impending death. If you then meet a dying person who is depressed, it is deduction from your general theory if you judge that they will shortly become accepting. Induction allows you to take ideas from a particular case or a small number of cases and test them to see if they apply to other circumstances. This enables us to transfer ideas from practice into more general theories. It allows social workers to contribute to theory from their own practice.

Sibeon (1990, p. 34) also distinguishes between three different types of theory, as shown in Table 1.1. Theories of *what social work is* are part of a

Table 1.1 Types of theory

Types of theory	'Formal' theory	'Informal' theory
Theories of *what social work is*	Formal written accounts defining the nature and purposes of welfare (e.g. personal pathology, liberal reform, Marxist, feminist)	Moral, political, cultural values drawn upon by practitioners for defining 'functions' of social work
Theories of *how to do social work*	Formal written theories of practice (e.g. casework, family therapy, groupwork); applied deductively; general ideas may be applied to particular situations	Theories inductively derived from particular situations; can be tested to see if they apply to particular situations; also unwritten practice theories constructed from experience
Theories of *the client world*	Formal written social science theories and empirical data (e.g. on personality, marriage, the family, race, class, gender)	Practitioners' use of experience and general cultural meanings (e.g. the family as an institution, normal behaviour, good parenting)

Source: Adapted from Sibeon (1990); Fook (2002); Gilgun (1994a).

discourse about the meaning of social work: people do not agree about this. Such theories relate to the material considered briefly here in Chapter 1 and in Payne (1996a): that is, different views of social work which, when you put them together, construct its nature. Theories of *how to do social work* are the practice theories that are the focus of this book. Theories of *the client world* are about the phenomena, the problems, the social realities with which social workers deal. An example is attachment theory, discussed in Chapter 4, which came out of psychotherapeutic work with children and bereaved people and was developed to become a theory of practice. Theories of the client world are sometimes referred to as knowledge for social work (see Barker and Hardiker, 1981; Sutton, 1994). Much of this material is contested in the field it came from. For example, there is a literature on child development, the sociology of families and organisations, which is vigorously debated. It is useful to know about each of these, and much more, as we deal within social work agencies with children in their families. However, using this material in social work means that we must transfer it from its original discipline into social work practice, while being aware that it is not final knowledge because there will still be continuing disagreement about it. Also, agencies, child development and family sociology interact in a particular way in social work, because social workers need this information for their particular purposes, which are different from those of, say, doctors. How that interaction between different sets of knowledge from different disciplines takes place and produces social work practice is the province of the practice theories discussed in this book. Practice theories may, therefore, be seen as a device for transferring knowledge from other purposes to the purpose of assisting social work practice (see Chapter 2 on learning transfer).

The social construction of welfare and social work

People do not agree about what social work is, and different groups within social work argue for and against different views. Moreover, what they do everyday as social workers creates social work. We call it a social construction because it does not exist as a reality, but as ideas, and what it is emerges from our debates and actions.

The idea of *social construction* comes from the work of the sociologists Berger and Luckmann (1971). They maintain that, in social affairs as opposed to the natural world, 'reality' is social knowledge which guides our behaviour, but we all have different views of it. We arrive at shared views of reality by sharing our knowledge through various social processes which organise it and make it objective. Social activity becomes habitual, so we share assumptions about how things are. Also, we behave according to social conventions based on that shared knowledge. So we institutionalise these conventions as many people agree about understandings of that aspect of society. Then, these understandings become legitimised by a process that attaches 'meanings' that, in turn, integrate these ideas about reality into an organised and plausible system. Social understanding is, in this way, the product of human understandings. For those humans, it is also objective, because the knowledge of reality is widely shared. Since people grow up within those social understandings to accept their reality, they are in a sense the product of society. So there is a circular process, in which individuals contribute through institutionalisation and legitimation to the creation of social meaning within the social structure of societies. In turn, societies through individuals' participation in their structures create the conventions by which people behave. We can see a spiral of constantly shifting influence, creating and recreating structures and these changing structures recreating the conventions by which people live within them.

Although Berger and Luckmann originated the term, recently it has been more widely used in social psychology to create a view of psychology critical of the traditional positivist psychology. Influential proponents of this view are Gergen and his colleagues (Gergen, 1994, 1999; Gergen and Gergen, 2003) and, in Britain, Parker (1998). To give you a flavour, this kind of psychology would cast doubt on the traditional view that there is a personality basic to our individual identity. This is because we all have the possibility of making changes, and then we become a different person. Traditional psychology emphasises the continuity of the person, and might lead a social worker to say that it is impossible to change someone's basic beliefs. Constructionist psychology emphasises the possibility of change, and might lead a social worker to be optimistic about the possibility of personality change.

Social construction creates a politics of theory (Payne, 1992, 1996b, 1997, 2002c). I refer to a *politics* of social work because particular theories have interest groups that try to gain our acceptance of theory within social work. This goes on in professions in the same way as in ordinary social life, as part of the constant interaction about what is reality. Groups seek influence in this way because it helps them shift our understanding of the nature and practice of social work and welfare in ways they think will be useful or which fit with their political and social beliefs. In this way, proponents and supporters for a particular point of view struggle for acceptance of it, and they use theories that support their premises to gain a greater contribution for it in the overall construction of social work. One of the ways in which they do this is to gain greater impact for it in workers' actions within social work as they daily construct it with their clients in their agency contexts. So in selecting a theory to use, workers contribute to how social work is constructed, because *what they do* in social work *is* or *becomes* social work through the process of social construction. Since, in this book, we are examining the different theories or parts of them that they might select, the choices that practitioners make between the theories in this book in part contribute to how they influence the future of social work.

Figure 1.1 presents three views (Payne, 1996a, 2000a, b) of social work at the corners of a triangle; the triangle represents a discourse between them. Discourses are interactions between what people or groups say or do that indicate important differences between them in the meanings they give to something. The important differences between these views of social work connect with different political views about how welfare should be provided:

- *Reflexive-therapeutic views.* Dominelli (2002c) calls these *therapeutic helping approaches.* These see social work as seeking the best possible well-being for individuals, groups and communities in society, by promoting and facilitating growth and self-fulfilment. A constant spiral of interaction between workers and clients modifies clients' ideas and allows workers to influence them; in the same way, clients affect workers' understandings of their world as they gain experience of it. This process of mutual influence is what makes social work reflexive, so that it responds to the social concerns that workers find and gain understanding of as they practise. In these ways, clients gain power over their own feelings and way of life. Through this personal power, they are enabled to overcome or rise above suffering and disadvantage. This view expresses in social work the social democratic political philosophy – economic and social development should go hand in hand to achieve individual and social improvement. This view is basic to many ideas of the nature of social work, but the two other views modify and dispute it.

■ *Socialist-collectivist views.* These see social work as seeking cooperation and mutual support in society so that the most oppressed and disadvantaged people can gain power over their own lives. Social work facilitates by empowering people to take part in a process of learning and cooperation which creates institutions which all can own and participate in. Elites accumulate and perpetuate power and resources in society for their own benefit. By doing so, they create oppression and disadvantage which social work tries to supplant with more egalitarian relationships in society. Dominelli (2002c) calls these *emancipatory approaches* because they free people from oppression. Others (for example Pease and Fook, 1999) call them *transformational*, because they seek to transform societies for the benefit of the poorest and most oppressed. Moreover, they imply that disadvantaged and oppressed people will never gain personal or social empowerment unless society makes these transformations. Value statements about social work, such as codes of ethics, represent this objective by proposing social justice as an important value of all social work. This view expresses the socialist political philosophy – planned economies and social provision promote equality and social justice.

■ *Individualist-reformist views.* These see social work as an aspect of welfare services to individuals in societies. It meets individuals' needs and improves services of which it is a part, so that social work and the services can operate more effectively. Dominelli (2002c) calls these *maintenance approaches*, reflecting the term used by Davies (1994). They see social work as maintaining the *social order* and social fabric of society, and maintaining people during any period of difficulties they may be experiencing, so that they can recover stability again. This view expresses the liberal or rational economic political philosophy – that personal freedom in economic markets, supported by the rule of law, is the best way of organising societies.

Each view says something about the activities and purposes of social work in welfare provision in any society. Each criticises or seeks to modify the others. For example, seeking personal and social fulfilment, as in reflexive-therapeutic views, is impossible to socialist-collectivists because the interests of elites obstruct many possibilities for oppressed peoples, unless we achieve significant social change. They argue that merely accepting the social order, as reflexive-therapeutic and individualist-reformist views do, supports and enhances the interests of elites. To the socialist-collectivist, therefore, the alternative views obstruct the opportunities of oppressed people who should be the main beneficiaries of social work. To take another example, individualist-reformists say that trying to change societies to make them more equal or create personal and social fulfilment through individual and community growth are unrealistic in everyday practice. This is because most practical objectives of social work activity refer to small-scale individual change, which cannot lead to major social and personal changes. Also, stakeholders in the social services who finance and give social approval to social work activities mainly want a better fit between society and individuals. They do not seek major changes. That is why individualist-reformists prefer their approach.

However, these different views also have affinities. For example, both reflexive-therapeutic and socialist-collective views are centrally about change and development. Also, reflexive-therapeutic and individualist-reformist views are about individual work rather than social objectives. Generally, therefore, most conceptions of social work include elements of each of these views. Alternatively, they sometimes acknowledge the validity of elements of the others. For example, socialist-collective views criticise unthinking acceptance of the present social order which is often taken for granted in individualist and therapeutic views. Nevertheless, most people who take this view of social work accept helping individuals to fulfil their potential within present social systems. They often see this as a stepping stone to a changed society by promoting a series of small changes aiming towards bigger ones.

So these different views fit together or compete with each other in social work practice. Looking at Figure 1.1, if you or your agency were positioned at A (very common especially for beginning social workers), your main focus might be providing services in a therapeutic, helping relationship, as a care manager (in managed care) or in child protection. You might do very little in the way of seeking to change the world, and by being part of an official or service system, you are accepting the pattern of welfare services as it is. However, in your individual work, what you do may well be guided by eventual change objectives. For example, if you believe that relationships between men and women should be more equal, your work in families will probably reflect your views. Position B might represent someone working in a refuge for women suffering domestic

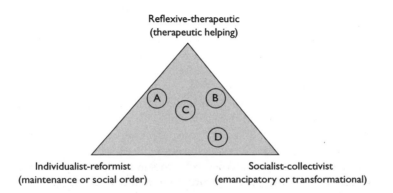

Figure 1.1 Discourse on the nature of social work

violence. Much of their work is helping therapeutically, but the very basis of their agency is changing attitudes towards women in society, and you might do some campaigning work as part of your helping role. Position C is equally balanced; some change, some service provision, some therapeutic helping. My present job is like that: to promote community development so that communities become more resilient about and respond better to people who are dying or bereaved, but I also provide help for individuals and I am responsible for liaison with other services so that our service system becomes more effective. Position D is mainly transformational but partly maintenance. This reflects the reality that seeking social change is not, in the social services, completely revolutionary, but will also seek to make the service system more effective. Many community workers, for example, are seeking quite major change in the lives of the people they serve by achieving better cooperation and sharing, but they may act by helping local groups make their area safe from crime, providing welfare rights advocacy or organising self-help playgroups in the school holidays.

Political aims in welfare, views of social work and particular practice theories link in complex ways. The links between, say, liberal or rational political theory and individualist-reformist social work and task-centred practice are clear, but the devisors of task-centred practice (Chapter 5) did not identify themselves as political liberals, and seek to devise a theory that expressed their ideas about the nature of social work. They did research, came up with an approach that seemed to work, and presented it to social workers to use. When we set it alongside other theories, we can see that it meets some of the aims and philosophies of social work and not others. The connections and commentary parts of many of the chapters in Part II of this book draw attention to some of the links and disagreements between theories that express these philosophies of welfare and views of social work.

There will never be a final answer that says social work is one thing, but we can see by looking at the discourse the sort of areas in which it operates and the sort of issues that it faces. The answers vary according to the time, social conditions and cultures where we ask these questions, because these times, social conditions and cultures contribute to the construction of social work, as workers, clients and agencies interact with each other. Nonetheless, taking part in social work requires a view about your particular balance between these aims – your own construction which guides the actions you take. It includes values appropriate to doing social work, and theories about the nature of social work; for example, sociological theories about its role in society or its relationships with other occupational groups. This analysis helps social workers to think through their view in general, and also to see what balance of views they might take in a piece of work.

Practice theories fit into and support one or other of these views of social work. They appear to form alternatives which compete for attention, and exclude one another, competing for territory. However, part of this competition represents a politics of support for a view of welfare and social work which emphasises one or other of the views on social work. Critical, anti-oppressive, feminist and empowerment perspectives, for example, implement – and exemplify the possibility of acting in – a socialist-collectivist frame of action. Existentialist, humanist and social psychological perspectives represent a more reflexive-

Table I.2 Analysis of social work theories

Type of theory	Reflexive-therapeutic	Socialist-collectivist	Individualist-reformist
Perspective:			
Comprehensive	Psychodynamic	Critical	Social development
Inclusive	Humanist, existential	Anti-oppression	Systems
Theory	Construction	Feminist	Cognitive-behavioural
Model	Crisis	Empowerment	Task-centred

therapeutic emphasis. Task-centred and systems theories are more individualist-reformist in their assumptions. An analysis of the groups of theories discussed in this book along these lines is given in Table 1.2.

This table divides perspectives into comprehensive and inclusive categories. *Comprehensive* theories claim to offer a system of thought to cover all the practice that social workers might want to undertake. They do so by offering a view of the world that organises our thoughts and gives us priorities within the range of things that might be possible. These theories are more or less supported by an evidenced body of knowledge, and the extent to which this is so might be disputed. However, the literature about them contains a great deal of commentary, analysis and prescription that is able to form the basis of a social work practice on its own. *Inclusive* theories, while they are comprehensive in this way, also explicitly permit the inclusion within them of other theories and models, provided they are used consistently with the overall outlook of the perspective.

Before looking at trends and types of theory, I want to comment first on how I have allocated theories to different cells in Table 1.2. First, I must emphasise again that the ideas of discourse between views within social work and the need for all theories to have elements of perspective, theory and model within them means that no theory can be allocated wholly to any category. We are talking about centres of focus and strengths, not absolutes. On more specific points, I want to comment on the positioning of social development, critical and anti-oppressive groups of theories. I have placed social development theories as individualist-reformist because they are generally theories that accept the current social order. Some theories of development are socialist and seek social transformation, but, generally, social development practice theories seek reform or operate on individuals and small groups or communities, rather than seeking radical social change. Critical theories have increasingly become comprehensive, since some formulations do offer a worked-out practice model and in their own terms are based on a well-constructed and evidenced theory. However, some critical theory, for example Mullaly's (2003) structural social work, is very sketchy in its practice guidance, and leaves workers to include methodologies from anywhere provided they fit with the overall ideology. Also, it is more a well-constructed edifice of ideology than a theory evidenced from social science research. Anti-oppressive theory is supported by evidence of discriminatory social relations and provides a well-worked-out explanatory account, but has less evidence for its practice prescriptions. It seeks to be more a value base and approach to practice incorporating other practice methods and so leans towards being inclusive. Empowerment and advocacy have some explanatory and ideological content, but increasingly seek to promote a practical way of doing social work within cotemporary society. This makes them, among socialist-collectivist ideas, an important explanatory base for action, even though the implications of the structuralist ideology drawn from it are disputed.

To comment more generally on Table 1.2, the three groupings of theories show how theories take different views of social work; I will remind you of this in the separate chapters of Part II. The reflexive-therapeutic column represents the ideas within social work which concern personal development and fulfilment, with an emphasis on emotions and interpersonal responses. It is concerned with personal change. The socialist-collectivist column represents the ideas within social work which focus on its social purposes. It is concerned with social change. The individualist-reformist column represents those ideas within social work which focus on its response to social and political demands for order. It is concerned with maintaining social order. If we work within a particular group, rather than take ideas from everywhere, this will have consequences for how we understand social work and what we are doing within it.

Are there paradigms of social work?

Sometimes, views of professions and areas of knowledge such as social work are called *paradigms* (pronounced 'paradymes'). This concept means a pattern or template, something which is commonly reproduced in an activity. Kuhn (1970) uses 'paradigm' to describe a general view of the nature of physical or natural phenomena in science. His influential book on the history of science suggests that scientific activity (theory-making, experimentation, methods of research, debate and so on) always builds on a paradigm. Eventually, in a scientific revolution, a completely new world view of phenomena is constructed. This changes the conception of those phenomena and forms a new paradigm.

Some writers (such as Fischer, 1981) argue that such shifts in social work conceptions have occurred. Again, this is part of a politics claiming that their view of what social work should be like is replacing an older (and, it is implied, discredited) position. Kuhn questions (1970: 15) whether the social sciences are developed enough to have built a paradigm, let alone to have had a revolution. However, Kuhn (1970: 49) accepts that minor paradigms grow up in what he calls the 'ramshackle structure of specialities'. He accepts that some people will want to claim these as paradigms before they have found wide agreement. This seems to me to be the status of the three views in social work. I think, therefore, that debates between theories which fall mainly within each view are debates between these 'minor paradigms'.

Generally, though, seeing 'paradigm' as Kuhn mainly uses the term, I argue that there is one paradigm of social work, socially constructed in the discourse between the three views, the triangle of Figure 1.1. All current theory and practice fits into this paradigm. It is in practice accepted since most social workers do what most people would recognise as similar sorts of things with their clients. We accept that the different views are present within the social work discourse, because we debate them all the time.

If theoretical ideas all fit into one paradigm, they can be an important pillar of mutual understanding and identity among social workers. They would form an element in the *social*, that is, *shared*, construction of social work. One problem with this view is that the shared understanding derives from the wide influence of Western social work theories. There has been criticism since the 1970s (Yelaja, 1970; Midgley, 1981; Osei-Hwedie, 1990, 1993) about the way Western social work ideas have been used in other cultures, allowing the culture of Western countries, and in particular the USA, to dominate knowledge. The internationalist perspective in social work education (Payne, 2005) understands the development of social work as being one stream of progress, strongly influenced by American and other English-language perspectives.

The argument against this view has been that:

- value and cultural bases of different societies may be incompatible
- societies face different problems and issues
- concerns about cultural imperialism and the history of oppressive colonialism continue to be reflected in postcolonial social and cultural relationships between Western and non-Western countries, where domination is by cultural influence rather than physical force.

On the other hand:

- Many Western countries are culturally pluralist and there is interest in different ideas. However, criticisms of multiculturalism and ethnic sensitivity (see Chapter 13) suggest that this is sometimes tokenistic or shallow.
- Cultural hegemony (exercising power by influencing people through culture) does not only work in one direction, since different colonial powers operated in different ways and there was influence in both directions. Postcolonialism is the idea that colonial influence continues through economic and cultural dominance rather than political control; some people argue that its effect is exaggerated.
- Western cultural dominance is resisted, and the more there is interference, the more likely it is that alternatives will gain credence among non-Western cultures. Some people point to the growing influence of Islam as an example.

This debate suggests that we must be careful of assuming the shared understanding and shared theoretical base of social work. In this book, I have tried to introduce alternatives to Western social work theory, for example Gandhian social work from India, perspectives from China and Africa, and social pedagogy from Europe. I have inevitably used mainly literature produced in the West, because that is where I live and so it forms the perspective from which I am writing. However, I have looked for contributions from a range of Western countries, from Australia, Canada, and various European countries as well as Britain and the USA. My intention here is to draw attention to the issue that views of social work and practice theory vary in substance and application in different social and historical contexts. That is the consequence of social construction engaging with different realities. While accepting that formal theory as currently written often originates in the single Western viewpoint, I want to raise awareness that it is widely adapted for other cultures, and that new ideas emerge from other cultures. The West can learn new possibilities from these adaptations and ideas.

In summary, then, we must be cautious about saying that social work has one paradigm or that the three views of social work are competing paradigms. This is because, as a social phenomenon, any act of social work, any organisation of an agency or any welfare system represent a mixture of elements of all these views in a different recipe, reflecting social expectations and cultures. So social work theory and how it is used is different in different countries and different agencies. Although everywhere it shares many of the same elements, the way they are put together to create social work practice in context always varies.

Is social work theory 'modern' or 'postmodern'?

I refer to 'modern' social work theory for two reasons. The first is that the social construction view is that a phenomenon such as social work can only be understood for a time and social context in which the understanding arises. People will inevitably reconstruct theories as they are affected by social changes. So only what is modern in the sense of 'current' will be fully relevant, although we can pick things up from older sets of ideas, and it is often helpful to understand where ideas come from historically.

The second reason for discussing 'modern' social work theory is because of the idea of the 'postmodern'. This connects with the politics of social work theory, because postmodern ideas represent a particular view of knowledge. *Postmodernism* refers to changes in the way in which we think about our societies and the way in which we create and understand knowledge. One of Kuhn's scientific revolutions was the shift in thinking in Europe during the Enlightenment in the 1700s and 1800s. Prior to this, we relied on the authority of religion and monarchs to tell us how to think. The Enlightenment led to an emphasis on the *scientific* method, the idea that we could develop knowledge by observing and experimenting with the real world. Each observation and experiment builds up a picture of what the real world is like, which gives us evidence for how to act. Eventually, this led to less reliance on absolute political authority, and the successive British, American and French revolutions led the way in rejecting monarchy in their different ways and promoting rational democratic authority. It also led to a decline in the social importance of religion in the West. This emphasis on rationality and scientific method has been economically and socially successful; it is called 'modernist', to distinguish it from 'traditional' reliance on authority, even though to people living now it is a fairly ancient development.

Social work is a product of *modernism*. This is because it is one of the secular replacements for the welfare role of the Christian churches in Western countries (Payne, 2005). It is also modernist because it is based on the idea that we can understand and study social problems and societies, and take rational action to deal with the problems we see. The very idea of social work theory is also modernist, because it says that we can reach a rational understanding of human beings and society and decide how to act consistently to change both people and societies according to our knowledge. Having a theory that guides action is inherently modernist – it says that we can base our actions on evidence of the world around us.

Postmodernism suggests that there is an alternative way of thinking about knowledge and understanding. These ideas arose partly as a reaction to modernist thinking; this is why they are called 'postmodern'. However, they reflect a set of ideas, 'interpretivism' (Chapter 3), that have always been present in debates about knowledge. Postmodernism points out that knowledge is always socially constructed, because the choice of which knowledge is developed is not neutral. For example, a scientist chooses to observe or experiment with particular aspects of the real world out of personal choice and because society at the time is interested in that particular area of knowledge. Another example is that people are often psychologically disturbed and socially disrupted by their experiences of war, so psychiatry and social policy develop as a result.

Another point is that when we observe or experiment in social matters, we are part of the society that creates what we are looking at, so it is difficult not to take for granted the social arrangements that we see all around us. For example, we are all part of families, and society has approved ways of forming a family, such as a man and a women marrying and having children. So, is a couple of men a family, if they live together in a gay relationship? Would they be more of a family if they adopted or fostered children? This example draws attention to our language, to the word 'family'. By using it, we often refer to the conventional model of the family, a heterosexual couple with children. That is how we 'construct' an idea of what a family is, and we compare it with other examples and think they are 'not-family'. This then has consequences for behaviour: the gay couple and their children may resent not being constructed as a family; they feel excluded and calling their arrangement a 'family' is a political statement, which seeks to change other people's views of what a family is and of them. Using this item of language is an example of a social action to try to achieve change by changing language use.

How social ideas are constructed changes. To follow the same example, twenty years ago, most people in Western countries would have taken it for granted that a gay couple was not a family and would not have children. Language also changes: they would probably have been called homosexual rather than gay, which also means cheerful, and was widely used in that way until the 1950s. In the early 2000s, some people would accept that they might be a family and might adopt children, while others feel strongly that this extends the idea of family too far and that their having children would be potentially damaging to the children. In the physical or medical sciences, once we have found something out and confirmed it in experiment, it is generally accepted as true, and we can build other knowledge on that fact. In social matters, we know that our language and knowledge will change, so it is hard to build a structure of knowledge upon it, because we cannot generalise from how it is at one time or in one place to other times and places. Also, how researchers use the term 'family' will imply something about their own views and will offend or gain the support of others who have their views. People with particular views try to use language to emphasise their views; people who dislike the views may resist this. Some people resisted the appropriation of the word 'gay' to mean 'male homosexual', for example. Language therefore becomes part of the politics of discourse.

Postmodernism, then, taking it to the extreme, says that we cannot take for granted any social knowledge. There are no essentials or foundations for knowledge so postmodernism is *anti-essentialist* and *anti-foundationalist*. This is because all knowledge has the potential for change, and we must question it all the time. Of course, as we question it, we are using language in a way that raises the possibility of changing it. Postmodern knowledge must also rely on its historical and social context. It arises out of the social relationships in any society at any particular time. This has tremendous advantages for social workers for two main reasons. First, it emphasises that change is continuous and urges us to believe that we can achieve it through social interaction. Social work seeks to make personal and social changes through social interaction, so social construction ideas emphasise the possibility of effectiveness in social work. Also, social workers often have the job of finding out about people's personal and social histories to contribute to the work of other professions and official decision-making processes. Social construction ideas suggest why this is useful as a basis for understanding and action, because we cannot understand reality without understanding historical and social contexts. It also warns that how we use language in our report-writing may have a strong influence, for good or bad, on the outcome.

Social construction is a postmodernist idea, and so therefore my presentation of social work as a social construction accepts that it is ambiguous, contested and responds to social and cultural contexts. How, then, can we deal with producing practice guidance for a constantly changing activity? To understand this, we have to look more closely at how social work is constructed in particular societies.

Arenas of social work construction

Social construction in social work is a complex of social structures and individual participants influencing each other. I have suggested (Payne, 1999) that three arenas of social construction are important for social work, as set out in Figure 1.2. Each arena influences the others. One is the *political-social-ideological arena*, in which social and political debate forms the policy that guides agencies and the purposes that they are set or develop for themselves. Social workers engage in this through professional associations and other organisations, their involvement in social issues, as activists, voters or writers, and through the influence of their agencies. Another is the *agency-professional arena* in which employers and collective organisations of employees, such as trade unions and professional associations, engage in influencing each other about the more specific elements of how social work will operate. The third is the client-worker-agency arena, which I discuss more fully below, because it is the most important arena for the focus of this book on practice theory. Each of these arenas influences the others. People who are clients can, for example, influence the political-social-philosophical arena by their votes or by rioting and many other ways. They can affect the agency-professional arena by arriving at agencies in large numbers asking for service; this will lead to practical changes in policy and practice, even if it is to exclude them.

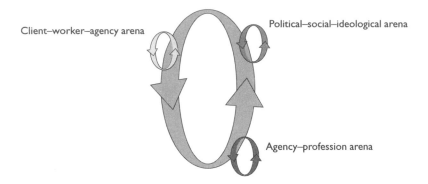

Figure 1.2 Arenas of social construction of social work

For example, in the 1980s, when HIV/AIDS first became evident, pressure groups and specialist agencies grew up to influence government and social debate. People with problems arising from HIV/AIDS came to social agencies and caused them to change their practice. These changes were negotiated in many different places, and these three arenas are only a limited selection, indicating important centres of influence.

Our focus, in this book, is on one aspect of the spiral of influences in social work, the theory that guides workers' practice: the client-worker-agency arena. At the beginning of this chapter, I suggested that in spite of cultural and national differences, social work was always constructed from three elements: client, worker and agency. So, general statements about social work and its theory must reflect an understanding about how that construction takes place. Social construction takes place in interactions with reality within social contexts.

The social construction of practice theory

We create practice theory within social work out of an interaction with social work practice, which in turn interacts with wider social contacts. Three sets of forces construct social work: those that create and control social work as an occupation; those that create people as clients who seek or are sent for social work help; and those which create the social context in which social work is practised. Evans and Kearney (1996) describe these as the central triangular relationship between worker, client and agency. Social work is a special activity where people interact in special social roles as 'social worker' and 'client'. Those roles thus partly define its nature. Sometimes other forms of social work such as care management (managed care) create the special role 'service user' instead. Understanding social work involves examining the factors which establish the social positions of these actors in a complex of social relationships. These interact over time and in a power context. There are process outcomes (for example caring and trust between the participants) which make the interaction effective in achieving desired results. These desired results in many cases produce the outcomes of social services within which practice takes place.

In encounters with clients social workers are constructed by occupational expectations, that is, the organised statements and understandings which say what a social worker is, and the social processes which define someone as a social worker. The various histories of social work, and its relationships with other occupational groups and social institutions, define its nature as an occupation. That nature changes, grows, perhaps declines in response to social changes. So, knowledge and ideas that workers use also respond to social changes.

Much professional writing ignores clients' influences on social work – they are merely the objects of an activity that theory has defined. In fact, I argue, they partly construct the activity through the process by which they become the special people called 'clients'. The client-making process is itself socially constructed, because it relies on general social understandings of the nature of social work. It is a slightly different process that would construct them as 'patients' or 'service users', if we prefer to call them that. As they bring the outside world with them into social work activity, clients change the nature of social work. In this sense, social work is a reflexive process in which clients change workers *and* the nature of social work *and* therefore also change the 'theory' of social work. Clienthood is not an invariable or absolute *state*, but is partly a matter of perception, so that if others see a person as a client, they may treat them as such. Such perceptions may be held by clients, workers, officials in the worker's agency, people in other agencies, the client's family or others in the client's social environment. Once we ascribe clienthood to someone, it often persists even if social work activity is intermittent or has stopped. Clienthood may be associated with certain sorts of people, for example those of a particular social class or living on a particular housing estate.

Since different people's perceptions of clienthood vary, we must see where those perceptions come from. This may be personal. For example, an Israeli study (Krumer-Nevo, 2003) identified three patterns of receiving help among women who lived in long-term social and economic deprivation:

- A calming pattern; help is perceived as an opportunity to escape, relax and calm down
- An empowerment pattern; help is perceived as a source of learning and strengthening
- A rebiography pattern; help is perceived as bringing a new self-awareness and personal development.

These patterns connect with the three views of social work, discussed above, being respectively individualist-reformist, socialist-collectivist and reflexive-therapeutic.

It is likely that the social institutions and their history that we examined as originators of the definition of a social worker are also influential in defining clienthood. Terms such as 'child in need' or 'vulnerable adult' in British social work gain official status through legislation or government guidance. However, 'child', 'adult', 'need' and 'vulnerable' are all words that might easily be interpreted differently in other societies, and in different agencies with varying priorities.

This brings us to defining clienthood as a process. Since clienthood is hard to understand as a state, understanding it as a *process* is more appropriate. People are becoming, acting as and moving away from being clients of social work (Payne, 1993). *The route to clienthood* only begins when someone becomes aware of some issues in their lives which need resolution. The definition of a problem, the social pressures, the route to the agency and options which were closed off on that route which led to the selection of this agency, all these may arise from general social perceptions about a problem and the agencies available. Becoming and being a client leads also to the process of ceasing to be one. This, again, involves recognising circumstances which lead to an impulsion – this time away from the agency. Understanding when it is appropriate to stop involvement with an agency is also an important factor. In any of these moves, clients are again affected by their own social understanding, information gained from the worker, legal pressures and knowledge and attitudes derived from the client's social circle.

Social work characteristically takes place in an organisational context of agencies, that is, associations of people constructed to achieve particular purposes. This is true even of private practice or working with self-help groups, which form simple, less structured agencies. Agencies are another set of social relations through which social constructions influence social work. They are formally controlled by management boards representing the communities served, by political election with government agencies, or through another nominating process with private or voluntary agencies. As organisations, they are subject to influences, whether economic, political, organisational, bureaucratic or theoretical, different from those affecting workers and clients. I have explored these points more fully elsewhere (Payne, 1996a).

The social construction view of social work that we are exploring presents the relationship between workers, clients and their agency context as *reflexive*; each affects and changes the others. A major feature of any acceptable model of social work theory, therefore, is the extent to which it can offer explanations of and guidance in dealing with the pressures put by clients on the perceptions of workers of their social circumstances. A theory which is inadequate in representing the real needs of clients as presented to agencies is likely to be only partially accepted or become supplanted.

So far, I have argued that social work *itself* is reflexive because it responds to people's demands on a service affecting workers. Theoretical development reflects this, because we reject or amend theories which fail to meet the demands actually made. So theory is constructed in an interaction between ideas and realities, mediated through the human beings involved. How clients experience their reality affects how workers think about their practice theories; agencies constrain and react to both and together they make some social work. The social work they make influences what social work is and how it is seen elsewhere.

A social work theory must therefore respond to the contemporary social construction of reality both by clients and workers and their social environments; if it fails to do so, it will be unsuccessful. The recognition of the need for theory to be reflexive like this is a feature of more modern social work theories such as ecological systems approaches, where the interaction with the environment is strongly recognised (see Chapter 7), and critical approaches (see Chapters 11–14).

According to this view of social work, its theory must be constantly changing in response to practice constructions by its participants. Therefore, accounts of its nature cannot be universal. Instead, it is a variety of activities which have common features in most social constructions of it. In saying this, we must remember Berger and Luckmann's (1971) view that a social construction is an (at least partially) *agreed* view of the world which is accepted within a social group as a 'reality'. That is, it is agreed to be at least a reasonable representation of the world which helps us to deal with things external to us. Since theory describes and explains what workers do, it must also respond to the realities of its social constructions, otherwise, we would reject or amend it. So theory is both flexible and allows us to change and develop it through practice, but it is also settled between us and changes and develops through a process of creating 'formal theory' as opposed to 'informal theory' (see Table 1.1).

CRITICAL PRACTICE FOCUS

The Gargery family

Mr Gargery, a migrant to the town from Africa, was admitted to the hospital intensive care unit following a coronary incident, received intensive treatment, then moved to an ordinary ward in the hospital, where, still being quite ill and with such a large family visiting, he was placed in his own room. The family had many teenage children, the room was always noisy, there were arguments, senior nurses had to break up a fight between two family members in the doorway of another patient's room, the television or music was often on and loud. Several members of the local church visited regularly and prayed and sang hymns for Mr Gargery's well-being, disturbing other patients. The multiprofessional team caring for Mr Gargery discussed the situation, and wondered about limiting visitors on health grounds, although this was not strictly necessary, and Mr Gargery appreciated having his family around him.

The social worker in the team has to carve out a role relevant to the team's wishes which also respects the social work role. To apply theory, the worker must select an aspect of the complicated situation. Looking at the three views of social work, you might see your role in maintaining the quiet peaceful 'social order' of the hospital for the benefit of other patients, you might be aware of the cultural and family strengths that Mr Gargery can call on and needs to maintain, you might see an opportunity for social learning or personal development for some of the younger children, whose distress at their father's illness is plain to see but is cheerfully downplayed by the senior members of the family.

Establishing your professional role in a multiprofessional situation, where the concerns are for a social institution, the hospital and Mr Gargery, the patient, is commonplace in present-day social work. You also have to accept the social work focus on the patient's interaction with his social environment and its cultural and structural effects on him and his family. What balance of approaches might you think appropriate?

What do you think the route to clienthood for Mr Gargery and his family might be? You would need to bear in mind the experience of migration and his being part of a minority ethnic group. How will that route interact with the hospital and its policies, the requirements of social work ethics and practice? How will it interact with your route to being a social worker to construct your particular social work for and with this family? Thinking about another social worker you know, how would it be different constructing social work for him or her?

Conclusion

In summary, then, I have argued that social work is socially constructed through interactions with clients, because they themselves become defined as clients by social processes, through its formation as an occupation among a network of related occupations, and through the social forces which define it through its organisational, agency and social context.

Going on from these points, the social construction of social work suggests that its theory at any time is constructed by the same social forces that construct the activity. Theory for practice will inevitably respond to current social realities, so that present interests and concerns colour it. Yet it also reflects the histories of theoretical, occupational and service context. The strength of influence of those histories in constructing contemporary theory varies from time to place to person, but they are always there, alongside present social forces.

The implication of a social construction view is that social work theory should be seen as a representation of more or less agreed understandings within various social groupings within social work, presented through the medium of language in texts which contain accounts of those theories. The struggle between competing understandings and constructions of social work is manifested in the differing theoretical constructions and languages which form the theories discussed in this book. That struggle is a politics: people and groups seek influence over social constructions of social work and thus over the actions of workers in their profession by seeking broader professional acceptance of particular theories expressed as coherent, agreed forms of understanding. In turn, this may influence perceptions of social work within welfare services and the wider society, which will start the spiral of influence again as these perceptions will affect how social workers act within their work. I explore the politics of social work theory further in Chapter 3.

I have argued that these constructions become, as a context for present construction-making, a reality for the participants. These constructions react to a real world that affects these participants. Social work, then, is created from two realities, the one constructed as a context for our present activity and the real natural world that affects us all and on which our constructions build. Consistency and continuity in what social work is and how it may be done comes from the social and natural realities that underlie our constructions. Therefore, although I am concerned to recognise how social workers construct social work in their interactions, I am also concerned to show how there is a social work to be understood, known and researched. Social work theory is a construction, interacting with a real world of social relations, but because it is a construction,

we are able to adapt and develop it as we practise, just as we can
develop and adapt by our practice. To do so, we need to have ide.
manage and inform what we do. These ideas are the social work practice
reviewed in Chapters 4–14 of this book. However, to use them, we have tᵕ
able to work in practice with those ideas, and this is the focus of Chapter 2.

FURTHER READING

Burr, V. (2003) *Social Constructionism*, 2nd edn (London: Routledge).
An accessible account of social construction theory in social psychology.

Jokinen, A., Juhila, K. and Pösö, T. (1999) *Constructing Social Work Practices* (Aldershot:
    Ashgate).
A useful collection of papers, many research-based, demonstrating how social construction ideas may be applied to social work, and how effective social construction research
may be in researching practice.

Payne, M. (1996) *What is Professional Social Work?* (Birmingham: Venture).
An extended discussion of the points summarised in this chapter about the social
construction of social work within three perspectives, and examining the construction
of practice from ideas about social work, its values, its organisational setting and dealing
with issues such as globalisation, power and professionalisation. An updated second
edition is forthcoming from Policy Press in 2006, dealing particularly with the relationship between social work and social care, that is, social work as part of wider provision
in the social and human services.

Payne, M. (2005) *The Origins of Social Work: Change and Continuity* (Basingstoke: Palgrave
    Macmillan).
This book examines the development of social work and continuing themes in its social
construction as a profession within different welfare regimes.

What is Professional Social Work? and *The Origins of Social Work: Change and Continuity* are
related to the present book and its account of how practice theory constructs social
work. Jointly, they give an extended account of the social construction of social work as
a social phenomenon, a practice activity and a profession.

WEBSITES

http://www.swap.ac.uk/
The Social Work and Policy (SWAP) website has a comprehensive, searchable set of
links to a wide range of social policy and social work websites, and gives a good picture
of social work generally.

http://www.elsc.org.uk/
The Electronic Library of Social Care contains access to a wide range of resources
included the Caredata searchable bibliography of recent social work literature.

http://www.ifsw.org/
The International Federation of Social Workers website provides access to national
associations of social workers and codes of ethics across the world, many of which have

useful resources, and contains the international definition of social work and international codes of ethics.

http://www.socialworksearch.com/
http://www.nyu.edu/socialwork/wwwrsw/
'Social work search' and 'World Wide Web resources for social workers' are useful directories of websites relevant for social work, from American bases, but with reasonable world coverage.

http://www.geocities.com/kieranodsw/index.html
'Surfing social work' – a good New Zealand-based directory.

CHAPTER 2

Using Social Work Theory in Practice

What this chapter is about

The aim of this chapter is to help workers use social work theory in their practice. This book reviews different theories proposed by various writers as useful in practice, but many workers find it hard to connect theories to the situations they come across as they practice and understand how the theories fit together as a full picture of social work.

MAIN POINTS

➤ The connections between practice and theory form a politics in which groups seek influence over social work practice.

➤ Practice/theory politics focus on four issues: application (how do we apply theory in practice?), relevance (can practice change theory?), accountability (does theory support accountability in agencies or independence?) and legitimation (is social work distinctive and socially valuable?).

➤ Learning transfer takes place between general theoretical perspectives and social work theory and vice versa.

➤ There are complex relationships between theory and practice, each having the potential to influence the other.

➤ Practitioners need to resolve issues in selecting a theory to use or being eclectic.

➤ Reflective, reflexive and critical thinking are ways to use theory in practice.

PRACTICE ISSUES AND CONCEPTS

➤ *Reflective, reflexive* and *critical thinking* as ways of making connections between theory and practice.

➤ *Learning transfer* as a way of understanding the use of theoretical knowledge in practice and practical knowledge in theoretical work.

➤ Being *selective* and *eclectic* in using ideas from different theories in a team, agency or individual practice.

The politics of theory/practice relationships

Chapter 1 examined the idea of a politics of social work theory and suggested that interest groups within social work support the adoption of particular theories to push forward their view of social work. A similar process goes on in debate about how theory relates to practice. The politics of theory and practice relationships revolves around four issues:

- *application* – can we apply theory to practice?
- *relevance* – can practice change theory and vice versa?
- *accountability* – does theory support accountability in agencies or practitioners' independence?
- *legitimation* – is social work distinctive and socially valuable?

As adults, we have a good deal of experience of human interaction, so we do not come completely new to social work. We know how we meet other people; we have worked out practical ways of understanding what other people are thinking and feeling, the 'informal theories' of Chapter 1. Once we start doing social work, we find ways of working, often fitting in with what we see around us. How are you supposed to fit a formal theory into that? Harrison (1991), an American studying British social workers, found that they did not experience work as highly programmed or ordered, but as a 'seamless integration of thought and action' following from their own typical way of thinking things through.

Sometimes, people talk about the application of theory to practice. However, Chapter 1 argues that social work is not like this. Clients and workers meet together in agencies and have an impact on each other. Other arenas of political and social life also have an influence, often through what workers, clients and agencies bring to the interaction. It is more accurate to see theory and practice as having an influence on each other.

Mutual influence also implies the interaction of interests and the use of power. During the 1980s and into the 1990s, there was considerable debate and some research (Carew, 1979; Curnock and Hardiker, 1979; Hardiker, 1981; Barbour, 1984; Harrison, 1991) about whether the theory available could be applied to practice. Carew (1979) identifies several different issues of concern: social work should be scientific, inclusive, incorporating a reasonable range of ideas, and organised in a way that permits application. As Smid and van Krieken (1984) point out, we may reasonably see arguments about application as a struggle between academic and practice institutions for influence over the nature of practice. Agencies or governments might see social work theory as being inadequate to provide the kinds of services they want to offer or social work education as not helping social workers to transfer knowledge effectively. Hindmarsh (1992) studied 22 new graduates of social work in New Zealand, and summarised much of the world literature. She argues that many people are motivated to come into social work by a sense of opposition to the status quo. Through helping others and supporting social change, they seek to act on this feeling of opposition. Their training gives them confidence, self-awareness and a personal framework of practice and identity as a worker. They experience agencies as creating barriers, through their formal management systems, to putting that confidence and identity into practice. As a result, workers become alienated and isolated. Their experiences in agencies and training play out the oppositions they experience in their view of the world.

These experiences of social workers connect with *accountability*. Workers use theory within the politics of their daily practice to offer accountability to managers, politicians, clients and the public; students are accountable to these people and to their teachers as well. Theory does this by describing acceptable practice sufficiently to enable social work activities to be checked to see that they arc appropriate. Theory may also offer justification for particular explanations of their activity. For example, it may show that the practice is effective, or in accordance with conventional guidelines for practice, how social work values are incorporated into practice, how social justice or other social purposes are implemented or how social work theories connect to wider theories used in society. In these ways, theory becomes a politics because it is used by different groups to account for or justify their work or practice to each other. Equally it might be used to criticise another group. Social workers, for example, might complain that managers fail to provide the resources to enable them to do their work as theory prescribes while managers can look at theory to ask whether social workers are doing the 'right' thing according to theory.

Another politics is about *legitimation*. Social work is expanding and taking on additional roles in many societies. However, many political and social priorities see social work as part of health and education services rather than valuable to society in its own right. Perhaps some related activity might perform social work's social roles. So, is social work practice and its theories truly of social work alone, creating a legitimate, identifiable theoretical base for social work?

I have argued elsewhere (Payne, 1996a) that social work is part of a network of occupations working in a territory or social space concerned with interpersonal and social action. These occupations, such as counselling, nursing, development work, teaching, police work and medicine, have social roles, theories, social, legal and political contexts for their practice, systems of professional organisation and education which may overlap but which also have distinctive features. Professionals may move among these occupations, or stay within the boundaries of one throughout their careers. The boundaries between these groups are more or less permeable, more or less negotiable and shift according to social expectations and preferences as they are constructed within societies.

Therefore, related professions are likely to share some aspects of their theoretical base. For each, this may be strengthening. A social worker in a psychiatric setting, for example, may be supported in daily practice by sharing a theoretical base with a professional colleague. It also helps the colleague. The availability of a range of theoretical perspectives in social work enables appropriately trained workers to work in agencies using specialised techniques, and this helps the penetration of the profession into various settings from which it might otherwise be excluded.

However, ideas as implemented within social work become distanced from the literature in related professions. Books focusing on counselling or clinical psychology, for example, deal with cognitive, behavioural and psychodynamic theories with virtually no recognition of the social work literature, although some importation from these areas is made into social work literature. There are also substantial areas of thinking, particularly from sociology, which social work incorporates but which are not represented well in related literatures. Each profession creates its own focus and interpretation of bodies of knowledge. The particular characteristic of social work is to bring together reflexive-therapeutic literature and perspectives, socialist-collectivist objectives and thought and individualist-reformist ideas into a nexus of practice theories.

We saw in Chapter 1 that practice and theory influenced each other through social interaction. Therefore, I expressed the issue of *relevance* as being about the possibility of practice changing theory and theory having an impact on practice. Clearly because they are in a social interaction, they must do so; the question is how the processes of this interaction works. This leads us to the issue of learning transfer. Theories might derive from academic, practitioner or managerial sources, and recognise the primacy or balance of one or several of those sources. This suggests that we should be looking for a number of ways of joining theory and practice from different positions. We should avoid a struggle between different elements of occupational control for influence, concealed as a debate about the 'true' nature of social work theory. Hearn (1982) contends that we should avoid seeing theory and practice as two ends of a dumb-bell, but rather as always intertwined and relating to each other in a variety of ways.

Learning transfer

Transfer of learning is about the possibility of using ideas and knowledge gained from one area of practice in another (Cree and Macaulay, 2000). People often discuss transferring ideas from one country or culture to another, one profession to another or one intellectual tradition to another. Learning transfer examines the adaptations and organisational requirements that are needed to move an idea from one area to the other.

Social work occasionally develops its own theoretical perspectives from their outset. Task-centred work is an example. More commonly, however, its theories select from, embroider and develop external ideas. These come from wider ideologies in society and theoretical perspectives from related academic fields of study and may pass into social work through intermediate professional arenas, such as clinical psychology or counselling. Systems theory originally developed in social work based on writings from psychology and management theory. These processes are one of the ways in which social work relates to social movements in society and is constructed through the political and social construction processes outlined in Chapter 1.

Accreting theory in this way means that social work ideas connect to and originally came from wider bodies of knowledge and theory and may contribute to those wider bodies (see Figure 2.1). For example, an important aspect of feminist theory has been influenced by studies in social welfare and policy. Social work adapts ideas to its use over time, within social work literature and debate. Much of this may be decoupled from developments in the main body of theory. Thus, social work's distinctive view of a theory has the same view of the world

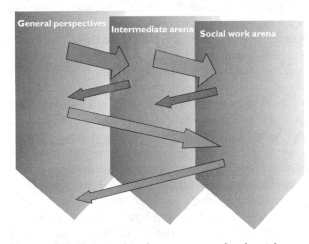

Figure 2.1 Relationships between general and social work theories

and may share some of the same original literature with the external body of literature. Some influence may continue in either direction. Usually, though, for workers in everyday practice, the connections are relatively sparse.

However, specialist agencies, which are often multidisciplinary, using particular theories, also exist. Social workers there have more contact with the wider theoretical world of this perspective. They may borrow and adapt new ideas to their practice as social workers. Joint contributions to both social work and the wider literature may be influenced by this experience. This is one way in which new ideas filter into social work. The broader the literature, generally speaking, the more influential it will be. Partly, this is because widely debated ideas will influence both clients' and workers' social contexts. So, clients may be more aware of sets of ideas in common currency, and colleagues in other agencies may be more able to interact with social workers about them. Thus, feminist or humanist ideas have a broad constituency within philosophy, literature and the social thought. Debates are part of the currency of everyday discourse. Cognitive theory, on the other hand, is a technical psychological theory that few outside psychology and medicine have heard of. The flow of ideas from the feminist and humanist thought into social work (or into anything) is likely, therefore, to be stronger.

We can, therefore, conceive of two situations in which social work theory transfers from wider bodies of theory. First, in the politics of social work theory, it may have become incorporated within a general approach to social work that most workers carry out or within one of the three views discussed in Chapter 1. For example, most social work is fairly open-minded and non-directive towards clients. There are practical reasons for this, because clients might not cooperate with someone who was too directive. But this general approach also comes from the long-standing influence of psychodynamic theory (Chapter 4) on social work. Second, this general approach to social work may be applied in theoretically specialised settings. The particular perspective and its wider theory then becomes more important in what the worker does in that setting than it is in general social work. A worker in a women's refuge, for example, might be closely in touch with and committed to feminist theory. A worker in a therapeutic community for mentally ill people might be in touch with aspects of psychoanalytic theory on groups and institutions. Workers in an acute psychiatric unit might be actively involved in behavioural and cognitive treatment regimes. These specialist settings may then have an influence on social work more directly than the wider bodies of ideas. Social work theory, therefore, is often at some distance in time and interpretation from ideas in wider theoretical debate. For example, realist theory, discussed in Chapter 3, has only begun to influence social work in the early 2000s, whereas the first discussion within sociology was in the late 1970s and 80s.

Wider bodies of theory need to be considered, but they may have no direct or influential relationship with the usual use of the related social work theory. This book focuses on the social work theory used in non-specialist social work. Workers in specialist agencies or with particular theoretical interests will have greater knowledge of and commitment to that theory than the average worker. In general social work, theories that would be clearly distinct, and perhaps incompatible in some debates within wider theoretical bases, have become entwined or connected in various ways. Attempts to relate systems and psychodynamic theories of various kinds are an example. Debates and conflicts also exist within social work. The mutual criticism of traditional (psychodynamic) and radical (socialist-collectivist) theories is an example.

Figure 2.1 sets out in diagrammatic form some of these connections. In addition, each set of social work and its wider theories have connections and disagreements with other social work theories. The focus of this book is, in each case, with the social work theory and its literature. Connections elsewhere are acknowledged rather than explored.

The range of theories: selection or eclecticism

Why have social workers come up with so many theories, if research shows that workers mainly operate according to one or two basic styles? Presented with the array of theories discussed in this book, can or should a worker choose to use just one, or are there many for different purposes? Hartman (1971) argues that we must each make our own definition of theory in order to practise. One of the characteristics of the theories presented in this book is that they are generic: they claim that they may be used in a variety of situations. Using them does not depend on working with a particular social group or in a particular way. Is there then some basis for choosing between them, for example that one is more effective than another for particular purposes or more generally? This would lead to *selection*, an approach that reviews the theories and then selects one theory or a group of similar theories to use as the basis of practice. The problem with selection is that a particular theory may not be the best one for our circumstances. In contemporary practice, selection works best in specialised agencies, often with a multiprofessional staff, where the theory works well for their specialism. Crisis intervention, for example, although theoretically capable of being used in a variety of situations, is mainly used in agencies dealing with emergencies, often involving psychiatrists, psychiatric nurses and others as well as social workers. In the USA, other emergency services, such as the police, use it in dealing with disasters and emergency work with a strong emotional component, such as rape and domestic violence.

Alternatively, can we just pick up some ideas from several theories and put them together to produce a style of work that suits our agency and our own capabilities and preferences? This raises the issue of *eclecticism*. There is research evidence of a degree of eclecticism in the 1970s and 80s (Jayaratne, 1978; DHSS, 1978: 134–6; Curnock and Hardiker, 1979; Kolevson and Maykranz, 1982; O'Connor and Dalgleish, 1986; Hugman, 1987; Olsson, 1993; Olsson and Ljunghill, 1997). Some of these studies indicate an inexplicit or what Olsson (1993) and Olsson and Ljunghill (1997) call 'naive' use of theory. Debate has led to wide acceptance that general social work practice is eclectic, but that this should be managed to avoid using theories in ways that are internally inconsistent or debase the full theory. It is difficult to keep hold of a full range of the possible ideas, and use them with credibility. It is also not practical to use many theories in depth without going into them in considerable detail, and having supervision and support in their particular application.

Therefore, being eclectic is something that that we should do consistently, in a planned way, and testing out our decisions with a team of people working together rather than on a casual or individual basis (Epstein, 1992: 321–30). This would be consistent with a social construction approach, which argues that constructions are shared rather than personal. Because of the danger of confusion in combining and adapting theories, if we pick up ideas from different places, it is important to be aware of the sources, values, methods and objectives of the basic theories we are borrowing from, and prohibitions and encouragements to combination with other ideas.

How to be eclectic

From this discussion, it is possible to summarise a reasonable approach to theory selection and eclecticism, as follows:

- Workers will work with people according to professional and agency expectations.
- Building on these expectations, they will use theories following their team's precepts and these will be adapted as new ideas become available.
- Although there will be a basic theoretical model, this might be varied using a range of practice concepts from different theories, for example, in appropriate circumstances, the idea of crisis and the basic model of crisis management might be used. For this reason, I identify major practice issues and concepts at the outset of each chapter and present a basic model in diagrammatic form wherever possible.

How to use selection

The corollary of this is a reasonable approach to using selection:

- Specialist agencies might use a realm of theory, for example a women's refuge might use feminist theory explicitly. The agency might attract workers already committed to feminism, or workers might go there to develop this theoretical emphasis in their repertoire.
- Within general agencies, workers might, possibly individually but more likely

as a group, decide to use a particular theory in greater depth with appropriate people. This would be backed up by supervision, support and training.

■ As many social workers now work in multiprofessional settings, it may be necessary to use or at least understand something of theories similar to the approaches used by other professionals. It may also be necessary to be explicit about the theories that social workers are using.

A cautious, coordinated and planned approach should help to overcome the problems with eclecticism. We can thus use ideas where they effectively meet workers' and clients' needs, taking account of the range of possibilities, avoiding unhelpful options and seeking to develop ideas from the basic theories. The purpose of this book is to provide the resource of a starting point with access to the literature on theories likely to be useful to facilitate thoughtful rather than casual eclecticism.

Process knowledge and reflective, reflexive and critical thinking

How, then, can workers find a way through these complexities to think theoretically in practice? Increasingly, *process knowledge* about the way in which professionals make decisions and judgements helps with this. Sheppard et al. (2000) report an empirical study in which workers pursued two processes: critical appraisal of the situation and then hypothesis generation, which allowed them to work out ways of acting. Critical appraisal included focused attention, querying information and not taking it for granted and making causal inferences about what is going on in a case to enable workers to make sense it (Sheppard and Ryan, 2003). Hypotheses were partial, about particular aspects of the case, whole-case, trying to analyse the total situation that the worker faced, and speculative, in which the worker thought out which interventions and legal or administrative procedures might be required. They then create rules of action, which give them guidelines to follow.

Contemporary debate on this topic particularly focuses on critical and reflective thinking. Fook (2002: 43) comments that *reflective thinking* is particularly concerned with identifying a process of working things through, while *reflexive thinking* is concerned with the stance of taking into account as many different perspectives on a situation as possible, and especially different perspectives among clients and their social networks. *Critical thinking* means not taking for granted the present social order, but actively looking for social change. I have been working recently with a dying man whose relationship with his wife has become more conflictual, because he is blaming her behaviour for some difficulties in their marriage. I have been, in a reflective way, thinking through possible reasons why this might be and talking over explanations with him. His wife has another perspective, that he is projecting some of his behaviour onto her (to use a psychoanalytic term, see Chapter 4). Their various children think different things; being reflexive means putting these ideas into the discussions with him. Thinking critically, I am aware that some of the conflict reflects changes in attitudes to what is acceptable in gender relations; things he took for granted as acceptable ways for men to behave are no longer acceptable in contemporary attitudes. Part of what I am doing is getting him to acknowledge changes in the social order of gender relations, so that both he and his wife can agree about the right attitude, and he can say 'sorry' before he dies.

Reflective thinking originates from the work of Argyris and Schön (1974; Schön, 1983, 1987). This body of work is another aspect of the literature that seeks a way to represent the reality of the way professionals use knowledge in working with people. 'Technical rationality' describes the use of evidence in a positivist way (Chapter 3) in professions such as engineering, where people use natural substances that perform in the same way in similar conditions. Even medicine uses medication, which has predictable effects on the human body; this is a technical rational application of knowledge. However, other aspects of medicine, such as communicating with patients, like social work, nursing, teaching and similar professions, use knowledge in a more flexible way. Argyris and Schön suggest that workers have guidelines for good practice and use these to carry out their work in a practical way. When they come across a new situation, they try new responses, 'practical experiments', which then adapt the guidelines. Education for such professions involves helping people to identify when a new situation has arisen and how to develop new guidelines using practical experimentation. This approach has been widely used and systematically developed in teaching education, nursing and social work.

There are criticisms of Schön's approach. First, it assumes that variations in the situation are all amenable to changes in guidelines for action that fit within the present social order. However, many situations might involve changing the present social order, or experimenting in ways that conflict with existing guidelines. Related to that, it assumes that a professional has enough discretion to carry out experiments, whereas many professional jobs are constrained by agency policies or government regulators. It also might make us think that all problems are within the capacity of some rethinking by a professional, whereas some require additional resources. To deal with these points we should as part of our practice be looking for situations where wider change and additional or different resources are needed. Critical theory (Chapter 11) particularly takes up reflective thinking and uses it in this way.

Reflective practice involves more than carefully thinking things through and taking all aspects of the situation into account (Payne, 2002b). It implies a structured system for thinking things through either as we are taking part in the situation (Schön calls this 'reflection-in-action') or as a learning or review technique after the event ('reflection-on-action'), which might improve future practice. Figure 2.2 brings together, partly using Jasper's (2003) account, four models of reflective practice, her own, Borton's (1970), Boud and Knights's (1996; adapted by Payne, 2002b) and Gibbs's (1988). Jasper's (2003) ERA (experience-reflection-action) model provides an underlying structure: you experience something, you reflect on it, and this causes you to take action in a particular way. All see it as a cycle, starting from describing the situation, through analysing it and ending by working out the implications of your analysis for taking action. Boud and Knights usefully emphasise the importance of attending to different aspects of the situation. Social work practice theory operates in the

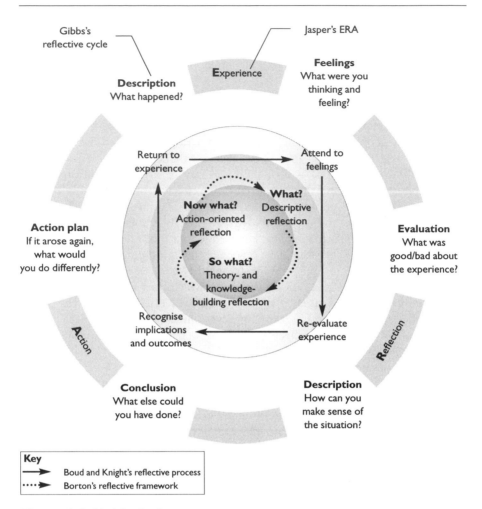

Figure 2.2 Models of reflective practice

Source: Adapted from Borton (1970); Gibbs (1988); Jasper (2003); Boud and Knights (1996); Payne (2002b).

area between Borton's (1970) 'so what?' and 'now what?', where our conclusions about the situation in front of us are converted into a plan of action that takes our assessment into account. We could ask whether a particular theory has something to tell us about situations like this, or we could apply a theory's practice prescriptions to tell us what actions we could take, or both. Theories of the client world are relevant to the description part of the diagram, to the right, because they might give us information about clients and their social environments that would inform our assessment.

It is not easy to develop reflective practice. Goodman (1984, cited by Jasper, 2003) suggests that skills in doing so might be explicitly developed through three stages:

■ Reflection to achieve specific objectives, such as fitting in with agency practices and policies

■ Reflection on the relationship between principles and practice, the area where practice theory becomes integrated into practice

■ Reflection to incorporate ethical and political concerns, which might be particularly relevant to critical and feminist practice but include concerns for the underlying politics of all theories.

In nursing, where reflective practice is incorporated into learning development systems, ideas such as using diaries and journals, and selecting 'critical' or particularly significant incidents from a case or area of practice can help to focus reflection (Jasper, 2003, 2004). Martyn's (2000) study shows, through a series of case studies in work with families and children, how different workers applied theoretical perspectives they already pursued to reflective practice, considering both theories of the client world and practice theories. Darlington et al. (2002) showed that the explicit use of theory, particularly through effective supervision, could enhance use of evidence in child abuse cases.

Two developments of reflective practice have come into use during the late 1990s and early 2000s: reflexivity and critical thinking. They have had a strong influence, particularly on critical and feminist theory (Chapters 11 and 12). Reflexivity derives from qualitative research methods, particularly as applied in feminist research. It means a cyclical process in which we openly study how what we observe affects our thinking and how that then affects what we do. Parton and O'Byrne (2000) describe reflexivity as a way of responding to the uniqueness of each individual. That involves thinking about both our response and the uniqueness; we are not being reflexive unless we seek to find the uniqueness of the individuals we deal with and also respond to it. While we may generalise about issues, reflexivity tells us that as soon as the generality is applied to an individual, it is adapted. So, as in realist thinking (Chapter 3), every general point is the context for the way the individual is. As we see what is individual about that person, we compare it with the general, and adapt our response to our understanding of both the general (the theory) and the particular (the individual we are working with). So, with the dying man I was working with, I know (the general point) that dying people often think about the past and try to set things right in their relationships. In his particular case, this meant looking at changing social values and thinking about setting things right with his wife according to new rather than old values; reflexively including alternative ways of looking at things.

During the 1980s, feminist researchers were concerned to explore unexamined power imbalances between researchers and the people being researched. Traditional research methods assume a neutral observer looking at social situations from outside, while, as we saw in Chapter 1, critics pointed out biases arising from the social assumptions and constructions of researchers. Feminists, followed by researchers in disability and more generally in health and welfare and the social sciences, moved towards research methods that involved the people who were being researched more actively in the process. Ethnographic methods, where the researcher is a participant observer in the events and situations being researched, included specific attention to how researchers were affected by their observations and how this then affected their behaviour. Feminists and disability researchers sought to develop collaborative methods in developing research objectives, carrying out research, analysing data and disseminating results. These approaches included building interpersonal relationships with the people being researched rather than maintaining a stance as a neutral observer, carrying out research managed or influenced by representative groups of the people being researched and working with people affected by the research as collaborators (Finlay and Gough, 2003).

Finlay (2003) identifies ways of being reflexive as follows:

- Introspection, looking into our own mind and working out how we are thinking and why
- Intersubjective reflection, that is joint reflection involving the participants
- Setting up systems for mutual collaboration, so that processes are established and agreed for influencing each other's thoughts
- Using reflexivity as a social critique, where disseminating the fact of having worked reflexively criticises those who have not taken the trouble to do so
- Using reflexivity as ironic deconstruction, where the process of thinking together identifies where the use of power and authority by the people involved has affected neutrality. In this process, we begin to question taken for granted patterns of sharing thinking, for example a husband and wife's normal power relations.

Taylor and White (2000) discuss a number of studies in health and welfare that use such methods to uncover systematic behaviour that is not typically prescribed by practice theory. For example, they show how, in interviews, clients established their credibility, entitlement to services, 'moral adequacy' and gave their story authenticity by giving details. Such findings might have implications for how to practice according to theory. For example, crisis intervention theory suggests that workers should find out how people have coped with previous crises in their lives. However, detecting this intention, clients may feel that they should assert their 'moral adequacy' by showing the worker that they have managed well in the past. Seeing the application of the theory from a potential client's point of view draws attention to ways in which workers should present what they are doing: making it clear in this case how the theory says that past experience affects what we do in present crises. It also draws attention to possible failings in the theory.

Secker's (1993) study of social work students applying theory shows how useful taking a reflexive approach may be. Students in the middle and latter parts of training used theory extensively. Most had great difficulty in integrating theory in practice, kept finding conflicts between different theories and were unable to make connections between theory they were taught and informal sources of theory. A few were fluent in integrating theory. These were students who had particular social skills. They listened well, and tried to tie ideas to what they heard when meeting with clients. They could develop ideas, drawing on a range of different courses and seeing connections, rather than seeing pieces of knowledge as separate. Also, they discussed their ideas effectively with the clients concerned, so that they could test out the validity of their application. So, instead of keeping their thinking to themselves, they tested out ideas with their clients by saying things like: 'Do you think your husband could be showing his own guilt about his behaviour, by saying that you are just as guilty in your own way?' They did not use the technical term 'projection' here, but explained what they thought might be happening in ways that might help the client to understand what was going on in her relationship with her husband. It may be, then, that successful use of theory requires social and interpersonal skills, and the self-confidence to discuss ideas reflexively so that clients are participating in the construction of practice. Crawford et al. (2002) used student reflection in groups with practice teachers (field supervisors) to help interweave theory, practice and reflection.

Gardner (2003) developed a mode of critical reflection in community work situations, involving:

- seeking subjective histories and narratives from people involved
- making sure that those least likely to be heard are included
- enabling participants to make connections between broader structural issues and their personal experience, a feminist approach (Chapter 12)
- paying attention to processes as well as outcomes.

What all this work draws attention to is the importance of involving clients, service users and members of the community as well as multiprofessional colleagues in reflection. It need not only be a professional or only a social work activity, indeed it cannot be if it is also to be reflexive. Clients may also transfer learning from one experience to another.

Critical thinking

Ideas of reflexivity have been applied particularly in *critical thinking* on practice. This term has two meanings. One refers to the study of logical use of language in the best way to guide thought processes. Such studies focus on use of language and the practical application of rhetoric and logic (Bowell and Kemp, 2002). The second refers to the incorporation of critical social science into how we think about our practice. Brechin (2000) identifies the two guiding principles of critical practice as respecting others as equals and having an open approach, not taking things for granted. Her approach identifies reflexive principles as basic: forming effective relationships so that workers can incorporate multiple perspectives in their thinking, seeking to empower clients by increasing their opportunities and making a difference so that the client's experience of life is better. In Payne et al. (2002), reflecting a more critical social science approach, the principles of *critical practice* were set out as follows:

- To identify situations of openness and uncertainty as opportunities for creative practice
- To seek opportunities to extend personal empowerment towards collective relationships and social change
- Being alert to the use of language

- Being alert to who has and uses power to set agendas
- Examining the content and methods of making judgements and assessments
- Questioning the ideology underlying particular services and decisions
- Paying attention to the detail of different perspectives on a situation
- Contextualising evidence by understanding theoretical and value positions
- Developing an overview of processes and events, so that this may be seen by everyone involved
- Making sure that all involved understand the perspective and context.

I have devised elsewhere (Payne, 1996b) some ideas which may help to make concrete some possibilities for critical practice. They form the basis of the 'critical practice focuses' presented in each chapter. These invite reflection on the ideas presented in the chapter applied to a case situation, and then invite wider reflection, using ideas from different theories to criticise what the present theories might suggest. These reflective ideas are as follows:

- *A dualities approach.* Many concepts, especially value concepts, include within them implicit references to their opposites. For example, when we have a problem with confidentiality, we can ask ourselves: 'What is the difficulty about openness which this confidentiality issue implies?' Again, with self-determination: 'What rule-following is being required of the client that raises this problem with her self-determination?' Berlin (1990) argues that dichotomous thinking of this kind is a useful habit of mind, but highlights extremes and suggests that it may be insufficiently complex to deal with real-world problems. Critical and feminist theorists (Chapters 11 and 12) particularly raise concerns about dichotomous thinking, since it tends to reduce complexity and places people and issues in opposition to one another. It is important to use a dualities approach to see alternatives as operating together, not one excluding the other.
- *A thinking-emotions approach.* We tend to think about people on a rational level in theories such as task-centred casework or cognitive-behavioural work. In psychodynamic and humanist approaches, on the other hand, we tend to concentrate on emotional motivations. We need to beware, in practice, of seeing people's problems as solely concerned with their thought processes or perceptions, their emotions or lack of self-control. Where we find this happening, we should ask ourselves, 'What are the emotions (or what ideas does this behaviour represent) here?' This is a special case of the dualities approach.
- *A power analysis approach.* The analysis of power relations in any situation enables us to consider the political issues present. It is useful to consider the pathways of client and worker and the development of the agency situation in which they meet as giving a history of the political factors that form their interaction (Payne, 1993).
- *The alternative perspectives approach.* Chapter 1 introduced the idea that all social work is constructed from three different perspectives. However, these perspectives are typically all present to some degree and we should explicitly seek them out as a way of questioning our own approach to a situation. For

instance, where we find ourselves implementing the agency's requirements and trying to get clients to fit in (individualist-reformist), we can ask how we can collaborate to change the situation (socialist-collectivist) and what personal power and development the client can be enabled to achieve (reflexive-therapeutic) to gain other perspectives on our work.

CRITICAL PRACTICE FOCUS

The Burmans

Mr Burman is a resident in an old people's home, having been admitted recently because Alzheimer's disease has led to restless and aggressive behaviour, such that Mrs Burman can no longer cope with him at home. She visits every day and stays with him much of the time, but this means that she is no longer readily available to help her daughter, a single parent with three small children, who has recently separated from a violent husband. Mrs Burman's brother has recently had a leg amputated because of circulatory disease, linked to smoking, and is, bad-temperedly, convalescent at home; his wife has relied on Mrs Burman for support also and is very depressed. Mr Burman formerly chaired a local community association, several of whose members ask Mrs Burman's social worker how they might help.

Who might be involved in a reflective process? What experiences or events might reflection focus on? How might different people involved transfer learning from previous experiences?

Conclusion

I argued that theory is practically useful, and that its variety and confusion can be organised and understood. Critical reflection and thinking are useful ways of doing so. The relationships and oppositions between theories provide a context in which their value can be assessed against one another, and against the modern social context in which they must be used. However, my emphasis on reflection, reflexiveness and criticality as an approach to using social work theories in practice does not answer the question of which theories may be most effective in giving us answers about the realities of the worlds that we deal with. This issue is the focus of Chapter 3.

FURTHER READING

Epstein, L. (1992) *Brief Treatment and a New Look at the Task-Centered Approach* (New York, Macmillan).
A useful summary of various methods of brief treatment, but also containing an excellent account of eclectic practice.

Finlay, L. and Gough, B. (eds) (2003) *Reflexivity: A Practical Guide for Researchers in Health and Social Sciences* (Oxford: Blackwell).
A useful discussion of reflexivity, covering theory and application to research.

Jasper, M. (2003) *Beginning Reflective Practice* (Cheltenham: Nelson Thornes).
An excellent practical account of reflective practice, derived from nursing, but very applicable to social work.

Schön, D. A. (1983) *The Reflective Practitioner: How Professionals Think in Action* (New York, Basic Books).
The classic, but very readable book on reflective practice, but it needs to be updated by a work such as Jasper's.

Taylor, C. and White, S. (2000) *Practising Reflexivity in Health and Welfare: Making Knowledge* (Buckingham: Open University Press).
A comprehensive research-based account of reflexivity applied to practice.

JOURNAL

Reflective Practice, London: Taylor and Francis/Carfax.

CHAPTER 3

Issues in Social Work Practice Theory

What this chapter is about

The aim of this chapter is look at recent debates about social work theory. What theories are important? I summarise the range of practice theories that are available. How we assess their value leads us to important debates about epistemology and whether we have the knowledge to back up what practice theory tells us to do.

MAIN POINTS

> ➤ A wide range of theoretical ideas have generated social work practice theories.
>
> ➤ There are various comparisons of different theories in casework, groupwork and community and macro social work.
>
> ➤ Theory in family therapy and residential care are relevant to wider social work theory.
>
> ➤ Research in the 1950s and 60s raised questions about whether social work interventions had the effects claimed for them by theory; more recent research has shown that focused, limited work is effective for many purposes.
>
> ➤ However, recent research looks mainly at services or particular objectives, rather than theories, so research validation of particular theories is limited.
>
> ➤ Positivist and interpretivist views of knowledge represent two different sets of ideas about where theory comes from and how it represents the world outside ourselves.
>
> ➤ This has generated four views of the way in which knowledge affects practice theories: evidence-based; social construction; empowerment; and realist views, each of which has an influence on practice.

Recent debates about social work theory

Most practitioners do not keep up daily with theoretical development. Mainly, they are concerned with practice within the policy and management requirements of social work agencies. New projects and new services grow up, but practice within them changes only slowly. Occasionally, major new insights arise: in the early 2000s the main new area has been the development of practice theories using social construction ideas (Chapter 8).

Social work theory in the early 2000s has maintained the main areas of social work theory, with new presentations, new adornments, but no substantial innovations. In addition to the innovation of constructive practice, three areas of strong development have been in cognitive-behavioural and critical practice, and in the concern for spirituality as a theoretical issue. This latter concern is partly related to cultural and ethnic sensitivity because culturally different approaches to spirituality are significant in important cultural conflicts. Cognitive-behavioural practice continues to excite interest because of empirical support for its effectiveness, and creative new techniques and applications, using behaviour and thinking scales, and interesting new ways of implementing its ideas in practice have been developed. Its impact on related professions means that support and supervision are available to some social workers for developing the precise techniques. There is also political support for its use because of evidence of its effectiveness. In critical practice, creative new presentations of practice possibilities and strong debate have ignited interest and commitment.

Other areas of development have seen confirmation of their established position. Most other chapters in this book present new interpretations or renewed and developed presentations of established theoretical ideas in virtually every theoretical position. Therefore, there is evidence that social workers continue to find them useful and develop them.

The major area of debate about social work theory in the late 1990s and early 2000s has been epistemological, that is, how we know and organise our thinking about the knowledge we use to back up theory. As Webb (2001) points out, it is a long-standing philosophical debate that goes back to the 1700s. Debate between theories has been quiescent. In the early 1990s, separate theories were disputed, and there was debate about whether eclecticism meant that social workers twisted the basic ideas of particular theories to make them fit with other inconsistent sets of ideas. The theory wars of the 1970s left an aftermath of separate presentations of social work theory and some conflict about whether one was better than another. However, this has died away to the point where Applegate (2000) presents a postmodern conception of alternative theories as alternatives 'stories', narratives or representations of the activity 'social work'.

Pragmatically, many practitioners in general social work settings have picked up ideas according to their interest or use. This book reflects that reality, in identifying in each chapter major practice ideas that often engage social workers' interest. This partial engagement may inform workers who move on to specialised settings where a particular theory is most relevant. In the UK, for example, the government has (unknowingly) encouraged interest in crisis intervention because it has promoted crisis resolution teams in the mental health services of every area. This is not because of the achievements of crisis intervention theory, or research findings supporting its effectiveness, although there are some, but because of a demand from related services and the public for an effective response to people with acute mental illnesses in their community. The people involved needed some idea what to do. In clinical settings, on the borders of psychotherapy and counselling, working with people with severe difficulties, it continues to be possible to practise using psychodynamic theories and other therapies and draw on the richness of their social and psychological ideas.

Analyses of social work theories

Practitioners reflecting critically on practice, selecting or incorporating theories in a personal or team construction have a wide choice among apparently comparable and useful theories. The purpose of Part II of this book is to offer information about some of those theories, to enable comparisons of their value and see how they may be selected and combined. Some doubt whether this is a useful enterprise. Solomon (1976), for example, considers that theories and models of social work are not comparable because they often deal with different things (for example the functions of practice, the process of change, the sequence of helping processes, the nature of problems to be dealt with). Some, she argues, are based on particular methods of change, while others extend into fields of therapeutic change beyond social work. This sort of criticism shows why it is so important to consider carefully how we select and group theories.

Work with individuals and families

Several writers and editors try to review and compare a range of social work theories. Table 3.1 summarises the coverage of some of these, compared with the coverage of the present edition of *Modern Social Work Theory*. This is not a complete analysis, since many of these works specifically deal only with casework or what, in the USA, would now be called 'clinical social work' (for instance Roberts and Nee, 1970). This reflects a separation between settings where most social work is concerned with facilitating social protection and service delivery, and those where interpersonal and group therapeutic work is a major part of the role, where practice would be more likely to be called 'clinical'. Two companion books of Roberts and Nee (Roberts and Northen, 1976; Taylor and Roberts, 1985) review and compare group and community work theories; these are considered later. I include some discussion of group, residential and community work in chapters with related general theories. Some of these works of review, while not defining their coverage as casework, concentrate on this field (for example Howe, 1987).

I have included Roberts and Nee, the first such review of theories, as a benchmark of American conceptions of 'theory wars' at the outset of the period in which alternative theories became sufficiently separable for their differences to be debated. Turner's first edition was published shortly afterwards, and he has continued to produce new editions periodically, the book lengthening and reflecting the current American preoccupations on each occasion. He is the only modern reviewer to differentiate such a wide range of psychotherapeutic theories. This reflects a large and diverse population of social workers in the North American social work profession, which is also partly integrated with counsellors and other mental health professionals, so that distinguishing varied forms of psychotherapeutic activity is far more important than in European welfare regimes.

Table 3.1 Alternative reviews of social work theories

Categories of theory	Roberts and Nee (1970)	Howe (1987)[1]	Lishman (1991)	Kumar (1995)	Turner (4th edn) (1996)[2]	Stepney and Ford (2000)	Cooper and Lesser (2002)
Psychodynamic	Psychosocial Functional Problem-solving	Psychoanalytic	Psychodynamic Erikson's life-cycle approach to development Psychodynamic counselling	Problem-solving	Psychosocial Psychoanalytic Functional Problem-solving Ego psychology	Psychodynamic	Psychodynamic (object relations) Self-psychology
Cognitive-behavioural	Behavioural modification	Behavioural social work	Behavioural social work Cognitive-behavioural		Behaviour therapy Cognitive (Family treatment)	Cognitive-behavioural	Behaviour therapy Cognitive
[Family treatment] *Crisis theories*	Family therapy Crisis intervention		Crisis intervention		Crisis	Crisis intervention	
Task-centred		[allies with behavioural approaches]	Task-centred practice Written agreements		Task-centred	Task-centred	
Systems theories	Socialisation	[not seen as a major category]		Systems	Life model systems	Ecological	
Social psychological/construction			Attachment theory Bereavement/loss		**Constructivist** Communication **Narrative** Neurolinguistic programming Role theory		Narrative Solution-focused
Sociological/social development			Community social work	Social development		Community social work	
Humanist/existential spirituality		Client-centred [groups a number of existential ideas under the heading of 'seekers after the self']		Gandhian Existentialism	Client-centred Existential Gestalt **Hypnosis** Meditation Transactional analysis **Transpersonal**	Existentialist Counselling	
Critical theories		Marxist radical/radical structuralism consciousness-raising	Structural approach	Marxism Radical	**Materialist** (Marxist)		
Feminist		[includes feminist social work]	[includes feminist social work]	Feminism	Feminist		Women's psychology
Anti-discriminatory sensitivity theories					**Aboriginal/Cree**		Cross-cultural
Empowerment and advocacy					Empowerment	Empowerment	

Note: 1. Square brackets denote author's comments. 2. Brackets denote a theory covered in Turner's (1986) previous edition, excluded from the present edition; bold denotes theories covered in this edition but not previously; the chapter on Marxism was renamed 'materialism'.

Kumar (1995), an Indian text, is included as an example of a book published outside the European and American professions; it includes Gandhian practice, an important influence in India, emphasises social development perspectives and, while retaining a general problem-solving model to cover practice with a psychological emphasis, focuses on transformational practice, including and differentiating radical and Marxist perspectives. Lishman (1991) distinguishes between 'models of understanding human development' and models of intervention. The first group includes what I have called 'perspectives', such as psychodynamic or structural approaches, as well as fairly restricted theories of development such as attachment theory and Erikson's (1965) life-cycle approach to development. Since her book is explicitly for practice assessors or teachers (fieldwork supervisors), it presumably reflects concepts she thinks will be unfamiliar to practice assessors.

Frameworks for analysing theories

Some writers have attempted more than just description of social work theories. They have tried to group them to show connections, or underlying principles which different theories share. One possible way of doing this is to analyse the content of each theory according to a standard set of categories. Turner (1996) offers this as an adjunct to his theory review, but this, and other similar attempts, often produce lengthy lists of headings without helping to decide between theories in practice. An alternative and more sophisticated method has a conceptual scheme placing theories in relation to one another.

Whittington and Holland's (1985) classification of social work theories has been influential, particularly since Howe's (1987) review of social work theory takes it up. It is based on Burrell and Morgan's (1979) sociological work. They propose that philosophical positions about the nature of society range from subjective (humanist, postmodernist, constructionist) to objective (modernist, positivist, scientific). An alternative dimension ranges philosophical positions about the nature of order in society. It deals with whether they understand society

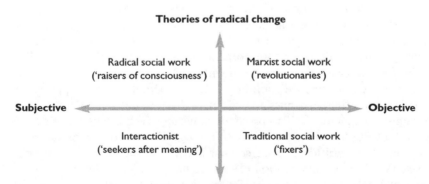

Figure 3.1 Analysis of social work theories
Source: Whittington and Holland (1985); Howe (1987).
Note: Howe's labels for each grouping are given in brackets.

as changing in a radical way or as a regulated set of social interactions. We can assess social work theories according to where they fit into these two continua. Figure 3.1 gives some examples of how this works. We may criticise such approaches to categorisation because they set arbitrary continua for analysis and it is always possible to question where theories are placed within the axes (Stenson and Gould, 1986). For example, theories regarded as mutually exclusive are neatly set in a particular position, whereas often they overlap and share things in common. Equally, conflicts of ideology which do not relate to these axes may not be represented. Howe (1987) treats both psychodynamic theory and behavioural approaches to social work as both representative of functional ideas, whereas there are considerable differences between them.

Groupwork

Some attempts to classify groupwork theories are set out in Table 3.2. Roberts and Northen (1976) present an analysis that includes several forms of groupwork allied to casework theories, such as functional and problem-solving groupwork. Their book attempts to parallel the models of practice covered in their book on casework theories. More recent classifications rely on the ground-breaking article by Papell and Rothman (1966), and there is broad agreement about this perspective which is based in current groupwork ideology (see for example Bundey, 1976; Brown, 1992).

This offers three approaches. The *remedial model* presents the group as a place in which individuals who have problems, often of how they function in social roles, are brought together in a group to help them change their deviant patterns of behaviour. We might regard any therapeutic model of groupwork as remedial in approach. A contemporary approach is, for example, to implement solution-focused therapy in groups (Sharry, 2001). The *reciprocal model* emphasises mutual support according to a programme devised by group members alongside a worker. The *social goals* model, associated with youth and community work, uses groupwork to pursue external goals, such as education or community activities. Brown's (1992) account of theory development includes other more recently devised models. These include *mediating model* groups that help people examine and establish their social roles in a safe, supportive but challenging environment. Encounter groups are normally regarded as a separate humanist and gestalt form of groupwork concerned with personal growth (Chapter 9) but might also be regarded as mediating in philosophy. Developmental approaches aim to understand group dynamics, the group's behaviour independent of actions and thoughts of its members. This psychodynamic approach is based particularly on the work of Erikson (1965) and ego psychology, theories of group dynamics and social psychological ideas about conflict and group membership (Balgopal and Vassil, 1983). The work of Bion (1961) could also broadly be described as developmental. Glassman and Kates (1990) offer a humanist groupwork model combining mediating and developmental approaches.

Douglas (1993) has also offered a wide analysis of groupwork theory. There have been several attempts to develop groupwork approaches carrying out wider therapeutic ideas, such as task-centred groupwork, humanist and feminist. I deal

Table 3.2 Classification of groupwork theories

Roberts and Northen (1976)	Feldman and Wodarski (1975)	Papell and Rothman (1966)	Douglas (1979)	Balgopal and Vassil (1983)	Brown (1992)
Generic Organisational	Traditional		Eclectic		Time-limited 'Mainstream'
Psychosocial Functional Mediating		Remedial Reciprocal	Remedial Reciprocal/mediating	Remedial Mediating	Psychotherapeutic Person-centred models/ gestalt/psychodrama/ transactional analysis Problem-solving/task-centred/social skills
Developmental/humanist	Group-centred		Group-centred/process/ developmental/ maturational stage/ personal growth	Developmental	
Task-centred			Task-centred		
Socialisation crisis Intervention Problem-solving	Behaviour modification	Social goals	Behavioural Social goals	Behavioural	Guided group interaction Social goals/social interaction/self-directed self-help/ mutual support Empowerment Intake/assessment/ induction

with these in Chapters 5, 9 and 12 respectively. Heap (1992) argues that in Europe, groupwork is becoming more multidisciplinary (although I think this is a worldwide trend) and is less central to social work practice. He also points out the growing importance of self-help groups. Supporting and stimulating these has become a major focus of groupwork development, and begins to merge with community work. It is an important part of Mullender and Ward's (1991) self-directed groupwork (see Chapter 14).

Brown's (1992) account of groupwork theories extends the range of ideas in a looser but more differentiated analysis. In some situations, clients meet as a group, but the worker does not try in an organised way to achieve change (Feldman and Wodarski, 1975). Instead, it is assumed pragmatically that the presence of people possibly with shared circumstances or problems would be beneficial and that they could help one another. Self-help and mutual support groups also do not seek to promote therapeutic change. Brown has with colleagues (Brown et al., 1982; Brown, 1994) tried to develop such a pragmatic use of groupwork. This involves time-limited groups with the aim of meeting agency objectives by achieving individual change in clients, using a sharing approach and co-leadership.

Community work, macro-social work and administration

Analyses of community work recognise the fluidity and range of activities in this field. In the USA, a recent significant development in social work practice is a specific focus on 'macro' (for example Brueggemann, 2002) or 'contextual' (O'Melia and Miley, 2002) social work. These concepts pick up the importance of social workers seeking change indirectly in wider social systems and within the present social order. These ideas have many overlaps with the aims of empowerment and advocacy theories, and recent books make significant use of social network theory (for example Hardcastle et al., 1997); this and the term 'macro' indicate the connection with the dominance of systems theory in the USA. These materials also overlap with social services organisation development and administration, for example in Brueggemann (2002) and Hardcastle et al. (1997), and the social work role of advocacy within their organisation. This reflects the tendency of American social work to include management as an element or role of social work, whereas in European welfare regimes this is often seen as separate from the professional role. Some of the professional skill elements of this work is paralleled in British literature on community work, for example the recent updating after a long gap of Henderson and Thomas's text (2001) and Gilchrist's (2004) text on networking in community development.

York (1984) suggests that several conceptualisations of community work divide it into three types. He categorises these as concerned with organising community agencies, developing local competences and political action for change. He argues, however, that all community work involves facing a series of dichotomies:

- directive versus non-directive work (Batten, 1967)
- task or problem versus process approaches
- initiating versus enabling roles for the worker

■ treatment versus reform.

Many of these issues are represented in distinctions made between different types of community work. I summarise three analyses in Table 3.3, with my explanation of the meaning of the categories identified. The distinctions between

Table 3.3 Models of community and macro-work

Taylor and Roberts (1985)	Popple (1995)	Brueggemann (2002)	Explanation
Community development	Community development	Community development	*Community development* Helping groups come together and participate in gaining skills and confidence to promote services and facilities in their locality
Political action	Community action	Social policy advocacy Social movements activist	*Social action* Direct action often at local level to change government or official policies and practices or attitudes of powerful groups; in Europe, often class-based
Programme development and coordination Community liaison	Community care Community organisation	Programme developer Community organisation	*Community organisation and liaison* Cultivating social networks, voluntary services to achieve better working of and coordination and participation in welfare services
Planning	Social/community planning	Social work planning	*Community planning* Concerned with participation in better planning of services, analysis of social problems and policy goals; evaluating services and policies
	Community education		Concerned with participation in and developing opportunities for involvement in education for deprived groups
	Feminist community work		Improving women's welfare; challenging and changing gender inequalities and enabling women's participation in resolving policy and social issues of concern to them
	Black and anti-racist community work		Challenging racism; enabling black people's participation in resolving policy and social issues of concern to them
		Social work administration Organisation development	Working to make social work agencies more effective and responsive in serving clients

community development, social action, community organisation and liaison and community planning are widely acknowledged internationally. Social development (Chapter 10) incorporates a range of these approaches in developing economies, in an attempt to incorporate social objectives into economic development.

Community work is a distinct form of practice, which calls upon a theoretical and knowledge base that is more sociological and less psychological than casework and groupwork, although many social workers practise it and a community orientation is important in many agencies. The social development model (Chapter 10) has significant elements of community work within it. Some views of social work give importance to using community approaches as part of social work, particularly critical, feminist, anti-racist and empowerment approaches (see Chapters 11–14).

Other aspects of social work

Some writers include *family therapy* within social work theory (see Table 3.1), but this trend of the 1980s is now receding. This is a form of practice in which all or several members of the family are treated together on the assumption that their problems arise from interactions among them all. These therapies are excluded from this volume as they are from most similar books, although their use in social work and connections with social work theories are considered in relevant places. One reason for this exclusion is that there are several schools of thought in family therapy, and exploring them would extend the length of the book (and the competence of the author). Also, family therapy is more a multidisciplinary area of practice in which several occupational groups operate and to which several, including social work, have made contributions. It is reasonable to regard it as a form of practice from which some social workers borrow as part of social work, or an occupational grouping into which they move, rather than as an activity that has been adapted to social work (see Payne, 1996a). Many social workers see themselves as practising social work with special relevance to families, and taking into account the family context as part of the 'person-in-situation/environment'.

Residential care can be viewed as a setting in which other treatment theories are used (for example Jones 1979; Ward, 1980), in which case no separate theoretical perspectives are relevant, or as a distinct form of social work activity justifying theories of its own. Writers such as Ainsworth and Fulcher (1981; Fulcher and Ainsworth, 1985) regard residential care as a form of groupwork carried out in residence and call it *group care*, a term which they extend to day care, and settings in health care, education and criminal justice systems outside the social services. They see group care as an occupational focus, a field of study and a domain of practice in each of these settings.

Sinclair (1988: 162–3) reviewed the evidence presented to the British Wagner committee on residential care and detected three ideologies within it:

- *Christian love* proposes that care should be guided by a recognition of the importance of every individual. This is similar to the social work philosophy of respect for persons.

- *Therapeutic value of communal living* espoused by therapeutic communities who argued that 'living together' must be used as part of therapy in order that removal from normal environments can be appropriate. This is similar to the radical view outlined above, except that supporters of therapeutic communities would not necessarily agree that the purpose of communal living should be to enhance people's experience of cooperative living in order to combat the alienating effects of isolation in capitalist societies.

- *Individual rights*, the normalisation approach, which suggests that the aim of residential care should be to return people to life styles which are valued by ordinary people in that culture.

Such ideologies have a bearing on possible theoretical perspectives in residential care. Clough's (2000) typology of theory in residential care is as follows:

- Theories of the resident world are like theories of the client world
- Theories of function and task in residential care are like theories of the nature of social work
- Theories of intervention are like social work practice theories and are often connected to them or other psychotherapeutic theories
- Theories of residential homes as systems, refer to the organisational context of residential care.

Theories of intervention are mainly connected to other theoretical approaches discussed in this book, and are dealt with in the relevant chapters, as follows. *Therapeutic environment* theory is psychodynamic in origin and is dealt with in Chapter 4. *Behavioural* approaches (see Chapter 6) often use token economies, but increasingly cognitive methods are being used, particularly to manage depression and anxiety in residential care. *Reality* therapy is a form of cognitive therapy having residential care origins (see Chapter 6). *Systems* theories have been applied to residential care (see Chapter 7). *Radical* approaches connect to critical theory (see Chapter 11). *Empowerment* theories include self-directed group-work, which is also relevant to residential care (Chapter 14). The applicability of general theories of social work to residential care is, then, possible. However, the pragmatic nature of much residential care literature and variable uses of theory suggest that there is as yet a very unclear theoretical basis for residential work to be claimed as a completely separate form of theoretically supported social work activity.

A key European perspective, which has important relationships with residential work, is *social pedagogy*. This is a general theory of social work that concentrates on social work as an educational and developmental process. It is considered in Chapter 10 on social development, therefore, but is not given a chapter on its own, because extended texts are not translated into English; however, some papers and discussion are available.

Effectiveness of social work theories

So far, we have been looking at the range and types of social work theory available. But are they all equal, or is one more useful than another? Is it important, therefore that social work is effective, and according to which points of view? In many societies, social work is used increasingly for more social purposes. The number of countries where it is developing is increasing too. Of course, more does not necessarily mean better. Social work has critics and detractors, but so too have doctors, journalists, lawyers, politicians or priests, all of whom are universal. It is a less deferential, more critical age and we are the better for it, because it means we must constantly be alert to improve our performance. So social workers have sought to see whether our theories are effective as part of that search for improvement. This section considers the outcome of such attempts, which generally do not help us to say that one theory is better than another. Recent research has not tried to answer that sort of question. This is unsatisfactory, because it does not help us to evaluate the theories against each other, and we need these theories to help us to practise. Instead, research in social work has tried to identify services or procedures that are useful, mostly without looking at what practitioners do within those services and procedures. This leads me, in the next section, to explore current debates about the kinds of questions that social work should try to answer.

Early evaluations of social work in the 1950s and 60s either failed to demonstrate that it achieved the results it set out to achieve, or produced uncertain results (Fischer, 1973, 1976; Mullen et al., 1972; Wood, 1978). However, research produced ideas about methods from work on person-centred practice (Chapter 10), behavioural methods (Chapters 5 and 6) and other psychological knowledge, such as communication and social construction research (Chapter 8). A strong focus of this approach, following behavioural models, lies in single-case or single-system research designs. These start from a baseline at the beginning of a piece of intervention, and check for improvement in intended directions during and after intervention. Social work objectives became more highly specified and testable, goals were more limited, assessment was more thorough, evaluation gave better feedback to workers, intensive and focused activities were used, clients rehearsed behaviour instead of just being counselled, special projects were staffed by enthusiasts instead of evaluations being made focusing on routine services, attempts were made to restrict outside interference which limited projects' effectiveness and services were located to encourage clients to come early for help (Sheldon, 1987). All these led to clear evidence, mostly from the USA, that in well-designed agency programmes or individual work demonstrable success was achieved (Reid and Hanrahan, 1982; Thomlison, 1984; Rubin, 1985; Videka-Sherman, 1988; MacDonald and Sheldon, 1992; Gorey, 1996). Most interventions were cognitive-behavioural, but about half the investigations of ordinary casework, non-behavioural groupwork and much family therapy were also successful (MacDonald and Sheldon, 1992). American surveys of groupwork (Tolman and Molidor, 1994) and residential care (Curry, 1995) show that research techniques have been less strong in these areas, but some successful results have been achieved. A number of studies have shown that service developments including or focusing on social work have been successful (Goldberg, 1987). This includes some aspects of community social work and case management with elderly people as part of community care services.

From this brief account of research into the effectiveness of social work, there is research evidence to support cognitive-behavioural and similar theories, and probably fairly focused practice based on task-centred work. Research after the 1980s is into problems or social programmes (Brawley and Martinez-Brawley, 1988) rather than attempting to validate theoretical approaches (Jenkins, 1987). This may be partly because explicit use of theories is not a characteristic of most social work, hence the use of special projects for evaluative research. Smith's (2004) collection of research supporting particular practice interventions does not include any accounts of whether one theory is more effective than another. In any case, Sainsbury (1987) makes the point that often research does not produce changes in practice because individuals' commitments and political impetus lies behind agency practice. There is also a problem of dissemination between those who generate and those who might use research findings (Brawley and Martinez-Brawley, 1988).

Research in social work, then, fails to explain whether one practice theory might be more effective than another. One reason for this is that governments fund most research, mainly to explore the effectiveness of services that meet their objectives. It is not their objective to try out practice theories; therefore this is only ever incidental to the research. Consequently, practitioners are not helped to know how to work in the services that are so carefully evaluated.

Social work theory, therefore, increasingly has a problem, and solution-focused practice is an example of it. This form of practice has been well evaluated in initial trials by its founders, and like many other forms of psychological therapy before it, has been taken up enthusiastically by social workers. However, its formal implementation in social work settings by social workers has not led to research to validate it as a theory. On the other hand, research into organisational settings for social work has got to the point that, for example, a review of day centre settings for mentally ill people can say that this is more effective than inpatient care, employment rehabilitation or outpatient care (Marshall et al. 2001). The problem for practitioners is: what do they do in those settings in order to make them effective for the individuals involved? The largely unresearched theories are the only way to decide. And when the research tells you that day centres are more effective, the context of this judgement is in treatment for mental illness. This is valuable in itself and it is pleasing that social work contributes to it, but curing mental illness is not the purpose of social work. Caring for people with long-term mental illness or dealing with the social aspects of recovery may be. But the same study excluded informal social provision because there was no evidence of its effectiveness. Perhaps not, but it may be welcomed by people with long-term mental illness and contribute to social cohesion by involving people from the community in informal care for their neighbours. These are different objectives from the aim of better care in mental illness. However, the emphasis on effectiveness for health care objectives and the political priority given to them conceals the possibility of other objectives and other priorities not emphasised by politicians and their voters but, in this case, emphasised by the citizens who receive the service. Thus, Wodarski and Thyer's (1998) extensive two-volume survey of effective empirical practice focuses in the first volume on specific mental health diagnoses and in the second volume less easily on 'social problems and practice issues', where much less evidence of what is effective can be adduced.

A remaining area of theoretical debate is between the three views of social work reviewed in Chapter 1, connected to critical, humanist and liberal theories of welfare, and, lying behind these, the related views of humanity. Critical theories continue to assert the importance within welfare services of a transformational approach, trying to achieve social change. Liberal theories continue to assert the validity of practice within and reform of the present social order. Humanist views continue to assert that it is the human beings that matter and they have the possibility of making change work for themselves. Under attack for its weak practical prescriptions, and possibly because of its political unacceptability in the Thatcher–Reagan age of the 1980s, radical theory declined but is now renewed as critical theory. As a result, there is, first, a clearer strategic view of how it is possible to practise critically. There is a broader conception than class-based radical theory, drawn particularly from feminist theory, of possible objectives and ways of practice that seem possible and engaging for both practitioners and clients. There is a method drawn from the postmodern concern with language and social construction, which suggests there are things that will make a real difference and are very acceptable, according to the solution-focused research, to clients.

However, there remains a cleft in social work between this critical position and the liberal view. We can see it most clearly in Chapter 12, where anti-discrimination holds to structural views, while sensitivity theory, aiming to achieve many of the same objectives, incorporates an understanding of the impact of structural ideas, but acts within the present social order. It also exists in empowerment theory, which in principle many critical theorists would support, but whose practice prescriptions mostly do not incorporate structural objectives.

The politics of knowledge in practice theory

Positivism and interpretivism

So far, we have seen that, while theory is important for helping practitioners to decide what to do, recent social work research has not tried to evaluate social work theories, and we can only make general statements about the sort of thing that is usually useful, often drawn from psychological rather than social work research and not covering the full range of social work activity. Why has this situation arisen? As we saw in Chapter 1, groups concerned to promote particular views of social work seek influence for related practice theories. Connected to this is their view of what knowledge and theory count as useful in practice. To understand this, we have to understand different views about epistemology, that is, how we understand and write about human knowledge.

Brechin and Sidell (2000) usefully explain the distinction between interpretivist and positivist views of knowledge. *Positivists* believe that the world is orderly and that how it works follows natural rules that we can come to understand. The world exists independently of human beings and we can stand outside it, that is, be *objective*, and observe it. Human beings are like objects, animals in a natural world, and behave according to rules that apply to objects of that kind. If we do so systematically, we can understand how the world works and the rules that affect its inhabitants, just as we can understand other aspects of the natural world. Then we can apply that knowledge to create desired changes. In doing so, we can be effective, because we can explain how one action causes another. Human beings are complicated, so it will be difficult, but it must be possible.

Interpretivists believe that human beings are independent, free to follow their will as part of the world, in relationships with other human beings, so that they cannot be objective. Society is separate from the individuals it contains, so we can be most effective by relating to and understanding how other human beings understand the world in relation to ourselves. Participation in human relationships means that we influence the world we are studying, and in turn our understandings about the world will influence how we behave, that is, we are *subjective*. Human beings are subjects, so their actions affect others, but in doing so also change themselves. This is so, even though they may be constrained by the natural and social order of the environment around us. This view says that it is just not possible to collect all the necessary information to understand the rules of human life, so it is better to think about the world in a more flexible way.

For example, if I shout at my children and upset them, my perception of their reaction will change my future behaviour to be less aggressive, assuming that my personal values and social objectives in dealing with my children lead me to want to avoid upsetting them. Therefore, as social workers, we need to enter into relationships with people and engage in mutual exploration of what is happening to gain a full appreciation of the situation. People's social objectives and values in their relationships are always a factor. My own view of the construction of social work and its theories, explained in Chapter 1, is interpretivist: I emphasised how social workers, their agencies and clients change each other through their interactions.

Disputes around these two positions have created the debates in social work. There are four main views about how knowledge should be used in social work to provide the basis for theory, which I describe here in an order that I hope will make them easier to explain. Then, I discuss the politics between them and present a view of the debate.

Evidence-based practice (EBP) views

Evidence-based views argue that to be ethical, social workers should use knowledge that has been gathered and tested empirically in the most rigorous ways possible to provide evidence of the form of action that is most likely to achieve its objectives for the benefit of clients. In social work, these ideas are represented in the work of Gambrill, Macdonald, Sheldon and Thyer and are associated particularly with cognitive-behavioural theories.

The traditional view of a profession is that it develops expert knowledge, and understanding this knowledge is what defines a member of that profession. EBP supports and extends this traditional position about the role of knowledge in social work, and so I start with it. Orcutt (1990), Kirk and Reid (2002) and Reamer (1994) provide historical and analytical accounts of social work knowledge development, the first two particularly focusing on the role of science in producing social work knowledge.

A number of approaches exist:

- *Classifications.* These try to classify by logical analysis the kinds of problems that social workers deal with and their treatment methods. Examples include psychodynamic ideas such as 'differential diagnosis' (Turner, 1995), in which problems that people experience influence the approach to practice taken; Hollis and Woods' (1981) casework treatment classification; the American medical diagnostic and statistical manual for mental disorders (DSM); and person-in-environment (PIE) associated with ecological theory (Karls and Wandrei, 1994).

- *'Research-minded' practice* (Everitt et al., 1992). This proposes that social workers should be aware of and influenced by empirical research about the problems and effectiveness of services they provide. Kirk and Reid (2002) consider at length the problems of disseminating research for practitioners to use and ways of overcoming them.

- *EBP* (Thyer and Kazi, 2004). This proposes that social workers should practise using the best available evidence of what actions will be effective to achieve the intended outcomes. If evidence provides a causal explanation and is generalisable, in the positivist tradition (Brechin and Sidell, 2000), evidence-based practitioners prefer it. This means that they prefer research designs that suppress subjectivity as far as possible, such as surveys or experiments (Gomm, 2000a, b) where statistical and other techniques prevent subjective influence. Random controlled trials of treatment techniques that mimic the tests used to see if medical drugs are effective are ideal. Single-case designs (Kazi, 1998), where workers establish present levels of behaviour and retest after intervention to see what changes have taken place, apply this method to individual cases. Standardised scales are used for assessment, so that we can see how people compare with a wider population. Using all these techniques together is sometimes referred to as 'empirical practice' or 'empirical clinical practice' in the USA (Faul et al., 2001). Research studies are collected and analysed to accumulate results to increase the generalisability of research to a wider range of circumstances. For example, Franklin et al; (2001) used accumulated single-case designs to demonstrate the effectiveness of solution-focused work with children in school.

- *Evaluation of service programmes.* These propose that actual services should be evaluated as a whole, rather than the component parts of practitioners' actions. This would produce evidence about what patterns of provision are effective, but I argued, above, that it does not help us to decide what to do as we practise as part of those services. Hence, understanding of and research on theory is still important, and rather neglected now in favour of service evaluation.

- *Practitioner research.* This approach suggests that practitioners should research their own practice, by carrying out small research projects and single-case studies that cumulatively could produce useful evidence of what is effective. Doing their own research might also make them more research-minded, and more able to evaluate the results of research for its potential impact on their practice.

- *Practice guidelines.* This approach is a form of dissemination; it proposes that research findings should be incorporated into and interpreted by guidance for practitioners. In the UK, the Social Care Institute for Excellence (SCIE) is an example of what governments, official bodies and professional associations do around the world. Its guidelines on managing practice and assessing the mental health needs of older people (SCIE, 2001, 2002), for example, incorporate research findings but are produced with reference to a panel of experienced practitioners to convey what has been found to be useful in practice. Howard and Jenson (1999a) suggest that guidelines are an effective way of transferring research findings into practice. Rosen et al. (2003) propose that such guidelines should contain a taxonomy, that is, an ordered classification of the outcome targets and interventions associated with them. Richey and Roffman (1999) suggest that they need to incorporate practical values and organisational requirements so that they fit with agency programmes. This is the approach taken in many of the practice texts reviewed in this book. However, from an evidence-based practice viewpoint, Kirk (1999) argues that they include too much unsubstantiated opinion and policy, although Howard and Jenson (1999b) argue that many of these practical problems can be overcome. As with Epstein's cautions on eclecticism (see Chapter 2), in Wambach et al.'s (1999) view careful collaboration and discussion is required, rather than personal implementation and the creation of guidelines.

These approaches interconnect, as the account of practitioner research shows, and most proponents of positivist approaches to social work knowledge would support many of these developments. Classification, however, is criticised (for example by Kirk and Reid, 2002) as producing complex distinctions based on practitioners' opinions that are hard to use in practice and have little evidence to back up any prescriptions for action. Research-mindedness has been criticised for lack of rigour, since practitioners might choose congenial theories that they are aware of, rather than systematically evaluating all the evidence available. EBP has been criticised, from an interpretivist position, for its failure to recognise the limitations of the positivist position in a human activity and more broadly for its tendency to examine small-scale psychological interventions with individuals, which form only a small part of the social roles performed by many social workers. As we have seen, research into the effectiveness of service programmes is often not detailed enough to give practice guidance, so that there is wide variation in how apparently similar programmes actually work. Practitioner research has been criticised for producing large numbers of poorly constructed studies reflecting the personal interests of researchers, rather than an overall plan for systematic knowledge development. Practice guidelines have been criticised for incorporating material to comply with the policy demands of governments and agencies or professional opinion or trends rather than evidence of effectiveness.

An important stance for EBP is that it should derive from rigorous research, where subjectivity is limited as much as possible, and identify causation, so that effective practice may be derived from it. Also, its results should be generalisable, so that its findings may be used in a variety of situations.

Social construction views

This is the view of social work practice theory discussed in Chapter 1; here we are meeting it in a more generalised form referring to all knowledge and understanding.

Social construction views argue that knowledge and understanding about the world come from social interactions among people. Knowledge is therefore constructed within cultural, historical and local contexts through the language used to interpret social experiences. This comes to form and represent social experiences because it is the only way in which those experiences can be understood. In social work, this position is represented most directly in the work of a group of Finnish researchers (Jokinen et al., 1999; Karvinen et al. 1999; Hall et al., 2003) and Parton (1996; Parton and O'Byrne, 2000) and is associated with social construction practice theories (see Chapter 8).

Social construction is an interpretivist, postmodernist theory proposing that understandings about the world come from interactions between people as part of many interchanges in a social, cultural and historical context.

A useful aspect of social construction is its distinctive approach to research, which uses detailed analysis of human interaction, particularly conversation analysis, relying on video- and audio-taped records of interactions. These are systematically analysed to reveal patterns of communication and behaviour that may be hidden.

An important issue for social construction research is that it should engage people who are the subject of research in an equal relationship with researchers, so that complex human understandings about the situation may be explored from different points of view and the outcomes should represent as full a picture of complex human situations as possible. Social constructionists argue that supporters of EBP produce results that do not reflect this rich, complex reality. It is even naive; a wider range of methods that examines how people make sense of the social situations they face is more helpful (White, 1997). The social and historical context in which situations develop and knowledge is researched must have an important impact on our understandings of individuals, society and research as a source of knowledge. An important idea is 'tacit knowledge', the practical understanding of how things work in our social arrangements, which is often not turned into formal, researched knowledge (Polanyi, 1958).

Empowerment views

Empowerment views argue that knowledge primarily comes from clients and that to be ethical social workers should use knowledge according to clients' wishes in order to empower them further. In social work, these ideas are most clearly represented in Beresford and Croft's work (1993, 2001; Croft and Beresford, 1994) and are associated particularly with social and community development, ethnic sensitivity, empowerment and advocacy theories (Chapters 10, 13 and 14 respectively).

Empowerment views of knowledge argue two things:

■ The purposes of social work require workers to seek social justice (a socialist-collectivist position) and therefore to empower people by responding to their knowledge and understanding about the world.

■ Clients (in this view often called consumers or service users) often have the best knowledge about their circumstances and objectives, which should therefore be followed.

These views give priority to the views and wishes of service users. Since they are often oppressed, disadvantaged and marginalised, empowerment views of knowledge argue that their understanding of their situation should be what guides social work practice. Feminist social workers argue that social workers reinforce oppression of women through the role of social work in surveillance and enforcement of conventional patriarchal relationships (Dominelli, 2002a). Many perspectives on practice say that it is not practically possible to pursue activities contrary to service users' wishes. Alternative views about knowledge emphasise the worker as an expert, whose knowledge should set the direction of work, and this diminishes their valuation of their client's knowledge. In democratic societies, professionals and governments should respond to the social demands of the citizens. This view about knowledge is different from value positions such as self-determination, which argue for the client's right to set the direction of the work. Empowerment views of knowledge propose that service users' knowledge is best and should be empowered. One way is through working in a dialogue that incorporates their views as a critique of professional knowledge (Sellick et al., 2002). Such views partly rely on 'epistemic privilege', the view that the person or social group that creates knowledge or experiences particular aspects of life has an advantage in understanding and describing their knowledge or experience. This view is also espoused in relation to people from minority groups; it is claimed that only they have the experience of oppression that gives them the full understanding of it. Empathy is not enough.

This approach also produces a useful research perspective. The development of action research proposed a technique by which social projects could be evaluated as they developed, the results influencing how the project changed. Because of its interpretivist view, this was criticised for its lack of rigour by positivists, although it has proved practically useful in evaluating experimental projects. It was also criticised by empowerment writers for viewing projects from the point of view of the funders or professionals involved in projects. This led to the development of participative action research in resource-poor countries (Whyte, 1991). More individual work also produced alternative research approaches. De Shazer and Berg (1997), for example, emphasise the importance of whether solution-focused therapy meets clients' objectives, rather than agency purposes. Early research by Beresford and Croft (1986), evaluating the introduction of a community social work management system in a large social services department, seeks to evaluate this professional development, through clients' perspectives and argues that clients' irrelevance to the innovation or active dislike of it is an argument against it.

Realist views

Realist views are a fairly new perspective and argue that evidence of reality is not always available to empirical observation, so that knowledge *emerges* or is generated from human interpretations of successions of events that can be captured empirically. In social work, these ideas are represented in the work of Morén and Blom (2003) and Kazi (2003). Although often described as 'realist' for convenience, many writers prefer to talk about 'critical realism', because this particular view of realism seeks to question taken-for-granted assumptions about theory and research, and this connects the ideas to critical social science theory, which tries to achieve this critical position. EBP is realist in another way, because it accepts that there is a reality to research, but we have seen already that critics of EBP do not see this as critical in a social science sense.

Realist views argue that social phenomena exist beyond social constructions (Houston, 2002), but that the constructions are nevertheless important to understand. Their current importance originates from the work of contemporary social scientists, in particular Bhaskar (1979) and Archer (1995) and researchers such as Pawson and Tilley (1997), whose approach has been discussed and elaborated in social work by Kazi (2003). The following account is based on the discussions by Sayer (2000) and Houston (2001), with additional material. Bhaskar (1979, cited in Sayer, 2000: Ch. 1) distinguishes between things we study empirically, such as a man's behaviour, and our explanations of that behaviour. For example, psychodynamic and behavioural theories both offer explanations of the man's behaviour as a consequence of empirical study and practice experience, but there is also a discourse between them about which is a more valid and helpful explanation for various purposes, including social work. This discourse about validity is a different issue from the man's behaviour.

The crucial point about this distinction is that the 'real' man and his behaviour exists, however we explain it. Real things have structures and causal powers, that is, they have the capacity to make things happen. A social work agency, for example, has a chain of command, a social mandate to carry out particular tasks and employs social workers to do the work. The social workers are able to do the work if they are properly educated and skilled in what they might do. This is so, even if the agency is closed for the night; it still exists in its social relationships and our understanding of its existence.

The 'real' is different from the 'actual'. For example, suppose the agency is new and will start work on Monday. During the weekend before the opening, the agency and workers are still real. Its structure, for example the relationships between workers and between the agency and wider social structures, still exists. They have the real capacity (causal power) to do social work, but they are not actually doing it. They only become an actual social work agency when they open on Monday morning.

The 'empirical' may be real or actual, and depends on what we can observe and experience. If we visited the agency after opening, we could see the workers and what they are doing, compare it with what we know social work to be and decide whether these are social workers in a social work agency. But suppose we arrive in the city on the Saturday before opening, hoping to visit the agency. If nobody knows where the office is, we might have little confidence of the agency's reality, but it is real nevertheless. Most people have had the experience of getting an address wrong and then walking round and asking themselves: 'Does this place exist at all?' A building with a notice about opening hours on Monday might give us more confidence that the agency is going to be actual. Meeting a social worker and hearing them talk about their future work might give us more. We might be able to see that they have the capacity (causal power) to become a social worker, but today and tomorrow they are not an 'actual' social worker. So we may build up more and more confidence in something that is real but not, at the time, actual. Finding extensive evidence of the existence of the agency would be very difficult, so a positivist approach is not helpful. We rely more on a human sense of how much information is accumulating that the agency is there. Houston (2001) points out that all human activity takes place in open systems, which are in constant change, and depends on human beings' decisions, which are not fully determined by their own psychology or social circumstances. Therefore, expecting to use evidence to predict human activity is impossible. We should refer more to events containing tendencies and being influenced by psychological and social mechanisms. By examining the tendencies and influences, we can see the mechanisms at work.

Archer (1996) argues that culture in societies influences people's individual behaviour, and in a circular process their behaviour collectively generates their culture. This is similar to Berger and Luckmann's (1971) account of social construction. Archer (1995) proposes that existing social constructions form the social context within which new social constructions are formed. As these emerge, they form a new social context within which continued social construction takes place. Her model of this process makes it clear that, of course, social construction not only brings about change, but may also lead to reproduction, that is, the present social construction is maintained. This is as you would expect from Berger and Luckmann's (1971) account: constructions form a stable reality to the people involved. You would also expect this from critical thinking, which makes clear that the existing social order is hard to change. So, social construction does not, as its critics often say, always lead to instability, uncertainty and constant change. Usually it leads to stability and continuity. This makes it possible to use positivist research to some extent, but within an awareness that there are lots of complexities and possibilities.

This concept of *emergence* is important in understanding the realist critique of EBP, which often ignores emergent properties. EBP assumes that either we can observe everything that exists or what actually happens is all that might happen. However, we cannot empirically observe our social work agency, although we can see some information suggesting that it is there in the possibility that these people may come together on Monday, for it to emerge in the new week. Realist theory therefore allows for emergent possibilities. Archer (2000) proposes, moreover, that although language and interaction are important, it is our practical experience of the world that allows our humanity to emerge and become our personal identity. So what we do in relation to other people is what mainly gives us an identity. In turn, this emphasises that practice is what produces reality, not what we think or theorise about.

Pawson and Tilley (1997) describe research and evaluation on crime prevention and reduction projects. Each project is in a different area and social context, so its initial social structures vary, and the outcomes of similar project activities will also vary. However, by examining a number of projects, researchers can identify the different factors that might have an effect on how projects work. However, it will not usually be possible, as EBP assumes, to identify particular interventions that will always have the same effects. Moreover, as society (the initial contextual social construction) changes, what will be needed will emerge towards a different pattern. But, for a limited period, relevant factors that might be helpful in setting up a crime prevention project would be identifiable. Many people would argue that this is a reasonable approach to take to social work. We have some knowledge and information to guide us, but we have to apply it with an awareness of the change that is going on all around us. Therefore, flexibility and following the principles and guidelines of practice theories are more practical than expecting clear statements from research that we can apply to the variety of human situations we are likely to meet.

Following this principle, a social work researcher could see how a social work technique works in a number of different settings. It might work well in some circumstances but not in others. As you accumulate information, you can identify those circumstances that affect how it works. This would then tell you how the use of the technique is likely to change as social changes affecting the context in which the technique is used change.

Realist ideas amend, rather than replace, EBP by accepting social construction and the need to understand the cultural and social origin of much human action, but they also question social construction views. The strict social construction view that everything is contextual and depends on the concepts used ultimately ignores the need to explain and take into account the physical reality of the world and the way it affects how we act (Best 1989; Bhaskar 1979, 1989). It also ignores the reality of pre-existing social constructions that affect us. The social construction 'social work' presupposes the existence of human communication through physical means. We have to interact to do social work, and it presupposes social ideas like helping others and problem-solving. These change over time and you can trace the changes, but they have a good deal of stability and are the basis on which many people carry out their social interactions. As Berger and Luckmann (1971) originally described social construction, it is a social construction of what is, to its participants, a social reality.

Assessing the politics of social work knowledge

How can we assess these various views about social work knowledge? First, is this debate important or can practical people ignore it? The distinction between positivist and interpretivist views of the world is a well-recognised, long-standing philosophical distinction going back several centuries and it is still making a difference to people. Robbins et al. (1999) argue that the choice to focus on scientific theory and knowledge is a recent and ideological one for social work. It is a powerful difference, as we can see from the debate that has affected social work in the late 1900s and early 2000s. It is crucial to major political and social beliefs. For example, critical and feminist theorists value shared human interaction and reject positivist approaches as technological knowledges that manipulate human beings in favour of existing social orders, because they accept the general social context in which we live and mainly seek to change individuals. Halmi (2003), to take another example, argues that social work models of explanation must take account of chaos theory and non-linear thinking, the view that simple cause-and-effect explanations of human social behaviour of the kind that EBP assumes are insufficiently complex to reflect the reality.

Table 3.4 outlines points made by Gibbs and Gambrill (2002) summarising some arguments against EBP, drawing on a paper referring to EBP in medicine, and includes points made for and against EBP by other writers. They also attack Webb (2001), who concludes that evidence in social work is:

- mediated by organisations, availability of resources, communication and social relations
- situated in complex decision-making environments
- provisional, since most social situations cannot be fully understood
- pragmatic, arising from an interaction between clients', agencies' and workers' understandings of particular situations rather than being concerned with formal, therapeutic decision-making.

He suggests, in a realist way, that research could usefully focus on how all these factors impinge upon social work decision-making, and how the EBP approach has become a socially valued way of dealing with these issues.

Table 3.4 shows how EBP focuses on particular approaches to obtaining evidence, while opposition to this view points to the way in which EBP gives priority to a particular way of thinking about social work, as a therapeutic process in which explicit decisions about workers' actions are designed to have therapeutic consequences. They also point to how this connects with the managerial and social control aspects of the role of social work, rather than the liberating and transforming aspects. Critics of EBP acknowledge the value that information from evidence can have, but propose that EBP neglects the practical and moral aspects of social work and the role of emotion, attitudes, judgements and discretion (Taylor and White, 2001). In this view, knowledge is not the only thing: how it is applied and the political and social processes through which it is applied are just as important. There are and will continue to be different approaches to gaining and using knowledge. In particular, both interpretivist social construction and positivist EBP commentators seem not to acknowledge the many aspects of validity in the other alternative approach to knowledge.

Table 3.4 Arguments about evidence-based practice (EBP)

Arguments against	Arguments for
EBP is based on optimal behaviour in a planned, organised environment; life is not like that.	EBP allows for a planned and systematic approach to understanding complex situations, even though it does not have all the answers.
Social workers deal in reflexive understanding of complexity, not decision-making about certainties.	Complexities can often be disentangled if you ask the right questions. EBP allows for an organised approach to uncertain situations.
By separating 'facts' and 'values', EBP undermines professional judgement and discretion.	Professional judgement should be based on evidence, not values.
EBP restricts social work to a narrow, linear rationality, connected to managerial objectives, encouraging cost-cutting and limiting flexibility.	Service management should develop and follow evidence of what is effective. Applying the research consistently will often be more expensive.
There is nothing new; EBP is common sense; we are already doing EBP.	EBP involves identifying the issue, searching for research, critical review and decision-making with clients. This inspires confidence.
By proposing how to think, EBP proposes what to think; evidence can be found for any view.	EBP proposes critical evaluation of the evidence and opposes misuse of evidence to make inappropriate claims.
EBP restricts practice innovation.	Innovation should be based on evidence, not untested ideas.
EBP is reverence for the researchers' authority.	EBP gives the client the authority. Other practice guidelines give authority to agency policy or teachers who are able to engage support.
EBP ignores client preferences in favour of research by professionals (the empowerment view).	EBP requires incorporating client views and being open about professional and research information.
There is no organisational support to use EBP rather than policy or political decisions.	This means that actions may not be effective; ultimately evidence will be influential.
EBP damages flexibility in therapeutic relationships, neglecting artistic, spiritual issues by focusing on workers as rational thinkers.	Rational thinking and critical evaluation of research findings are preferred over opinion and worker preference; artistic and spiritual matters should be the client's preference rather than the worker's.
EBP neglects tacit knowledge and social constructions, which have an impact on social relations (the social construction view).	EBP would include evidence of such constructions in its evaluations (but constructionists would say it takes particular constructions for granted).
EBP assumes that what there is evidence of is useful in practice.	EBP is concerned with testing if what is being used in practice is true, and finding truths that may be useful in practice.
Many issues that social workers deal with (for example poverty and oppression) are not susceptible to research evidence.	Some EBP focuses on effective ways of resolving wider social issues. Well-constructed questions about what clients want to achieve will often produce relevant evidence.
EBP is a cookbook approach, encouraging application of 'effective' ideas from theoretically inconsistent sources.	A critical appraisal of the value of a particular intervention in a particular case includes its theoretical consistency.
In practice, extensive reviews of the research are not practicable.	With particular clients, research-based practice guidelines and agency policies, daily research reviews are not required.
Clients' needs are unmet if there is no relevant research.	Absence of research should be reviewed with clients, so that they can understand the basis of what the worker is doing.
Random controlled trials (RCTs), the favoured method, are inappropriate for much social work practice.	RCTs are a robust research method, but other methods are required for different purposes, and a wide range is available (but EBP tends to regard other methods as not robust enough).
Effectiveness is a matter of opinion.	Clients' opinions should be consulted about the evidence.
EBP is derived from discredited logical positivism and behaviourism.	EBP originates from health care. Cognitive-behavioural practice has been subjected to rigorous research and so contributes strongly.
EBP privileges one research paradigm above others. It limits or is inconsistent with the range of methods, evaluation approaches and teaching options in education and practice.	EBP raises important issues and offers useful tools that may be integrated into many kinds of education and practice, and may be applied in many different situations. Inconsistency is not an argument against innovation using research.
Research courses in social work education are not sufficient as a basis for EBP.	Existing reviews and guidelines may be used, and evaluation of research does not require training in using the research methods.
EBP pathologises people, associating them with their condition and blaming them; it is indifferent to diversity.	EBP (and behavioural practice) assumes that all explanations apply to everyone, so it does not label people with their problems and large-scale research does not produce good results for minorities.

Source: Gibbs and Gambrill (2002); Heineman-Pieper et al. (2002); Raynor (2003); Sayer (2000); Webb (2001, 2002); with adaptations and additions.

Positivist commentators, for example, reject the idea of tacit knowledge; all knowledge is knowable and researchable to a positivist. EBP commentators claim to include interpretivist evidence, but they rarely do, since they do not think it sufficiently rigorous compared with evidence gained through positivist approaches. However, this decision is made on positivist criteria, not criteria about different kinds of validity. An example of this is Reid's (2001) acceptance of pluralistic research methods, but only in a context of common standards for appraising research knowledge. Marsh (2003) comments that EBP commentators reject the value of theory as a way of organising evidence into useable systems of thought. The evidence-based caution with practice guidelines is another example of the resistance to practical means to incorporate and interpret evidence-based knowledge in practice.

Interpretivist commentators, similarly, do not accept the validity of the possibility of independent rigorous observation, without which the EBP arguments have no foundation. Smith (2000) points out that research into effective outcomes ignores the importance of process. Social factors are usually so complex that success in achieving outcomes is usually not evidence of the effectiveness of what is done; many other factors might have caused the success. Outcome measurement does not usually measure what is done as part of the work. In a related point, Mahrer (2004) suggests that helping requires knowledge and understanding to have an effect in real situations; what can be proved as true through empirical means is not necessarily useful, and useful information and theory may be less easily proved, but still useful in practice. Gambrill (2001) argues from an EBP viewpoint that social work does not involve clients in decision-making, instead relying on the authority of agency mandate and professional assumptions as guides to practice. In this view, EBP aligns with empowerment views, but, rather than relying on clients' attitudes and opinions directly, seeks to use the research evidence as a way of making rational decisions with the client. Empowerment commentators would argue that this gives too much importance to professional interpretations of evidence.

Understanding human and social situations will inevitably be complex and consequently we need a wide range of methods of research and understanding, depending on the purposes we will use knowledge for. Närhi's (2002) Finnish study shows that workers gain practical, value, factual, procedural and tacit knowledges from a range of sources, including their daily experience of how agencies work and from their clients' attitudes and beliefs. They share this with colleagues regularly, building up a pattern of local knowledge, which interacts with more formal knowledge. An appreciation of the complexity of this process of building up knowledge suggests that a shared reflective process, as discussed in Chapter 2, is a good way of collecting and using knowledge in practice. Rosen (2003) argues that we should use knowledge of whatever kind systematically, giving argued rationales for decisions (Osmo and Rosen, 2002), avoiding transferring lay assumptions about clients and their circumstances when good evidence is available, adapting evidence to 'practice-friendly' systems of guidance and applying evidence to empowerment and social justice objectives as well as psychotherapeutic interventions. Webb (2002) suggests that prescriptive implementations of cognitive-behavioural frameworks do not offer the flexibility for responsive practice, and suggests acceptance of a range of sources of knowledge, provided it is tested and decisions are made carefully. Since our purpose is to be effective in practice, we will sometimes be able to use detailed experiments on individuals providing evidence of causation that will give us rules for practice, but we will often have to take into account the importance of clients' views of what they want, the aims of social and policy thought, and hidden and taken-for-granted tacit elements of understanding and the historical and social context in which we are placed.

CRITICAL PRACTICE FOCUS

The Gargery family 2
Looking back at the account of the Gargery family (Chapter 1), what alternative practice approaches do the different theoretical perspectives in Figure 3.1 suggest. What would be needed from interpretivist and positivist points of view to understand the situation better? What are the differences and similarities in how you would research the case from EBP, empowerment, social construction and realist points of view if you wanted to use the case to contribute to social work knowledge? In what ways would these different approaches to knowledge help you to work with the Gargerys?

The future politics of social work theory

Social work theory must have a future, because all activities are informed by theory, even if it is covert or inexplicit. What trends, then, can we see?

Social work theory trends are leading in similar directions to a reformation of social work ideas. Cognitive ideas – from psychodynamic ego psychology, behaviourist approaches and existentialism – draw attention to the rational control that human beings have over their environment and their own behaviour. If we accept this movement, it rejects the traditional psychodynamic view that clients are driven by irrational and unreasonable needs; that view has almost disappeared from social work. It rejects the traditional radical view that clients are unable to overcome the oppression that characterises all capitalist societies, or the systems view that energy to make changes in a system must come from external influences. Those views have been replaced by the influence of constructive, critical and ecological theory in devising ways of showing what possibilities exist within the situations we see, while acknowledging a heavily constrained world. The patient, client, service user, citizen is clearly seen as a crucial actor, even *the* crucial actor, in achieving whatever outcomes are desired in the social work process. Thus, social work must be more participatory, rather than therapeutic. This is the success of task-centred work. Social work must also recognise the particular social and personal characteristics of clients, rather than treating them as all of a kind, or all needing the same model of practice. This is the success of feminist and humanist approaches to social work. It must also recognise the way clients are treated in social systems, without denying the possibility of action. This is the success of sensitivity and empowerment approaches to social work. And if the client is the crucial actor, the social relations between the worker and the context created by the agency are the means of the change that theories increasingly optimistically say will be possible.

Social work, therefore, is forming round a new nexus: we can see this from its theoretical movements. It is accepting the reflexive-therapeutic element of itself, but moving towards the reflexive, away from the therapeutic. It is accepting the individualist-reformist element of itself, but the individualism is not of the kind that says that only the individual, not the social, counts. Social work theory is saying that the needs and wishes of the individual served must count in any morally valid practice that intervenes in the social. Social work theory is, finally, accepting the socialist-collectivist part of itself, but with an emphasis on the social and political position of clients within critical, feminist and empowering practice, rather than seeking to form their needs into false collective interests.

We have shifted towards a positive and optimistic theory. In their practice social workers implement different views of the social role of their profession, implying different analyses of their social world. This book's account and analyses of their practice theories present some of the possibilities for using those theories to draw ideas from various theoretical traditions and understand their competing perspectives. Social workers use critical and reflective practice to create theory, by practising reflexively with their clients. This is how their work becomes part of the critical debate among the ideas that inform social work action in the arenas that construct theory in a complex social world.

Part II of the book looks at groups of practice theories representing different theoretical traditions in social work. Each chapter:

- identifies the main perspectives offered by the theory
- draws out some important practice ideas that social workers have found useful
- explains important debates about that theoretical tradition
- shows how one or two important writers in this tradition have recently presented it in systematic practice guidance for social workers
- presents a case study to permit a focus on critical practice and asks some questions about how the ideas in the chapter might be applied to the case study and what alternative theories might offer to produce a different perspective or contribution to practice
- tries to draw out the important features of the theory for practice in the commentary and conclusion.

FURTHER READING

Beresford, P. and Croft, S. (2001) 'Service users' knowledges and the social construction of social work', *Journal of Social Work*, 1 (3): 295–316.
A good statement of the empowerment position on social work knowledge.

Gibbs, L. and Gambrill, E. (2002) 'Evidence-based practice: counterarguments to objections', *Research in Social Work Practice*, 12(3): 452–76.
An EBP response to criticisms, and, if read critically, particularly for what it does not say and the way it represents its opposition, a good account of the weaknesses in the EBP perspective. It also usefully connects to the medical origins of the EBP approach.

Gomm, R. and Davies, C. (eds) (2000) *Using Evidence in Health and Social Care* (London: Sage).
An excellent edited text on the critical use of evidence, which reviews clearly and neutrally the debate between positivist and constructionist thinking.

Karvinen, S., Pösö, T. and Satka, M. (1999) *Reconstructing Social Work Research*, (Jyväskylä: SoPhi).
A ground-breaking book, by Finnish authors, applying social construction research in social work, with an excellent theoretical discussion.

Kirk, S. A. and Reid, W. J. (eds) (2002) *Science and Social Work: A Critical Appraisal* (New York: Columbia University Press).
An excellent account of a range of scientific and evidence-based approaches to social work.

Morén, S. and Blom, B. (2003) 'Explaining human change: on generative mechanisms in social work practice', *Journal of Critical Realism*, 2(1): 37–61.
A good statement of the critical realist position on social work knowledge.

Smith, D. (ed.) (2004) *Social Work and Evidence-Based Practice* (London; Jessica Kingsley).
A collection of recent British research and sceptical commentary on evidence-based practice.

Stepney, P and Ford, D. (eds) *Social Work Models, Methods and Theories: A Framework for Practice* (Lyme Regis: Russell House).
An edited collection reviewing social work theories in a British practice context.

Thyer, B. A. and Kazi, M. A. F. (eds) (2004) *International Perspectives on Evidence-Based Practice in Social Work* (Birmingham: Venture).
A good review of various applications of evidence-based practice from across the world, demonstrating some applications in non-Western countries and some community applications.

Turner, F. J. (ed.) (1996) *Social Work Treatment: Interlocking Theoretical Approaches*, 4th edn (New York: Free Press).
The latest edition of a long-established USA-centric text, containing authoritative accounts by enthusiasts for the main American models of social work practice, although its edited structure underplays comparative and critical insights into the theories, and it does not explore issues about the construction of social work knowledge.

Webb, S. A. (2001) 'Some considerations on the validity of evidence-based practice in social work', *British Journal of Social Work*, 31(1): 57–79.
A good statement of the constructionist critique of evidence-based practice.

WEBSITES

http://www.campbellcollaboration.org/
The website of the Campbell Collaboration, which provides systematic reviews of evidence about social interventions, most of them agency- or service-based, and therefore wider than social work practice interventions.

http://www.cochrane.org/index0.htm
The website of the Cochrane Collaboration, an organisation similar to Campbell covering health care.

http://www.elsc.org.uk/socialcareresource/tswr/tswrindex.htm
The website of the 'Theorising Social Work Research' seminar series, which positions debate about social work research around the year 2000.

http://www.scie.org.uk/
The website of the Social Care Institute for Excellence, the UK government organisation that sets and reviews standards of practice; contains links to various resources and organisations that disseminate practice research.

PART II
Reviewing social work theories

CHAPTER 4

Psychodynamic Perspectives

What this chapter is about

This and the next three chapters focus on 'individualist-reformist' theories, working with individuals, families and groups and focusing on improving their situation within the present social order, or achieving changes in the policies and practices for the benefit of clients and others like them. Psychodynamic perspectives are particularly individualist, since they have little focus on social change.

Psychodynamic perspectives are based on the work of Freud and his followers, and developments of their work. They are called 'psychodynamic' because the theory underlying them assumes that behaviour comes from movements and interactions in people's minds. The theories use various techniques to interpret how people's minds are working by observing their behaviour. Psychodynamic theory emphasises the way in which the mind stimulates behaviour, and both mind and behaviour influence and are influenced by the person's social environment. These ideas are a crucial historical starting point for understanding social work theory because they were influential during the period 1930–60, when social work was becoming established. Therefore, they are the basis for the 'traditional social work' that many other theories oppose or develop from, and elements of their approach still influence everyday practice, partly because psychoanalysis is well known in Western culture and most people have some awareness of its basic concepts. However, in their most complete form, they are mainly used in specialist, psychiatric settings.

MAIN POINTS

> ➤ Psychodynamic perspectives are an important historical source for basic social work skills.

> ➤ Their long history means that application to different forms of practice is fully developed.

> ➤ Recent developments in attachment theory are relevant to child care and protection and loss and bereavement.

> ➤ Recent developments in ego psychology have influenced therapeutic work with adults, particularly in the USA.

> ➤ Psychodynamic ideas are a rich source of complex ideas for interpreting behaviour.

> ▶ Wide understanding and study of psychodynamic theory makes for good connections with other professions and across national boundaries.
>
> ▶ Lack of a strong evidence base and the use of models of internal thinking have led to criticism.
>
> ▶ The historical, Eurocentric and Jewish cultural origins of psychodynamic theory lead to victim-blaming and stereotypical assumptions about women and homosexual behaviour.

PRACTICE ISSUES AND CONCEPTS

> ▶ *Anxiety* and *ambivalence*, derived from inadequate resolution of problems in an earlier period of life, which in turn lead to powerful feelings of aggression, anger and love.
>
> ▶ *Coping*, the ability to manage present problems without anxiety.
>
> ▶ *Defences* and *resistance*, psychological barriers to working on life issues, again derived from poor resolution of past problems.
>
> ▶ *Transference* and *countertransference*, interpreted for social work to mean the effect of past experience on present behaviour patterns, reflected in the client's behaviour in relation with the worker. The worker helps people to see where past problems are leading to present difficulties and find practical ways of overcoming psychological and practical barriers to taking effective action.
>
> ▶ *Relationships* with people to model effective thinking and self-control and as a vehicle to gain influence and confidence to explore psychological issues. Contemporary writers often refer to psychodynamic work as 'relational', which emerges from the 'object relations' theories of psychodynamic work (Ganzer and Ornstein, 2002).
>
> *Sources:* Partly from Kenny and Kenny (2000); Froggett (2002).

Wider theoretical perspectives

Psychoanalytic theory has three parts: it is a theory of human development, personality and abnormal psychology, and treatment. Two important basic ideas underpin the theory (Wood, 1971; Yelloly, 1980):

- *Psychic determinism* – the principle that actions or behaviour arise from people's thought processes rather than just happening
- *The unconscious* – the idea that some thinking and mental activity are hidden from our knowledge.

These ideas are widely accepted. For example, both ideas include the assumption that slips of the tongue (colloquially, Freudian slips) and jokes reflect hidden or unknown confusions in people's thought processes. Common-sense meanings do not always fully represent the complexity of psychodynamic ideas. Yelloly (1980: 8–9) gives the example of the meaning of 'unconscious' to show how full psychodynamic ideas are. *Resistance* arises when some thoughts and feelings are not compatible with other beliefs that we hold strongly. Here, the mind does not allow the contested ideas into the conscious by a process called *repression*. Many repressed thoughts are dynamic, in the sense that they cause us to act even if we are unaware of them. The psychodynamic unconscious consists of these forcibly hidden ideas, which are there whether or not we think about them, and are often deeply concealed. *Aggression*, where people turn destructive impulses against others, is important.

In the *developmental theory* of psychoanalysis, children are thought to go through a series of developmental stages. These occur as *drives* (originally translated as 'instincts') which are mental pressures to relieve physical needs such as hunger or thirst. Having such a need creates tension or *libido*, which gives us the energy to act in order to meet the need. Among physical needs sexual tension, even among young children, is very important in creating drives.

At each stage, particular behaviours are important, but as we progress through the stages we use the behaviours associated with previous stages. So, in an early stage, babies gain satisfaction from sucking (for example at a mother's breast to satisfy the need for food). Later, sucking can also be satisfying, for example in the use of cigarettes or sweets or in sexual activities. However, adults have a wider range of satisfying activities to choose from. Some people become unconsciously attached to behaviour associated with particular stages (*fixation*). They are driven to seek that form of satisfaction to an unreasonable degree. Consequently, they cannot use the full repertoire of behaviour available to them.

Children start in a stage of *primary narcissism*, seeking only gratification of their own needs. They learn through social interaction, at first with parents, that they must compromise. In each stage the focus of attention is on a different need; oral (hunger), anal (excretion), phallic (identification with same-sex parent), Oedipal (attraction to opposite-sex parent), latency (drives are managed through resolution of Oedipal conflicts) and puberty (social learning). Erikson (1965) has expanded on the stages of development. He suggests that at each stage the rational mind deals with a maturational crisis presented by the social circumstances of our life. His work, which has influenced social work, especially crisis intervention, emphasises cultural and social pressures rather than inner drives (Yelloly, 1980: 12).

Associated with the stages of development is the idea of *regression*. This occurs when people who have progressed through the later stages fall back on behaviour associated with earlier stages under some present stress. Regression is contrasted with fixation, when individuals are stuck in the behaviour of the early stage.

Psychoanalytic *personality theory* assumes that people are a complex of drives forming the *id* (literally 'it', an undifferentiated pressure from an unknown source – Wood, 1971). The id pushes us to act to resolve our needs but our actions do not always bring the desired results. Development of the *ego* follows from this. It is a set of pragmatic ideas about how we may understand and manipulate the environment. The ego controls the id. For example, children control the excretion of faeces as the ego learns that disapproval and discomfort follow inappropriate excretion. The ego manages relationships with people and things outside ourselves: *object relations*. The *superego* develops general moral principles which guide the ego.

Among important features of the personality is how the ego manages conflict. The need of the ego and superego to exert control over the id in the cause of social responsibility creates further conflicts. *Anxiety* results from such conflicts. The ego deals with anxiety by bringing into play various *defence mechanisms*, of which repression, already mentioned, is one. Other important ones are as follows:

- *Projection* – unwanted ideas associated with something the ego wants to protect become attached in our minds to another person or thing.

- *Splitting* – contradictory ideas and feelings are kept in separate mental compartments, and applied to different people or situations with inconsistent results.

- *Sublimation* – energy (from the id) which is directed towards unwanted activities (often sexual) is redirected towards more acceptable activities.

- *Rationalisation* – we believe acceptable reasons for particular activities, repressing emotionally unacceptable reasons for behaviour.

Freud's later work concentrated on ego and object relations. This was picked up after his death (in classic works by Anna Freud and Hartman) and has been influential as the basis of much psychoanalytic thought today. Ego psychology and object relations theories consider that children have the capacity to deal with the outside world (object relations) from an early age. Development of the ego is the growth of our capacity to learn from experience. This especially uses rational parts of our minds through using thinking (cognition), perception and memory.

Certain psychodynamic theorists and practitioners have achieved widespread and sometimes criticised influence on social work, pre-eminently Melanie Klein (1959; Salzberger-Wittenberg, 1970), Winnicott (1964) and Bowlby (1951). Their influence comes from their focus on work with children. Klein discusses two emotional life 'positions' that emerge in early childhood. One is a persecutory position, which comes from fear of being alone and failing to survive; the other, depressive position arises later from fear of destroying the mother. Experiencing these helps people to learn tolerance of ambivalence, and anxiety about being destructive. Winnicott's work is concerned with object relations. It is about how children learn to adapt from focusing on their inner world to developing a capacity for dealing with the outside world. Bowlby directed the psychoanalytic interest in early mother–child relationships towards research and theory about maternal deprivation. This is the idea that if we deprive children of contact with their mothers, their personal development is impeded. In recent years, this has developed into a more extensive theory about the importance of attachment (Bowlby, 1969, 1973, 1980; Aldgate, 1991; Howe, 1995; Howe et al., 1999). Attachment is particularly to the mother but also elsewhere. Experience of it affects the development of other relationships subsequently. The effects of loss of attachment are especially important. Such loss extends from death to loss of a parent by divorce (Garber, 1992). Evidence suggests that deprivation and disadvantage have major damaging effects on children's development and later life. However, relationships between children and parents, and a variety of other factors, including the social environment, are relevant, not just maternal deprivation. Many social and psychological factors help to protect against the damaging effects of deprivation (Rutter, 1981).

The idea of loss has a wider importance in psychoanalysis, and there are several different approaches to bereavement and grief (Berzoff, 2003). Mourning is regarded as a response to all kinds of loss, not just the death of someone close (Salzberger-Wittenberg, 1970). Parkes (1972) interprets bereavement in many situations as regression to childhood experiences of stress due to loss. Pincus (1976) argues that, in typical family reactions to death, hidden feelings about past relationships may be disclosed. The intensity of feeling when grief takes hold is particularly susceptible to psychoanalysis. However, Smith (1982) argues that much behaviour in bereavement and loss comes from social expectations of behaviour in such situations. She proposes that a phenomenological or existential interpretation of bereavement is more appropriate (see Chapters 8 and 9).

These more modern psychoanalytic developments link with sociological ideas, especially the idea that people are part of social systems and play a social role. Recent work in the object relations tradition, particularly by Kohut (1978; Eisenhuth, 1981; Lane, 1984; Lowenstein, 1985; Klugman, 2002), emphasises that children develop a perception of their 'self' and their difference from the surrounding world at a very young age. *Self-psychology*, particularly based on Kohut's work, has become increasingly important in psychodynamic social work since the 1980s, as will be evident in accounts of practice in the example texts discussed below. Elson (1986), for example, explores the process of formation of identity and disorders of self-perception.

Treatment theory in classic psychoanalysis required therapists to be 'blank screens', making themselves as anonymous as possible so that patients project their fantasies onto the therapists. *Transference* occurs when patients transfer unconscious feelings about their parents onto the therapist, and treat the therapist as though they were that parent. This is a way of revealing unconscious ideas. By stimulating transference, conflicts arising from early relationship difficulties with parents and causing present behaviour difficulties are revealed. Social work adapts this idea, referring more generally to how the emotional remains of past relationships and experiences affect our present behaviour, especially in relationships (Irvine, 1956). Countertransference occurs when analysts irrationally react to patients bringing in past experiences to the relationship. An example is given later in this chapter.

Some psychoanalytic treatments are concerned with revealing hidden thoughts and feelings. Undesirable behaviour may be caused by repressed conflicts leaking out in various ways, requiring more than ordinary attempts to disclose its origins. Once revealed and properly understood, the conflicts would no longer cause difficulties in behaviour. Thus, traditional psychoanalytic therapy is concerned with giving people *insight* into their repressed feelings. This is another emphasis which has been altered in ego psychology. It often concentrates on how people manage their relationships with the outside world through extending rational control of their lives.

Connections

Understanding psychodynamic theory is a prerequisite to examining other social work theories, since its influence is pervasive. A variety of schools of thought and applications or developments have grown up. Although most use psychodynamic ideas in general, there is, mainly in the USA, interest in applying ideas from psychodynamic theorists who are a long way from Freud and the mainstream development of psychoanalysis (such as Borensweig on Jung, 1980; O'Connor on Adler, 1992). Modern psychoanalytic theory has moved away from the idea of drives as the basic influence on behaviour (Lowenstein, 1985). It is more concerned with how individuals interact with their social world; it has become more social than biological. Brearley (1991) usefully summarises these concerns as about three key relationships: between self and significant others, between past and present experience and between inner and outer reality. Rasmussen and Mishna (2003) argue that psychodynamic social work usefully contributes to social work a focus on social context in which interpersonal relationships take place, multiple perspectives on reality and disjunctions in learning about reality. This has come about through the influence of ego psychology (Goldstein, 1984, Goldstein, 1995), increasingly seen as providing a *relational* model (Horowitz, 1998; Meyer, 2000; Cooper and Lesser, 2002: Ch 7) for improving human relationships. This focus on how the person interacts with the environment emphasises both intersubjectivity, how people experience and react to each other in relationships, and also expressing relationships in language (Saari, 1999). These are important connections with constructive theory (Chapter 8). Ego psychology is an important basis of ecological systems theory (Germain, 1978a; Siporin, 1980) and crisis intervention.

An appraisal of the role of psychoanalysis in social work (Pearson et al., 1988) shows that there is a range of developments, and in different countries various streams of thought. Ego psychology, for example, has been much more strongly influential in the USA than elsewhere, whereas object relations theory has two differing streams of thought: one British, based around the work of psychoanalysts such as Fairbairn (1954; McCouat, 1969) and Guntrip (1968; Hazell, 1995); and a different approach in the USA (Goldstein, 1995). Lacan (1979) has developed a line of psychoanalytic thought which has enabled some writers to make links with Marxism (see Bocock, 1988: 76). This is because he reinterprets the unconscious as a structure of symbols like language, to which our conscious behaviour points; Lacan has also had an important influence in cultural theory. Our society and culture impose these symbols upon us (Dowrick, 1983). If this is so, we can make ideas from Marxist historical materialism fit with some interpretations of psychoanalysis. Such ideas are closely related to postmodern ideas, which stress how language interprets and structures our experience of the world. Feminism, another radical ideology, has also attempted an interpretation of psychoanalysis as an explanation of patriarchy (that is, male domination of social relations and oppression of women). Leonard (1984), in his attempt to construct a Marxist approach to individual psychology, is doubtful of the intellectual viability of these attempts to interpret psychoanalysis in a radical way.

The politics of psychodynamic theory

Psychoanalytic theory has influenced social work theory in three phases (Payne, 1992). Before the 1920s in the USA, and the late 1930s in Britain, it had little impact. Then there was a period in which it was dominant, until the end of the 1960s. During this period it formed so powerful an influence that it created approaches within social work that remain to this day. Since then, it has been one of many contested theories, used by specialists, but retaining influence because of the strength of its influence on basic social work practice. Meyer (2000) sees its influence as a 'legacy'. Therefore, its theories of development, personality and therapy are not explicitly practised in a widespread way. Its influence is more complex and indirect through Freud's influence on Western culture.

Psychodynamic therapy has influenced social work's permissive, open, listening (Wallen, 1982) style of relationship (indeed, the emphasis on relationship at all; see Perlman, 1957b) rather than a directive and controlling style. It also encouraged seeking explanation and understanding of personality rather than action. Psychodynamic theory influenced social work's emphasis on feelings and unconscious factors in particular (Yelloly, 1980) rather than events and thought. Many ideas such as the unconscious, insight, aggression, conflict, anxiety, maternal relationships and transference come from psychodynamic theory. These are terms which are often used in watered-down strength as a common language in social work and everyday life. Psychodynamic theory gains in importance by their continued availability to practitioners. The important focus in social work on childhood and early relationships and maternal deprivation comes from psychodynamic theory and this has led to the importance of attachment theory. The emphasis on mental illness and disturbed behaviour as a focus of much social work comes from the importance in the 1920s and 30s of social work's association with psychiatry and psychodynamic treatment. Insight as an important part of social work understanding and treatment comes originally from psychodynamic theory. We give less emphasis to social factors in social work than to psychological and emotional ones because of psychodynamic theory's influence (Weick, 1981).

The theoretical sophistication and complexity of its ideas make it attractive and interesting to explore, as compared with newer and less-developed theories (Fraiberg, 1978; Lowenstein, 1985).

Early psychodynamic social work statements

Diagnostic theory (Hamilton, 1950) led to *psychosocial theory*, whose main exponent was Hollis (Woods and Hollis, 1999). The crucial elements are the idea of the *person-in-situation* (some writers, following ecological theory, now refer to the 'person-in-environment' – PIE) and the *classification of casework treatment*. Detailed classifications were developed of both direct work with the client and indirect work with other agencies. An important aim was to reduce 'stress' and 'press' from the environment on the personal capacity to live life satisfactorily. The empirical base of the theory is accumulated practical experience, and quantitative research methods are considered inappropriate to individual responses to human difficulty. Also, social workers may have a role where measuring effectiveness by conventional indicators would be difficult.

Functional theory (Smalley, 1967) arose in the USA during the 1930s, contesting pre-eminence with diagnostic theory. It is not a significantly distinct form of practice even in the USA (Dunlap, 1996). However, Dore (1990) argues that functional theory's lasting influences on social work include the idea of self-determination, the importance of structuring practice around time and the emphasis on process and growth. The term 'functional' is applied because it emphasises that the *function of social work agencies* gives practice in each setting its form and direction. Functional social work stresses that social work is a process of interaction between clients and workers rather than a series of acts or procedures as psychosocial casework has it.

Problem-solving casework (Perlman, 1957a) is psychodynamic because that was the accepted psychological base of social work at the time it was written (Perlman, 1986). It emphasised dealing with the presenting problems of the client and current difficulties in the environment. There is less emphasis on irrational and internal motivation. Clients are assumed to have failings in their capacity to solve problems and need help in overcoming obstacles to improving their coping capacity. This approach is rooted in ego psychology (Perlman, 1970: 169, 1986: 261), with its emphasis on how the ego manages outside relationships. Perlman's (1957a) book concentrates especially on study and diagnosis of the problems; treatment is ill-defined. Perlman (1986: 261) claims that this is intentional since 'the essential elements of the total helping process ... are to be found ... within the first few hours'. Perlman's model is an important forerunner of task-centred case-work, which has developed the idea of problem analysis (see Chapter 5). It is still used as the conceptual basis of important texts, such as that of Compton and Galaway (1999), who expand it with a more detailed analysis of the stages of practice, drawing on task-centred work and systems perspectives. Kumar (1995) discusses the use of the sequence of problem-solving activities in an Indian context, and claims that the focus here is on social problems such as poverty, unemployment and the lower status of women, rather than psychological and emotional problems.

Major statements

In addition to the historical texts, discussed above, the major texts in attachment theory are Howe's (1995) *Attachment Theory for Social Work Practice,* representing the main present-day British usage of psychodynamic theory. Howe et al.'s *Attachment Theory, Child Maltreatment and Family Support* (1999) provides a briefer but similar account of attachment theory focused on child maltreatment, containing more detailed description of behaviour to be found in different patterns of attachment. It also has a more detailed discussion of assessment and intervention applied to child maltreatment and family support.

In ego psychology, Goldstein's (1995) *Ego Psychology and Social Work Practice,* represents the main American use of psychodynamic theory. A more detailed account of object relations theory is contained in Goldstein's *Object Relations Theory and Self Psychology in Social Work Practice* (2002), which is in many ways an update of Goldstein's 1995 text, with a focus on object relations rather than the more general topic of ego psychology.

Howe: attachment theory

Howe's account of attachment theory starts from the extensive research into early childhood development and relationships between parents and children. The theory is based on evidence of the ways in which early experiences of attachment to secure and responsive adults, usually parents, are an important foundation for later social competence. Froggett (2002) connects attachment with solidarity between human beings. People form their identity, or self, in social relationships as, through learning how to deal with other people, the brain makes sense of what is going on around it. Through experience, it develops expectations that form a social reality. Some early relationships and experiences are formative, that is, they are particularly sensitive for creating effective relationships and learning later on. How we are depends on how we experience these early relationships. Warmth, mutuality, support and security are qualities of relationships that tend to produce coherent, well-organised later selves. Babies have an innate desire and capacity to communicate, and it is through this that they gain emotional experiences that help them to understand how they and other people feel. We build up explanations about why people are reacting as they do, so that we can interpret the meaning of other people's behaviour within our social and cultural context.

Young children gain an awareness of their own psychological states before they understand other people and begin to understand others by comparing them with their own feelings. Therefore, they develop their understanding by sharing experiences with others through intimate relationships and learn that different people bring different mental states to relationships, and that this affects others' reactions to them. Important understandings come from talking with their parents about feelings and learning to interpret social relationships so that they fit in with the expectations of the culture that surrounds them. This grows as they develop through childhood, and increasing language use allows children to learn through interactions with peers and others.

Children learn to work out what other people feel by trying to understand their behaviour, and they begin to develop emotional empathy with others as they do this. They use imagined relationships, make-believe and pretend play with dolls and toys to experiment with relationships. This kind of play helps them to gain the ability to imagine what other people are thinking and how this will affect their behaviour.

The psychoanalyst Bowlby (1969, 1973, 1980) developed a theory of how seeking attachment to others is a basic drive. When children feel under stress, they seek attachment to others in three important ways:

- *Proximity-seeking*, where a child seeks to be near a parent or other secure person
- *Secure base*, where a child feels able to take risks because a secure person is present
- *Separation protest*, where a child tries to prevent separations from secure people.

Bowlby's (1951) early work was concerned with how children deprived of their mother in the early stages of life (maternal deprivation) later experienced separation anxiety, feelings of loss and eventually disturbances in behaviour. The child first protests, then withdraws from relationships and finally becomes detached from relationships. Early experiences of loss, together with the quality of present relationships affect how we react to later losses. Children have a strong predisposition to attachment behaviour, and parents, particularly mothers, are also predisposed to interact with their children. Usually, considerable two-way interaction occurs and the quality of this interaction, its warmth, responsiveness and consistency, helps later development. Communication and shared social experiences give children the basis for social competence later on.

This does not wholly come from the parent: children have different temperaments, that affect how the social relationships develop:

- *Difficult* temperaments show withdrawal, intense expression of mostly negative mood and slow adaptation to change
- *Easy* temperaments have the ability to deal with new situations, high adaptability and express mostly positive mood
- *Slow-to-warm-up* temperaments show withdrawal from unfamiliar situations, low adaptability and mild expression of mood.

These temperaments and the consequent quality of relationships may be changed by the social environment, although there is some evidence that temperament is genetic.

Through the communication and social interactions that attachment behaviour generates, children develop competence in dealing with social situations, and, by experiencing the responses of others to them, gain a sense of self-worth and self-esteem. This allows them to develop working models of how the world works. They internalise models or pictures of:

- The self
- Other people
- The relationships between them.

If the important attachment relationships are coherent and consistent, children learn the skill of relating to others and experience themselves as 'potent', that is, they feel they are able to have an impact on the situations they are in. On the other hand, a child cannot develop a good working model where relationships and attachments are inconsistent, because there is no pattern to establish. Also, where communication is not free-flowing, they do not accept the risk of expressing emotions that may cause problems for the other person. This leads to withdrawal where there is experience of loss and separation.

The Ainsworth attachment classification system (Ainsworth et al., 1978) involves watching young children with attachment figures to see how they behave with the caregiver when there is a 'secure base', and how they deal with separation and return of the caregiver. Five types of attachment experience are identi-

Table 4.1 Types of attachment

Types of attachment	Attachment experience and behaviour
Secure (type B)	Some distress at separation, positive reaction at reunion, with some physical contact or comfort sought. Secure play; responsiveness between caregiver and child; caregiver preferred to strangers; caregiver alert and responsive to child's signals; child confident that the caregiver will be available and help where there are difficulties.
Insecure or avoidant (type A)	Few signs of distress at separation, ignore or avoid caregiver at reunion. Children do not seek physical contact. Play inhibited; children watchful of caregiver and wary generally; will interact equally with others; parent indifferent, insensitive or rejecting of child's signals.
Insecure and ambivalent or resistant (type C)	Highly distressed at separation and difficult to calm at reunion. Contact sought, but they still do not settle; will run after caregiver if they walk away. 'Ambivalent' children demand and resist attention; display both need and anger, dependence and resistance; nervous of new situations and people; caregiver is inconsistent and insensitive, but not rejecting or hostile.
Insecure and disorganised (type A/C or D)	Some elements of avoidant and ambivalent behaviour. Confusion and disorganisation (may 'freeze') on separation and reunion, shows little emotion on reunion. Parents experienced as frightening or frightened, and therefore do not calm child's anxiety.
Non-attachments	Little distress on separation. People are interchangeable, as long as needs are met; difficulties in controlling impulses and aggression. No opportunity to experience attachments, typically children who have had institutional care for early infancy or whose caregivers are emotionally unavailable (for example serious alcoholics or abusers of drugs).

Source: Ainsworth et al. (1978) cited by Howe (1995).

fied, set out in Table 4.1. Considerable research in many different countries has found this classification useful, with about 60 per cent of normal children in the USA and UK displaying secure attachment behaviour, although many fewer where there are identified problems.

Experience of *separation* is often a source of anxiety or anger for children. How they react helps them to adapt to the situation they are in, but if it becomes ingrained, may produce problems later, because social competence to deal with uncertainty and ambivalence is weakened. Reactions to separation are defence mechanisms: type B children tend to move towards people and be compliant; type C children move against people and are aggressive; type A children move away from people and withdraw and avoid others.

Patterns of attachment behaviour and defence mechanisms are often maintained across the life cycle and affect relationships with parents and family, peers, society, partners and children. Howe (1995: 105–77) reviews evidence of the effects of attachment behaviour on forming new relationships, with adoptive parents, peers or partners and children. For example, someone who has developed aggressive responses will find relationships with others more difficult and someone who avoids contact may have difficulty in creating intimate relationships. Howe also examines some of the factors relevant to particular difficulties, such as sexual abuse. The importance of the effect on the self, for example when there are losses and bereavements, is also clear.

An important concept is the idea of *resilience*, that is, the capacity to resist or rebound from difficulties. Three factors are important in generating resilience:

- Intelligence and being reflective
- Alternative psychological support
- Removal from risk environments.

Attachment theory practice

Practice using attachment theory involves an assessment looking at:

- *Present relationships:* their content and quality, function and structure
- *Relationship history,* and how it displays various types of attachment behaviour
- *Context:* particular stresses of the environment on present relationships.

Content and quality look at the affective tone of relationships, whether there is an emotional bond between people, and their operational style, that is, how they regulate the relationship. For example, a single mother developed a close relationship with her only daughter and controlled her behaviour by trying to explain rationally why her daughter should behave or react in desired ways. In childhood, this often led to lengthy conflict or impasse, but in adulthood, the daughter found it easy to ask for support and help from others and developed effective relationships. In another similar relationship, the mother was absent a great deal and relied on a series of instructions and the daughter's 'duty' to behave appropriately and not embarrass her mother. This also used rational means, but was not allied to the loving relationship and constant interaction of explanation, and in adulthood, this daughter avoided intimate relationships and had very little contact with her mother.

Workers intervene by providing understanding, support and psychotherapy. They should be receptive and demonstrate efforts to understand and explain what is going on for clients. They should be tolerant and not be surprised or hurt by aggression or avoidance, using their intellectual understanding and assessment to see how this behaviour has developed. Support involves practical support, such as improving social security benefits or helping to provide services that reduce the burdens of everyday life, and emotional support provided by being available when needed as a confidante and recognising, accepting and valuing the client's experiences and feelings. Giving status: 'you are trying hard to be a good mother' 'you are helping the family by bringing home a good wage-packet'; information about useful services and a degree of social companionship can also be helpful. A good, nurturing relationship between worker and client can help to compensate for some of the particular defence mechanisms used by a client.

Five therapeutic tasks identified by Bowlby are:

- Providing a secure base to explore unhappy events
- Assisting clients in their explorations

- Recognising how attachment behaviour is being imported into the present relationship (a development of the traditional psychodynamic idea of transference)
- Helping clients to understand how past attachment experiences relate to present difficulties
- Helping clients to use their understanding of how present relationship patterns reflect past attachment experiences to reconstruct their ways of thinking about and behaving within relationships.

While Howe's (1995) and Howe et al.'s (1999) accounts are the main extended discussion of practice within social work, other therapeutic developments continue. For example, Heard and Lake (1997) discuss attachment theory as an approach to supporting companionable caregiving, particularly focusing on the development of the self and looking at adults' capacity for attachment and companionship.

The connections with psychodynamic theory are clear from this summary of attachment theory and social work mainly deriving from Howe's account. The focus on emotions, early childhood development as the basis for later relationship and emotional problems and practice based on understanding and insight are typical of many psychodynamic theories. Attachment theory may be important for work with children, where it is well supported by research in child development but its application to adults is less well evidenced. Moreover, its social work application produces only a sketchy set of ideas for practice, although it gives a good basis for confident explanation of childhood problems. It takes up some ideas from cognitive and learning theory, particularly on its emphasis on therapy as learning. This is a point at which practice ideas from cognitive-behavioural therapy might be included in the general approach set out for practice in attachment theory.

Goldstein: ego psychology

Goldstein's account of social work using ideas from ego psychology starts with 12 functions of the ego, as set out in Table 4.2. In giving examples of each function, I have tried to emphasise both the complex psychological elements of the ego and less complex reactions. This list also emphasises the importance of the ego as channelling energy and motivation, as well as providing controlling, regulating and rational processes. People are said to have strong egos when they can manage relationships with other people in a consistent, rational pattern. If they can do this, they achieve *ego mastery*. People gain pleasure from being able to explore, understand and change their environment, so gaining ego mastery is a good motivator. People want efficacy in their interactions with others. However, developing social competence also involves social transactions, so is affected by the environment, social structure and culture. The ego is a mental structure, which is a metaphor for the mechanisms in the brain that manage the interaction of the needs and impulses of the person and the pressure of the environment. Ego mastery achieves both effective adaptation by a person to the social environment and also competence in adapting the environment to the person's needs.

Table 4.2 Functions of the ego

Ego function	Explanation	Example
Reality-testing	The ego allows people to distinguish reality from their own wishes and fantasies	A woman fears that her husband's lack of affection shows he has a lover; reality-testing makes her realise that he has always been undemonstrative and there is no evidence of changes in his pattern of absence from home.
Judgement	The ego allows people to judge appropriate reactions to events according to social and cultural expectations	A jealous wife wants to argue with her husband at the front door, but delays so that he is not publicly embarrassed in front of the neighbours. A wife with less good judgement might display her anger in public.
Sensing reality	The ego allows people to sense the reality of the world in relation to their self	A man may feel alienated from work after a strike for more pay has been unsuccessful, in spite of the fact that the job and his interest in it is unchanged.
Regulation and control	The ego regulates and controls drives, emotions and impulses	People may feel angry about something at work or sexually attracted to a colleague, but would not display these feelings to avoid disturbing work relationships.
Object relations	The ego manages interpersonal relations in relation to the 'object' in people's minds	A man sees a colleague as unreliable, so the 'object' (image of the man he has internalised) causes him always to check arrangements made with this colleague when, in a particular instance, the colleague is clearly committed to carrying out the task. Good ego control would allow the man only to take precautions where the colleague is likely to be unreliable.
Thought processes	The ego moves people from primary to secondary process thinking	Primary process thinking allows unrealistic wishes or impulses to be expressed directly, leading to unrealistic ambitions, whereas secondary process thinking means that people plan to achieve their wishes and react cooperatively to allow others to meet their responsibilities.
Adaptive regression	The ego allows people to regress to less sophisticated ways of thinking and acting to achieve objectives	A man is angry with his partner, but pounds the pillow with his fist until his anger is contained, while he thinks of a way of discussing alternative plans with the partner.
Defensive functioning	The ego generates psychological mechanisms to protect people from painful experiences	A man is distressed after the death of his teenage daughter after a drug overdose. He creates a shrine in the child's bedroom, with mementos of successful family holidays and starts a campaign against drug abuse using an attractive picture of his daughter; thus idealising the child compared with the reality of her later life.
Stimulus barrier	The ego defends people from over- or understimulation	A man who has a boring job organises a series of intellectually stimulating hobbies to engage his attention.
Autonomous functions	The ego manages primary and secondary autonomy	Managing primary autonomy controls the consequences of unavoidable psychological damage, for example where concentration is associated with a bombastic teacher; and secondary autonomy is where people develop a capacity, for example a hobby, to avoid painful psychological issues but these become separated from the original event, for example where someone becomes involved in breeding pigeons as a way of dealing with bereavement, but becomes successful with racing pigeons.
Mastery-competence	The ego motivates people to gain control over what happens to them and competence in dealing with their problems	A teenager from a poor household develops good relationship skills in order to make links with a wide range of friends, to improve the opportunities for social and job opportunities.
Synthetic-integrative	The ego integrates diverse experiences to contribute to self-perceptions of the person as whole and integrated	A social worker is able to transfer knowledge about behaviour gained in working with children to a new job working with people with disabilities.

Source: Adapted from Goldstein (1995).

The ego generates defences to protect people from anxiety when their impulses conflict with a rational assessment of what is possible in the real world; *defence mechanisms* help to achieve mastery by limiting the impact of the world on the impulses of the person. Defences originate at particular developmental stages, and if they do not work well, a person may have become stuck at an earlier developmental stage than is now desirable. Compared with coping mechanisms, defence mechanisms are more rigid and may become inappropriate to effective social relationships. *Coping mechanisms* create more of a social transaction between the person and the environment. Table 4.3 compares defence with coping mechanisms.

Erikson (1965), working originally in the 1940s and 50s, identified the importance of gaining mastery of developmental tasks and identified a series of eight developmental 'crises' (see Chapter 5). Levinson (1978), in work during the 1970s, also identified life eras. These are compared in Table 4.4. Erikson's earlier account gives a detailed account of stages in childhood, but is sketchy about later ages, filled in more completely by Levinson (1978) from more recent research. However, even his account assumes relatively little change in later years and this does not really reflect the changes that many people experience in the decade or two that they live after 65. Goldstein (1995) identifies criticism from feminist writers that Erikson's work assumes a mainly male focus and that different developments may be relevant for women. Walter and Peterson (2002), for example, discuss from a postmodern feminist perspective how Erikson and other psychoanalystic writers such as Kohlberg (1984) based their developmental research on adolescent boys. This leads adolescent young women to be regarded as 'emotionally disabled', when often their behaviour represents a different view or voicing of their experience and aspirations. Goldstein also notes that many diverse social groups, including ethnic groups, may develop differently, and seriously disturbing life events or traumas may also have an important impact on slowing or speeding up the completion of life tasks. The importance of the way people 'cope' with crises in their lives is an important factor in psychodynamic theory, and influenced the development of crisis intervention (see Chapter 5).

Ego psychology focuses on *object relations* and ego development. There are two views about object relations. One view is external: the ego's role is to form sustainable relationships with others with little hostility; the others are the

Table 4.3 Defence and coping mechanisms

Defence mechanisms	Coping mechanisms
Compelled, rigid	Flexible, purposeful
Pushed by the past	Pulled by the future
Distort present reality	Connected to present requirements
Primary process thinking and unconscious elements	Secondary process thinking and conscious and pre-conscious thoughts
All disturbing effects can be changed	Problems may be managed
Subterfuge and misdirection	Open, ordered, transparent

Source: Kroeber, cited by Goldstein (1995: 76).

Table 4.4 Erikson's and Levinson's psychosocial developmental stages

Erikson's (1965) life stages	Psychosocial crisis (Erikson)	Explanation	Levinson's (1978) life seasons/eras
1. Infant	Basic trust vs mistrust	Through effective relationships with caregivers, children gain confidence in the predictability of the world as it reacts to them.	1. Childhood and adolescence (0–17)
2. Toddler	Autonomy vs shame and doubt	Children seek more autonomy, requiring faith in their competence, but in doing so must learn to manage fear of failure and ridicule.	
3. Early childhood	Initiative vs guilt	Children enjoy expanding their horizons and activities, requiring support and help, but struggle with overcoming control by caregivers and others.	
4. Later childhood	Industry vs inferiority	Children work at education and skill development, thus gaining a view of their effectiveness at work tasks, which may be discouraging.	
5. Adolescence	Identity vs role confusion	Adolescents seek continuity with their childhood identity while experimenting and consolidating an independent identity, risking confusion if social relationships and support do not permit both continuity and development.	Early adult transition (17–22)
6. Early adulthood	Intimacy and distantiation vs self-absorption	Young adults are able to achieve intimacy with others, using their new sense of self, which if not achieved leads them to focus on self-interest.	2. Entering the adult world (22–28) Age 30 transition (28–33) Settling down (33–40) Midlife transition (40–45)
7. Middle adulthood	Generativity vs stagnation	Adults accept responsibility for involvement in society and supporting it and others, continuing and developing social life, which if not achieved leads to self-obsession and stagnation.	
8. Later adulthood	Integrity vs despair and disgust	Ego integrity develops a sense of completeness in adults' contributions to life, or despair and feelings of disgust at ageing in the absence of contribution and completeness.	3. Entering middle adulthood (45–50) Age 50 transition (50–55) Culmination of middle adulthood (55–60) 4. Late adulthood (65+)

Source: Adapted from Goldstein's (1995) comparison of Erikson (1965) and Levinson (1978).

objects. The other view is intrapsychic: the ego forms representations of itself in relation to others through experience, internalising others, and manages the relationships of these with external reality. Attachment theory is one explanation of the development of this capacity to manage the outside world. The American preference is for Mahler's (Mahler et al., 1975) theory of *separation-individuation*, in which the task of the child is seen as separating psychologically from parents and creating an individual identity. Critics would argue that this American preference reflects a view of childhood that seeks to create independent adults, rather than the interdependence with family and community that is preferred in many, particularly Eastern, societies. A series of phases in early childhood lead to a separate phase in adolescence. Again, the focus here is on childhood and there have been feminist critics of the lack of differentiation between women and men. Goldstein (1995) notes several other ideas about object relations, in particular the British school of Fairbairn, Guntrip and Winnicott and the work of Melanie Klein, and the self-psychology of Kohut (1978) and Stern (1985).

Ego psychology practice

The main issue in ego psychology practice is whether to be ego-supportive or ego-modifying. Generally, social work is ego-supporting, while counselling and psychotherapy is ego-modifying. Ego-supporting work focuses on current thoughts and behaviour rather than searching out the past, aims at improved ego mastery and learning, uses the relationship with the worker to give a positive experience, uses direct, educational methods, works with the environment and finds additional resources for the client and works on traumas, life transitions, people with poor patterns of behaviour and poor control of anxiety and impulses. Ego-modifying work focuses on the connections between past experiences and the present, insight to resolve conflicts, uses a non-directive and reflective approach, tends to work with the client rather than indirectly on the environment and concentrates on people with good ego strength who have poor patterns of behaviour and inappropriate defences.

To decide the approach, a full ego assessment is required. The basic questions to ask are about the extent to which problems come from:

- Difficulties in current life roles or developmental tasks
- Stress in the environment or traumas
- Impaired ego capacities or developmental difficulties
- Lack of resources or support or poor fit between internal capacities and environmental requirements.

Workers also assess internal capacities and environmental resources that can be mobilised to help deal with the problems. Data for the assessment will come from clients, their families and other people important to them, organisations in touch with clients such as schools or workplaces, other agencies, official records, observing the client's behaviour with the worker and in the agency and the use of psychological tests and assessment scales.

The outcome of the assessment will be to decide whether the worker should be focusing on:

- Inner capacities
- Environmental conditions
- The fit between inner capacities and environmental conditions.

The concern with 'fit' underlies the application of ego psychology to ecological systems theory (see Chapter 7), but Goldstein's use of this term probably reflects the influence of ecological systems theory on American social work. The assessment will also decide on short- or long-term intervention, although agency requirements may affect this. Short-term work would focus selectively on key issues in the client's life or would test hypotheses about the client's problems for later work. It might use less detailed evidence about the client, along with a preparedness to revise the assessment if intervention reveals other issues that are more important.

Social work based on ego psychology gives great importance to the relationship between the worker and client. This is crucially based on purposes determined by the client's needs, rather than aims arising from agency purpose or the family's wishes. Workers use themselves in a disciplined way; this develops the psychoanalytic technique of the blank screen. Workers focus on responding to clients' behaviour, helping them to see how they might deal with situations differently, learning explicitly what behaviours and ideas may be getting in the way of using their ego strength. Workers try to create a working alliance with clients to agree to try to overcome unrealistic behaviour and ideas and identify and practise realistic ideas. This approach has many connections with cognitive therapies in its focus on realistic thinking. However, ego psychological social work looks for examples where, in the relationship with the worker, clients display aspects of the unreality that is affecting them more widely, and use the alliance to point up the problems. For example, a client had difficulties in her relationship with her husband because they talked across each other and so could not communicate because they did not hear each other's point of view. I pointed this out as it came up in our discussions, and suggested that each practised listening quietly to the other for a set period of two minutes, making notes, because the woman had a memory problem, and then replying, taking turns to speak and listen. In this way, they learned to take turns in conversation.

Factors that affect the client–worker relationship are, from the client's point of view, their motivation and expectations, their values, experience and social and cultural background, their ego functioning and current life situation. The main factors that affect the worker's side of the relationship are the capacity to understand what is happening in the connection between thinking and behaviour, and responding to the client in ways which help to identify this and ways that problems in thinking may be dealt with. The agency will also have an effect on clients; its treatment of them affects their expectations and motivation and whether they find the experience helpful. For example, quiet confidential places for interviews, good timekeeping and efficient administration indicate respect for the client.

The worker uses the relationship to carry out the assessment, and then the focus of the work will be:

- Sustaining hope and motivation
- Enhancing autonomy, problem-solving and the capacity to adapt to the environment
- Providing a role model and a good experience that may correct past bad experiences
- Promoting personality change
- Mobilising resources to help the client
- Modifying the environment
- Mediating, educating, collaborating and advocating between the client and other services.

The relationship needs to be terminated in a way that allows clients to move on from dependency on the worker and the agency, while giving confidence that they would be helped again.

Various psychological techniques drawn from Hollis and Woods (1981) may help to explain how the worker does this:

- Sustaining techniques: sympathetic listening, receptiveness, acceptance and high valuation of the client
- Direct influence: suggestions, advice
- Exploration, description and ventilation: eliciting and valuing the client's perceptions and feelings about the situation
- Person-situation (or environment) reflection: focusing on current situations and relationships and seeking better understanding of others, insight into reasons for the client's and others' behaviour; evaluation of feelings associated with the situation and behaviour
- Pattern-dynamic reflection: identifying patterns of behaviour and how these connect with patterns of thinking and perception
- Developmental reflection: helping the client to see how present experience connects with what happened in the past
- Education: providing information, contacts with others
- Structuring: dividing problems, identifying priorities, setting time limits and organising actions.

Therapeutic environments: an application to residential care

Psychodynamic theory has been applied to residential care work through a variety of theoretical developments. Righton (1975) shows the theoretical relationships between three different theoretical positions:

- *Planned environment therapy* (Franklin, 1968; Wills, 1973) was based on work with maladjusted adolescents originally in the Second World War. It has its roots in psychoanalytic theory, and radical education, including the work of Homer Lane (Wills, 1964), Neill (1964) and Lyward (Burn, 1956).

- *Milieu therapy* is a mainly American concept, used in the work of writers such as Polsky (1968), applying psychodynamic groupwork with maladjusted young people. It also includes ego psychology and the ideas of Lewin (1951) on field theory and life space (that is, the total physical, social, cultural and psychological environment surrounding a resident) as a way of understanding interactions between individuals and within groups, particularly in residential care with adolescent offenders (Redl, 1959). Keenan (1991) shows how life space work focuses on the purpose for clients being in residential care.

- *Therapeutic communities*, which derive from the work of Jones (1968) and Clark (1974) in psychiatric hospitals and had important origins in Second World War attempts to deal with the psychological consequences of warfare (Kennard, 1998). This has also been applied in community settings, including day hospitals (Whiteley, 1979), and in hostels and housing schemes of various kinds through the worldwide work of the Richmond Fellowship (Jansen, 1980; Manning, 1989).

The psychodynamic groupwork of Bion (1961) influenced some of this work. A related area of influence is the work of psychodynamic organisation consultants, particularly those from the Tavistock Clinic and Institute (Brearley, 1991). Foulkes (1964) introduced the idea of 'group matrix', the totality of communications and relationships in a group, which forms the basis for developing a shared meaning of events for group members. It is associated with the idea of 'group spirit' and Bowlby's concept of a 'secure base' in attachment theory (Rawlinson, 1999). Froggett (2002) discusses how psychodynamic group approaches assist the containment of problems in secure bases with the matrix. Well-known contributions include Menzies-Lyth's (1988) work, particularly showing how staff facing difficult emotional situations in hospital settings used psychological defences to maintain their emotional equilibrium. Bettelheim's (1950) influential and atmospheric accounts of psychoanalytic residential care practice with disturbed children calls on his wartime concentration camp experience.

Perhaps the most widely influential of these models of residential care practice is the therapeutic community. Kennard's (1983, 1998) account of its main attributes offers a useful summary of the practice of all three forms of work:

- Informal and communal atmosphere.
- Group meetings are a central aspect of therapy, for information-sharing, building a sense of cohesion, making decision-making open, offering a forum for personal feedback and allowing the community to influence its members.
- All participants share in the work of running the community.
- Residents have a therapeutic role with each other.
- Authority is shared between staff and residents.
- Common values, are that individual problems are mostly about relationships with others, therapy is a learning process (insightful learning – Hinshelwood, 1999) and members share a basic psychological equality as human beings.

Katie and Jarold

Katie (7) and Jarold (9) are referred by their school for child protection work because of a risk of emotional and physical abuse and neglect. Their parents are Juliana (28) and Alberto (31). There was a history of late development in preschool years, and Alberto left Juliana several times, apparently to work in the Middle East, but also because he found the children's demanding behaviour difficult. The school has experienced behaviour problems of aggression from Katie – taking property from other children, denying it loudly in the face of clear evidence of her behaviour and then assaulting the accusing child. Jarold often sits quietly in the background watching what goes on in the classroom, but he is not learning much. There have been complaints from other parents, both to the school and Juliana and Alberto, which has sometimes led to arguments between Alberto and other parents in the street. The children have both been left behind at school on several occasions for teachers to look after when one or the other of the parents have failed to call for them. The school does not yet have an after-school club. Health care records show that there were fears that the children were being neglected or heavily disciplined. Juliana and Alberto's parents migrated from the Caribbean, and have returned there.

Think about how you, the child protection worker, might make a beginning with this family: make some notes about how you would present your role to the different members of the family.

Would you concentrate on the parents or the children? Thinking about attachment theory, how would you set about an assessment of the children? What kinds of behaviours would you look out for? What kinds of facilities would help you to assess their behaviour? What could you do to intervene using attachment theory?

How would ego-oriented practice help you to work with the parents? What kinds of factors might you look for in taking their histories? What kinds of behaviours and attitudes might cause you to be concerned about their ego strength?

Having thought about the possibilities of attachment theory for beginning work with the children and ego-oriented practice for beginning work with the parents, how might anti-discrimination, ethnic sensitivity and feminist theory add to or criticise what you intend?

Commentary

Features of psychodynamic social work that arouse critical comment are as follows:

- Developments such as managed care (USA) or care management (UK) require social work to emphasise effective *provision of services* rather than a psychosocial emphasis (Brandell, 2002).

- Focus on *evidence-based practice* and biological explanations of behaviour (Montgomery, 2002), through genetics and the search for chemical changes in the brain to explain behaviour, have directed models of explanation away from the more interpretive and metaphorical account of behaviour offered by psychodynamic theory (Brandell, 2002).

- Even so, it has been criticised as a *scientific*, and originally biological, approach to explanation, in a theory which cannot be easily tested in conventional scientific ways. Many argue that these scientific methods do not reflect respect for human self-determination (Strean, 1979).

- Originating in middle-class, Jewish Vienna, it is very limited in its *cultural assumptions*, so that it assumes that deviations from a limited, white, middle-class norm are abnormal behaviour to be cured. This has been controversial, in that psychoanalysts may see variations due to ethnic difference as abnormalities needing treatment. Similarly, its attitude to homosexuality as requiring treatment and as associated with maternal relationships has been regarded as objectionable (Strean, 1979: 56).

- Many current social ideas about *ethnic, cultural and gender issues* could enrich psychodynamic theory, but since it does not now form a central basis for social work, these ideas are not incorporated, but develop separately from what is now a minority, specialised interest. Clarke (2003) argues that psychoanalysis can offer insights into the complex emotional responses within racism, giving us insight into the complex personal responses that lead to racist behaviour.

- Psychodynamic theory's account of female development and personality has been criticised for reinforcing *stereotypes of women* as domestic, child-bearing, socially, intellectually and perhaps morally inferior, although some use has been made of the account in developing feminist perspectives on psychology. Mitchell (1975), for example, argues that psychoanalysis is a useful means of understanding how men achieve and maintain supremacy in a patriarchal society. Sayers (1986, 1988) contends that not enough attention has been given to explaining women's resistance to subordination in a patriarchal society and that psychoanalytic theory can also be helpful here. Similarly, Bonner (2002) argues that ideas about intersubjectivity, ethnocultural transference and racial enactments could enrich psychodynamic theory in dealing with minority ethnic groups.

- Related to its scientific approach, psychoanalysis operates on a *medical model* which assumes the patient's sickness, which an expert therapist cures, rather than a more equal model of relationships between client and worker. Perlman's (1957a) idea of social work as problem-solving, in which problems are identified and solved, is similar to a medical model of curing illnesses.

- The use of *insight* as a major therapeutic technique may lead psychodynamic workers to stop at the point where clients have understood what is happening to them emotionally. This does not help them to take practical action to do something about it. Since psychoanalysis is non-directive, this tends to make workers' help insubstantial.

- Its use of concepts sometimes induces workers to *blame the victim* for social problems of agency inadequacies, by interpreting the client's behaviour as maladjusted if it conflicts with the assumptions of the worker or agency. Gitterman's (1983) example is the use of psychological 'resistance' to avoid responsibility when clients are unhappy with aspects of the agency's service.

- It is a theory for a *talking therapy*, preferring verbally able clients with psychological problems, who can take part in discussion and self-examination. This plays down the importance of less articulate, working-class clients with more practical problems (Strean, 1979).

- *Environmental factors* are given less prominence than internal psychological ones. This limits the possible range of interventions, and narrows the assumptions from which workers start (Strean, 1979).

- Psychodynamic ideas have limited concern for *social reform*, which excludes a major element of social work (Strean, 1979).

On the positive side, understanding psychodynamic perspectives helps us understand many of the origins of important ideas in social work: 'conflict', 'aggression', 'concern for mother–child relationships', 'ego', 'sublimation', 'repression' and 'resistance' are all terms we use, often without a thought for their technical meanings in the theories from which their use originates. These perspectives have proved a rich source of ideas and understanding (Dean, 2002). Many people value them because, with all their limitations, they give a sense of the complexity of human lives and developments and how our minds and bodies interact with each other and the social environment.

OVERVIEW

- Psychodynamic theories have provided a rich source of ideas and metaphors for practice in more therapeutic or clinical settings.

- Attachment theory, working with loss and ego psychology have developed a practice that has moved away from traditional psychoanalytic ideas.

- Psychodynamic ideas are historically important as the source of many practices in social work.

- They are weak in dealing with social change and excluded or oppressed groups since they presume an existing social order to which individuals adapt, although they encourage concern for changing the immediate situation of individuals.

- They are used in specialist settings and a good knowledge of them enables connections with other professionals.

FURTHER READING

Goldstein, E. G. (1995) *Ego Psychology and Social Work Practice*, 2nd edn (New York: Free Press).

Goldstein, E. G. (2002) *Object Relations Theory and Self-Psychology in Social Work Practice* (New York: Free Press).

These two books provide a comprehensive overview of current American psychodynamic social work practice.

Howe, D. (1995) *Attachment Theory for Social Work Practice* (Basingstoke: Macmillan – now Palgrave Macmillan).

Howe, D., Brandon, M., Hinings, D. and Schofield, G. (1999) *Attachment Theory, Child Maltreatment and Family Support* (Basingstoke: Macmillan – now Palgrave Macmillan).
These two books provide a good review of attachment theory applied to social work, mainly in relation to work with children.

Parkes, C. M., Stevenson-Hinde, J. and Marris, P. (eds) (1993) *Attachment Across the Life Cycle* (London: Routledge).
A good account of practice applications of attachment theory at various life stages; not specifically about, but applicable to, social work.

Pearson, G., Treseder, J. and Yelloly, M. (eds) (1988) *Social Work and the Legacy of Freud* (London, Macmillan – now Palgrave Macmillan).
A good theoretical analysis of the role of psychoanalysis in social work.

JOURNALS

Journal of Social Work Practice, Group for the Advancement of Psychodynamics and Psychotherapy in Social Work: Carfax/Taylor and Francis.
Psychoanalytic Social Work, Haworth Press.
Smith College Studies in Social Work, Smith College School of Social Work/Haworth Press.

CHAPTER 5

Crisis Intervention and Task-centred Models

What this chapter is about

Crisis intervention and task-centred practice are two different theories that were historically developments of, respectively, ego psychology and problem-solving casework. They are thus in the individualist-reformist tradition, with little focus on social change. Initially, their development reflected a need to provide brief methods of intervention, since psychodynamic work emphasised open-ended and sometimes prolonged work with people. Both models developed using cognitive-behavioural methods, and so they form a link with the theories considered in the next chapter. Although they are theoretically separate, they are presented together here to offer a comparison between two well-established brief practice models. You can use the approach of one to point up the different features of the other.

MAIN POINTS

> ➤ Both crisis intervention and task-centred practice reflect a contemporary trend towards brief, focused and structured theories that deal with immediate, practical problems and may be criticised for avoiding long-term individual problems and social issues, leading to social exclusion.

> ➤ Crisis intervention assumes that we live in a steady state, able to cope with changes in our lives. Crises upset the steady state and provide an opportunity for developing improved skills at managing problems or a risk that we will fail and our capacity to manage life will deteriorate.

> ➤ 'Situational crises' are brought about by particular events. 'Maturational crises' occur regularly during our life cycle as our personal circumstances and relationships change and develop.

> ➤ Psychodynamic ego psychology is used in crisis intervention to emphasise people's emotional strengths in dealing with crises. Contemporary cognitive and solution-focused methods are used to challenge irrational thinking and build on strengths.

> ▶ Crises are turning points in people's lives when precipitating hazardous events lead to rising distress, upsetting the steady state in which previous coping mechanisms dealt with problems. This process leads to a state of active crisis.
>
> ▶ Crisis intervention involves an initial concern with people's safety and then assessment of affective, cognitive and behavioural reactions to the event.
>
> ▶ Strong emotional reactions are dealt with and then practice builds on people's strengths.
>
> ▶ Research has identified specific problems that task-centred casework is effective with; these are described and put in order of priority by clients.
>
> ▶ In task-centred work, client and worker agree a contract to carry out specific tasks to contribute to resolving the problems.

PRACTICE ISSUES AND CONCEPTS

> ▶ *Crisis*, as a focus for work and a commonly occurring element in life, setting a series of maturational tasks for us to complete.
>
> ▶ *Brief* interventions.
>
> ▶ *Structured, planned and directive programmes* of intervention.
>
> ▶ *Tasks* as both structured elements of an intervention and elements of life that have to be completed for emotional and social satisfaction.
>
> ▶ *Contracts* or *agreements* with clients to help them to participate and structure treatment plans.

Wider theoretical perspectives

The classic formulation of crisis intervention as a technique is that of Caplan on preventive psychiatry (1965). The method's origins, therefore, are in mental health work, and on prevention rather than treatment of illness. Parad and Parad describe the development process (1990b: 12–16). Lindemann's (1944) paper dealt with grief reactions in various groups of patients, showing how people coped with bereavement crises. They managed better if they had coped with previous crises in their lives, less well if they had not resolved past problems. A group of mental health workers around Lindemann and Caplan constructed the ideas of crisis intervention while working with several community mental health problems. Their work continues concerning preventive networks, and has led to a variety of developments influencing networking ideas (see Chapter 7).

Crisis intervention uses elements of ego psychology from a psychodynamic perspective, and recent developments have included cognitive therapy. It focuses on emotional responses to external events and how to control them rationally. Young (1983) analyses crisis intervention concepts alongside parallels in Chinese philosophy, suggesting that we might transplant the theory to Chinese culture.

She points to the 'doctrine of the mean', that is, maintaining our system in balance leading to a state of harmony and the Chinese assumption that people naturally gravitate towards fulfilment. The idea of *wu wei* proposes that life is constant change, which people should study and with which they should harmonise. The emphasis on seeking harmony in this Chinese application of the theory could be a useful element in Western theory.

Task-centred work originated wholly within social work, from a famous series of studies by Reid and Shyne (1969), Reid and Epstein (1972a, b) and Reid (1985). See Marsh (1991) for an account of them. In these it was discovered, first, contrary to expectations at the time, that truncated long-term treatment was as effective as long-term treatment which ran its full course, second, that 'planned short-term treatment' was effective and, third, that the task-centred model of practice devised as a result was effective. In its focus on problems, it had links with Perlman's problem-solving approach to casework (see Chapter 4), which it has largely displaced.

Both models and cognitive-behavioural methods are probably the most widely used examples of a range of 'brief treatment' approaches in social work that have become more important in recent years. Epstein (1992: 41–2) compares ten different models. She contends that among them the criteria for selection of clients, the organisation of treatment procedures and the approach to terminating contact vary considerably. Compared with longer term and particularly psychodynamic models, however, she argues that generally the focus is on 'upfront' problems. Also, advice and guidance are given, contrary to convention in more psychotherapeutic approaches.

Connections

These two models of social work have some common features. Both stress brief interventions, although they may string these together in a series. Epstein (1992: 102) treats both as examples of a range of brief treatment methods, all the others being described as psychotherapy or therapy. Reid (1992: 12) acknowledges the influence of crisis intervention on the development of task-centred work. Golan (1986: 309), viewing the relationship in the opposite direction, holds that research on task-centred work supports practice interventions in crisis intervention. Roberts and Dziegielewski (1995) treat crisis intervention as a form of brief cognitive therapy. Gray (1987) describes task-centred work within a crisis intervention psychiatric team. Both crisis and task-centred work are structured, so action is planned and fits a preordained pattern. 'Contracts' or other explicit agreements between worker and client are used. Circumstances in which each may be used are specified. MacNeil and Stewart (2000: 241) suggest that task-centred practice can help to formulate plans for action in crisis work.

Task-centred work also links with behavioural approaches (Howe, 1987). Some suggested links include the use of contracts, but these are widely used outside behavioural work (Corden and Preston-Shoot, 1987a; Hutten, 1977). Neither approach is formally connected with behavioural approaches. Crisis intervention is explicitly based on psychodynamic ego psychology. Task-centred casework rejects any specific psychological or sociological base for its methods and seeks to be 'eclectic and integrative' (Reid, 1992: 13; see also Reid, 1990; Epstein, 1992: 327–39). Many basic behavioural ideas, such as conditioning, play no part in task-centred work, and it deals with broader classes of behaviour than behavioural work normally covers. However, Gambrill (1994) argues that, as it has developed, it has increasingly used behavioural methods and its reformulation of these confuses the development of theory by denying its origins.

Both the circumstances in which crisis intervention and task-centred work should be used and the focus of work differ. Crisis intervention is, classically, action to interrupt a series of events which lead to a disruption in people's normal functioning. It only deals with the consequences of the one major issue, as defined by the situation. Task-centred work and other therapies do not necessarily focus on an immediate situation; rather they seek to identify and respond to major continuing problems in life. Task-centred work focuses on defined categories of problems. Both try to improve people's capacity to deal with their problems in living. Crisis intervention uses practical tasks to help people readjust, but an important focus is their emotional response to crises and long-term changes in their capacity to manage everyday problems. Task-centred work focuses on performance in practical tasks which will resolve particular problems. Success in achieving tasks helps emotional problems. Crisis intervention has a theory of the origin of life difficulties. Task-centred work takes problems as given, to be resolved pragmatically.

Task-centred work rejects the long-term involvement between worker and client assumed by insight-giving and supportive therapies, and concentrates on exposed problems rather than their underlying causes. Reid and Epstein (1972a: 26) specifically distinguish the approach from crisis intervention. They say task-centred work deals with a wider range of problems, and emphasises clear definitions of target problems, tasks and time limits. They stress links with functional casework, with their emphasis on time limits, client self-direction and having a clear structure and focus in the process of work. They use Hollis's classification of casework procedures (Chapter 4).

The main early writers on crisis intervention are represented in Parad's text (1965a), which introduced the subject to the social work literature and was later updated (Parad and Parad, 1990a). We can usefully combine crisis intervention with support systems work and networking (Mor-Barak, 1988; O'Hagan, 1991: 144–5). Roberts (1995; 2000; Roberts and Dziegielewski, 1995) focuses on cognitive treatment because of his emphasis on changing clients' perceptions and interpretations of the events that cause the crisis as the main focus of work.

The politics of crisis intervention and task-centred theory

The success of these two approaches to social work comes from the attractiveness and practical usability of the basic ideas of 'crisis' and 'task'. The theoretical models were developed at the time of social work's translation from a small-scale, undeveloped profession into being a servant of extensive welfare states. Parad and Parad (1990: 4–5) reject 'theory' as a description of crisis intervention, reserving this term for 'scientific' theory – see Chapter 3. The focus and brevity of these treatments offered an economic approach in this expansion, compared with longer term methods, which would have stretched costs and the size of the workforce to an impossible extent. Moreover, involvement in the front line of public services put social workers in touch with the crises in people's lives, in a way that trying to deal with longer term problems or offering care in the workhouses of the Poor Law and their successors did not involve. Task-centred work offered clearer accountability and a focus on outcomes for an influx of less experienced, less well-qualified and less supervised workers employed in settings requiring public scrutiny. It is also generic and can be applied in any setting with any person (Doel and Marsh, 1992: 6). The research-demonstrated effectiveness of task-centred work also strengthened its political acceptability to agency managers and funders, and supported a profession which was at times embattled about its effectiveness. Some research support for crisis intervention also exists (Parad and Parad, 1990b: 16–18). Task-centred work has also been popular with clients because of its clarity and sense of direction, and because it involves people actively in a sense of partnership (Gibbons et al., 1979). However, its simple concepts belie its complexity, and it is hard to train people to use it well (Marsh, 1991: 167). Ford and Postle (2000) examine its application in service systems such as care management (USA: managed care), and suggest that its structured approach permits it to incorporate social work practice within administrative responsibilities.

Neither model focuses on social change, and may be criticised as being mainly technical responses to immediate problems. This makes them attractive to public agencies and supporters of individualist-reformist views of social work, compared with those favouring the explicit political focus of critical theories which also had a currency as these models arose. Crisis intervention and task-centred theory have had greater staying power. The partnership approach and clarity of task-centred work and the emphasis on looking at environmental pressures have led to claims that they are both effective in use with anti-discriminatory work, offering empowerment and dealing with structural oppression (Ahmad, 1990: 51; O'Hagan, 1994).

Although crisis intervention seems specific in focus, dealing with 'situational' crises that are affecting someone at the present time, it is a general technique for dealing with people's problems. For example, a young man had difficulty in coming to visit his father when he was seriously ill, possibly dying, because it reminded him of his anger when his father had left the family during his divorce. During normal social relations, these feelings were hidden, but being aware of his father's possible death pressed him to resolve his anger by telling his father of them. Major social transitions such as birth, marriage, divorce and death tend to raise such previous conflicts within families, providing an opportunity to deal with feelings left over from the past or cement existing conflicts. One issue is that sometimes children are not involved in decisions at the time, so their feelings are not fully understood and talked through, being left to be dealt with at the time of a later crisis.

Parad (1965b) argues that people approaching agencies do so when they experience crises in their capacity to manage their lives. The crisis is what motivates them to come, or leads other agencies to refer or require them to seek help. Thus, everyone coming to an agency for help can be seen as 'in crisis', so that crisis intervention is relevant to all social work. The use of Erikson's (1965) analysis of developmental crises through which we achieve resolution of basic psychosocial life tasks (see Chapter 4) makes clear the concept's relevance to many personal difficulties.

Crisis intervention has been used in mental health services. It became associated with the idea of using multidisciplinary teams of doctors, nurses and social workers to visit people at home in an attempt to avoid damaging and unnecessary admissions to psychiatric hospitals (Fisher et al., 1990; Chiu and Primeau, 1991). Its methods of work with psychiatric emergencies have also been extended for use with assertive outreach for patients in the community with long-term problems. Such services respond to emergencies, but also ensure that contact is maintained by services with patients who might otherwise fall out of contact and then present as emergencies. Helping people to deal with severe reactions to loss and bereavement on death, for example, or when divorce or child care problems lead to the break-up of families are other common uses of the techniques. They are also relevant in many medical and other situations where loss or traumatic changes arise. More recently, in the USA, crisis intervention has been used in a range of emergency services that have a focus on emotional reaction to serious life events. These services reflect the inclusion of psychological and mental health responses to serious events, where previously concern about psychological difficulties after life events such as accidents was less well provided for. James and Gilliland (2001) discuss applications in services dealing with post-traumatic stress disorder, suicide and euthanasia, sexual assault, partner and domestic violence, addictions and personal losses, such as bereavement and grief. They also consider violent behaviour in residential care institutions, behaviour problems in schools and hostage crises. Kanel (2003) and Roberts (2000) cover similar lists. Kanel's analysis suggests crisis services as being useful where there is danger, victimisation, loss and developmental crises. While these last two are the traditional focus of crisis intervention, she also points to developmental crises that extend beyond the difficult transitions within the life course. These are where danger and victimisation may arise at a particular time of life, for example, teenage runaways and elder abuse.

In the UK, the term 'crisis intervention' is sometimes misused to refer to 'a crisis for the worker or the agency' (Browne, 1978: 115). Similarly, it is often used by radical or critical writers to refer to contemporary conflicts about the role of the state in welfare (see Chapter 11). These usages should not be confused with the concept in crisis intervention. O'Hagan (1986) treats 'crisis intervention' as an overall term referring to work in emergency and night-duty teams and some intake teams in the local authority social services. He regards it as particularly relevant to child protection work and mental health emergencies (O'Hagan, 1991). The classical usage of the term is retained in several services designed to respond to mental health emergencies (Davis et al., 1985; Parad and Parad, 1990a; Roberts, 1995) and the emotional aftermath of major public disasters (Sefansky, 1990).

Major statements

The classic statements of crisis intervention theory are those of Caplan (1965a) and, in social work, Parad (1965a), the latter being updated by a comprehensive review by Parad and Parad (1990b). Golan (1978) was the major international text for many years, and O'Hagan's (1986) account was useful as an introduction based on UK practice. All these, particularly Golan, whose work is generic and comprehensive, contain valid practice guidance and a similar approach. However, the development of crisis intervention as an aspect of emergency and disaster services, particularly in the USA, has led to a new generation of books providing extensive accounts of practice in wide ranges of emergencies aimed at a multiprofessional audience, prefaced by accounts of crisis intervention principles. These are all broadly similar, and the one most connected to social work is that of Roberts' (2000) *Crisis Intervention Handbook*, which is therefore the main text given here as an example of the present literature. Kanel's (2003) *A Guide to Crisis Intervention* is less comprehensive and more about principles, but is primarily aimed at a non-professional counselling readership, since many such services (for example suicide prevention services and rape crisis centres) rely on trained volunteers or paraprofessionals. Myer's (2001) *Assessment for Crisis Intervention* provides useful guidance on assessment. The following account of crisis intervention relies mainly on Roberts (2000), but includes material from Kanel (2003), Myer (2001) and James and Gilliland's (2001) *Crisis Intervention Strategies*.

The definitive statement of task-centred casework is in Reid's books (1978, 1992) and in Epstein (1992), and Reid's account is the main focus of the account presented below. The pioneer statement is in Reid and Epstein's *Task-Centered Casework* (1972a). It has been explicitly applied to groupwork and family work (Reid, 1985; Fortune, 1985). More recent accounts (Tolson et al., 1994; Reid, 2000) have elaborated and updated the model. A British interpretation, Doel and Marsh's (1992) *Task-centred Social Work*, elaborated in Marsh (1991) and Doel (1994, 2002), offers a comprehensive account using less technical terminology (included below for comparison) and full bibliography.

Roberts: crisis intervention

Roberts (2000) sees crises as turning points in people's lives. The model is shown in Figure 5.1. People function normally in a steady state (Rapoport, 1970: 276), that is, as things happen to them, they can 'cope', responding to events and changing and developing as they do so. 'Steady state' implies that people can manage new events in their lives, unlike the idea of equilibrium in early conceptualisations of crises, which saw people's lives as in a balance, with the crisis knocking them off balance, implying that people were not able to manage new events. In this way, contemporary accounts of crisis intervention incorporate a degree of social change.

As Figure 5.1 shows, a crisis is not a sudden or disastrous event, but a process: the model focuses on how people react to the *precipitating hazardous event*. Events that are meaningful or threatening to them are likely to lead to attempts

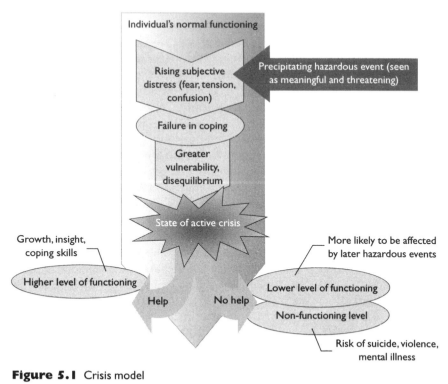

Figure 5.1 Crisis model
Sources: Caplan (1965); Roberts (2000); Kanel (2003); Parad (1965a).

to manage both the events and the reaction to them, using coping mechanisms that have worked before. Fear, tension or confusion rises as they try these. However, if it seems to them that the usual methods do not work on this occasion, they will experience a high level of discomfort and this leads to a state of active crisis. The disequilibrium will be seen in confusing and powerful emotions, physical complaints, such as sleeplessness and stomach upsets, and erratic behaviour as the person tries to find ways of dealing with the problem.

James and Gilliland (2001: 3) define a crisis as 'a perception or experiencing of an event or situation as an intolerable difficulty that exceeds the person's current resources and coping mechanisms'. Roberts (2000: 3) points out that a crisis may be personal (such as a the death of a loved one) or public (such as a major fire). It may be a personal crisis as a result of a public event, for example if your loved one died in the fire. A personal crisis may be potentially public. For example, a woman who has been raped has to decide whether and how she will report it to the police, and this will have public consequences, for example for other women who may have been raped by the same man, in having to give evidence. There may also be public policy consequences, for example the police may fail to protect women from rape if they do not have sensitive ways of dealing with women who have been raped or if the courts humiliate them in the process of the trial, leading women to fail to report rapes. Similarly, if a high level of drug abuse or escalating rates of HIV/AIDS in the community are matters of public controversy, people facing the personal crisis of addiction or infection may become elements in public debate or elements of their personal crisis may be affected by their views of the public debate.

The state of active crisis, according to Caplan (1965), continues for four to six weeks: Roberts clarifies that this is the period of disorganisation, resolved for better or worse during this period. If resolution is unsuccessful, a person will function less well in the future, and be more liable to bad reactions to later hazardous events. For example, someone who loses their spouse unexpectedly and does not have a successful bereavement will react unexpectedly strongly to later bereavements. Extremely poor resolutions may lead to serious difficulties, pushing someone towards suicide, drug abuse, violence to others or mental illness (Kanel, 2003). Crisis intervention, to Roberts, also includes:

- Establishing the new coping mechanisms as part of the client's repertoire
- Working through the feelings and experience of the problem so that longer term changes can be made
- Mobilising resources for support
- Reducing continuing unpleasant effects and emotions
- Thinking through events and their aftermath and integrating them into the client's personal life narrative.

James and Gilliland (2001) identify three models of crisis intervention:

- *The equilibrium model* – Caplan's (1965) original approach; people are seen as being in a state of psychological disequilibrium and need to return to a steady state in which they can deal with issues in their life effectively
- *The cognitive model* – Associated with Roberts (1995); people are seen as thinking in a faulty way about events that surround the crisis
- *The psychosocial transition model* – Associated with developments of Erikson's (1965) model of developmental crises arising as people move through life stages; people are seen as going through a particularly important psychological or social change as part of their development.

Treatment models are organised in stages, as shown in Figure 5.2. Each has their particular points of emphasis. Kanel's A-B-C model focuses initially on 'attending to' the client, to establish rapport, as Roberts has it. He emphasises the speed of reaction necessary in dealing with a crisis. Both he and James and Gilliland stress ensuring the safety of people involved from risk, further attack or emotional reaction leading to suicide or extreme reactions. James and Gilliland emphasise that assessment should be a constant part of crisis intervention, because of rapidly changing emotions. Myer's assessment model covers affective (emotional) reactions, and severe emotional reactions are a significant aspect of crisis intervention; Roberts stresses dealing with emotions first. Myer also separates out cognitive reactions, equally important to Roberts, and behavioural reactions.

Roberts suggests that the first two stages go together: conducting a psychoso-

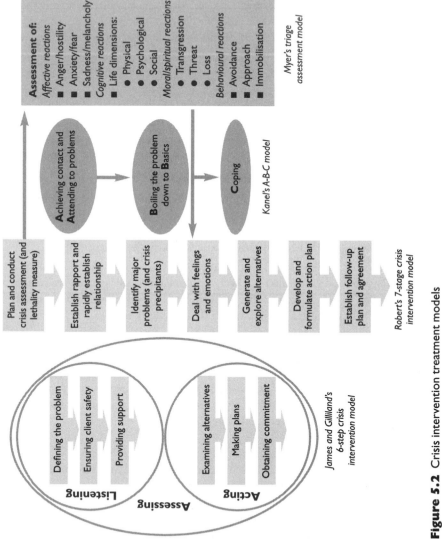

Figure 5.2 Crisis intervention treatment models

Source: Kanel (2003) (adapted); James and Gilliland (2001); Myer (2001); Roberts (2000).

cial and lethality assessment should be done in such a way as to establish rapport and relationship. Although one person may have been referred or have presented themselves at an agency, they may not be the person most at risk: it may be someone in their family or social network. Assessing lethality involves checking:

- whether someone needs medical attention
- whether someone is thinking of suicide or self-harm
- whether someone is a victim of violence whose attacker is nearby
- whether violent or dangerous individuals are nearby
- if a child is in danger
- if someone needs transport to safety
- if someone is under the influence of drink or drugs.

Where this is not immediate danger, risk should be assessed more fully, as follows:

- where there is violence, examine past attempts at self-protection, in order to assess victims' present capacities to protect themselves
- where there is violence, examine the perpetrator's history of violence and criminality
- where there is violence, has the victim a history of physical abuse, drug or alcohol overdose or suicide or self-harm attempts?
- are there dangerous weapons or objects in the vicinity?
- have weapons or dangerous objects been used against the victim?
- is the victim suffering from a major mental illness, particularly depression, anxiety or post-traumatic stress disorder?

Rapport is achieved by genuine respect for and acceptance of the people involved. Sometimes reassurance that behaviour is not unreasonable or unexpected may help. James and Gilliland include being supportive to those involved.

The third stage involves understanding the problem so that the hazardous precipitating event and the process by which the crisis developed may be identified. Myer's distinction between affective, cognitive and behavioural aspects of the reaction to the crisis are also relevant here. On affective aspects he suggests looking at verbal and non-verbal behaviour, using the client's voice quality and questions. Severity of reactions need also to be assessed. The main distinctions are between anger and hostility, anxiety and fear and sadness and melancholy. On cognitive reactions, he distinguishes between feelings of

- *threat*, where needs or integrity are in danger. This refers to a future possibility and in a mild form may be seen as a challenge
- *loss*, where people experience acute deprivation of, for example, a relationship, job, emotional well-being. This refers to comparisons with *past* experience

- *transgression*, where people's rights are being violated, for example violence, burglary, discrimination; personal standards of behaviour may also be violated, for example a spouse being unfaithful. This refers to *present* experience.

Assessing behavioural reactions involves looking at coping mechanisms. Previous coping mechanisms may fall into three categories:

- *avoidance*, for example repression, denial ('I can't believe he's dead')
- *approach*, for example rationalisation, sublimation ('I keep thinking it through, but I can't seem to move on')
- *immobilisation*, for example restitution, compensation ('I can't think what to do').

Roberts identifies the fourth stage of active work on feelings and emotions because in trying to deal with an immediate problem, it is easy to miss out or avoid a focus on feelings. However, the opportunity to ventilate feelings will release energy for coping later.

The fifth stage involves looking at past coping mechanisms. Here, Roberts recommends using solution-focused techniques (see Chapter 8). Greene et al. (2000) suggest that this helps to build on strengths. In their approach, engagement, or 'joining', by treating people as experts in their own situation allows problems to be exposed and defined, goals set, using 'miracle' and 'dream' questions ('if a miracle happened or you could have your dream, what would it be like?') and by scaling ('on a scale of 0–10, what is it like now, and where would you like to be?'). Exceptions to failings in coping and evidence of past successes should be reviewed. Successes should be highlighted and reinforced.

In stage six Roberts emphasises the cognitive element of restoring functioning. Thus, people could work on understanding why the hazardous precipitating event was so distressing and thinking about ways of mastering the past experience by looking at how to manage similar situations in the future. Workers might note and question unrealistic and distorted thoughts and beliefs about the event. Then, restructuring involves replacing the unrealistic beliefs with new beliefs. People might be given homework to try out new forms of behaviour and report how they experienced that.

In the final stage, people should be helped both to feel able to return if further problems arise and also to identify likely stress points in the future, such as the anniversary of the hazardous event.

Task-centred casework: Reid and Epstein

In task-centred work, workers resolve problems presented by clients. Any social work theory should, therefore, show how problems arise, what they are and how we may deal with them. Brief work with explicit time limits is an essential feature of the approach. The aim is for a collaborative relationship, where both worker and client make contributions to a standard process, set out in Figure 5.3. The systematic nature of planning is also effective for care management (managed

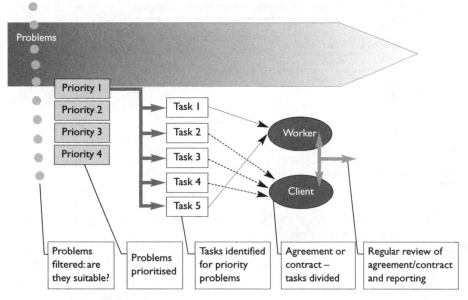

Figure 5.3 Task-centred work

care), where multiple providers need to be integrated into shared objectives and practices (Reid, 1996).

Task-centred work is concerned with problems that:

- clients acknowledge or accept
- can be resolved through actions taken outside contacts with workers
- can be defined clearly
- come from things that clients want to change in their lives
- come from clients' 'unsatisfied wants' rather than being defined by outsiders. For Reid (1992: 18–19), only acknowledged problems offer the necessary degree of partnership. Doel and Marsh (1992: 23) also include problems imposed by formal processes, such as courts.

People share some problems with others in their lives, who may acknowledge and define the problem in the same way. Agreement does not always exist about shared problems; people in the situation may see them differently. For example, with Joan, a young woman, the worker discovered that her inability to find a job was worrying her most, and began to work out a plan for undertaking a series of tasks to share the task of finding one. Before completing this, however, she visited the home to find that Joan's mother preferred her to remain at home to help domestically with the elderly grandparent who was also living with her. Also, Joan's father felt that working in a shop, which she preferred, was not socially acceptable. He wanted her to learn office skills at college. The worker had first to resolve different perceptions of Joan's family duties before being able to continue with job-finding.

Table 5.1 Problems with which task-centred work is effective

■ Interpersonal conflict
■ Dissatisfaction in social relationships
■ Problems with formal organisations
■ Difficulty in role performance
■ Decision problems
■ Reactive emotional stress
■ Inadequate resources
■ Psychological and behavioural problems not otherwise categorised, but meeting the general definition of problems in the model

Source: Reid (1978).

Reid classifies the types of problems with which task-centred work is effective into eight categories, as shown in Table 5.1.

Workers should try to understand people's problem-solving behaviour, especially where explanatory theories account for how problems are caused and resolved. We should assess the direction and strength of clients' *wants*. Some wants support one another, while others are in opposition. Wants start action off, but *belief systems* shape the wants and the acceptable ways of fulfilling them. In Joan's case, for example, the desire for a job was enough to start her seeking the worker's help. However, the type of job she believed was possible – shop work – and her lack of desire to spend time in college to gain qualifications for office work meant that the direction of job-seeking had to be changed from the father's preference. Alternatively, her socially conditioned expectations might be raised, so that she would look for more interesting and demanding jobs.

Beliefs guide action and are changed by interactions between the worker, client and others. Such beliefs are *points of leverage* which can help to change beliefs, as in cognitive therapies. Points of leverage are as follows:

- *Accuracy*, where workers help people to understand how accurate their beliefs are.

- *Scope*, where workers help people to see the implications or range of beliefs which they think are more limited.

- *Consistency*, where distortions due to dissonance between one belief and another can be removed by the worker.

Again in Joan's case, the worker found it useful to explore whether her assessment of her capacity to gain better qualifications was accurate, by discussing the different perceptions of father and daughter. She also explored with Joan how she might limit the scope for moving on to more interesting jobs in the future if she failed to gain qualifications now, since she might get used to having a wage coming in and be loath to return to college. Joan and the worker also explored the mismatch between Joan's desire to do something interesting (as shown by her wish to find a job more stimulating than her domestic responsibilities and her wish for the independence deriving from having a job and a wage) and the likelihood that a low-grade job would prove boring very quickly.

Emotions arise from the interaction between beliefs and wants. Fear or anxiety arise because people believe that a want is lost or threatened. Unconscious motivation may affect beliefs or wants but not (directly) behaviour. Joan, for example, was afraid of getting stuck at home and was reacting too quickly and to her disadvantage as a result.

Action is behaviour carried out with intent, so understanding actions involves understanding intentions. *Plans* are descriptions of intentions formed by the interaction of beliefs, wants and emotions. Planning means assessing alternative options, preferably away from the situation in which action is needed. When a plan is acted upon, the outcome gives feedback to the actor. Actions often occur in *sequences* and the problem may lie early in the sequence. For example, if my son misbehaves, I might shout at him and then feel guilty because I believe that shouting in this situation is wrong. Is shouting appropriate to stop the misbehaviour? This may be so if he is overactive today and needs a warning and a reminder to think about and moderate his behaviour. But suppose the problem is that I ignored him, causing him to misbehave to gain attention. Deciding not to shout would not be effective as a resolution of the problem of inappropriate shouting, because this plan mistakes the problem, and he would probably misbehave more to get attention, which the early misbehaviour did not achieve. A better way to solve the problem of inappropriate shouting would be to play with him and show him that I have more time for him.

Clients may not have *skills* to perform actions needed in particular circumstances. Skills may be learned directly or generalised from other situations. Going through a series of small steps may help such learning.

Some *social systems* generate or affect people's beliefs, or respond to actions providing feedback in ways that distort further actions, whether for good or ill. The environment surrounding people may therefore be important. Action sequences may in this way become *interaction sequences*, so that actions affect one another in circles or spirals. This idea comes from communication theory. *Organisations* may form a context for actions, labelling or categorising people or generating 'collective beliefs' about certain sorts of people. For example, staff in a school may come to believe that children from a particular housing estate are disruptive. This may in turn affect what the children believe about themselves, and what their parents and other agencies think about them. Going further, this may then affect how people involved act towards one another.

The *intervention strategy* has two aims:

- helping people to resolve problems of concern to them
- giving a good experience of problem-solving so improving clients' future capacity to deal with difficulties and willingness to accept help.

Worker and client identify *target problems*, carry out *tasks* outside the agency setting and *rehearse and review* achievements.

This account of general principles shows how the model's ideas come from a variety of psychological and sociological sources. Social learning theory influences the mode of action, identifying targets and tasks and rehearsal. Communication theory is present in the concern for sequences and interactions of behaviour. The emphasis on belief shows a cognitive element. The identification of influence from the environment, and particularly organisations within it, suggests ideas borrowed from systems theory. As with psychodynamic theory, which influenced task-centred work's predecessor, problem-solving, focusing on distinct problems to be solved is a medical model of practice. Solving problems is a social work analogue for curing illness (see Chapter 4).

The aim of *assessment* is not, as in psychodynamic theory, to study clients' responses or life history, but to identify

- action requirements
- obstacles to action
- unchangeable constraints.

People wanting less formal, more friendly or more personally involving relationships should seek alternative forms of therapy. Where people cannot maintain a focus on a limited range of problems, less structured or more exploratory methods such as crisis intervention should be used. Task-centred work helps in protective work (for instance with the parents of abused children) but should not be used where authoritarian protection or social control are the main priorities. People's own actions will not change some physical and mental illnesses, so task-centred work can only be part of interventions here. However, it may help to deal with the social consequences of illness or disability.

Problem specification is the first step, taken early on through agreement with clients to undertake a short period of assessment. Doel and Marsh (1992) use a newspaper metaphor. We look first at the front page for the main news, then scan for headlines, identify the story lines (details of the problems) and client quotations (putting the whole issue in the client's words). The social context of the problem and others' responses to it are important. The process presented by Reid (1978) is as follows:

- *Identify potential problems* by helping people describe difficulties in their own way. Summarise and test out workers' perceptions of problems.
- *Reach tentative agreements* on how people see the main problems.
- *Challenge unresolvable or undesirable problem definitions* (for example where the client unreasonably wants a deserted spouse to return).
- *Raise additional problems*, having first accepted the client's definition of priorities, where the client does not understand or accept additional problems.
- *Seek others' involvement* if necessary.
- *Jointly assess the reason for referral* if someone else compels the client to attend.
- *Get precise details* of when and where problems arise.
- *Specify the problem*, usually in writing.
- *Identify clear baselines* of the level of present problems (see Chapter 6 for further discussion of baselines).
- *Decide desired changes.*

In the phase of *contract creation* – Doel and Marsh (1992) call this making an *agreement* – worker and client reach specific agreements on action. The process is as follows:

- Agree to work on and specify one or more client-defined problems (Doel and Marsh – the selected problem).
- Rank the problems in order of priority.
- Define the desired outcome of treatment (Doel and Marsh – goal; Epstein, 1992, limits goals to specifiable outcomes).
- Design the first set of tasks.
- Agree the amount of contact and time limits.
- Reid prefers oral contracts to written ones because they are less frightening, unless several people are involved or the problems are complex. Doel and Marsh (1992) prefer written agreements in order to make goals less fuzzy and invoke the client's commitment.

Task planning takes place in regular sessions with clients. Tasks are explicitly planned, practicable for clients to do outside the sessions and agreed between worker and client. They may involve mental or physical action (for example to decide this or do that). *General tasks* set a policy for the treatment process, and *operational tasks* define what the client will do. Tasks may be *unitary*, involving just one action or a series of actions, or *complex*, involving two different actions (for example to find a new flat and take part in occupational therapy). They may be *individual*, undertaken only by the client; *reciprocal*, so that if the client does this, the worker or a relative will do that; or *shared*, so that the client and another important person will do it together.

The *task planning process* is as follows:

- possible alternative tasks are identified, through generating *task possibilities* (Reid 1992: 57–8)
- an agreement is made, and explicitly secured with the client (Reid, 1992: 60)
- implementation is planned
- the task is summarised.

Task implementation then takes over the sessions between worker and client. This involves the following:

- A recording system is set up, especially where a sequence of or repeated actions are required.
- Strategies are identified (for example a series of increments, setting limits, setting precise targets, mental tasks, use of paradox, tasks to be done by client and worker concurrently, involving other people).
- Incentives for finishing a task are agreed if these are not built in.

- The client's understanding of the value of the task and how it helps to meet the goal is checked. This helps to establish motivation.
- Relevant skills are practised, by simulation (for instance the worker acts out an employment interview) or guided practice (such as helping a person with disabilities try out a new adaptation to her home in a day centre). Reid (1992: 50–3) calls these *session tasks*, that is, they are work undertaken among clients or between client and worker in the session. They include planning and expressing and dealing with anxiety and other feelings.
- Obstacles are analysed and removed. These may relate to motivation, understanding, beliefs and emotions such as anxiety or anger and lack of skill (Reid, 1992: 73–94).
- The worker's contribution is planned.

The *worker's tasks* may involve the following:

- working with people other than clients to help clients to complete their tasks (such as preparing the way with another agency)
- arranging for rewards and incentives for success
- sharing tasks with clients where they have insufficient skills or resources to do them alone.
- Worker and client review achievements jointly in each session.

Mr and Mrs Knowles were an example of some of these processes. They were referred to a mental health advice service, with the problem that Mrs Knowles had become slightly agoraphobic, and now was unable to go out, except with her husband in the car. She was, for example, unable to do the shopping or go out on her own to see friends. She felt a little embarrassed by this. There were no resources to carry out a behaviour modification programme involving the worker. Instead, he explained the basic principles of doing things in stages, having Mr Knowles alongside for support, and with the idea of getting relaxed before moving on to the next stage. They then discussed a series of events in which they would go out in the car and Mrs Knowles would get out of the car, then later would go part of the way to a small shop, then all the way, later still buy some things, and then progress in stages to going to the supermarket. The contract included the worker being available on the phone if any difficulties arose. This programme worked effectively without further interventions.

The *ending phase* involves client and worker in the following actions:

- describing the target problem as it was and as it is now, including checking whether it was the most important problem (Doel and Marsh, 1992: 81–2)
- assessments by the worker, client and others involved of any changes and achievements

- planning for the future (for example how people will use any skills learned or cope with changed circumstances) and helping people to manage evident future problems
- additional contracts, to extend the process to finish off properly, or establish new problem and task definitions
- an explicit end where (as in residential care or continuing supervision of someone subject to legal requirements) contact with the worker or agency continues
- movement to a long-term treatment process, or arranging for follow-up to check that progress is maintained
- referral to another agency for additional or alternative help.

CRITICAL PRACTICE FOCUS

Mr Hardy

Mr Hardy has mild learning disabilities but holds down a routine job. He lives in a Housing Philanthropy Association flat. His support workers have set up a routine with him, with his salary being paid into a bank account, and a regular programme of shopping, cooking and some entertainment. He attends a local church and takes part, with the support of church members, in some social events. Unfortunately, the area in which he lives is becoming run-down, and a group of young neighbours, who initially seemed friendly, have turned out to be drug users. On one occasion a group of them pushed their way past his front door, into his living room, threatened him with knives to get him to take them to his bank's ATM and take out money for them. He resisted them, so they took him into the bathroom and held his head under the water until he agreed. They told him not to inform anyone 'or else' ... . The threat was unstated, but real to him. His fears are confirmed: this happens several times, until he is unable to pay his rent. The housing association contacted his support workers, who found out what has been going on and referred it to the social worker/care manager. A report was made to the police, who picked up some of the youths, but this led to more threats outside the house, and Mr Hardy now fears going to work. He says he will commit suicide – there is nothing left for him. A multiagency adult protection strategy meeting is called to consider what actions might be taken to protect him. Moving house and 24-hour police protection are not practical. In the longer term, some action might be successful with the youths.

Considering Mr Hardy's position, what contribution might crisis intervention and task-centred practice offer the social worker member of the meeting? There might be practical measures that could be susceptible to task-centred practice. Alternatively, Mr Hardy's distress should perhaps be the main focus, as crisis intervention would suggest. In this complicated situation, where is the best place to start? How would you decide on your social work role in relation to the multiagency team? Who must be incorporated into what you do? Who might help?

Commentary

The general success of both these models of practice may conceal areas where they are not effective. In both cases, they are not effective where constant debilitating crises and long-term psychological problems are the main issue. They may be used in child protective work or in a long-term case to achieve results with a specified problem or a particular crisis. Often in such cases, however, supportive work, provision of services and longer term efforts at change or supervision to prevent deterioration or risk will be required. Neither model works well with people who do not accept the right of the worker or agency to be involved. Many workers find that the clarity of the process is one of the great attractions, but this may simplify the complexity of the issues in people's lives. However, they may help with finding a way of entering a complex situation and demonstrating the worker's effectiveness in helping by resolving feelings around a crisis or particular aspects of a problem. The short timescale may also help where people are limited in commitment or capacity to focus on important issues

Both theories represent a trend in social work to clearer, more focused activity than the long-term, non-directive, insight-giving methods of psychodynamic work. Kadushin (1998) proposes that adaptations to conventional interviewing and practice techniques are required to implement brief, focused therapies of this kind. For example, the need to establish a relationship rapidly means that presenting a warm, intelligent impression from the outset is important. Focusing on the present and on solutions rather than exploring problems and their history in detail are also important. Workers are not attempting an overall 'cure' but resolution 'for now' of specific issues.

Both theories, however, are in the traditional lineage of social work problem-solving, using a conventional social work individualising relationship with clients who are treated on a medical model: problems are seen as like illnesses and the worker's job is to solve them, as it is the doctor's job to cure illnesses. Crisis intervention, with its more psychodynamic roots, offers a greater emphasis on emotional responses and irrational or unconscious behaviour than task-centred work, which assumes greater rationality on the part of clients. However, the impact of cognitive-behavioural practice on both is shifting brief practice using either model towards cognitive practice (Chapter 6).

The idea of a contract has been criticised. Rojek and Collins (1987, 1988), using concepts from discourse analysis, argue that it offers a false sense of equality between workers and clients; false because it neglects the position of social workers who have all the power and authority of the state, profession and class to impose their will. They propose that in using terms like 'contract', workers imply an equality that in a sense enables them to take greater power in the relationship. The fact that this power imbalance exists makes it difficult to use contracts in the way proposed by activities such as task-centred work; it prevents the mutual cooperation which the model assumes and which is the origin of its success. Replying to this, Corden and Preston-Shoot (1987b, 1988) argue that the contract can benefit client–worker relationships by helping to make these explicit, and at least more specific so that each knows more clearly what is going on. In fact, contract work does achieve results in allowing people to attain desired ends.

More broadly, Gambrill (1994) argues that task-centred work – and by extension many forms of brief therapy – provides a minimal response to severe social problems. It thus conceals resource inadequacy and the failure of political will to respond realistically to deep-seated problems of poverty and social inequality. Its effectiveness in dealing with presenting problems may result in society avoiding longer term and more deeply seated responses to social oppressions.

OVERVIEW

- Both models reflect a contemporary emphasis on brief, structured forms of therapy and dealing with immediate rather than long-term problems.

- Crisis intervention is a model to describe the process by which serious events have an impact on people's thinking about themselves and emotional reactions.

- It provides a useful basis for services that help people to deal with major situational events or developmental life transitions, incorporating other modes of practice, including cognitive and solution-focused methods.

- While it helps to deal with the immediate problem in focus, and offers a theoretical underpinning for services, providing help in disasters, violence, victimisation and particularly psychiatric emergencies, it has lost its original preventive emphasis.

- Crisis intervention is also unable to help people whose whole life is characterised by continual crises because of poverty and social exclusion.

- Task-centred practice is a structured, short-term model of working with specific problems, providing good guidance and well supported by research.

- Like crisis intervention, it may ameliorate the consequences of more generalised social failings and fail to deal with important social issues affecting people's lives as a result.

FURTHER READING

James, R. K. and Gilliland, B. E. (2001) *Crisis Intervention Strategies*, 4th edn (Belmont, CA: Wadsworth).

Kanel, K. (2003) *A Guide to Crisis Intervention*, 2nd edn (Pacific Grove, CA: Brooks/Cole).

Roberts, A. R. (ed.)(2000) *Crisis Intervention Handbook,* 2nd edn (New York: Oxford University Press).

These three books are up-to-date and comprehensive alternative resources on American crisis intervention practice.

Doel, M. and Marsh, P. (1992) *Task-centred Social Work* (Aldershot: Ashgate).

Tolson, E. R., Reid, W. and Garvin, C. D. (1994) *Generalist Practice: A Task-Centered Approach* (New York: Columbia University Press).

Good accounts of task-centred practice from, respectively, America and Britain. Doel and Marsh's book is soon to be updated.

Payne, M. (1998) 'Task-centred practice within the politics of social work theory' *Issues in Social Work Education*, **17**(2): 48–65.
An analysis of the development of the debate about task-centred practice.

JOURNAL

Brief Treatment and Crisis Intervention Journal, Oxford University Press/High Wire Press.

WEBSITE

http://www.task-centered.com/
American site for enthusiasts; links to other international sites.

CHAPTER 6

Cognitive-behavioural Theories

What this chapter is about

This chapter deals with two related sets of theories, which are now usually treated as one:

- Behavioural models of therapy, deriving from psychological learning theories
- Cognitive models of therapy, deriving from psychological theories of perception and information-processing.

Since they are mainly psychological and do not seek general social objectives, they are, like psychodynamic, crisis and task-centred theories, primarily individualist-reformist.

MAIN POINTS

> Cognitive-behavioural work focuses on defining and addressing people's problem behaviours, particularly social phobias, anxiety and depression.

> Careful assessment and monitoring of progress often uses behavioural measurements.

> Research evidence of effectiveness is strong and important to theory and practice.

> The main techniques are well defined and technical, including respondent and operant conditioning, social learning and skills training and cognitive restructuring of people's belief systems.

> Social learning techniques such as assertiveness and skills training are widely used, particularly as part of groupwork and are taken up in feminist practice.

> More specific techniques are used in clinical settings where supervision and training in their use are available.

> The use of cognitive-behavioural models of practice have been controversial because of their association with politically controversial 'what works' and professionally controversial 'evidence-based practice' perspectives and the

sometimes intemperate critique by its proponents from a scientific and evidence-based perspective of pre-existing and broader perspectives on social work practice.

➤ There has also been cautious concern about potential ethical problems and these theories have not been widely used in Eastern countries, where scientific methods are less influential, and countries where broader social work aims are more relevant.

PRACTICE IDEAS AND CONCEPTS

➤ *Behaviour, cognitive* and *cognitive-behavioural therapy*, focusing on specific behaviours and thought patterns.

➤ *Social learning theory*, focusing on people learning from their perceptions of social experiences.

➤ *Generalisation* of learned behaviour from treatment to ordinary life.

➤ *Extinction* of unhelpful behaviour patterns.

➤ *Assertiveness training* enabling people to practise behaviours to give them confidence.

➤ *Reinforcement* of useful behaviours.

➤ *Modelling*, a form of social learning where people understand and copy useful behaviours from a valued role model.

➤ *Shaping* behaviour by reinforcing small changes.

➤ *Token economies* reinforce behaviour in residential care using tokens of rewards that will be given later.

Wider theoretical perspectives

Overview

Cognitive and behavioural ideas come from two related streams of psychological writing. Historically, learning theory came first, and developed into clinical psychology using a behaviour therapy based on psychological research. Sheldon (1995) expresses the underlying ideas of *learning theory* as a separation of behaviour and mind, the totality of the person's psychological identity. The psychodynamic and perhaps conventional view is that behaviour comes from a process which goes on in our minds. This has connections with philosophical ideas about what the mind is, and whether it is the seat of our humanity, what Christians call a 'soul'. A related question is whether environmental influences limit people's freedom or whether they are free to act according to their will, that is, what their mind wishes. Learning theory does not deny that this may be so, but argues that we cannot know what is happening in someone else's mind. Therefore, we can only study and influence the behaviour we can see. We learn most behaviour, except some inborn reflexes, that is, it originates from influences outside ourselves. Therefore, we can learn new behaviour to meet our needs or replace existing behaviour if it is causing us problems. The therapy, therefore, focuses on doing things that consistently lead to changes in behaviour. It does not concern itself with what changes may take place in our mind during this process.

Social learning theory (Bandura, 1977) extends these ideas by arguing that most learning is gained by people's perceptions and thinking about what they experience. They learn by copying the example of others around them. Helping this process can enhance therapy.

Cognitive theory is in part a development of behaviour theory and therapy, recently building particularly on social learning theory. It also grew out of therapeutic developments of a pragmatic kind, devised by writers such as Beck (1989) and Ellis (1962), who were concerned with psychiatric conditions such as anxiety neurosis and depression. In social work, Glasser's (1965) *reality therapy*, which originates from residential work with young women, has been important. Because the originators of behavioural therapies were dealing with disorders of the mind, they moved towards trying to incorporate thinking within their model of therapy. Cognitive theory argues that behaviour is affected by perception or interpretation of the environment during the process of learning. Apparently inappropriate behaviour must therefore arise from misperception and misinterpretation. Therapy tries to correct the misunderstanding, so that our behaviour reacts appropriately to the environment. According to Scott (1989), different approaches include Beck's concern with distorted thinking about ourselves, our lives and our future leading to depression or anxiety, Ellis's focus on irrational beliefs about the world and Meichenbaum's (1977) emphasis on threats we experience. This latter idea, particularly, relates to some ideas in crisis intervention.

Gambrill (1995) identifies the main features of *behavioural work* as follows:

- It focuses on specific behaviours that worry clients and others around them. If behaviour is changed, we remove the concern.
- It relies on behavioural principles and learning theory.
- Workers make a clear analysis and description of problems, based on direct observation. Assessment, intervention and evaluation methods are explicitly defined.
- Factors influencing behaviour are identified by changing factors in the situation and looking for resulting changes.
- Clients' assets are discovered and put to use.
- Important people in clients' environments are involved.
- Intervention is based on research evidence of effectiveness.
- Progress is monitored using subjective and objective measures, comparing data about the present with data about the situation before intervention.
- Workers are concerned to achieve outcomes valued by clients.
- Workers help clients to use changed behaviours in many situations (generalisation) and maintain improvements after intervention has ceased.

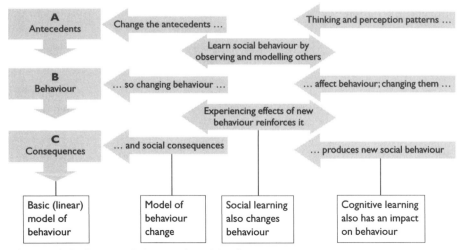

Figure 6.1 Cognitive-behavioural models of practice

Consistent with the scientific approach of behavioural work, it uses a linear model of explanation: one thing leads to another in a straight line of explanation. This may be criticised from realist and social construction perspectives for reducing the complexity of interacting social factors in many situations to an over-simplified model of behaviour. Behaviour is caused by antecedents, that is, things that have happened previously, and when we behave in particular ways, this has consequences for us, which then form antecedents for later behaviours. Figure 6.1 illustrates this, and then shows some of the different approaches to changing the contingencies that might affect our behaviour; these are discussed in more detail below. Gambrill (1995) argues that the basic form of behavioural work is concerned with changing contingencies that affect antecedents and behaviours. She discusses several connected approaches to doing this. Social learning theory focuses on how we learn from social situations by learning how others act successfully (vicarious learning). *Cognitive-behavioural* methods are therapeutic procedures which focus on changing thoughts and feelings alongside, instead of or as a precursor to, changing behaviours. *Radical behaviourism* includes thoughts and feelings as behaviours, treating them as the cause of other behaviours. This prevents seeing thoughts and feelings as emerging from unknown areas of the mind. Thoughts and feelings are, therefore, caused and we can change them like any other behaviour. *Neo-behaviourism* is behavioural treatment particularly concerned with stress and anxiety disorders. Cognitive and behavioural ideas have much in common with models such as task-centred work, and there is a degree of mutual influence. Humanist and constructivist ideas also have relevance because of the concern with ideas of the mind and cognitive attempts to link thinking with doing, and because behavioural ideas emphasise scientific methods of research as the basis for therapeutic action and humanism discounts non-rational evidence.

Processes of cognitive-behavioural practice

Some basic ideas from learning theory and behavioural treatment are necessary to understand the approach. Sheldon (1998) identifies several important ideas underlying behaviour therapy:

- respondent or classical conditioning (the stimulus-response approach – Jackson and King, 1982)
- operant conditioning
- learned helplessness
- social learning and modelling
- cognitive factors such as disorders of perception or attribution (the meaning attached to events and experiences) and catastrophic thinking.

All are directly applicable in social work. The following account relies on Sheldon (1998) and Fischer and Gochros (1975).

Respondent conditioning is concerned with behaviour (anything we do) which responds to (is produced by) a stimulus (a person, situation, event, or thing usually in the environment). *Conditioning* is the process by which behaviour is learned, that is, connected more or less permanently with the stimulus. When we have learned a response to a stimulus, we have modified our behaviour. For example, if a young child gets into trouble regularly because he gets muddy at the park, he may learn to associate going to the park with the disapproval, rather than being muddy. Respondent conditioning is also known as *classical conditioning* because it derives from the first experiments in the field by Pavlov; famously, he trained dogs to salivate (the natural reaction to seeing food) when they heard a bell, even though there was no food, because he first associated the sound of the bell with seeing food.

Many behaviours are *unconditioned*. They happen naturally. An unconditioned stimulus produces an unconditioned response, for example people's eyes water in a high wind, they salivate when given food, they withdraw their hands sharply when burned, they are sick when they eat a noxious substance.

Behaviours are *conditioned* when responses become *associated* or paired with a stimulus that does not naturally produce the response. An example would be if our eyes were trained to water when we were given food. We call these *conditioned stimuli* and *conditioned responses*. Conditioned responses become *generalised*, that is, the person applies them to similar situations. So the child who avoids going to the park because of disapproval may eventually find it difficult to go out at all. Such responses are the mechanism of many social phobias and post-traumatic stress disorder. People develop a response to one stimulus and it begins to affect them in other situations.

Extinction occurs if the association between conditioned responses and stimuli is not kept up. The conditioned response fades away and loses its connection with the stimulus. This provides an important basis for treatment, since both the connection between stimulus and response and generalisation can be extinguished. For example, the child might be taken to the park in easy stages, to learn by experience that there is no disapproval associated with it.

Some kinds of behaviour are incompatible with other behaviour. For example, a completely relaxed person cannot be anxious or violent. *Counter-conditioning* seeks to associate desirable responses with particular stimuli, in competition with undesirable responses.

The most commonly used counter-conditioning technique is *systematic desensitisation*. Clients are taught the practical techniques of relaxation or are offered other means of personal support. Then they are slowly introduced to the unwanted stimulus, using the relaxation or support to fight against their anxiety. This is often used with school phobia or agoraphobia. We saw a simple example of this in the case of the Knowles in Chapter 5. Here, relaxation and Mr Knowles's presence counter-conditioned against Mrs Knowles's agoraphobic anxiety. *Assertiveness training* is another technique used where people lack confidence. Workers help them to practise appropriate forms of behaviour in a supportive environment, so that they are enabled to use these in, ideally, increasingly difficult real-life situations.

Counter-conditioning is used in sexual therapy. Pleasant sexual responses are learned in supportive surroundings and gradually introduced into more ordinary sexual situations which had previously caused anxiety. For example, a man who ejaculates prematurely learns to control ejaculation while stimulated by his partner when full sexual intercourse is not permitted, until he feels confident of control. Transfer to sexual intercourse follows later.

One example of these techniques is in conditioning children who are enuretic, that is, they wet the bed when they should have learned not to do this. A loud buzzer or bell is connected to an electrical contact placed within soft mats under the child. The buzzer sounds when some urine reaches the mats, and the child wakes and can complete urination in a toilet. This process has two effects. First, the child is conditioned to wake when the bladder is full, so avoiding bed-wetting. Second, the tone of the bladder muscle is improved, strengthening the capacity to get through the night without wetting. These responses are set up as a form of counter-conditioning to the natural process of reflex urination when the bladder is full (Morgan and Young, 1972).

Most behaviour does not develop from unconditioned stimuli, and *operant conditioning* deals with a wider range of behaviours. It is concerned with behaviour with operates on the environment, and can be used with complex and thought-out behaviour. In contrast, respondent conditioning is mainly concerned with learned automatic responses.

Operant conditioning was the original form of behavioural practice focused on changing the contingencies that affected behaviours, leading to new consequences, set out in the first sequence in Figure 6.1. Something happens (an *antecedent* event – A – which produces a behaviour – B – which tries to deal with the event, and because of that behaviour, consequences – C – arise. Workers manage *contingencies* which affect the relationships between behaviour and consequences which strengthen or weaken behaviour by *reinforcement* and *punishment*. Reinforcement, whether positive or negative, strengthens behaviour. Punishment, whether positive or negative, reduces behaviour. Positive always means doing something; negative always means taking something away. Both can be used together. More information is given below, in discussing Sheldon's (1995) account of cognitive-behavioural work.

Extinction is also an operant learning technique. It differs in principle from extinction in respondent conditioning. It means removing the relationship between behaviour and its consequence. In negative punishment, we may remove a consequence which has nothing to do with the behaviour, as in the example given above. Extinction might be used where avoiding homework led to arguments between child and parents. The arguments positively reinforce not doing homework, because they take up time and emotional energy which can then not be applied to the homework. Instead of arguing, parents put child and homework in a room, thus withdrawing the reinforcing behaviour. Unlike extinction in respondent conditioning, this is not solely avoiding making a response. It is positively removing the relationship between a consequence and the behaviour which led to it.

Positive reinforcement is usually preferable to or should be used with other techniques. For example, extinction gives no control over the behaviour that might replace the undesirable behaviour; it might be equally undesirable. Positive reinforcement allows the encouragement of favoured behaviour alongside extinction. Also, unwanted behaviour may increase temporarily to test out the new response and this is hard to cope with, so encouraging useful behaviour makes the process easier.

The main process in *social learning* is *modelling*. Hudson and MacDonald (1986) describe it as follows:

■ A person sees someone else performing an action and pays attention to it.

■ Observers 'form an idea' or code in their mind how the behaviour is done, including some rehearsals in practice or in their mind.

■ Observers identify circumstances in which the behaviour occurs and has its consequences.

■ When an appropriate situation arises, observers repeat the behaviour according to the 'idea' of it which they have formed.

Seeing a feared behaviour performed by a role model helps many people to appreciate that there are no adverse consequences. Sheldon (1998: 20) emphasises that most people do not learn by reading books or being told what to do; getting a demonstration of what to do, experimenting while in a supportive environment and getting feedback and encouragement are important. This work has led to skills training programmes, anger management and similar ways of helping people to learn new behaviours. Priestley and McGuire (1978, 1983) describe practical projects to help offenders to learn better social skills to avoid getting themselves into difficult situations and how to respond to conflict and relationship problems, and describe exercises that workers may use to work with people using skills training.

Sheldon (1998: 23) summarises the important factors in *social skills training* programmes as follows:

■ Specify problems where there are gaps in a client's behavioural repertoire and ways in which new behaviours would help to fill the gaps

■ Divide the problems into small components or stages

- Help clients to identify mistaken thinking (cognitions) that may hinder them
- Demonstrate the desired behaviour, then get the client to rehearse it
- Connect chains of small behaviours together to make more complex behaviours
- Help the client to understand how to discriminate between situations where it is useful and not useful to use the behaviour
- Introduce real-life difficulties
- Set real-life practical assignments and get clients to report back.

Scott and Dryden (1996) classify *cognitive-behaviour therapies* into four categories:

- *Coping skills* contain two elements, a 'self-verbalisation', that is, an instruction to ourselves, and the behaviour that results. Difficulty in coping with situations may come from an inability either to work out what to do to self-verbalise or to act on our instructions. Meichenbaum's (1985) stress inoculation training (SIT) aims to reduce and prevent stress by teaching clients what to say or do in difficult situations. Ronen (1998) suggests that focusing on skills in self-control may be helpful in direct work with children. Also, we make changes to reduce stress in the client's environment.

- *Problem-solving* is different from Perlman's (1957a) psychodynamic social work theory (Chapter 4). That is concerned with seeing human life as a process of resolving life issues. Here problem-solving is more like task-centred work: clients are encouraged to 'lock on' to and define a problem, generate solutions to it, choose the best, plan ways of acting on it and review progress.

- *Cognitive restructuring* is perhaps the best-known form of cognitive therapy and includes Beck's cognitive therapy (CT) and Ellis's rational-emotive behaviour therapy (REBT, formerly RET). In CT, clients collect information about how they interpret situations, and the worker questions and tests out how these work. In REBT, irrational beliefs dominate clients' thinking which leads to 'awfulising', that is, seeing things as unreasonably negative; low frustration tolerance, that is, feeling that bearing uncomfortable situations is impossible; and 'damnation', that is, feeling that you are in essence bad because you have failed at something. Workers question and attack the irrational beliefs which underlie these reactions. Sheldon (1998, 2000) emphasises attending to disorders in perception and attribution. Perception affects how someone sees what has happened to them; attribution is the judgements they make about the meaning of experiences. Thus, a lorry driver who has been threatened with dismissal because he was seen driving unsafely may perceive this as unfair, which may be a misperception, or he may think that the manager is determined to dismiss him to save money, thus attributing explanations to behaviour that have not been stated and may even be unconsidered by the manager.

- *Structural cognitive therapy* is concerned with three 'structures' of belief in clients' minds: core beliefs are assumptions about ourselves; intermediate beliefs are explicit descriptions people make of the world; peripheral beliefs are plans of action and problem-solving strategies used daily. Workers focus on beliefs at the periphery which cause problems, but use the process of change to explore the origins of these beliefs in deeper ideas.

Connections

The main aims of behavioural social work are increasing desired behaviours and reducing undesired behaviours, so that people respond to social events appropriately. This increases their capacity for leading a full and happy life. Insight into people's problems often helps because it speeds learning, but there is no evidence that it is necessary or that it is enough to get people to change. Warm personal relationships between worker and client help in behavioural work as in other forms of social work. Behavioural social work can be used in many social work situations. Authors in Cigno and Bourn's (1998) edited collection describe direct work with children and child protection, people with severe learning disabilities, offenders, carers, addictions, mental health, and in residential and group care for elders.

Thyer and Hudson (1987: 1) usefully describe the relationship between general behavioural work and behavioural social work as follows:

> Behavioral social work is the informed use, by professional social workers, of interventive techniques based upon empirically-derived learning theories that include but are not limited to, operant conditioning, respondent conditioning, and observational learning. Behavioural social workers may or may not subscribe to the philosophy of behaviourism.

The implication of this view is that workers do not have to import the model whole into all their work. They may use aspects of the model where it is useful. However, this approach suggests that there is nothing of other aspects of social work contributing to the model as it is used in social work. It is, in this formulation, the use of borrowed techniques. This suggests that behavioural approaches may not serve well some wider social purposes and issues within social work. Thomas (1968, 1971) in the USA and Jehu (1967, 1972) in the UK were the first significant interpreters of the psychological literature within social work.

Cognitive theories established a position in social work theory during the 1980s primarily through the work of Goldstein (1981, 1984), who sought to incorporate more humanistic ideas in them. This possibility is suggested by the concern of basic behavioural ideas with the nature of the mind. Humanist ideas (Chapter 9) claim that perceptions and their processing legitimately vary and the only reality is what is perceived and understood. Allied to cognitive ideas, this allows an acceptance of the accuracy of the client's understanding of the world. There is, therefore, no need to see clients' perceptions as wrong and attack them. This element of acceptance renders cognitive and behaviourist therapies in ways which seem more natural to the conventions of social work. Including the humanistic element is, then, the crucial aspect of Goldstein's work and the later writings of Werner (1982, 1986).

Cognitive-behavioural theories are primarily a Western model of practice, since they emphasise psychological change of individuals, rather than broader social purposes that might be more relevant in developing countries, and use the Western model of scientific method, which is less influential in many Eastern countries. This group of theories is, for example, not covered in Kumar's (1995) Indian review of social work theories. An Eastern interest in evidence-based practice is claimed in Thyer and Kazi's (2004) edited text about evidence-based practice, which includes chapters from Hong Kong and South Africa. However, these chapters are primarily about evaluation of social projects and social development, rather than cognitive-behavioural practice.

The politics of cognitive-behavioural theory

Controversy surrounds cognitive and behavioural models of treatment, because they have been at the centre of the debate about evidence-based practice (Chapter 3). Behaviourists mounted a trenchant attack on psychodynamic models of social work. They criticise its ill-defined outcomes based on assumptions about psychological structures within the mind which we cannot examine empirically. The strong argument for behavioural and cognitive methods, which is pressed continually in writing about them, is their empirically tested success in attaining results. Accepting this argument requires acceptance of the scientific method and modernist ideas about knowledge and linear models of explanation. One advantage of doing so is the acceptability of scientifically proven methods when working with other professions, particularly medicine and psychology, whose knowledge base is scientific. In this way, behavioural and cognitive methods contribute to arguments for the professional standing of social work in comparison. Again, accepting this argument means accepting the assumption that this is a desirable attainment.

Cognitive-behavioural methods have attained a limited use in specialised settings with particular client groups. They are often used for school phobia, childhood problems and in psychiatric settings, particularly, in the case of cognitive methods, with mild anxiety and depression. One reason for this is that clinical psychologists, and to a lesser extent other medical and nursing staff in such settings, can offer supervision and provide a sympathetic environment and a patient-centred setting for therapeutic methods. Such advantages are rarely available in conventional social work agencies.

Incorporating cognitive methods is disputed. Some writers (such as Sheldon, 1995) treat these as a development in basic behavioural methods, much as social learning theory has been. Others, such as Scott (1989), have more directly incorporated the ideas of cognitive theorists in social work formulations. Hudson and MacDonald (1986) were dubious about the incorporation of cognitive approaches into behavioural models of therapy. Most contemporary writers consider them a major new and different set of techniques, which have to some extent developed independently. Because they introduce a concern for internal mental processes, some think they damage the scientific credibility of behavioural methods, although in practical terms they have achieved their own research validation (Scott and Dryden, 1996). The focus on thinking and perception also connects to a range of other social work theories, which have had an impact because much social work practice deals in people's perceptions and reactions to social experiences. A strict focus on behaviour chimes less well with the social demands made on social work.

A major difficulty with cognitive-behavioural methods is their technical character, with many jargon terms and formal procedures, apparently worked out in set systems. To some workers this seems non-human. However, such an approach may suit some clients or workers who like to see an ordered, explicit approach to problems which can be clearly explained and justified.

There are also objections on ethical grounds, since the worker manipulates behaviour rather than it being under the control of the client. This could lead to behaviourist techniques imposing workers' wishes on unwilling clients, in pursuit of social or political policies which could, at the extreme, be used for authoritarian political control. Behaviourists argue that people's consent is ethically required and practically necessary to success. Also, the most ethical treatment is one that works best, and behaviourist approaches are well validated as effective. All techniques can be abused in the wrong hands. Many other techniques are manipulative in a way that is hidden from the people involved. An example might be the use of paradox, where a couple having many arguments might be encouraged to argue for an hour a night, thus learning to find other ways of behaving at other times and becoming aware of the social factors that stimulate their arguments. Watson (1980: 105–15) argues that this is not a sufficient answer to the ethical problem. Behaviourism inherently assumes that all behaviour is caused. If people decide that they want changes which might be achieved by behavioural methods, then they are acting using their own reasoning freely, in the sense of deciding without constraint on their decisions. However, what happens if behaviour is considered socially undesirable, by a court or people able to put social or other pressures on a client? They might be persuaded that their behaviour is right, good or adaptive to social conditions. In such cases, we are moving from unconstrained reasoning to decisions being made in pursuit of social goals. The only ethical position, which maintains clients' rights to self-determination, is to use the technique only where the client's own purpose is to free themselves from behaviour, for example where it is compulsive, and clients wish to but cannot control themselves.

Sheldon (1995: 232–4) argues that no social work methods, including behavioural methods, are so powerful that they can overcome resistance, and other kinds of work also involve control and limitation of freedom. However, this seems a weak protestation when behavioural methods particularly claim that they are successful beyond other social work or therapeutic techniques. Moreover, we should not put people in the position of having to resist, but should protect them from this. Sheldon further argues that we should measure any disadvantages alongside the model's advantages, and this would apply to the weaknesses of other theories: the evidence for effectiveness of cognitive-behaviour methods is not found in other theoretical models.

Behavioural models have sometimes been misused. Residential care homes, for example, have used the reward and punishment aspect of behavioural methods in oppressive or abusive ways. One instance is the 'pin-down' scandal in residential homes for children in Britain (Levy and Kahan, 1991). Here, certain behavioural ideas justified locking children up for long periods without day clothes. Sheldon (1995: 237–41) argues that in this sort of situation, some methods are used where the people concerned are already motivated to oppress clients. Any method could be misused to do so.

Behavioural social work has had considerable influence, particularly in the USA, but it has not succeeded in gaining widespread usage, except in specialist settings or for particularly relevant problems.

Major statements

Most behavioural writers cover similar ground. Sheldon's (1995) *Cognitive-behavioural Therapy* is used here as an example text to show how cognitive-behavioural ideas are implemented in social work because it offers a full account of behavioural practice but also takes some account of cognitive contributions, advancing from his previous edition. Additional material is included here from Scott (1989) and other writers. Other significant recent writers are Cigno (2002) and Cigno and Bourn (1998) in the UK and Gambrill (1977, 1995) and Thyer (1987, 1989) in the USA. Many accounts of empirical or effective practice are informed by cognitive-behavioural theories.

Sheldon: cognitive-behavioural therapy

The basic principles and methods of behavioural work were described above. These are applied in the therapeutic situation. Large changes of behaviour should be divided into small steps. A schedule of reinforcement should be worked out, as follows:

- *Continuous reinforcement* of every instance of the desired behaviour will work quickly.
- *Shaping* means reinforcing small steps towards the desired behaviour. For example, Joe is a mentally ill man who often speaks loudly and threateningly to people in his household. We start by reinforcing slightly less loud behaviour. When this is more commonplace, we only reinforce much less loud behaviour, then keeping quiet for longer periods, then being less threatening, then being more friendly and so on. Eventually, we can achieve quite complex changes of behaviour.
- *Fading* means steadily reducing the amount or type of reinforcement once the desired behaviour is achieved, so that behaviour can be transferred to a new setting. For example, Joe might be reinforced at first by a cigarette, then by verbal encouragement. Eventually, we want him to respond just to people showing how uncomfortable they are by a piece of his behaviour. Unless we do this, we are 'training and hoping' and we are likely to get a shift back into past behaviour patterns when we stop reinforcing. This is why people in residential care often seem to do well, but fail when discharged.

- *Intermittent reinforcement* is used when a behaviour is not always reinforced.
- *Ratio schedules* of intermittent reinforcement reinforce after a set number of occurrences of the desired behaviour.
- *Interval schedules* reinforce after a set period of desired behaviour.

Ratio or interval schedules may be fixed (completely regular) or may vary around a typical period or number of behaviours. Variable schedules are most resistant to extinction (particularly variable interval schedules) and more practical, since very consistent reinforcement may not be possible.

Modelling or vicarious learning (described above) both reinforces existing responses and creates the possibility of using new or unused responses by observing how others behave and how successful or otherwise the behaviour is. We do this generally, and at certain stages of our lives, for example in teenage years or when there are many changes, we pick particular people as models. We then combine and edit observations from different sources to create our own identity. Workers can have an input at each stage of modelling (see above). Bandura (1977) emphasises the importance of *perceived self-efficacy*, that is, our own view of how good we are at things like this. These are made up of two aspects: the outcomes we expect from certain sorts of behaviour, and the efficacy that we think we have in doing tasks like that. For example, someone who abuses drugs and is part of a subculture of people who share the habit may not see many beneficial outcomes from giving up (outcome expectations). However, even if they would like to be back in the 'straight' world, they may feel that they do not have enough strength of purpose to give up (efficacy expectations). There are criticisms of Bandura's theories. They are less parsimonious than operant and respondent theories, which explain all these things much more simply. However, they do offer a way of understanding more complex aspects of behaviour that social workers are likely to be dealing with.

Sheldon (1995) moves on to point out that much learning through modelling is cognitive, that is, we think ourselves into the situation we are observing, work out how we would act and so on. In practice, stimulating such thinking in people is useful. Feeling what it would be like to act as the model does through *empathetic learning* can be an important part of this. *Cognitive-mediational theories* concern how the performances we observe are coded into a series of images and words and then retrieved. This works better if people 'speak-along' with what they are doing as they reproduce the performance.

Assessment is a crucial aspect of cognitive-behavioural work, because it depends on detailed understanding of sequences of behaviour. Also, different reinforcers will affect different people, so each case must be carefully individualised. Therefore, assessment and definition of the antecedent events, the specific behaviours and detailed consequences are all important.

Sheldon's analysis of the distinguishing features of cognitive-behavioural assessment is set out in Table 6.1. Cognitive interviews use techniques based on the psychology of memory to help to stimulate accurate recall in situations where evidence of child abuse or similar traumatic circumstances is required (Westcott, 1992).

Table 6.1 Sheldon's distinguishing features of cognitive-behavioural assessment

Focus	What to assess
Emphasis on visible behaviour causing problems, or the absence of expected or adaptive behaviour	Who, what, when, how, how often, with whom. What is done, what is not done, what is done too much, what too little, what is at the wrong place or the wrong time.
Attributions by people of meaning to stimuli	Doubts, worries, fears, frustrations, depressions explained by people involved and revealed by behaviour or absence of expected behaviour.
Present behaviour and thoughts and feelings that go with it	Looking for past causes distracts work: try to control the size of the problem to limit action. Explore what maintains the behaviour in present repertoire. Learning history (for example inappropriate responses, inability to learn, inability to discriminate between crucial aspects of situations) may be explored.
Target sequences of behaviour	What behaviour needs to be increased or decreased? What new skills or reduction in emotions are needed to perform alternative behaviours?
Identify controlling conditions	Where do the problems occur? What are the antecedents? What happens during the sequences? What happens afterwards?
Identify people's labels, but avoid prejudiced attributions	How do the people involved describe or explain the problem? How far is it prejudiced or name-calling, rather than explanatory?
Flexibility in listening leading to a clear hypothesis about behaviour.	Do not be so task- or behaviour-centred as to squeeze out the complexities of the people's stories. Explore things that they might not see as relevant or have excluded. Come to a clear statement about a piece of behaviour that can be changed, and how it will be changed.

Source: Sheldon (1995: 111–18).

A suitable *assessment* sequence is as follows:

- Gain descriptions of the problems from different viewpoints.
- Get examples of who is affected and how.
- Trace beginnings of problems, how they changed and what affected them.
- Identify different parts of problems and how they fit together.
- Assess motivation for change.
- Identify thought patterns and feelings which come before, during and after incidents of the problem behaviour.
- Identify strengths in and around the client.

Throughout any work, it is important to continue monitoring what is happening. This is particularly so where there may be damage to clients or others. Workers constantly need to examine factors that may have changed the levels of risk. Being involved in a complex sequence of changing behaviours can blind us to changes in social factors that create risk.

Problems must then be reduced to their component parts. A chart covering antecedents, behaviour and consequences for specific events can be useful in doing this. Workers should focus on precise descriptions of behaviour, rather than judgements about it. For example, 'he banged his fist on the table' is a better description of behaviour than 'he became frustrated', because it is precise, observable, changeable and not arguable (he might have been angry, not frustrated).

Problems then need to be put in hierarchies. In doing so, we need to consider agency priorities, clients' views, their capacity and motivation to make one change rather than another, the availability of mediators (people in the environment who can record behaviour and administer reinforcement) and whether goals are fair, feasible and non-discriminatory.

The next stage is to find a basis for evaluating change. This is often based on 'single-case' experimental designs (Gingerich, 1990; Nelsen, 1990; Kazi, 1998). Careful definition of target behaviours is followed by measuring in a planned way how often it occurs in a 'baseline' period. The intervention follows. Occurrences of the behaviour during and after intervention are also measured. Sometimes after one period of intervention, there is a 'reversal period' in which the worker returns to their own baseline behaviour and the target behaviour is again measured. Intervention then starts again. In this way, we can test whether the intervention is indeed affecting the behaviour. Follow-up visits are also important, to check that changes are maintained and provide a motivation for maintenance. If the worker has limited aggressive behaviour through behavioural work in a day centre, and discovered that this is also maintained at home, a visit every month and then every two months for a while to check up may be an important motivational factor.

Following this, workers use various techniques for working behaviourally. These fall into two groups, response control and contingency management. *Response control* techniques involve activities such as modelling, social skills training, assertiveness training, various cognitive approaches discussed above and techniques such as systematic desensitisation. These have already been discussed as examples explaining the wider theoretical perspective of behavioural therapy.

In *contingency management* the following possibilities might be achieved:

- Identify and reinforce to amplify the frequency or force with which a client uses an existing piece of behaviour.
- Shape existing behaviour towards desired ends.
- Where there is an excess of unwanted behaviour, use one of the following techniques:
  - reinforce incompatible preferred behaviour
  - negatively reinforce the unwanted behaviour (as by withdrawing an aversive stimulus when the client does something preferred)
  - reduce the frequency by extinction (that is, withdraw reinforcement of the unwanted behaviour)
  - punish unwanted behaviour
- Change the stimuli that elicit the behaviour.

Choosing *reinforcers* is a crucial part of deciding what to do. Ideally, reinforcers should arise naturally from the situation, help clients understand the reasoning behind reinforcers, especially if they are a bit artificial, and focus on non-material generalised reinforcers such as praise, affection and attention. Reinforcers must be seen to work. We can find them by seeing clients in their day-to-day life and seeing what reinforces them and asking them and people around them. Premack's principle means using behaviour that the client likes and carries out frequently as a reward for less common behaviour that we want to encourage. For example, if a youngster enjoys chatting with friends on the street corner and we want to encourage homework, we can make agreeing to going out conditional on doing an hour's homework first. Then the amount of homework can be increased and the amount of chatting allowed decreased. Sometimes we can consult a checklist of possible reinforcers. Reinforcers have to be strong enough to compete with the unwanted behaviour, they must be practical to present, using mediators – that is, the therapist's agent in the everyday situation.

Scott's (1989; see also Scott and Dryden, 1996) account of cognitive-behavioural work contrasts with Sheldon's by focusing on cognitive interventions. His argument for using cognitive therapies is that they are brief, widely applicable, highly structured, easily learned and effective. This makes them understandable to client and worker and usable in a hard-pressed agency. He examines four areas. These are child behaviour problems, emotional disorders, such as anxiety and depression where cognitive therapy has had most influence (Scott and Stradling, 1991), interpersonal problems, such as marital problems or lack of social skills, and self-regulation disorders, such as controlling drug abuse.

In child behaviour problems, Scott describes groups for working with parents. These focused first on consistency and used a social skills approach to building up parents' capacity to deal with their children. Parents role-played dealing with difficulties, so that both parents in a household learned the same approach. This was then practised at home. Praise (reinforcement) was given for success. Parents then learned about time out, fines and penalties when dealing with their children. Again, there was practice and homework. Later sessions reviewed these experiences, then rehearsed parents in thinking through future problems. Although the focus here is on helping parents think out their problems, we can see many aspects of Sheldon's accounts of behavioural work used in these sessions to reinforce parents' successful behaviour and avoid unsuccessful behaviour. Work on anger control is also described. Ronen (1994) argues that cognitive-behavioural work can be effective in direct work with children in enabling them to exert stronger self-control over behaviour.

With emotional disorders, Scott expounds the practicalities of using Beck's (1989) cognitive therapy for dealing with depression. The precise aspects and degree of depression experienced by clients are carefully assessed, and there is a well-tested instrument for doing so. Early work with clients is behavioural, trying to develop and shape more appropriate behaviour. This gives immediate progress. Later sessions focus on cognitive therapy. Clients keep a record of 'automatic' thoughts in particular situations which lead to depression. These are thoughts which come into their head as they experience emotions. Each of these is 'tested in a laboratory' of questions. These are: 'How realistic is it?', 'Who gives the authority to hold that view?' and 'Does the assumption help achieve a goal?' Workers and clients together look for self-defeating thought patterns. With anxiety, clients may be demoralised; overvigilant to see problems and failures; avoid situations where they are anxious, which obstructs normal living; and have physical consequences, such as muscle tension, or emotional problems such as procrastination, so that they can never make a decision.

In marital therapy, Scott proposes a programme with three elements: behavioural exchange; cognitive restructuring; and communication and problem-solving training. Assessment is by interview, exploring the problem behaviours, much as Sheldon (1995) proposes – see above. Also, a variety of scales and questionnaires is used. These structured forms of assessment are much more common in cognitive-behavioural work than in other forms of social work. Early parts of the programme are designed to change specific, clearly defined behaviours which are easily changed. This helps couples to realise that it is possible to derive satisfactions from their partner. Each partner makes a behaviour exchange. Each gets something they want, and is helped by the other to achieve it. There is a written contract, with a penalty if it is not achieved and a reward if it is. The rewards are not at first made contingent on one another, because if one fails, the whole contract collapses. Eventually, the behaviours can be made to connect. For example, Sally and Peter disagree, among many other things, about his spending all his time in the garden and her spending too much money buying clothes. His redundancy has caused him to spend more time in the garden. However, because they rely on her part-time wage, they have less to spend, but she resents this because it means she cannot spend so much on her clothes. The contract is that she will help for an afternoon in the garden to plant vegetables to aid the household finances and he will come with her to buy something cheap but nice: a silk scarf. Both agree to limit their complaints about the other around these activities. The rewards are the tasks themselves. The penalties, if they fail to control their behaviours, are his doing all the housework alone for a week, or her spending all her non-work time at home for a week. A regular review and exploration of difficulties can lead to a better understanding of what each wants from the other and how to communicate effectively.

Cognitive restructuring can take place around troubleshooting when behaviour exchanges go wrong or other relationship difficulties arise. This involves the worker pointing up and debating issues, using the 'laboratory' questions discussed above. Communication training involves a sequence of treatment in which first the worker provides feedback, using specific examples, of communication patterns which do not work. Then, the worker offers alternative communication patterns. Finally, the couple rehearse the different communication patterns before trying them out as homework.

Cognitive-behavioural approaches are burgeoning and being imported into social work. Guided self-change (Tubman et al., 2002) is a typical example of the use of cognitive-behavioural elements. It includes elements of motivational work, which has been used and demonstrated to be effective for drug users and alcoholics where engagement in and motivation for change are sometimes difficult. There is a 'decision to change checklist', in which clients explore 'good' and 'less good' aspects of their present situation and the changed situation they hope to achieve. A 'goals for change questionnaire' is also used. Progress is checked every time the client comes to a session. Clients are also asked to identify triggers for problematic behaviour and situations in which they are at risk.

An influential application of cognitive therapy is the 'reasoning and rehabilitation' programme used in the probation service and other criminal justice settings. Devised by Ross and colleagues (Ross and Fabiano, 1985; Ross et al., 1988, 1989) in Canada, it has been applied in the Welsh STOP programme (Straight Thinking on Probation) (Raynor and Vanstone, 1994, 1998; Raynor et al., 1994) and elsewhere in the UK. It is prescriptive, following a detailed manual of action, using an explicit teaching programme. This covers self-control techniques, thinking skills, social skills, teaching about thinking of others, victim awareness, creative thinking, critical reasoning, thinking about others' perspectives, offenders' effects on others, emotional management and giving offenders experience of being a helper of others themselves. This gets offenders out of stereotyped thinking about their own needs and position, and allows them to see situations more broadly and from different perspectives. They are also able to think out their problems more rationally and find alternative ways to deal with them. Although successful, the approach has been criticised for its racism and lack of flexibility, since it forces workers to comply with strict procedures, treats people as machines and does not respond to the real causes of much offending which lies in poverty and the deficiencies of capitalism (Neary, 1992; Pitts, 1992). The way the programme gives priority to managing its general objectives, rather than individuals' needs and wishes, has also been criticised (Oldfield, 2002; Raynor, 2003). This approach fits well with an increasing emphasis on 'offence-focused' work with offenders. Such work concentrates on offenders reviewing their offences and patterns of behaviour which lead to them. Another example is Fishbein and Adzen's (1975) theory of reasoned action.

Group and community behavioural techniques

While Sheldon's account is almost entirely about individual work, both Fischer and Gochros (1975: 115–19) and Hudson and MacDonald (1986: 165–6) quote a variety of studies to show that behavioural approaches can be effectively used in groupwork. This may be by using a conventional group as a supporter and reinforcer to individuals undertaking behavioural programmes or by undertaking interventions with several people at once in the group. Such arrangements may help people with similar problems, for example alcoholics, or those who come from the same background, such as a local group of teenagers with offending problems, or people who are within the same family or social group. Typically, according to Hudson and MacDonald, the group works together on problem assessment, goal-setting, discussing and deciding on strategies and modelling and rehearsal. Social skills training is particularly useful. Rose (1991) discusses behavioural groupwork with a cognitive approach using social learning about 'self-defeating' and coping cognitions. However, Hollin (1990), discussing work with offenders, points out that social skills may only be one reason for clients' problems, so effective training should be part of multiple approaches to clients' problems. Wright (1995), discussing residential work with young boys with behaviour problems, showed consistent improvements with a cognitive-behavioural skills training programme. However, she emphasises the importance of recognising and dealing with other problems and developing a clear shared treatment philosophy involving a range of staff.

Burgess et al. (1980) describe the use of social skills training with a group of sex offenders in prison, which gives a good example of the range of techniques that may be applied. Three techniques were used in varying combinations:

- Micro-teaching of small elements of skills in interactions with others, such as use of voice, eye contact, posture.
- Assertiveness training to help prisoners express their opinions and seek their interests without interfering with others.
- Role-playing of increasingly complex events which might occur in the prison.

It then moved on to situations which might arise outside the prison. Workers' modelling of skills was important, and prisoners were given homework to practise with. At the end of each group meeting, a winding-down session of social conversation was arranged. A similar group for adult psychiatric patients is described by McAuley et al. (1988). Here, quite damaged clients learned to understand their own behaviour through explicit interventions in time-limited groups.

Although most community work is not oriented towards individuals, Mattaini (1993) shows behavioural analysis used to support community work practice. He proposes techniques for changing antecedents of behaviour in community settings, changing consequences and reducing behaviours which do not help the community achieve desired objectives.

Residential work

Behavioural approaches have been an important grouping of theories of residential work (Ryan, 1979; Hudson, 1982), although they have been used in very few social care settings. Few contemporary residential care homes use full-scale cognitive-behavioural regimes, but an increasing number use cognitive-behavioural techniques with individual residents.

The most common full-scale approach is the use of *token economies*. These are systems for managing the total programme of a residential establishment, in the same way that therapeutic environments, discussed in Chapter 4, manage the total experience of residence. Thus, they are not treatment programmes for individuals that happen to be carried out in residence, but represent an approach to residential work in the round. Token economies have been used in schools and residential homes for adolescents with behaviour problems and for offenders. They have also been used with people with mental illness and learning disabilities (Birchwood et al., 1988).

Token economies are an operant conditioning system using interval (or sometimes intermittent ratio) reinforcement. Staff in the establishment agree (according to Sheldon, 1995) a list of behaviours to be strengthened. Tokens are given for continuing these behaviours for a certain period or for performing behaviours a set number of times. Clients collect the tokens and exchange them for desired goods and privileges. There is, in effect, a price list of rewards, each reward requiring a specified number of tokens. Unskilled staff can be used to maintain the system (Fischer and Gochros, 1975: 288–9).

Token economies are also useful for *discrimination training* (Fischer and Gochros, 1975: 287; Sheldon, 1995). This helps people to learn what sorts of behaviour are appropriate to particular social circumstances.

Pizzat (1973) gives an extended account of a residential programme using a variety of reinforcers. He shows that in the early stages, or when residents are first admitted with extreme behaviour difficulties, they need a phase of immediate reinforcement to gain quick improvement. This can then be backed up by a system giving tokens at specified times of day. Later still, the establishment offered a weekly allowance unconnected with specific behaviours for good conduct. Otherwise, social and self-reinforcement were adequate at this stage. This is a helpful account of a range of behavioural techniques used in a residential setting, and shows the importance of developing the various forms of reinforcement carefully.

Sheldon (1995) notes that, although token economies are successful in changing behaviour, there are problems in maintaining them over a period. In most residential establishments, residents are not carefully selected, and most are not large enough to offer several separate stages, as Pizzat's was. As a result, staff have too wide a range of problems to deal with. It may also be hard to ensure that staff and others impose the system uniformly, and not all may believe in it sufficiently. Supporting staff adequately is important. Outside pressures such as courts, health or local authorities may limit the degree of control necessary to impose a consistent system. Birchwood et al. (1988), in a review of the research, support these comments and claim that social modelling may be an equally effective form of treatment.

The sum of these difficulties may lead to excessive rigidity or rewarding residents for acquiescence rather than progress in appropriate behaviour. Behaviourial systems can be used for part of an establishment or during a phase of particular difficulty, to gain quick results. Goldapple and Montgomery (1993) describe a programme which used cognitive and behavioural methods with serious drug abusers in residential care. This improved the drop-out rate, so that no residents left, although long-term treatment goals were not always achieved. Possibly this is because residents were rewarded by the practical attention to everyday activity, while longer term work was needed for substantial improvement in behaviour.

The alternative approach to cognitive-behavioural interventions in residential care is to use the range of therapies with individuals. Kazi and Mir (1998) describe social learning approaches in residential care with young people and single-case designs to evaluate interventions. Cigno (1998) describes using operant conditioning and social learning with elders in residential care. Davis and Broster (1993) describe successful cognitive-behavioural-expressive interventions in residential care with aggressive young people. These used a logbook of perceptions in individual sessions, stress management techniques and behavioural learning of coping skills. They warn that workers should avoid allowing expression of violent ideas, if this seems to lead to strengthening them, and that workers and regimes may stimulate violence through their actions. De Lange et al. (1981) describe a group in a residential care setting for young offenders using cognitive-behavioural methods through role-playing solutions to common problems on video.

The Goldman family

Mr Goldman works at a local factory that is at risk of being closed and the work transferred to an Eastern European country, while Mrs Goldman works part time in a local supermarket, for low wages, and is receiving medication for depression from the family doctor. Gary, their 19-year-old son, has been diagnosed as suffering from schizophrenia and of the two younger children, Kayleigh (12) has started missing school and Donovan (8) has mild learning disabilities; he is under consideration for moving from a special class in the local school to a specialised school. A social worker from the community mental health team is involved with Gary, trying to establish a new pattern of life after discharge from his first period in a psychiatric hospital. An education social worker is to be involved to resolve Kayleigh's behaviour. The family doctor employs a part-time counsellor and the education department of the local council has allocated a psychologist to consider Donovan's case.

This complicated situation, with many different problems and involvement from different professionals, presents a common problem for social workers – their agency gives them a particular role but the issues that the family face interweave and require more complex actions to intervene. Various cognitive-behavioural interventions might be possible, but might also be balanced against long-term intervention from a psychodynamic or brief intervention approach such as task-centred or crisis intervention work. One of the issues for workers is to decide a focus or focuses of intervention, and an appropriate combination of roles and theories to apply. What are the possibilities for cognitive-behavioural intervention, with whom? How would you balance these against the possibilities offered by other styles of intervention?

Commentary

Both behavioural and cognitive approaches are clearly valid and widely applicable forms of treatment, whose effectiveness is supported by research (Scott et al., 1989; Stern and Drummond, 1991; Sheldon, 1995), but whether good outcomes are maintained over time is more uncertain. Typical of the evidence is Malkinson's (2001) review of the literature on a range of bereavement therapies. Cognitive therapies have been found to be effective particularly with complicated grief, where people have an irrational prolonged preoccupation with a dead person. Cognitive techniques help them to reconstruct their thinking so that the loss is woven into normal living. However, careful work is needed to connect the work with clients' broader social aims.

In general, the effectiveness of cognitive-behavioural treatments depends on how careful workers are helping clients to generalise behavioural and cognitive learning to ordinary social situations. Much practice and research into it is by psychologists and the social work contribution to the general literature is marginal even in the USA. It is questionable whether the almost wholly individualistic therapy presented by some writers, such as Sheldon (1995), easily transfers to general social work settings, although it clearly could do so. One difficulty is that it requires skill and experience to construct behavioural programmes, and this requires supervision by someone already expert in the procedures. Where there is no existing group of practitioners, this is difficult to provide. Thus, behavioural work is used in pockets, and particularly in clinical settings where psychologists and other professional groups with training in the techniques are available for training and support. See Wong et al. (1987) for a discussion of this point in relation to chronic psychiatric patients in hospital.

Among the advantages of cognitive work is the explicit, structured guidance on practice which is offered and the assessment instruments often employed. This gives stronger guidance to workers lacking in confidence in trying a new technique. On the other hand, it may become constricting and limiting to flexible responses by workers to clients' problems where there are broader issues. One advantage is that looking at particular behaviours means that we do not label the whole person as abnormal, as psychodynamic theory might do. Different behaviours may be adaptive in different environments and cultures. So, behaviour which is appropriate to and comes from different genders and ethnic cultures is not assumed to need changing in learning theory. In psychodynamic theory, behaviours are considered acceptable according to that theory's ideas of the origins of that behaviour, so behaviour which does not fit in with the dominant culture but might be acceptable in a minority ethnic culture or an oppressed gender comes to be disapproved of. While Fischer and Gochros (1975) note this point about learning theory, they do not note that the idea of adaptive behaviour might still require a minority or oppressed culture to align itself with the majority culture. There is still a risk that a therapy which seeks to change behaviour so that it adapts to an environment undervalues minority forms of behaviour and less dominant aspects of the culture.

Cognitive practice has developed strongly in the 1990s and 2000s, because of its effectiveness and clarity, and probably also because of its structured assessment and action sequences, which can help to engage clients, focus practice and command management and policy support. It has been particularly influential in mental health services and in settings that need to be concerned with clients' anxiety and depression, where its effectiveness is well validated. Psychological and counselling professions have embraced it strongly, and an understanding of it helps to integrate social workers in multiprofessional teams with psychological and psychotherapeutic roles. Cognitive methods also connect with psychodynamic ego psychology, since both are concerned with rational responses to the real world, and with constructive therapies that have a focus on the processing and interpretation of perceptions (Chapter 8).

Social learning methods, especially social skills training, are more widely used than conventional behavioural methods. The reasons for the lack of impact of these techniques are threefold. First, the explicit attack on the conventional psychodynamic form of social work and the alliance of behaviourists with the positivist critique of the effectiveness of social work seems to have led to a degree of defensiveness. Second, the specific techniques are distant from the standard non-directive approach of social workers, and have a mechanistic terminology and procedure which they may feel uncomfortable with. Third, there have been some ethical criticisms which, while not wholly valid, might have reinforced the reserve of social workers and the feeling that this is not in the style of social work. However, an alternative critique comes from a sociological perspective, systems perspectives, and it is to this that we devote the next chapter.

OVERVIEW

- Elements of cognitive-behavioural practice, particularly social learning theory, have had a wide influence in social work.

- Traditional behavioural practice has had limited usage, partly for practical reasons of the need to have specialised supervision and deal with clearly specified problems.

- The time-limited, focused and planned approach of cognitive-behavioural practice has been important.

- Many elements of the practice are empirically well validated.

- It has had most use in multiprofessional health care and mental health teams, where it is particularly valuable for work on depression, anxiety and other psychological reactions to social stresses.

- It continues to generate ethical and intuitive doubts because of its technical, rational approach to humanity.

FURTHER READING

Cigno, K. and Bourn, D. (eds) (1998) *Cognitive-behavioural Social Work in Practice*, (Aldershot: Ashgate).
Useful collection of theoretical and practice articles.

Sheldon, B. (1995) *Cognitive-Behavioural Therapy: Research, Practice and Philosophy* (London, Routledge).
Sundel, M. and Sundel, S. S. (2004) *Behavior Change in the Human Services: Behavioral and Cognitive Principles and Applications*, 5th edn (Thousand Oaks, CA: Sage).
Comprehensive British and American texts.

CHAPTER 7

Systems and Ecological Perspectives

What this chapter is about

Systems perspectives are important to social work because they emphasise its social focus, as opposed to counselling, psychotherapy or many caring professions, whose emphasis is on individual patients or clients. However, their approach to social issues is mainly one of working with individuals to fit in with the present social order, so that they are mainly individual-reformist. Social work's concern is with people's social connections and relationships, and social objectives such as social justice or social change as well as interpersonal work. Systems perspectives represent this view, seeing social work as concerned with evolving a more effective social order, rather than promoting radical social change. It also balances, in clinical and health care settings, the emphasis on 'the patient' or 'the client'. In such settings, social workers are often the members of the multiprofessional team most concerned with better functioning of families and communities as a whole. However, Anderson et al. (1999) emphasise that systems theory integrates the atomistic-holistic continuum. That is, it requires us to think about the social and personal elements in any social situations as well as, and at the same time as, seeing how those elements interact with each other to integrate into a whole.

MAIN POINTS

- ➤ Systems theory focuses on individuals as part of and incorporating other systems, and so it integrates social with psychological elements of practice.

- ➤ Systems interact with each other in complex ways, Exploring these helps to understand how individuals interact with other people in families and communities and in wider social environments.

- ➤ Systems ideas have been particularly important in work with families.

- ➤ Systems theories had a strong impact in social work during the 1970s, responding to a movement for the integration of different practices and the creation of larger social agencies, but, except in the USA, its influence has waned as trends towards specialisation and protective administrative responsibilities of states made it less relevant to practice.

> ➤ In the USA, ecological systems theory became a predominant practice model, through its incorporation of elements of traditional psychodynamic practice, which permitted the continued integration of social work professional practices.

> ➤ Ecological 'life' and ecosystems perspectives seek to incorporate social elements alongside practice aimed at psychological problems and use concepts such as adaptation drawn from ecological ideas.

> ➤ European eco-critical theories criticise the failure of American ecological systems theories to incorporate the growing ecological critique of unsustainable Western civilisations. Sustainable social development is also relevant to practice in developing countries.

> ➤ Systems theories are criticised for assuming that everything fits into a social order, a fundamental social structure that establishes accepted relationships between people, groups and organisations in society.

> ➤ Developing support through and by social networks is an important outgrowth of systems ideas.

PRACTICE ISSUES AND CONCEPTS

> ➤ *Systems* focus on connections between and resources of families and groups and their effective functioning, rather than, as with health work or counselling, seeing the family as helping or hindering the function of improving the health or well-being of the individual patient.

> ➤ *Life stressors* apply energy in the form of stresses to a system; this may be a person or more commonly a family or community.

> ➤ Fit or *adaptation* between individuals and their social environments.

> ➤ Working to initiate, maintain and improve social *networks* and mutual support.

Wider theoretical perspectives

Overview

Systems ideas in social work originated in general systems theory developed in the 1940s and 50s in management and psychology, and were comprehensively formulated by von Bertalanffy (1971). This biological theory sees all organisms as systems, composed of subsystems, and in turn part of super-systems. Thus, a human being is part of a society and is made up of, for example, circulation systems and cells, which are in turn made up of atoms which are made up of smaller particles. The theory is applied to social systems, such as groups, families and societies, as well as biological systems. Hanson (1995) argues that the value of systems theory is that it deals with 'wholes' rather than with parts of human or social behaviour as other theories do.

Mancoske (1981) shows that important origins of systems theory in sociology lie in the social Darwinism of Herbert Spencer. Siporin (1980) argues that the social survey research of the late nineteenth century in England (for example the work of Booth and Rowntree), information theory and the ecological school of the Chicago sociologists in the 1930s were also antecedents.

Systems ideas and their applications

Concepts about the *structure* of systems are as follows:

- Systems are entities with *boundaries* within which physical and mental energy are exchanged internally more than they are across the boundary.
- *Closed systems* have no interchange across the boundary, as in a closed vacuum flask.
- *Open systems* occur where energy crosses the boundary which is permeable, like a teabag in a cup of hot water which lets water in and tea out but keeps the tea leaves inside.

Concepts on *processing* in systems, the way systems work and how we may change them (Greif and Lynch, 1983) are as follows:

- *Input* – Energy being fed into the system across the boundary.
- *Throughput* – How the energy is used within the system.
- *Output* – Effects on the environment of energy passed out through the boundary of a system.
- *Feedback loops* – Information and energy passed to the system caused by its outputs affecting the environment which tell it the results of its output.
- *Entropy* – Systems use their own energy to keep going, which means that unless they receive inputs from outside the boundary, they run down and die.

A simple example of these processes is if you tell me something (input into my system). This affects how I behave (throughput in my system), my behaviour changes (output) and you observe this change. So you receive feedback that I have heard and understood what you said (a feedback loop).

The state of a system is defined by five characteristics:

- Its *steady state*, how it maintains itself by receiving input and using it. This idea suggests that systems, such as human beings or social groups, can incorporate change without changing their fundamental identity.
- Its *homeostasis* or *equilibrium*. This is the ability to maintain our fundamental nature, even though input changes us. So, I may eat cabbage, but I do not become cabbage-like. I remain me, while the cabbage is digested and gives me energy and nourishment. Part of it becomes output, through heat, activity and defecation.

- *Differentiation*, the idea that systems grow more complex, with more different kinds of components over time.
- *Non-summativity*, the idea that the whole is more than the sum of its parts.
- *Reciprocity*, the idea that if one part of a system changes, that change interacts with all the other parts. They therefore also change.

As a result of reciprocity, systems exhibit both *equifinality* (reaching the same result in several different ways) and *multifinality* (similar circumstances can lead to different results) because the parts of the system interact in different ways. These ideas help to understand the complexity of human relationships and why outcomes of similar actions vary. Social systems may possess *synergy*, which means that they can create their own energy to maintain themselves. So, human beings interacting in a marriage or in a group often stimulate each other to maintain or strengthen relationships, which builds up bonds within the group and makes it stronger. This is an example of non-summativity, because these bonds could not be achieved without the interaction within the system. Without creating synergy, the group or marriage would have to be fed by outside energy or entropy would occur. Thus, synergy negates entropy, and is sometimes called *negentropy*.

Pincus and Minahan (1973) identify three kinds of helping system:

- *informal or natural systems* (such as family, friends, the postman, fellow workers)
- *formal systems* (like community groups, trade unions)
- *societal systems* (for example hospitals, schools).

Their analysis of the systems that workers use as part of their practice has been influential (see Table 7.1)

Evans and Kearney (1996) outline seven key principles of a systems approach to practice. Their analysis usefully shows how systems ideas can inform social work practice in a variety of settings. Their approach emphasises looking within

Table 7.1 Pincus and Minahan's basic social work systems

System	Description	Further information
Change agent system	Social workers and the organisations that they work in	
Client system	People, groups, families, communities who seek help and engage in working with the change agent system	*Actual* clients have agreed to receive help and have engaged themselves; *potential* clients are those whom the worker is trying to engage (for example people on probation or being investigated for child abuse)
Target system	People whom the change agent system is trying to change to achieve its aims	Client and target systems may or may not be the same
Action system	People with whom the change agent system works to achieve its aims	Client, target and action systems may or may not be the same

Source: Pincus and Minahan (1973).

the social networks and systems for possible targets for action, for power relationships and involving each in a social work process.

In their view, systems ideas can help to maintain *consistency* in practice; this is the reason why many people find it helpful in integrating ideas from different sources in practice. Systems theory suggests that you should start from the context in which you are operating, its opportunities and constraints, the aim of being involved, your powers and responsibilities and likely or intended effects or outcomes. For example, if you become involved with a family because of concerns about neglect of their children, you have a different set of aims and responsibilities compared with the referral of the same family for help with family relationships. However, the work you need to do may be similar in both cases. You need to recognise how pressures on the family create different aspects of their problem and respond to both the protection and relationship concerns.

Recognising the importance of *context* in defining what we are doing extends from the importance of consistency. Context defines what your aims and responses should be. For example, a disabled person in specialist housing might receive mainly practical services, but in doing so the worker identifies family relationship problems that might affect the stability of the situation in which those services are being provided. Again, the situation in which the client lives determines that a full service requires a response to both issues.

Adopting a *positive* approach again partly emerges from the importance of consistency and context. Workers may feel that it is hard to make progress with a mentally ill man in a secure unit for serious offences. However, activities such as improvements in education, relationships with others and renewing connections with estranged families may all make a significant difference to the client's life experience in care, even if it does not lead eventually to discharge.

Identifying *patterns* of behaviour helps to see positive possibilities, where behaviour in one social system has created learning for use in another. It also helps to identify where changes are needed. For example, a person having relationship difficulties with neighbours may reveal similar patterns of behaviour in a day care setting, or in a social setting, which may help the worker to identify where work on relationship or behaviour problems might be targeted.

Systems theory emphasises *process*, that is, how relationships and interactions occur, as well as content and outcomes. The worker may be able to identify positive skills and relationships in one part of someone's life that can be transferred to other situations where there are difficulties. It may also be helpful to identify how systems are interacting together to create problems in an unexpected area of life. For example, poor relationships within a family may reduce the influence of the family in helping a child to overcome difficulties at school.

Working with others is an important bonus of systems theory. It emphasises how working indirectly with other agencies or with families and networks permit influence on clients.

Joint working is also a product of systems thinking; the worker is seen as interacting with networks associated with clients and with colleagues and agencies.

Atherton (1989), applying systems theory to residential care, focuses on its concern with how people relate to one another within social situations, rather than as individuals. Because, in residential care, people are part of a group of staff and residents and all have contacts with an outside world as well as interrelationships within the residential unit, it is difficult to deal with the complex understanding needed to work effectively in this setting. The systems idea of *boundary* helps to limit the complexity to particular issues or relationships within the residence or within the network of the client. Similarly, the idea of *feedback loops* helps to identify the interaction of different factors in creating a situation which workers must deal with. Systems theory also helps to create a focus on present *communication* among people in residence, both as a way of explaining how problems are maintained in the situation and as a way of intervening. This avoids the complexity of trying to work on complex past causes of problems.

Residences are bounded by the fact that everyone lives together. This means that residences are *self-regulating systems.* This has advantages of security, but rather than exploring and trying to understand what is going on to develop people's skills and capacities to live their lives more effectively, staff and residents often focus on controlling events. They do this by establishing norms for how things *ought* to be done and attempt to minimise risk by reducing unexpected events adversely affecting the smooth running of the residence. In this way, residential units try to establish homeostasis or a balance, which enables them to manage external events and other factors which may upset their smooth running, rather than a steady state which allows them to incorporate change.

Atherton seeks to develop practice to help residents and the residential unit become more open and flexible in dealing with the outside world. It is a useful example of how systems theory can be applied to understanding complex interactions and provide guidance on worthwhile directions for social work intervention.

Connections

Systems theory had a major impact on social work in the 1970s and has been a subject of controversy for almost as long. Two forms of systems theory are distinguished in social work:

- general systems theory
- ecological systems theory.

Hearn (1958, 1969) made one of the earliest contributions, applying systems theory to social work. The greatest impact came with two simultaneously published interpretations of the application of systems ideas to practice, one from Goldstein (1973) and the other from Pincus and Minahan (1973). These gained considerable influence in the UK through interpreters such as Vickery (1974; Specht and Vickery, 1977) and Olsen (1978). The later development by Siporin (1975) and Germain and Gitterman (1980; Germain, 1979a) of ecological systems theory had considerable impact in the USA. Brown (1993) shows the application of the idea of 'boundary' and environment to groupwork. Elliott (1993) argues that systems theory can be integrated with social development ideas (see Chapter 9) to apply the latter to social work in industrialised countries. Kabadaki (1995) shows how the possibility of intervening at different levels in society is particularly relevant for social development work.

The politics of systems theory

Systems theory was an aspect of the reaction against psychodynamic theory in the 1970s. Its sociological focus seemed to counter psychodynamic failures in dealing with the 'social' in social work. Also, separate social work specialisms were being perceived as aspects of a generic social work. In the USA and the UK, separate social work professional organisations had been merged (in the 1950s and 60s respectively). In the UK, separate local government agencies had been merged in the Seebohm reorganisation. The systems theory focus on 'wholes' (Hanson, 1995) was thus an attractive contribution to social work. Roberts (1990) sees it as one of several integrating conceptual frameworks developing in social work then. For example, the influential writers Pincus and Minahan (1973) and Goldstein (1973) described their theories as 'integrated' and 'unitary' respectively. Another source of influence was its importance in family therapy, which also began to develop and influence social work in the mid-1970s. Here, systems theory is a major perspective, since it provides a way of understanding how all members of a family can affect and influence one another. This capacity to deal with analysis of relations among people in groups was also important in gaining usefulness in residential care (Payne, 1977; Atherton, 1989).

Compared with radical theory, the other sociological critique of traditional social work theory which was influential at this period, systems theory did not propose critical ideas that rejected many aspects of current social organisation and social policy. One reason for its success is that it accepts and analyses existing social orders rather than, as with radical theory, analysing and rejecting them. It thus fits well with a profession and agency structure that is part of the state and has authority and power. It gained influence when social work was expanding and taking up roles in state agencies in many countries. Unlike radical theory, it relates successfully to psychological theories, since it does not reject theories at this level of human behaviour, but permits their incorporation in its wider framework.

Its broad focus allowed it to incorporate many aspects of other theories. Leonard (1975: 48) writing from a Marxist perspective, argued that systems theory can help in understanding institutions, their interaction with one another, and how change might be brought about in a radical way, provided that the theory is not used simply to suggest that systems maintain themselves wholly stable. More traditional writers, such as Woods and Hollis (1999), incorporated it into their accounts of psychodynamic practice. Preston-Shoot and Agass (1990) attempt such a combination. They argue that psychodynamic theory (but this might apply to any psychologically based theory) offers a useful understanding of human emotions, interactions and internal responses to the outside world. Systems theories offer a context for such understanding, showing how the public and private interact, how various change agents might be involved and that workers and their agencies might themselves be targets for change. Together, these sets of ideas enable workers to manage the stress of emotional pressure from their interpersonal work by seeing it in a wider social context. They also highlight the fact that we cannot maintain awareness of complex social or interpersonal situations continually. Maintaining two related but separate ways of understanding enables us to switch between an interpersonal and social focus. The connections between the two theories are their emphasis on patterns of behaviour and social relations, which connect with each other and connect us to each other. Kondrat (2002) also emphasises the separate but connected elements of the large- and small-scale aspects of social work in her application of Giddens' (1984) structuration theory within ecological theory. She argues that this and other theories incorporating elements of social construction (Chapter 8) allow for a strong emphasis on people's capacity for influencing their social situation.

Major statements

Three major statements of ecological systems theories are:

- The eco-critical/eco-social/eco-feminist approaches in Matthies et al.'s *The Eco-Social Approach in Social Work* (2001)
- The life model in Germain and Gitterman's *The Life Model of Social Work Practice* (1996)
- The ecosystems perspective in Mattaini et al.'s *Foundations of Social Work Practice* (2002).

Discussion of critical ecological theories are outlined at the end of the account of ecological systems theories, since they are critical of the approach of these theories. The other two models are offered through general texts introducing American interpersonal social work. The life model is a long-standing development, with an extensive history, with some of Germain's papers (1976, 1977, 1978b) being first published in the mid-1970s. Although largely a presentation of American interpersonal social work with some usage of ecological concepts, the approach was been widely influential in North America, so there is considerable documentation from practitioners in American journals and some application to community and family settings. A related concept, the person-in-environment is also widely documented. I present the main features of Germain and Gitterman's (1996) text below, selecting it because it is the most widely influential of the three mentioned above and is a fully developed account, clearly focused on the perspective rather than research or teaching needs, and so therefore theoretically comprehensive. Some major points from the other two texts are added, in particular the German eco-critical focus of the eco-social approach by Matthies et al. (2001), which explicitly attacks the American work.

Also originally developed in the 1970s, but with its first major statement from Meyer in 1983, the ecosystems perspective in Mattaini et al. (2002) has been heavily reconstructed to comply with current American teaching requirements, so it covers community, group and family settings. An important characteristic is graphical representations of particular family relationships through eco-maps. Another consequence of the textbook approach is a more modern focus on diversity, social justice and human rights than the other works discussed here.

Germain and Gitterman: the life model

Germain and Gitterman's (1980, 1996) *life model* of social work practice is the major formulation of ecological systems theory; Germain edited a collection of articles demonstrating its application across a range of social work (1979a). She argues that there are close parallels with ego psychology in the importance given to the environment, action, self-management and identity (Germain, 1978a). However, both sets of ideas are conceptually distinct and can be used without each other.

The life model is based on the metaphor of ecology, in which people are interdependent with each other and their environment: they are 'people-in-environment' (PIE). The relationship between people and their environment is reciprocal: each influences the other over time, through exchanges. The aim of social work is to increase the *fit* between people and their environment.

Figure 7.1 sets out the life model. People are seen as moving through their own unique life course. As they do so, they experience *life stressors*, transitions, events and issues that disturb their fit with the environment. This causes an unexpected disturbance in their capacity to adapt to their environment, such

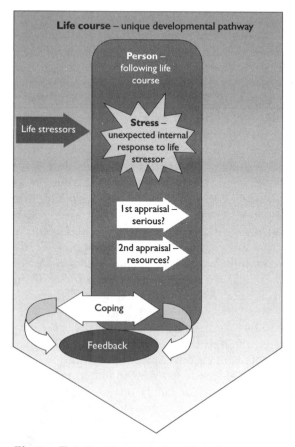

Figure 7.1 The life model of social work practice

that they feel they cannot *cope* with it. They move through two stages of *appraisal* of the stressor and the stress. First, they judge how serious the disturbance is, and whether it will cause harm or loss or be a challenge. Second, they will look at measures they might take to cope and resources they have to help them. They will try to cope by changing some aspect of themselves, the environment or the exchanges between them. Signals from the environment and their own physical and emotional responses give them *feedback* about the success of their efforts at coping.

Among the resources that people have in order to cope are:

- *Relatedness* – the capacity to form attachments
- *Efficacy* – their confidence in their ability to cope
- *Competence* – their sense that they have relevant skills, or can get help from others
- *Self-concept* – their overall evaluation of themselves
- *Self-esteem* – the extent to which they feel significant and worthy
- *Self-direction* – their sense of having control over their lives, alongside taking responsibility for their actions while respecting others' rights.

While these are presented in relation to individuals, personal responses are markedly affected by the influence of experiences in people's families and communities. An apparently poor community, for example, may offer significant resources of self-respect. The presentation of the model may be criticised for making the fine distinctions drawn here unnecessarily detailed for everyday practice.

The ability to use these interpersonal resources is affected by social factors. These are:

- *Coercive power* – where dominant groups withhold power because of personal or cultural features of client groups
- *Exploitative power* – where dominants groups' create technological pollution endangering health and well-being, especially of poor people
- *Habitat* – the physical and social settings of the client
- *Niche* – the particular social position held by the client
- *Life course* – unique, unpredictable pathways through life, and the diverse life experiences gained as a result of following them
- *Historical time* – the historical context in which the life course is experienced
- *Individual time* – the meanings that people give to their life experiences
- *Social time* – events affecting the families, groups and communities that the client is part of.

Germain's early work focused on space and time as aspects of social work practice, and these influences emerge in this element of the model. A criticism might be that, as with systems theory more broadly, these ecological metaphors do not add to the value of concepts such as social class, social status and discrimination on grounds of race and culture (Chapters 11–13), and that time is an unnecessary aspect of the three factors describing the impact of social contexts on people's relationships and personal responses to life. Ideas of social construction may deal with these concepts more effectively (Chapter 8).

The aim of practice in the life model is to improve the fit between people and their environment, by alleviating life stressors, increasing people's personal and social resources to enable them to use more and better coping strategies and influencing environmental forces so that they respond to people's needs. Practice must be sensitive to diversity, ethical and empowering, carried out through a partnership between worker and client that reduces power differences between them. Workers would come to shared agreements with clients about what issues are important, through listening to life stories and assessing in ways that allow clients to make informed choices about appropriate ways of responding. They would work in eight modalities: with individuals, families, groups, social networks, communities, physical environments, organisations and political action. Building up personal and collective strengths should be the main focus of action, which would emphasise clients taking decisions and action on their own account. The environment and the demands of the life course should be a constant factor in making decisions. Practice should be evaluated, and accumulated experience contributed to the professional knowledge base.

Three main phases of practice and the actions and skills involved in each are set out in Table 7.2. The detailed account of practice and skills contained in Germain and Gitterman (1996) provides useful examples of these bare bones. The book also explores practice with communities, organisations and seeking political change, although in less detail. An example of practice with environmental stressors may help to explain the approach. Mrs Evans, an elderly woman, lived in a small public sector apartment and experienced depression after her husband died. After discussion with the worker about her preferences, some mementos of Mr Evans were removed from her bedroom and displayed formally in the hallway. Other items of his property were donated to a charity shop, giving Mrs Evans more storage space. The flat was redecorated by volunteers from the local community centre. As a result of this contact, she started to attend an old people's club at the centre. Mrs Evans was worried by the behaviour of neighbours, and the worker went with her to complain to the housing department. This was ineffective, and the worker made an informal approach to the housing manager. This example demonstrates the importance of developing an effective relationship with the client, even though the focus of the work is mainly on environmental issues. Personal (better storage), semi-fixed (Mr Evans' mementos) and fixed space (redecoration and neighbours) problems were all addressed, and connections with external contacts were also achieved. There was also mediation with the housing department and in the end a more assertive advocacy.

Eco-social approach: eco-criticality

The eco-social approach argues that early American uses of ecology in social work focus on the social environment and in some degree accept an opposition between

Table 7.2 Germain and Gitterman's life model of practice

Phase	Helping process	Actions
Initial: beginnings	Auspice: create an accepting and supportive service environment	Demonstrate empathy in engaging with client; encourage client to express wishes and choices Describe service, agency and worker's role clearly Counteract effects of client group's experience of oppression
	Modalities	Select individual, family, group, community work according to client choice and type of life stressor
	Methods	Select episodic, emergency, short-term, time-limited open-ended service
	Skills	Assess person-environment fit: ■ background: basic individual and family data ■ define life stressors ■ identify client expectations of worker and agency ■ client's strengths and limitations ■ physical environment Agree plans
Ongoing	Helping with stressful life transitions and traumatic events	Enable by demonstrating 'being alongside' client Explore and clarify issues by giving focus, direction, specifying issues, seeing patterns, offering hypotheses, encouraging reflection and feedback Mobilise strengths by identifying capacity, reassuring, offering hope Guide by providing and correcting information, offering advice and discussion, defining tasks Facilitate by identifying avoidance patterns, challenging false engagement, confronting inconsistencies
	Helping with environmental stressors	Identify role and structure of relevant social welfare agencies Identify supportive social networks Explore effect of physical environment: appropriate personal space, change semi-fixed space (moveable objects); mitigate effects of fixed space (building design) Coordinate and connect clients with organisational resources; collaborate with client; mediate with organisations Directive, assertive and persuasive interactions with organisations Adversarial or advocacy interactions with organisations
	Helping with family processes	Identify functions provided by family: procreation and socialisation of children; shelter, for protection of members; nurturing acceptance and self-realisation; connections to outside worlds Join the family group: affirm positives, track different life stories; create therapeutic contexts in which family can make progress; monitor family's paradigm (world view and structure) Interact with family: reframe perceptions, assign homework; work on rituals and patterns of behaviour; offer reflection
	Helping with group processes	Identify group focuses: education, problem-solving, specific behavioural change, carry out tasks, social purposes Identify internal stressors: problems in group formation, structural and value issues Form groups: gain organisational support, identify composition and structure, recruit members Offer support, identify needs for being different and separate, mediate between members
	Reducing interpersonal stress between worker and client	Identify sources of stress: agency authority and sanctions, worker authority and power, worker's professional socialisation, social differences, struggles for interpersonal control, taboo content Prepare effectively for likely issues; explore with interpersonal barriers openly
Termination: endings	Auspice: organisational time and methods factors	Identify factors leading to ending in agency policy, timescale, and appropriate use of methods
	Relational factors	Changing client–worker relationship; differences in client or worker social background
	Phases	Identify and respond to negative feelings about ending and avoidance of ending Acknowledge sadness or pleasure at success; acknowledge release from responsibility of the work

Source: Germain and Gitterman (1996).

the person and their environment. Germain, Gitterman, Meyer and her colleagues merely use ecological ideas as metaphors for discussing clients' relationships with their environment. The eco-social approach uses ecological ideas politically to combat social exclusion, including such ideas as environmental impact statements (Matthies et al., 2000a, b, 2001; Närhi, 2004). Eco-feminism (Besthorn and McMillen, 2002) argues that political and social systems, including ideas such as ecological systems theory in social work, oppress women's concern for sustainable and sustaining environments.

Coates (2003) develops at length an ecological approach to social work that focuses on sustainable development in all societies, not only those that are resource-poor. He emphasises the connectedness of the world, that has been thrown into focus by the increasing speed and influence of globalisation. Subjectivity must be amended away from individuality to include a concern for the local communal responsibilities and people living in communities worldwide. We need to understand the complexity of interdependence and value the diversity of human as well as natural forms. He uses the systems idea of boundaries to emphasise that the earth is a closed system, with limited resources, and that our lives should be sustainable. The basic ecological ideas of social work should be:

- integration and connectedness
- the wisdom of natural things
- the importance of becoming, to see what realist theory (Chapter 3) calls emergent properties, rather than only what exists now
- maintaining diversity
- relationship in community.

Social work practice would focus on:

- developing caring communities
- identifying and developing activities that benefit the common good
- promoting active partnerships
- building capacity in individuals and communities
- promoting decentralised and localised decision-making and helping it to work
- promoting community health and social resilience
- promoting environmental as well as social justice
- reducing human and ecological stress, in particular through focusing on grief work and loss
- focusing on natural methods of healing and spirituality (see Chapter 8).

Närhi and Matthies (2001) call on a German discussion of the American literature to suggest that the person-environment relationship should not be seen as a dichotomy, but as an integrated whole. Moreover, the entire life context and not merely social relationships should be the focus of attention. This *eco-critical* approach in 1980s' Germany harnessed practical environmental and green projects, shared living and workshop projects for young people to enhance people's self-understanding of political and social relationships and develop social self-consciousness and concern for the environment. Conventional social work encouraged non-sustainable life styles based on employment that increasingly did not exist because of globalising social forces benefiting capital- and pollution-intensive industries. Moreover, sedentary life styles were unhealthy, using highly manufactured foods and encouraging smoking. Tester (1994) similarly argued that the life model takes the present, human-created environment as a given, rather than as one that should be modified to assist the social groups from which clients are mainly drawn. People should be helped to develop more inspiring, diverse and stimulating environments than the gloomy and excluding housing living conditions they are often given. This is a particular challenge for workers in day and residential care and in establishing care packages for community provision. Cultural and ethnic diversity provides opportunities for creating a richer social environment, but is often treated in a divisive and excluding way. Promoting social inclusion by proactively encouraging people to become engaged in mutual help and community involvement makes best use of human and cultural resources in any community. Boeck et al. (2001) propose that any eco-social approach to social inclusion should incorporate both the British emphasis on redistribution of resources and the French tradition of focusing on social capital, including the ways in which relationships can exclude social groups.

The main approaches to *eco-social* work are:

- *Holistic analysis*, drawing on the needs of the global environment and including environmental impact analysis of the social area in which workers operate, involving citizens in planning and social action relevant to their interests and needs
- Promoting *positive use of natural resources* and self-consciousness about life styles respectful of environmental resources
- Concern for the *social environment* and *cooperative networks* through which services are provided, especially schools, and health and social care agencies
- *'Adventure pedagogy'* to promote specific networks to promote life opportunities for people. Matthies et al. (2001) refer to young people, but it is possible to imagine such work with disabled, elderly, mentally ill and learning disabled people.

Networking and social support systems

Developing networks in social support systems emerged in mental health work as a way of supporting isolated people as psychiatric hospitals were deinstitutionalised in the 1970s (Caplan, 1974; Caplan and Killilea, 1976; Maguire, 1991; Biegel et al., 1994). Effective social support requires both planned formal support groups and also enabling 'informal' or 'natural' carers to help friends, neighbours and family members who are in need (Walton, 1986). The Italian theorist Folgheraiter (2004) suggests that all social problems derive from relationship problems and suggests that social work practice should consist of jointly working out helping plans. Where isolation from social support is short term, there is evidence that re-establishing previous links is effective, while long-term isolation requires group- and community-based work (Eyrich et al., 2003). A network, according to Seed (1990: 19) 'is a system or pattern of links between points ... which have particular meanings' for those involved. Social workers focus on clients' networks and agency links which form a pattern in clients' daily lives. The aim is to identify formal and informal social networks, extend them and make them usable in helping the client. Networks may be more or less dense or of varying quality, depending on, respectively, the amount of contact between particular parts of the network and the value placed upon it. They may also have a variety of features (such as being concerned with home, work, leisure, care).

Recent developments in networking attempt to develop a technology by which interpersonal work developing people's relationships can be connected to community work. Trevillion (1999) proposes networking as a basis for practice in developing partnerships with service users and the community, and I have argued similarly for its value in developing multiprofessional teamwork (Payne, 2000). Trevillion sees social workers as potential community brokers, able to link users with a variety of community resources. This has links with empowerment practice. Gilchrist (2004) combines network with chaos and complexity theory, suggesting that community development often seeks to recreate close interpersonal connections within communities that probably only exist in romantic notions of what communities used to be like. Meta-networking connects human-scale interpersonal networks together to create a pattern of links. This is better than integration of such complexity that it feels chaotic, is hard to grasp and understand.

Specht (1986) shows that social support applies to a wide range of social relationships and organisations, whereas social networks refer to a specific set of interrelated people. He argues that there is little evidence that there are untapped resources available in the community to support people with problems in the USA, and there is empirical support for this view in the UK (Abrams, 1984; Bulmer, 1987). Timms (1983) and Allan (1983) suggest that a supportive service to existing social networks is appropriate, but attempting to replace formal provision with informal care or change the existing patterns of informal care is likely to be unsuccessful. This is confirmed by Cecil et al. (1987) in a study in Northern Ireland.

CRITICAL PRACTICE FOCUS

Mr Hardy and his neighbours

Looking back on Mr Hardy's case (Critical Practice Focus: Chapter 5), would systems interventions be the best course, rather than interventions with Mr Hardy. If so, which systems would be the target systems and what agencies might be the action systems?

Turning to his neighbours, Mr and Mrs Garrett have two children, George (7) and Freda (4), and have moved to Philanthropy Housing from their birthplace in the country, several hundred miles away. The children are finding it difficult to build relationships in the city at their school and preschool centre, and George is presenting behaviour problems and his attainment at school has dropped. Although Mr Garrett has a well-paid job, Mrs Garrett feels isolated and depressed. Her elderly mother (82) has had several falls, but has a close network of friends and more distant relatives in their home town. Mr Garrett's parents , who are a bit younger, live nearby, but have few friends and ask for the Garrets to visit regularly. Mrs Garrett and the children would like to return home. A social worker attached to Mrs Garrett's doctor's health centre is asked to help her.

Looking at this situation from a systems point of view, what systems and social networks may be identified and how might intervention be developed? What different points of view would systems theories offer? What points might emerge from applying from eco-critical theories?

Commentary

Systems and ecological theories, with their attempts at structuring and technical terminology, form a very different style of theory from traditional social work practice, which emphasises individualisation and psychology. They are among the few comprehensive sociologically based theories of social work. Advantages of the systems approach are:

- More emphasis on changing environments than psychological approaches.
- It is interactive, concentrating on the effects of one person on another, rather than on internal thoughts and feelings. Cox (2003), for example, discusses helping grandparents offering care to children. She shows the importance of gaining a wide range of perceptions of the situation from people involved; there may be many different services, workers, neighbours and different generations of a family to be considered.
- It alerts social workers to the possibility of alternative ways of achieving the same object (equifinality and multifinality). This reduces the stigma arising from diversity of behaviour and social organisation which some psychological theories concentrating on normality and deviance tend to create (Leighninger, 1978).
- It is unitary (Goldstein, 1973), integrated (Pincus and Minahan, 1973) or holistic (Hearn, 1969; Leighninger, 1978), including work with individuals, groups and communities, and does not emphasise any particular method of intervention. Instead, it provides an overall way of describing things at any level, so that we can understand all interventions as affecting systems. Particular explanatory theories form part of this overarching universe. Workers choose theories appropriate to levels of intervention with which they are involved. They thus avoid sterile debates about whether they are concerned with individual change or social reform. However, selecting theories to use on any organised basis may be difficult.
- It avoids linear, deterministic cause-and-effect explanations of behaviour or social phenomena of the kind common in cognitive-behavioural practice,

because equifinality and multifinality show how lots of energy flows can affect systems in many different ways. Patterns of relationships and how boundaries are shared or *interface* with one another are important ideas.

- Wakefield (1996) identifies four arguments for ecological systems theory's combination of general and ecological systems: its ability to analyse circular connections in transactions between worker and client; its value in assessment; its integration of other social work theories; and its inclusion of social factors to balance individual casework. He concludes that all these arguments are flawed, for the reasons discussed below.

There are, however, problems with such claims:

- Because it is expository rather than explanatory (Forder, 1976), it sets out ideas in a novel way which makes them easier to grasp and makes connections between different levels of society and individual behaviour. However, it does not explain why things happen and why those connections exist. It is therefore hard to test empirically.

- It is not prescriptive (Germain, 1979b: 6), so it does not tell us what to do, where or how to affect systems (Mancoske, 1981). Also it does not allow us to control the effects of interventions in a system, because we do not know how each part of it will interact with the others. It assumes that affecting one part of a system will affect other parts, but in practice this does not seem to happen (Siporin, 1980).

- It is overinclusive. Not everything is relevant and it does not help to decide what is. Many things may not fit into a general schema, deciding on boundaries may be complex or impossible, and it may be assumed that things are related in a system without checking to see if they actually are (Leighninger, 1978). In encouraging social workers to concentrate on wide-scale issues, it may lead to the neglect of small-scale and personal issues (Siporin, 1980).

- Systems (particularly ecological) theory may overstate the importance of integrating parts of the system and assume that all the parts of a system are needed to maintain it, and are or should be interrelated. It thus tends to assume that systems are or should be conserved, and should maintain equilibrium rather than change or be changed. Also, systems theory tends to assume that conflict is less desirable than maintenance and integration, which may not be true in practice (Leighninger, 1978).

- The idea of feedback implies slow and manageable change, but what if radical change is needed? Systems theory makes little provision for this and does not deal with the problem that feedback sometimes amplifies deviance rather than reducing it (Leighninger, 1978).

- The ideas of entropy and survival as aspects of systems are analogies with the behaviour of physical systems, and, like many of the biological and physical analogies in systems theory, may not have a general application to all social systems (Leighninger, 1978). Should all systems (for example families torn by strife) seek to survive? Do they? Should entropy be exported to the environment, or cause a system to leach energy from what may already be an environment poor in energy? For example, should a poor family make demands on the resources of a poor neighbourhood, or should resources be redistributed from richer neighbourhoods? Such questions raise political issues that the model does not deal with, and it seems to assume a local, non-political resolution when applied to the daily round of social work.

- It has a complex and technical language which does not fit well with a human activity like social work (Germain, 1979b: 6) and often alienates workers as a result. This is a common criticism of borrowed technologies which systems theory shares with behaviour modification. By contrast, the ideas of conflict, need and drive in psychodynamic theory, or genuineness and alienation of humanist theory seem much more attractive.

- Because it is a generalised theory, it is hard to apply to any specific situations (Germain, 1979b: 7; Leighninger, 1978) and, on the other hand, applications might be very variable. One worker might interpret a situation in one way, another worker in another and it would be hard to judge which is right.

As well as these practical criticisms, there are also ideological doubts about systems theory. Many of these stem from criticisms of social systems theory in sociology because of its structural-functional perspective on society, and particularly that of Parsons (Evans, 1976). Mancoske (1981: 714–15) summarises these criticisms as follows:

> Critics claim that Parsons' action theory is less a systems theory than a statics theory, it is not empirically verifiable as developed, and is so abstract and vague that concepts are undefinable. The emphasis of action theory is on function, not process of interaction, and this negates the meaning of systems.

Mancoske argues that in its social work formulations, the criticisms of systems theory as static are weak, because usually considerable attention is given to change, both individual and social. In social work interpretations of systems theory, however, and particularly that of Pincus and Minahan, Evans (1976) argues that there is a hidden assumption that all systems are interdependent. This is only true of closed systems; open systems are much more flexible, and it is important to make the distinction clear. Siporin (1980) points to Marxist criticisms of systems theory which claim that it does not take account of the incompatibilities of class interests in capitalist societies and how these prevent any integration in such a society. Devore (1983) argues that the life model is better at dealing with social class, ethnic and cultural differences and life style than many other theories, but still lacks specificity in dealing with issues affecting black people. Eco-critical and eco-feminist approaches argue that ecological theory in social work does not concern itself with sustainable ecological systems, and thus continues to promote oppressive and damaging social relations. This connects with critical theory.

Critical, anti-discriminatory, advocacy and empowerment theories are the other major sociological theories of social work, but social psychological, role and social construction theory offer a more social psychological approach to social work activity, and the next chapter is concerned with these.

OVERVIEW

- Systems theory presents useful language and ideas for incorporating social and psychological approaches together in a single approach to social work

- In particular, it explains how social change and indirect practice may be incorporated into a practice mainly focused on individual change

- By including ecological elements, systems theory has developed a comprehensive theory of practice that has particularly engaged support in the USA

- It has led to useful developments in networking and social support systems as part of social work

- As a social order perspective, systems theory fails to incorporate critical, especially eco-critical, and transformational social ideologies

- It has been criticised for providing a framework of understanding that does not specify clearly the level and type of interventions required in particular circumstances

- Systems theory has begun to shift towards a model of social work that also includes broader ecological concerns as a part of social action and individual practice, but most social work accounts do not adequately reflect this perspective yet.

FURTHER READING

Coates, J. (2003) *Ecology and Social Work: Towards a New Paradigm* (Halifax, NS: Fernwood).
Useful discussion of ecological and sustainability ideas related to social work.

Germain, C. B. and Gitterman, A. (1996) *The Life Model of Social Work Practice: Advances in Theory and Practice*, 2nd edn (New York: Columbia University Press).
Mattaini, M. A., Lowery, C. T. and Meyer, C. H. (eds) (2002) *Foundations of Social Work Practice: A Graduate Text* (Washington DC: NASW).
Comprehensive American texts.

Matthies, A.-L., Närhi, K and Ward, D. (eds) (2001) *The Eco-Social Approach in Social Work* (Jyväskylä: SoPhi).
Useful account of theoretical and practice aspects of the eco-social approach.

Payne, M. (2002) The politics of systems theory within social work, *Journal of Social Work*, **2**(3): 269–92.
An analysis of the development of the debate about systems theory.

Wakefield, J. C. (1996) 'Does social work need the eco-systems perspective? Part 1: is the perspective clinically useful?' *Social Service Review,* **70**(1): 1–31: 'Does social work need the eco-systems perspective? Part 2: does the perspective save social work from incoherence?' *Social Services Review,* **70**(2): 183–213.
Helpful evaluation of American ecological systems theory in practice.

CHAPTER 8

Social Psychology and Social Construction

What this chapter is about

This chapter focuses on theoretical ideas used in social work mainly from social psychology, and in particular the impact during the 1990s of social construction theory. Social psychology has mainly been concerned with understanding how group relations construct social identity and has not developed therapeutic ideas that may be easily transferred to social work. However, concepts from role and communication theory, ideas that lie on the borders of psychology and sociology, have been widely used in social work. Social construction theories incorporating postmodernist ideas developed during the 1990s to form a critical psychology, generating ideas that are used in a range of successful therapies and have been imported into social work practice. While these theories are individualist, they represent a shift towards a reflexive-therapeutic position, emphasising flexibility and responsiveness to the views and wishes of the people involved.

MAIN POINTS

> ➤ Social psychology is concerned with the way relationships within and between groups create and maintain social identities.

> ➤ Its main influence in social work until the 1990s has been the adoption of concepts from role theory and communication studies.

> ➤ In the 1990s, a critical psychology based on postmodernist and social construction ideas has influenced the development of constructive practice theory.

> ➤ The main sources of social work's use of social construction thinking have been de Shazer's solution-focused therapy, White and Epston's narrative therapy and O'Hanlon's possibility thinking.

> ➤ The main approach to practice is identifying, through understanding patterns of language, how people construct their social world and helping them to reconstruct the world by using language differently to identify possibilities for change.

> Forming social *identity* within groups.

> *Role*, role conflict and role performance.

> *Communication* analysis and skills.

> *Reframing* intractable ideas by identifying alternative plausible interpretations.

> Reality is a *social construction* within historical and social contexts, and therefore permits a wide variability of cultural and social forms.

> *Narrative* is a focus for understanding and changing people's social identities, roles and social constructions.

> Existing successful behaviour is a basis for finding *solutions* to individual problems.

> *Exceptions* or *possibilities* give ideas for change in people's experiences.

Wider theoretical perspectives

The subject matter of social psychology (Hogg and Abrams, 2001) is the effect of relations within and between groups on creating and maintaining social identities. This includes ideas about how people behave in relation to, and therefore influence, others and the effects of social factors such as stigma, stereotyping and ideology on behaviour in groups. Social psychology generally has a lot to say about oppression and discrimination between groups.

Following from this, social psychology considers the effects of communication and therefore language and speech upon social interactions. A substantial area of 'communication studies' has grown up concerned with language and other symbols of communication between human beings as individuals, within groups and more widely in organisations and social collectivities (Tubbs and Moss, 2000; DeVito, 2002). Communications research involves understanding how human beings use language individually and in social situations to give meaning to particular views of the world. Power relations derive from the use of language to construct a view of the world which, if socially accepted, influences others. People such as social workers use language in this way to influence clients, which means that the processes through which they do so give power over clients. Equally, as Lyon (1993) argues in relation to the study of roles, creating roles is a process of constructing a place in social relations for ourselves.

Concepts from role theory, the idea of labelling and the whole area of social psychological research into human interactions have been important in social work. Breakwell and Rowett (1982) proposed a social psychological approach to social work. It emphasised in particular how relationships are formed and managed by people in social situations, issues of identity related to matters such as stigma, group behaviour, the effects of environments, territory, and the need for personal space, and material on social and personal change. Kelly's (1955) *personal construct theory* proposed that people manage their behaviour according to 'constructs' in their mind about how to behave, which have been developed from past experience. We construct events differently from one another. Therefore, looking at and changing people's constructs may help to change behaviour, in the same way that cognitive theory (Chapter 6) proposes. This approach may also be a useful way of understanding social interactions (Tully, 1976). It has relationships with phenomenological and existential ideas, considered in Chapter 9, which proclaim the variety of interpretations of the personal and social world that are possible.

Personal construct theory is different from social construction. Figure 8.1a illustrates how personal constructs are the internal pictures of the world that people build up through their own perceptions; each personal construct differs from other people's constructs. The study and therapeutic use of perceptions and interpretations of the world relates to cognitive therapies (Chapter 6) and such practice is often called 'constructivist'. D. Carpenter (1996), for example, focuses on the idea of 'structure determinism', that is, how structures like social role influence behaviour. Practice focuses on misperceptions and inappropriate thinking, which means that accurate perceptions are not well processed. Figure 8.1b illustrates social constructions as shared pictures of the world that people build up by interacting with each other in social and historical contexts; practice based on these ideas is often called 'constructionist'. Practice focuses on how the shared picture has been built up and how the impact of such shared conceptions or

the context in which they have their effects may be changed. Not all writers, particularly in the USA, make this firm distinction between constructivist and constructionist ideas, and see these practices as interrelated because they are all concerned with constructions and how they may be changed.

Figure 8.1a Personal constructs are individual perspectives

Figure 8.1b Social constructs correspond with shared social realities

Social construction theory proposes that people describe, explain and account for the world around them as part of interchanges between people in their social, cultural and historical context. Chapter 3 discussed how these ideas are important for epistemology, the theory of knowledge, because social construction says that people's knowledge does not come from reasoning and experiment, but by interpreting the discourse between people. Social construction ideas have also become important, in social work, through their use in psychotherapy.

Four areas of sociological social construction theory are important for social work (Payne, 1999):

- Berger and Luckmann's (1971) ideas about the social construction of reality (Chapter 1)
- the social construction of social problems (Kitsuse and Spector, 1973; Spector and Kitsuse, 1977)
- phenomenological sociology (see Chapter 9) and postmodernism
- the social construction of human categories, such as gender and 'race'.

The *social construction of reality* emphasises that shared social constructions contribute to the socialisation of individuals into society and into social groups within society, to the extent that social ideas are so widely shared that they become a form of reality to participants in that society.

Social problems arise when a social group successfully makes a claim about a social issue, particularly using mass media, that it is problematic, requiring social and political action. The argument is that social problems are not inherently problematic: they are created by 'claims-making'. For example, the fact that a high proportion of marriages in some societies end in divorce might lead to the suggestion that those societies have efficient ways of formalising the end of unsuccessful marital relationships. However, some groups claim that this constitutes a social problem, leading to social instability and conflict. We might point to their assumptions that marriage does create social stability and is desirable and that effective divorce leads to instability and is undesirable. Claims-making in social problem formation is a special case of the social construction of reality. It shows how groups work to create social constructions about particular social experiences.

Phenomenological sociology researches taken-for-granted aspects of behaviour to disclose underlying social assumptions. For example, ethnomethodology examines how apparently irrational behaviour follows logical rules tacitly understood by everyone involved. One study found that case records in a health care clinic are written to make it appear that workers followed the clinic's procedures, rather than reflecting what workers actually did (Garfinkel, 1970).

Work on *human categories* points out that many apparently physically determined human categories, such as men and women, become overlaid by social assumptions and behaviour. So, it is assumed that being caring is a female characteristic because only women can be mothers, when they are socialised and pressed into caring roles by the assumption that this is 'natural'. Extensive research through detailed conversation analysis demonstrates that assumed human categories are created by the assumptions of people involved, or the structural requirements of agencies (Jokinen et al., 1999; Karvinen et al., 1999; Hall et al., 2003). For example, Juhila (2003) points out that in a social work relationship, it appears that there are only two roles available, social worker or client, and that these are asymmetrical in power. That is, the participants have different kinds of power over different aspects of the relationship. The worker has institutional power drawn from professional knowledge and agency authority, while the client controls access to personal information and family relationships. More complex relationships are possible than this, and different kinds of social work relationships might be imagined. Feminists, for example, seek greater equality (Chapter 12) .

All this work draws attention to how careful analysis of human interactions may give access to a complex understanding of social relations and how identity and behaviour is created in them. It also gives access to the possibility of using the same kinds of interactions to change people's perceptions and social constructions and thus change their behaviour and social relationships. This possibility is the source of constructionist social work.

Social psychological ideas about social construction create a critical psychology of how groups and individuals form their identity. Conventional psychology assumes a fundamental personal identity, the 'self'; we saw in Chapter 4 that this is also important to psychodynamic psychology. Critical psychology says that consciousness and the self emerge from the meanings and practices in social relations (Wetherell and Maybin, 1996) through a reflexive cycle (see Chapter 2), which is influenced by our understandings, language and power relations. Thus, social construction in psychology emphasises the possibility of change in response to social relationships, such as those that a social worker or therapist might create, rather than an unchangeable basic personality. The French philosopher Foucault has been an important influence on the development of these ideas (Chambon et al., 1999). Irving (1999) argues that, building on the philosophy of Nietsche and the literature of Beckett, Foucault developed ideas that questioned the possibility of examining an external world empirically, and being internally able to be certain about how the outside world was. Since social work emerged from modernism, incorporating these ideas of 'radical doubt' into social work questioned important tenets underlying most social work practice (Irving, 1999). Much of Foucault's work connects with phenomenological sociology, in that his 'archaeology' of knowledge was concerned to uncover buried aspects of understanding hidden in everyday behaviour and events. He 'deconstructed' the language of surface interpretations of social institutions and activities, destabilising the assumptions that were included in the language, and then reorganised social knowledge about the issues that he studied. Lengthy and important studies examined prisons, mental hospitals and sexual behaviour, showing that social institutions and behaviour often have many facets that are not always immediately apparent. Important aspects of his work include the following points:

- Many apparently beneficial institutions are designed to maintain existing patterns of social power by disciplining and punishing transgressions against social conventions. The implication for social work is that its caring and therapy is part of patterns of power that also discipline and punish. As Foucault put it: 'social work is inscribed within a larger social function that has been taking on new dimensions for centuries, the function of surveillance-and-correction: to surveil individuals and to redress them, in the two meanings of the word, alternatively as punishment and as pedagogy' (Foucault, 1999: 92).

■ Social institutions are formed in a discourse between people and social groups about their nature and objectives, and patterns of social power are disclosed through the analysis of discourse. So in Chapter 3 I discussed a discourse between evidence-based and social construction views of social work knowledge. This discloses not only the issues in the debate, but the existence of the discourse shows us a meta-level of itself. That is, social work has a concern about effective forms of knowledge for practice, a concern that is unresolved. If we can identify this meta-level, we can ask questions and look for evidence about why social work has this concern.

Important ideas in social psychology have also come from the micro-teaching of personal and social skills (Marshall and Kurtz, 1982), which we have already encountered in relation to social skills training in behavioural approaches to social work. Similar ideas have also grown up around the development of counselling through the work of Rogers and Carkhuff (see Chapter 9) using experiential techniques. These enable clients to learn practically skills that counsellors are helping them to acquire. Micro-training grew up to offer a practical basis for using such techniques among the helping professions. It includes the use of video for viewing actual behaviours, and partly grew up as the technology became available and more sophisticated, and detailed attention to feedback on specific behaviours (Kurtz and Marshall, 1982). Groupwork and residential care have used many aspects of social psychological research into group and inter-group behaviour, and have constructed it from theories relevant to social work. Community work has also used this research to provide some basis for constructing work methods (Sutton, 1994).

Connections

Because of their psychological base, and experimental, research-based episte-mology, social psychological approaches to social work have close links with cognitive approaches to social work. However, the focus on interpersonal and inter-group behaviour and therefore on language and communication have led towards a more social learning and cognitive approach and away from traditional behavioural views (Heller and Northcut, 2002). As these forms of psychology have developed a more constructionist approach, the focus on language as a social creation and as a process for forming social structures and understanding have enabled the inclusion of ideas such as roles as 'performances' and communi-cation as a form of social construction. The importance of language as an aspect of social construction in postmodernist ideas has recently strengthened the interest in communication ideas, for example in Thompson's (2003b) book. This also makes connections with the importance of minority language and interpreta-tion for social work agencies and connects with anti-discriminatory and empowerment practice (for example Lynn and Muir, 1996). This, in its turn, brings connections to the humanist and existential models of social work (see Chapter 9). Feminist theory has found the ideas of the construction of gender and knowledge emerging from relationships and language helpful in understanding how female roles are created in patriarchal societies.

Nelsen (1980, 1986) argues that communication theory can offer a useful connection between many theories of social work. Much of the energy which maintains the equilibrium of a system (see Chapter 7), such as an individual, family or social group, consists of information and reactions to it. Ego psychology (Chapter 4) and cognitive behavioural theories are concerned with how the individual processes reality, and this too relies on communication. Communication is, therefore, an essential part of any worker's understanding. Communication theory and research have established knowledge and a framework for such understanding. Lishman (1994) and Thompson (2003b) select from this material to explore more pragmatically useful ideas for practice.

The politics of social psychology and social construction

It is perhaps surprising, in view of its social rather than individual focus, that no consistent development of a social psychological theory occurred within social work until the impact of social construction in the late 1990s. Saleebey's (1992, 1996) strengths perspective, Kelly's (1955) personal construct theory, narrative psychology (White and Epston, 1990), including oral history (Martin, 1995), and various aspects of family therapy have been adapted into social work. Particularly influential work has come from de Shazer (1985, 1988, 1991) where solution-focused work (Walter and Peller, 1992), like strengths-focused work, has a positive, rather than problem-solving, emphasis. Behaviours which are not typical of problems that people identify as their reason for seeking help are used as exceptions to the 'problem', and as evidence for the possibility of and a basis for building solutions. Change is assumed to be continual, with small changes building up to large ones. Clients' resources and existing cooperation with others are used to work towards solutions, with clients treated as experts in their situation. We impose meaning on outside events, which we then influence by the meanings we have constructed. This circular process is interrupted with meanings attached to the new solutions, which then form part of the reconstruction of the world. All these ideas have influenced the development of construction approaches to social work.

The main reasons for the weak influence of social psychology are threefold. First, its focus on inter-group and interpersonal understanding and its experimental epistemology were not easily converted to individual casework, which has dominated theoretical development in social work. Social construction ideas have made available an application that can be incorporated in casework. Second, partly because of its epistemology, there is no coherent theoretical model offering a set of principles of therapeutic action for transfer into social work, as there was in psychoanalysis or behavioural and cognitive theories. These were devised for therapeutic purposes and could therefore be quickly adapted. Again, the development of narrative therapy and its use in clinical psychology and counselling has made this possible (McCleod, 1997). Third, and as a result of this, specific knowledge has been acquired from social psychological work, especially for groupwork, without a model of action being created.

However, because of the importance of family therapy during the 1970s and 80s, the communication theory base of family therapy became more widely understood within social work. Greene (1996) emphasises the family therapy roots of much communication theory, and picks up ideas such as reframing, where the worker gives plausible alternative meanings to family and individual interpretations of social 'facts'. This helps people to see how these are interpretations, rather than realities, and connects directly to social construction practices that focus on language. Communication ideas offer a fairly comprehensive theory of action well supported by research and experience. It expresses many important values in social work, especially listening to clients and focusing on their behaviour and experience. However, it does not provide a coherent account of social work with wider social purposes. Therefore its use has been limited to mainly therapeutic or clinical situations, or explaining and understanding particular patterns of behaviour in general social agencies, rather than providing a general theory of action. This is how it has been used, for example, in Nelsen's (1980), Lishman's (1994) and Thompson's (2003b) books on communication in social work.

Role theory

Role theory has a long history in social work theory, because it is about our interactions with others and how their expectations and reactions cause us to respond in characteristic ways. Perlman (1968) argues that it offers social explanations complementing psychological understanding of personality (Strean, 1971; Biddle and Thomas, 1979; Davis, 1996).

Two types of role theory exist:

- *structural-functional role theory* assumes that people occupy positions in social structures. Each position has a role associated with it. Roles are sets of expectations or behaviours associated with positions in social structures. How we see our roles affects how well we manage change. Howard and Johnson (1985) give the example of single-parent families. American research found that people with traditional assumptions about the proper role to play in marriage find it harder to adjust to being a lone parent than people who experienced role flexibility in their marriage.

- Goffman's (1968b) *dramaturgical role theory* sees roles as 'enactments' of the social expectations attached to a social status. People pick up signs about others in social interactions. We influence others' views of us by managing the information they receive from us. *Performances* give an appropriate impression. Our performance is usually 'idealised' so that it includes common social expectations. Some aspects of the role are emphasised, others concealed. So, in another famous book, Goffman (1968a) is concerned with how stigmatised people manage the impressions other people have of that aspect of them which is socially disapproved, so that they can 'pass' as normal. People often work together in 'teams' to share the responsibility, particularly in organisations, of enacting socially approved roles, and they can share behaviour which is not in role 'backstage', as a relief when they do not have to put up a front. In a series of books, Goffman (1972a, b, c) extends these ideas into a comprehensive analysis of how socially expected roles can explain many different forms of behaviour.

The value of these ideas is that some behaviour can be understood as role conflicts and ambiguities. This is easy for clients to understand, it does not criticise them in a personal way, and so it is easy to intervene and create change. Moreover, role theory takes in a social perspective on behaviour, so it is a useful link between behaviour problems and social environment. Major (2003) proposes a six-step process for exploring role issues with clients, by negotiating about roles and role change, which I have generalised from her detailed work on caregiving for children:

- Identify the demands that new roles will make
- Define the role set, that is, others who will be involved and what their roles will be
- Recognise the barriers created by present roles and conflicts with a new role
- Negotiate in detail new roles: who does what, when and where
- Work on role integration, for example by creating timetables of who does what and when or create back-ups
- Renegotiate roles as feedback indicates that change is needed.

An example of role issues is Clare, a middle-aged woman, who was working as a secretary, having been divorced by her husband. She had brought up her children successfully alone. Her elderly mother, also alone, suffered from failing sight, was registered as blind and later had a fall in her home. The doctor to both families suggested that they should live together, so Clare could provide greater security for her mother. This arrangement became difficult and a social worker was asked to help. Using ideas from role theory helped to explain that there was *role conflict* here between Clare's working role, which was important for her self-esteem (this is often the case with work), and her role as a caring daughter. This was both inter-role conflict, because work and daughter roles conflicted, and intra-role conflict, because it appeared that the mother's expectations about the role of a caring daughter conflicted with Clare's and, indeed, those of the doctor and Clare's daughter who still lived at home. Looking more deeply into the situation, Clare was suffering from *role ambiguity*, because she understood and appreciated all these views of her role as daughter, so she was herself uncertain about how she should behave.

This approach can also be criticised from a critical perspective, because it fails to emphasise wider social pressures leading to the oppression of women as carers, when social provision to help them accept their responsibilities is not available. So, while role theory helps to explain how social patterns affect individual clients, its structural-functional approach may lead to our assuming that roles exist and are a necessary part of the pattern of society. If so, we may fail to question whether those patterns are appropriate and might usefully be changed. Moreover, role theory does not provide techniques for behaviour change and dealing with emotional and personal responses to role conflicts. It merely makes them apparent.

These ideas relate to symbolic interactionism (see Chapter 9). They emphasise how roles are formed by social expectations and *labelling*. Labelling originates from the work of Becker (1963) and Lemert (1972). According to Lemert, most people occasionally act in a deviant way, and the crucial issue is the response of the surrounding social environment to that act. Sometimes, people are put through a social system which labels them as 'deviant' or 'criminal'. Once labelled, they are likely to live up to the social expectations of their label, and to be encouraged to act in more deviant ways. This leads to an even stronger labelling process. Becker shows how social groups create deviance by making rules and deciding whom they are applied to, labelling them as 'outsiders' to normal social life. 'Moral panics' (Cohen, 1972) about particular forms of deviance, such as hooliganism or rowdy behaviour at sports events, mean that social concern about that form of deviance rises. This strengthens the labelling process. In turn, people are caught by the expectation that they will be deviant and this encourages deviant behaviour.

Their value as ideas, however, is that they draw attention to how official agencies, such as those employing social workers, may play a part in the social creation of problems they are set up to deal with. We need to take care, therefore, in assessing and providing services to avoid stigmatising systems and behaviour (Levy, 1981). There is research evidence suggesting that social workers often label clients negatively (Case and Lingerfelt, 1974; Gingerich et al., 1982).

Communication theory

Communication theory helps to develop some of the social psychological ideas discussed above and decide on appropriate direct interventions with clients. It brings together a number of psychological studies, particularly of a group of psychologists and therapists in Palo Alto, California, of whom the best known is possibly Satir (1964, 1972). Satir's work is about the complexities of human interaction particularly through speech and in attempts to change patterns of behaviour. Anthropologists and social psychologists such as Birdwhistell (1973), Scheflen (1972; Scheflen and Ashcraft, 1976) and Hall (1966) are also relevant. They are concerned with the micro-level of detailed physical movements associated with communication, and broader cultural issues, such as territoriality, personal space and proxemics, which is about how closeness and related factors affect relationships. Related to this work is neurolinguistic programming (Angell, 1996), which originates from the detailed study of the language interactions of therapists. It focuses on how information received from the environment is processed through language and then organised by an individual (Angell, 1996). Thompson (2003b) emphasises the importance of language as an aspect of culture and cultural studies as an increasing influence on communication studies. He also includes a focus on written communication. While there is discussion of the use of correspondence with clients in social work literature, the development of email and text messaging using mobile phones (cellphones) is likely to lead to greater use of written communication and require us to consider the special features of communication using new communication technologies. Certainly, awareness of the languages of communication by new technologies is required for working with children and young people.

According to Thompson (2003b), the basic model of communication is the transmission of information to a receiver. Communication may be interfered with by 'noise'. Networks of communication build up and how we communicate and with whom becomes part of our culture and social relations; for example ethnic and class divisions are marked by separation in communication networks and noise. Nelsen (1980) proposes that when we take some action, we always do so in response to some information we have received. Information might be facts, or other things that may be learned, such as emotion, memories, bodily sensations or an idea about how someone feels about you. We perceive the information, and then we evaluate it; this is information-processing. As we evaluate communications, we give *feedback* to the communicator, who thus gains some idea of how we have perceived and evaluated the communication. We came across this idea when discussing systems theory. We all have our own internal rules for processing information, which mean that we think some things are important and not others. This leads to *selective perception*, where we do not pick up communication that is not important or meaningful to us, but may be crucial to others.

Some communication is *verbal*. Feedback that we are listening to verbal communication can be comforting to speakers. *Non-verbal* communication, such as how we hold our bodies or move or how close we sit, also gives information to others. We are all always communicating. Even silence or absence is communication, because others interpret it. Relevant communication may be symbolic and non-verbal as well as verbal (Lishman, 1994). All communication must be evaluated within its context. Behaviour which is strange in one place at one time would be perfectly normal at another.

Most communication forms *patterns*. People become accustomed to balanced and predictable ways of communicating with those with whom they regularly have contact. This forms the basis of their relationship. Furlong (1990) argues that social workers fall into a pattern of using words such as 'help', 'support' and 'encourage' which imply positive relationships with clients. This implies cooperative endeavour of a therapeutic kind. He argues that on occasions more directive words would form a more effective pattern for getting clients to complete tasks. Pugh (1996) analyses the use of patterns of language within communication to show how they give evidence of attitudes, create identity and are used to express power in relationships and social structures. Communication always has *content*, which is its surface material, but in a relationship, the metacommunication may give added or different meanings to the apparent content. The way content is presented offers a proposal of a certain sort of relationship. So, how workers behave towards clients says something about how relationships between them are expected to be. Apparent distance due to professional roles might be misinterpreted. Some clients may think workers too formal, others expect them to be 'professional' and are surprised when they are informal. Patterns of communication often express power, domination or subordination. Communication theory may, therefore, help us to identify oppression and inequality.

Communication theory and understanding can be useful for:

- analysing and developing practice by improving communication skills
- working on communication problems experienced by clients
- analysing problems in teamwork (Payne, 2000).

Major statements

No major statement that specifically attempts to apply social psychology in social work has been produced since Breakwell and Rowett (1982). Applications of communication ideas provide useful contributions to practice, and are often closely linked to family therapy (for example Greene's 1996 discussion). Nelsen (1980) has produced the most comprehensive account of communication theory for general application to social work, but this is too old to cover recent developments in communication theory and incorporate cultural studies and recent developments in linguistics. Thompson's (2003b) practical and theoretical guide is a useful exposition of a range of up-to-date communication ideas, including cultural studies and postmodern linguistic issues, but does not attempt to provide an overall theory of communication in its application to social work.

Fisher's (1991) somewhat idiosyncratic account of the application of constructivism to social work, although extensive on constructivism, does not deal with social construction ideas and does not incorporate more recently developed practice insights from solution-focused and narrative therapy. McNamee and Gergen (1992) edited a ground-breaking text which applied developing ideas in psychological social construction theory to therapy; many of these papers were influential in social work. Franklin and Nurius (1998) provide an interesting range of articles, including case studies of practice in family and individual work and in teams and community work, but as an edited collection, it does not contain a coherent theoretical account or an application to practice. Therefore, Parton and O'Byrne's *Constructive Social Work* (2000), with its conflation of the main psychotherapeutic approaches to construction theory applied to social work practice, must be considered the major account of this perspective.

Parton and O'Byrne: constructive social work

While accepting that there are rational-technical aspects of social work, Parton and O'Byrne (2000) argue that it is as much an art. Consequently, processes are as important as outcomes, there is a plurality of knowledge and voices about the world, there are possibilities and opportunities as well as problems and barriers and knowledge and understanding derive from social relationships. Constructive social work seeks to open up alternative possibilities, from which people are often excluded by their 'stories': the way in which they have understood or experienced how the world deals with them. Constructive social work is constructive because it tries to build on the positives in people's lives and experiences and uses ideas drawn from social construction theory. The model of practice is illustrated in Figure 8.2.

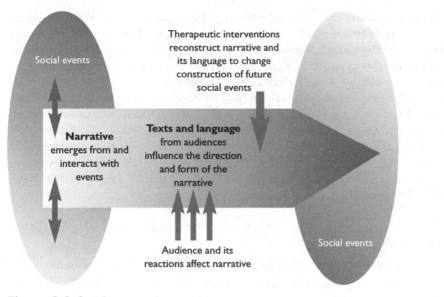

Figure 8.2 Social construction practice

The starting point of Parton and O'Byrne's account is *narrative*. People describing events try to make their story correspond with reality as they perceive it, so their narrative represents their reality. Stories also take into account the audience, so that the representation of reality is affected by the narrator's perceptions of the people listening. Thus every narrative is a social relation: it represents an event, but interprets it within a social relationship. However, every story raises the possibilities of alternative representations, but as it is narrated, it fixes the reality it represents and tries to impose coherence on the elements that comprise it. As a result, its coherence makes a *truth claim*, that is, it seeks to persuade the audience that its claim is true. Communication research shows that in conversations, people take turns and can question each other, but a narrative interprets knowledge and understanding to make it ready to be listened to. Humans interpret and give meaning to events, but must do so within a framework of agreed intelligibility, and the stories we create are formed by the collective narratives of our cultures and communities (Saleebey, 1994). Within cultures and communities, powerful people have more influence on which stories are accepted as truth.

If we are all shaped by cultural and community constructions, we can only achieve our own influence by being aware of how social structures and power construct our knowledge and therefore our world. In Foucault's analysis, our lives are shaped by *normalising truths* produced by the exercise of *power*. They are normalising because people with power have set these truths as conventional social expectations. Thus, these truths gain the respectability of objective reality, and we all join in policing them. Power operates through ideas that gain influence in cultural and social relations, and therefore through language, because ideas are expressed or *signified*, that is, made significant to us, by the language or *signifiers* that we use to express them.

What goes on in the world is, therefore, like reading a *text*. We hear events described and we interpret the narrative in the way that we read books, by bringing our own experience to them. We have experiences and we keep these in our memories as stories; we edit and polish them so that when required they make the points we want to make. So the language we use and the way we produce the text has an important impact on how we understand things. There is also the scope for misunderstanding and conversation allows us to question and take part in a discourse to clarify meanings for ourselves. We are also able to redirect the story by giving the narrator clues about what we are interested in; they will adapt their narrative accordingly. Three different types of narrative, from Gergen and Gergen (1986) and quoted by Parton and O'Byrne (2000: 58), are:

- *Progressive narratives*, where people describe themselves as moving forward to their goals
- *Stability narratives*, where people imply that things are unchanging
- *Digressive narratives*, where people imply that they are moving away from their goals.

Change is going on all the time, but knowing how we can make a difference is an important part of having agency, that is, an impact on things as they change. Being able, through conversation, to identify what has made a difference improves our agency. Thus, co-constructing a narrative with a social worker might help people to understand what things are new in their lives, how they came about and what they did to create them. The past may be a restraint on having agency now, but the most important thing in conversation is to identify *successes* and *exceptions* to problems.

The idea of resistance, used in psychodynamic theory (Chapter 4) is unhelpful. When people do not cooperate, they are showing how not to help them and the worker needs to identify alternative approaches. However, we may see resistance as creating stories of heroism in defeating problems, and this is good for building motivation and learning lessons.

What people talk about and in particular how they discuss problems and solutions is the main focus of practice. Constructive social workers attend to the words spoken about the problem and the desired goals. Some constructionist therapists see people as inviting problems into their lives, influenced by oppressive cultural narratives, For example, thinking that the man is the wage-earner and the woman stays at home may work fine until the man is disabled. By believing this cultural truth, a couple may have invited the problem to happen to them. However, others consider the problem not an important issue, because their constructions are not so affected by the inaccuracy of this cultural assumption.

The first important issue is to discuss desired goals. These should be clear, well constructed and relevant to the user. The worker starts from a position of *not knowing* and maintaining *curiosity*, without asking why. Workers have expertise in asking helpful *questions* and *reframing* stories. The worker will need to distinguish clearly between helping and controlling responsibilities, and help the user to understand this distinction. Sometimes, as where there are statutory responsibilities, an important goal for the user is to end the contact with the worker; the negotiation about goals can proceed on the basis of 'what will get me out of your hair?'

The basis for finding solutions is *exceptions* to the problem or *possibilities* for change. Exceptions (de Shazer's concept) are times when the problem was absent or less and the solution is to find ways of increasing those times, for example by looking at what circumstances brought the exceptions about. Also, the worker looks for talents or competences, no matter how small, and finds ways of *utilising* them. Workers listening to narratives communicate empathy with a 'twist', because they are always looking for ways of reframing the story. For example, if someone says: 'My daughter was so rude to me', a worker might pick up the word 'so' and ask: 'Have there been times when she was less rude?' The worker focuses on the distinction between emotions, thoughts and actions. She was rude, but what were the thoughts and emotions lying behind it? Was there something particular the parent did? Could she do it differently? *Relational reflexivity* means reflecting on the experience of your relationship with the user, being changed by your reflection and therefore responding in a way which incorporates their input to the relationship and your own considered response. Nothing is routine, nothing is defined in advance by an external science: you are responding to people in a relationship with them.

The practice guidance derived from construction ideas is set out in Table 8.1. This account of constructive social work by Parton and O'Byrne (2000) is an amalgamation of the work of O'Hanlon's 'possibility work', White's narrative therapy and de Shazer's solution-focused brief therapy. All these are psychological therapies focusing on careful study of the client's language and on thinking about and reframing possibilities and solutions in the future.

Assessment in constructive social work (Parton and O'Byrne, 2000: 134–51) emphasises taking the time to hear the stories told by clients and validate them. Discussing constructivist assessment, Neimeyer and Neimeyer (1993) argue that people 'make meaning' from narrative structures ('telling stories'). Neimeyer (1993) suggests *laddering*, whereby an interviewer helps someone to delve into the more complex implications of simple statements about themselves, taking a step at a time into more complex ideas. For example, someone who feels the need to keep her emotions controlled comes to see first the implication that she is therefore not relaxed in social situations, then that she can be uncomfortable and that this leads her to be lonely. Neimeyer identifies a number of similar devices, many of a cognitive nature, and some based on Kelly's personal construct theory, to enable people to tell their stories in a structured way. Similarly, particularly with people from different cultures, organised exploration of people's family and life histories through 'oral history' can allow people to examine in a structured way the meanings and constructions they give to their own experiences (Martin, 1995).

Table 8.1 Parton and O'Byrne's constructive social work practice

Process	Aim	Explanation
Introductions Brief social engagement Ask for the story of the problem Take time to get the full story	Attend to language Validate people's experiences/feelings Show how they don't have to feel that way	Acknowledge and validate how they feel Would you prefer some other way?
Ask about negative effects on life, relationships, self-image others' opinions	Question the 'viewing'; create uncertainty; your language opens the door to 'possibility'	Seeing merely the possibility of change Separate yourself from your own 'being-put-down'
Identify person's view of contrast between *this* way of being and the *preferred* way	Resist the problem Externalise the 'doing' (*not* where the problem is the person's violence/oppression of others) Alienating	See yourself resisting the problem Conversations include context and external effects on you Stress accountability for problems created by client Construct problem as outside: 'the sneaky feeling'
Challenge four types of problematic stories	■ Impossibility ideas ■ Blaming ideas ■ Invalidation stories ■ Non-accountability for action	'Can't change' 'She's all bad' 'I'm overanxious' 'I'm just like my father'
Promote externalising stories – times when there were exceptions to the problems **Seven steps:**	■ Naming ■ Effects ■ Exceptions ■ Personalise exceptions ■ New story evidence ■ Futures ■ Social dimensions	'Black dog' = depression Feelings, experiences of problem When things were better When successes led to approval/liking = new identity Past successes, explanations for exceptions Incentives: successful future Others who can support
Use externalising metaphors: ■ Oppression ■ Imprisonment ■ Spying ■ Sports ■ War/violence ■ Seduction ■ Supernatural ■ Crime	Deconstruct the problem: ■ Bullies, silences ■ Ties you up ■ Infiltrate, undermine ■ On the ropes ■ Attacks, defeats ■ Entices, promises ■ Bloodsucker ■ Steals, highjacks	Become the hero/heroine? ■ Resist ■ Liberate yourself ■ Find out the truth ■ Play fair, get a grip ■ Hold the ground, outflank ■ Keep your head, say no ■ Exorcise the ghost ■ Foil, catch, appeal
Storytelling	Tell stories of others' successes	Raises possibilities, helps decide what to do, shows what's OK
Shift from talking problem constructs to talking strengths	Check pre-session exceptions Use exception-finding questions Scaling: on a scale of 1–10 Coping	'Since deciding to ask for help …' 'Day after the miracle?' 'Any small part of the miracle?' Where are you now, where will you end? How could you 'get by'?
Negotiate goals: ■ *Visitors* (in unwilling contact) – focus on things they want ■ *Complainants* (want to change another person) – focus on things they can do ■ *Customers* – want to change	When will we be able to stop? Use active verbs	Specific and achievable: ■ 'Small rather than large' ■ Process: doing something ■ Here and now ■ Positive ■ In the person's control ■ In the person's language ■ Perceived to need hard work
Sessions to discuss progress/achievements (about 45 minutes)	Interweave 'goal-talk' and 'exceptions-talk' 'Future-talk'	What else? What could you be *doing* instead of feeling like that? What will your husband notice? Let's suppose – what would it be like?
Break during sessions	Study language and exceptions	Are exceptions deliberate (under client's control)?
Feedback after break	Compliments linked to tasks	What's gone well, how that contributed to goal
Set tasks	Maintains engagement Encourages practice Encourages thinking about problems	Notice and list things that they want to continue Pretend … or act as if … Predict: what would happen if exceptions occur again?
Subsequent meetings	EARS Repeat scales Focus by using 'too few' questions – the same points put in different ways	**E**licit exact changes **A**mplify changes: what difference did they make? **R**einforce change: compliment **S**tart again: what other changes?

Source: Parton and O'Byrne (2000).

Freddie and Christine

Freddie and Christine are in their twenties, disabled wheelchair-users and recently married. They live in a specially adapted ground-floor apartment provided by a specialist housing association near their parents. Freddie has had severe cerebral palsy from childhood, and Christine is paraplegic after a road traffic accident in her teens. She works as a secretary in a local school, he works as a computer programmer in a company producing specialist systems for insurance companies. Her parents resisted her marriage to someone who was so severely disabled. His parents felt it would be impossible for two such disabled people to live independent lives. Both sets of parents visit a great deal and take on some caring tasks. However, Freddie and Christine want to buy a house more convenient for his work, which has been recently relocated; she would change jobs. Their parents resist this; Freddie and Christine ask the social worker for the regional disability rights association to be their advocate.

Thinking about the situation in advance, what alternative narratives and constructions might be present here? Would role and communication theories have ideas to offer? What interventions might help to resolve people's feelings about the situation? Would psychodynamic, cognitive-behavioural or systems ideas be a better focus than constructive social work, in view of the depth and complexity of feelings? How should the social worker's role be affected by the request for advocacy, rather than help?

Commentary

This account of constructive social work drawing on psychotherapeutic models demonstrates its connections with other social psychological ideas. Reviewing research into various forms of constructionist work, Parton and O'Byrne (2000: 152–69) comment that research into de Shazer's work (de Shazer and Berg, 1997) focuses on whether there is evidence that clients' goals are achieved rather than more conventional outcome measures. Solution-focused work has been evaluated successfully as part of services in a range of agencies. For example, Franklin et al. (2001) report a study using its techniques effectively with school children presenting academic difficulties and classroom behaviour problems.

The advantages of social construction theories for social work (Payne, 1999) are:

- They are social *and* psychological, rather than just one or the other
- They are strong in explaining both social factors as well as personal factors
- Their research base, using detailed analysis of behaviour and language, relates well to practical needs in social work and are already present in social psychological contributions to social work
- There is evidence of successful application in psychotherapeutic practice

- The focus on reflexive, dialogic communication as the basis for practice fits well with the role of social work and critical and empowerment theories (see Chapters 11–14)
- Their emphasis on openness to change is valuable for social work
- Their social theory of influence is flexible and connects well with Eastern modes of practice that emphasise both individual responsibility and social connections (see Chapter 9).

The assets of social psychological models of social work are their incorporation of social psychological precepts about the contribution of social and group relations to the creation of social identity. This helps to understand important aspects of clients' lives. Crawford et al. (2002) suggest, based on work with reflection on narratives, that 'thick', that is, complex and rich, description of clients' lives can be achieved. The use of dialogues and conversation analysis can offer ways of understanding and working with families and networks in an equal and exploratory way (Seikkula et al., 2003). At least in general principle communication and construction models are useful and applicable in practice, and communication theory, in particular, is based on a long, rigorous research tradition. They are applied mainly to assist in clarifying interactions in practice. The theories and the research which lie behind these ideas give practical help in controlling and understanding relationships and interactions with clients and learning a technology of interviewing and interpersonal skills.

Role theory, about expectations around social positions, gives an understanding of social relationships which, allied to better understanding of how communication patterns create such social expectations, creates a useful model for understanding both social and interpersonal aspects of social life.

Communication theory also gives practical ways of intervening using such understanding. Communication theory is relatively neutral in major ideological debates between, for example, behaviourists and psychoanalysts or critical theorists and functionalists, for this reason. Role theory, however, is generally functional in character. Both accept a role for environment, and also for internal thinking and emotions. However, they may not always emphasise sufficiently, or permit intervention in, the emotional and social origins of behaviour.

Role theory, which sees roles as presentations of the self, and developments of communications theory, which are concerned with how language constructs meaning in social situations, present unthreatening ways of helping people understand behaviour. These ideas connect social psychological theory to the wider social aspects of situations. This permits, at least notionally, the possibility of using social psychological concepts in the understanding of the creation of social identity, rather than relying, as social work has tended to, on developmental psychology as the basis for understanding human development. Nelsen's (1980) account of communication theory creates a comprehensive theory of action at least in therapeutic situations but it has not succeeded in introducing communication and other social psychological concepts to wider use. This may be partly because her work was produced before more complex theories about communication, social identity and social meaning began to develop into social construction ideas. White et al. (1994) demonstrate that it is also crucial to participatory work in social development and more generally.

Problems with communication theory lie in its concentration on the style and nature of the interactions rather than the content. Although content is said to be important, how to assess it is not well articulated. We noted criticisms of psychoanalysis that it encourages workers to look for inferred thoughts and problems behind difficulties that clients expressly present. Social psychology presents similar problems. The worker is seen as relatively competent, compared with the client, and may even be a manipulative and devious figure. One feature of the model, the use of paradox, particularly gives rise to this criticism. Compared with psychoanalysis, however, interaction with clients is relatively open in a communication model. With the practical problems that many clients face, role and communication ideas have little to offer. Contacts with other agencies, and competence in everyday life may be enhanced for the client, but different techniques are presumably needed to gain social security entitlements.

The recent development of social construction to provide social work theory relies on work in clinical psychotherapy and partly builds on social psychological perspectives, but has much broader connections to cultural theory and phenomenological sociology (see Chapter 9). It provides a way of targeting many of the softer issues that clients face in an organised way, but deriving from clients' own accounts of what is happening, rather than imposing the various complex theoretical structures of cognitive theory. Lee (2003) argues that its focus on pragmatic change and people creating solutions for themselves allows workers to focus on cultural strengths and thus combat discrimination and cultural insensitivity. This has proved attractive as a way of engaging clients and effective in meeting their aims in therapeutic kinds of social work.

However, there are criticisms. If constructive ideas are taken to extremes, they assume that all perceptions and values are relative, and this makes it difficult for workers to negotiate on behalf of clients and family and community members or agencies that take different views, since all views are equally valued (Northcut and Heller, 2002). It may be less helpful for achieving welfare service objectives. For example, Parton and O'Byrne (2000) point to the value of construction ideas in finding creative, non-oppressive ways of working with children, young people and parents in child protection work, and construction ideas have been useful in developing creative assessments. However, its focus on openness to, and relativity in, people's perceptions of the world make it less easy to incorporate into care management (managed care) assessments and other situations. This is because formal assessments fitting in with agencies' and legal requirements do not fit with its openness to interpretation, and its focus on people's stories is liable to misinterpretation by seeing stories as 'fictions', rather than as views of the world.

OVERVIEW

- Ideas from social psychology provide detailed assistance in interaction with clients and understanding how their social relations interact with their psychological reactions. However, they did not stimulate a general model of social work practice until social construction ideas began to have an impact.

- Social construction theories have generated a practice model that responds particularly to clients' own views of their world and assessment of their problems.

- Constructive social work is a positive, forward-looking approach to clients' problems rather than a backward-looking, blaming one.

- However, its focus on variability and opportunity have raised doubts about its uses where social control and surveillance are important issues.

- Ideas such as solution-focused work, narrative, impossibility thinking, and looking for exceptions in clients' failed coping mechanisms, have been useful and positive and connect with contemporary social science developments.

- In social construction research, ideas such as conversation analysis could contribute to an understanding of interactions in social work.

- These ideas are not fully developed as social work theories.

FURTHER READING

Chambon, A. S., Irving, A. and Epstein, L. (eds) (1999) *Reading Foucault for Social Work* (New York: Columbia University Press).
A useful collection of articles showing how Foucault's work has been applied to social work.

Franklin, C. and Nurius, P. S. (eds) (1998) *Constructivism in Practice Methods and Challenges* (Milwaukee, WI: Families International).
Useful American practice text, particularly concerned with constructivism rather than social construction.

Parton, N. and O'Byrne, P. (2000) *Constructive Social Work: Towards a New Practice* (Basingstoke: Macmillan – now Palgrave Macmillan).
A useful account of the application of social construction ideas to social work.

Saleebey, D. (ed.) (2001) *The Strengths Perspective in Social Work Practice*, 3rd edn (Boston, MA: Allyn & Bacon).
This American model of practice uses some aspects of construction theory, and is well known in the USA, but not elsewhere. There is a website: http://www.socwel.ku.edu/publications/strengths/index.shtml.

CHAPTER 9

Humanism, Existentialism and Spirituality

What this chapter is about

Humanism and existentialism are well-established philosophies that have had a particular influence on social work and have influenced particular practice theories. Spirituality is a related aspect of humanity concerned with the common, some would say universal, human need to find in our lives meaning and importance that transcends, that is, rises above, mere survival. All these ideas have relevance to social work practice. They connect to approaches to social work in minority ethnic groups and particularly non-Western cultures that are increasingly influencing social work thinking. The concern with human experience and artistic and cultural aspects of social relationships have been seen as radical, in that they refuse to take for granted the modernist assumptions of evidence-based professionalisation; however, their approach is centrally reflexive-therapeutic since their main purpose is achieving human potential and growth, rather than social change.

MAIN POINTS

➤ Humanism, existentialism and spirituality are different interpretations of important elements of human experience and social work, concerned with the integrity of human experience and its personal and social purposes and meaning.

➤ Many non-Western religions give great importance to these issues, but their use in Western societies has led to a sense of importing exotic religions, whereas most cultural views see spiritual concerns as universal.

➤ Understanding the spirituality of many minority ethnic groups in Western countries is important to adequate understanding of their social and personal needs.

➤ Symbolic interaction, phenomenological sociology, Laing's view of mental illness, Rogers' client- or person-centred practice, gestalt therapy, Gandhian social work and transactional analysis are all relevant ideas focusing in different ways on human experience, social justice and social and ecological sustainability.

> ▶ Glassman and Kates' humanistic groupwork and Thompson's existentialist social work offer examples of interpretations of these ideas in systematic accounts of social work practice.

PRACTICE ISSUES AND CONCEPTS

> ▶ *Self-actualisation* and *self-fulfilment* as social work objectives.

> ▶ *Empathy, congruence, genuineness* and *unconditional positive regard* as attributes of the worker in successful practice.

> ▶ *Scripts* and *games* as patterns of behaviour.

> ▶ Spiritual ideas of *wholeness* and *connectedness* as human aims and values.

> ▶ *Decentralisation, sustainability* and *interdependence* as important social objectives.

> ▶ *Democracy* and *participation* as elements of practice.

> ▶ *Dread* and *alienation* in peoples' lives.

> ▶ The transactional analysis metaphor of people having a *parent, adult* and *child* interacting internally and externally.

Wider theoretical perspectives

Humanism and existentialism are ways of looking at life, based on well-established philosophies. *Humanism* believes in the capacity of conscious human beings to reason, make choices and act freely, uninfluenced by gods and religion. Because social work is part of the secularisation of welfare, as it separated from the churches in the 1800s, it is strongly associated with humanism, and leads people with a strong religious faith to question it. Humanism is different from being humane, which is the practice of treating people with kindness because we value their humanity. Humanism is also associated with democracy, because of its belief in the capacity of human beings to value and participate with one another in controlling their destiny. An example of such an association is Glassman and Kates's (1990) book on humanist groupwork, discussed below. They see groups as supporting democratic and humanist principles because they allow people's participation in working together on an equal basis.

Existentialism is concerned with the meaning for human beings of the fact of their existence. It focuses on the capacity of people to gain the personal power to control their lives and change ideas governing how they live. People are accepted as both 'subjects' and 'objects', that is, they both act on and are affected by the environment. It is accepted that the environment contains absurd and alienating experiences and suffering. Major streams of thought are based around the work of Büber, Kierkegaard and Sartre. Sartre's work has had most impact on social work theory (Blom, 1994). Thompson's (1992) book, discussed below, applies Sartre's ideas to social work.

Although social work is associated with Western secularisation, in many countries welfare has remained connected to religious faith, since many individuals take up social work as a way of putting their faith into practice, and many social work agencies are associated with or developed by churches and faith groups. Also, social work with individuals often raises or deals with spiritual issues in people's lives. *Spirituality* is a human search for meaning and purpose in life, to see being human as incorporating into a whole personality a wide variety of experiences. Stanworth (2004: Ch 2) connects this human wish for integrity of meaning in our lives with the heightened physical experience of people in sport or the shared experience of musicians playing together. She reviews evidence that many people experience spiritual events that induce awe, wonder and a sense of wholeness within them. People may feel this during the birth of their child, for example, or when going through personal difficulties such as divorce or bereavement, as they try to make sense of the experience as part of their whole lives. They may say that their child's birth made them or their family feel complete or that their husband suddenly leaving them is a mid-life crisis.

Many Eastern philosophies have relationships with spirituality and some of the elements of humanism and existentialism, especially Zen Buddhism, but also Hinduism and aspects of Islam. This is because they emphasise the process whereby human beings realise their capacity to enhance their own well-being through spiritual self-development. The high value given to religious faith is an important distinction of such philosophies from humanism and existentialism. Such religious philosophies have had direct impact on the thinking of many therapists, particularly in seeing people as 'awakening' aspects of their personality and gaining insight into their self (see for example Claxton, 1986; Young-Eisendrath and Muramoto, 2002).

Similarly, African and Caribbean spiritual perspectives have had a considerable influence on what Martin and Martin (2002) call the 'black helping tradition' in social work in the USA and elsewhere. In this tradition, the spiritual self interacts with a racial self and a communal self. Traditional caregiving in African tribes connected with black spirituality, which created a sense of the sacred and divine that gave African-American people a sense of dignity and self-worth as slaves. In particular, family relationships and child care were important sources of solidarity and maintained connections across the generations (Graham, 2002). These perspectives are considered briefly below.

Some relationships exist between humanist and existential ideas and 'green' political and social philosophies (George and Wilding, 1994). These emphasise the importance of human beings controlling their destructive capacities and living in harmony with their environments. Such ideas have had some impact on residential care through communes focusing on shared living (Pepper, 1991). These views have been marginal in their social importance and their influence on social work, but are increasingly influential on younger people through the impact of eco-critical ideas (Chapter 7).

Similarly, we can see relationships with feminist theories. This is because they focus on women's shared experience in developing a consciousness of their oppressed social position (see Chapter 12). Also the control of capacities claimed to be associated with men, such as violence, which might be destructive of equal and harmonious social relations, is an important feature of feminist ideas. Here again, we can see the importance given to humanist, participative self-development, while recognising the need to control the destruction implicit in existing social relationships. This also has connections to Kohut's self-psychology (see Chapter 4), which, while it focuses on the organisation of the self, also acknowledges the idea of the 'tragic man', in which imperfections and failings always interfere with self-organisation (Klugman, 2002).

Connections

While they have specific philosophical meanings, in social work theory, models of practice with certain features are grouped together as humanist. These models have in common ideas that human beings are trying to make sense of the world they experience. Also, social workers are trying to help people to gain the skills to explore themselves and the personal meanings they attach to the world they perceive and which affect them. Humanist models propose that people's interpretations of their own selves are valid and worthwhile. The importance of spirituality in many cultures, particularly non-Western ones, means that it is an important issue in understanding social work approaches in African and Eastern countries and where working with black and minority ethnic groups. Many ideas from spiritual perspectives in such cultures are consequently beginning to influence Western social work. Graham (2002), for example, presents aspects of African-centred world views as both a critique of Western social work theories and a way of understanding African Caribbean people. Wright and Anderson (1998) survey the considerable literature on the culturally based strengths of African-American families as a basis of practice. Mikulas (2002) seeks to integrate aspects of Eastern and Western traditions, particularly linking cognitive and behavioural ideas, which in some ways focus on self-control, with Eastern meditation as a form of control of the self. These views are still not mainstream approaches in Western social work and counselling, for the same reason that the impact of Western social work in Eastern and African practice has been criticised. That is, they do not connect well with the role of social work in Western welfare regimes and have been picked up mainly by counsellors with a particular interest. The connection with ecological ideas is an example of this. Ecological systems theory (Chapter 7) has been mainly concerned with intervening in social relations rather than harmonising human relationships.

Such concepts are closely related to constructivist and constructionist views of the world, considered in their psychological incarnation in Chapter 8. We saw in Chapters 1 and 3 that this precludes a focus on objective, neutral views of behaviour and social interaction (Allen, 1993). Workers generate multiple ideas by working with people on constructing a variety of meanings to their experiences (Dean, 1993) and creating a new idea of their 'self' (Fisher, 1991). One approach may be to identify contrasts and dualities in experiences, eliciting and reconstructing accounts which involve experiences of power, choice and change (Fisher, 1991). *Discourse analysis,* related to postmodernist and post-structuralist ideas (Rojek et al., 1989), similarly seeks to incorporate the reality of diversity and ambiguity into the way we represent people, their social world and the role of social workers through language. Rodger (1991), for example, shows how using the language of 'contracts' in negotiations with clients about who is to do what within a social work relationship introduces uncertainty and conflict into the negotiation because of differences between professional and everyday understandings of the meaning of 'contract' (see Chapter 5 for another area of this debate).

Well-known systems of practice and writers in social work and related fields are regarded as humanist or existentialist. Their ideas have filtered into more general use. Examples are Laing's views of mental health, Rogers' client- (more recently person-) centred therapy; and a variety of writers such as Brandon and Keefe on thought systems such as Zen and meditation, the gestalt therapy of Perls et al. (1973), and occasional enthusiasts such as Bradford (1969), Krill (1978, 1990) and Thompson (1992) have provided a literature applying these ideas to social work. Goldstein (1981, 1984) has attempted to adapt cognitive theory and make it more social work-friendly by adding an explicitly humanist element; much of his work included humanist, spiritual and artistic elements applied to both education and practice (Gray, 2002). Berne's (1961) transactional analysis, although its origins lie in psychodynamic theory, is also often regarded as humanist in approach, because of its focus on self-understanding through analysis of patterns of communication and behaviour.

The politics of humanism, existentialism and spirituality

Humanism is both basic and peripheral to social work theory. It is basic because many take it for granted as the fundamental attitude of social workers, for example Mullaly (2003) incorrectly treats it as a synonym for humanitarianism. It is peripheral in that it is not even treated as a perspective, since it is seen more as a general philosophical position informing practice than a way of defining a specific approach to practice. Existentialism and Eastern philosophies are even more of a fringe interest, taken up by only a few.

However, some writers have presented a critique of many social work theories and perspectives for being too technical and medical (individualist-reformist). In doing so, they are reasserting the importance of a belief in the capacity of humanity to improve itself, which we often see as central to social work. They often also rail against the tendency to make social work, especially in large state agencies, too technical and bureaucratic. Emphasising the humanity of the objectives and ideals of social work is a counter-position (for example Hugman, 1977). It seeks to re-establish the focus of social work as reflexive-therapeutic in character, and therefore in some respects opposed to socialist-collectivist and individualist-reformist. Nonetheless, existentialism particularly relates to radical-critical concerns about alienation, although the explanation of and approach to alienation are different, and the valuation of democratic processes and human participation also speaks to radical and feminist approaches to social work. Goldstein's (1981, 1984) attempts to humanise cognitive approaches to social work create some alliances with technical and individual-reformist approaches to social work. Again, therefore, we can see the tensions between and connections among these different perspectives on social work.

Crucial in many areas of work is the idea of working on people's self-esteem, and self-understanding towards empowerment objectives (see Chapter 14). This can be important where clients experience oppression due to ethnic difference (Greene et al., 1996). Family therapy and, through this activity, social work ideas have taken on social construction and constructivist aspects which are regarded as replacements or developments of systems ideas (Kelley, 1994).

Humanism, and such views of social work, are often taken as part of the cause of public criticism of social work for being vague and idealistic.

Some humanist influences on social work

Person-centred ideas

Carl Rogers (1951, 1961; Rogers and Strauss, 1967) is probably the most important humanist writer on therapy to have an influence on social work. His impact is, however, indirect, since his greatest significance is in the related field of counselling. Social workers' involvement in counselling work and training has moved his ideas into social work. Another significant influence is his formulation of the conditions necessary to successful therapy. These are that *clients should perceive* that workers act as follows:

- They are *genuine* and *congruent* in their therapeutic relationship (that is, what they say and do reflects their personality and real attitudes and is not put on to influence clients).
- They have *unconditional positive regard* for clients.
- They *empathise* with clients' views of the world.

Carkhuff and his associates (Truax and Carkhuff, 1967; Carkhuff and Berenson, 1977) have adapted these ideas into a more general concept. These are, first, honesty and genuineness; second, (sometimes non-possessive) warmth, respect, acceptance; and third, empathic understanding. Carkhuff's work proposes scales by which we may assess the extent of these in a therapeutic relationship. Empirical work has confirmed that these are the effective elements in therapeutic relationships. Rogers' development of understanding of the relationship and effective elements within it has been his major influence on social work.

The worker's approach, according to Rogers, should be non-directive, non-judgemental and, in later formulations, should involve 'active listening', 'accurate empathy' and 'authentic friendship'. Rogers developed a humanist perspective, concentrating on the importance of the 'self' seeking personal growth. There is an emphasis on the 'here and now' rather than on the history of clients' problems. Because of the belief in clients' uniqueness, diagnosis and classification of conditions is not accepted. Everyone must be treated as an individual. Rogers' later ideas extended into taking up these humanist ideas in community work, organisations and political change. He proposes that we should enable people to take up their 'personal power' which we all possess to achieve their objectives (Rogers, 1977).

Besides Rogers' work, there are several humanist psychologies and therapies which were influential in the 1960s and 70s. Carkhuff and Berenson (1977) suggest that five ideas characterise them all, as follows:

- We can only understand ourselves in relation to others.
- Our main anxiety in life is losing others and being alone.
- We are guilty because we cannot achieve a creative life.
- We alone have responsibility to act on our own decisions.
- Therapy aims to help us to act and accept freedom and responsibility in doing so.

Many ideas in humanistic psychology derive from Maslow's concern for 'self-actualisation' and the attainment of 'human potential' (Maslow, 1970). Maslow's basic theory, like psychoanalysis, supposes that the motivation to act for such purposes comes from a need which derives from something we are lacking. It has been applied to social care work in day centres, since it enables workers to see which clients' needs they are meeting and whether clients may move forward to achieve higher levels of potential in creative activities (Kennett, 2001). Frankl's (1964) logotherapy is typical in emphasising that we each must find our own meaning in life. A development of Frankl's work in family therapy proposes that the human search for meaning is best achieved within a family context (Lantz, 1987). Some writers (for example Keefe, 1996) promote meditation for exploring oneself and one's potential, and in increasing workers' capability to be empathetic with and conscious of clients' needs. Wolf and Abell (2003) tested the effects of Indian meditation with Americans with problems of stress and depression, and found it to be helpful as part of a more general approach to spiritual help.

Eastern, artistic and symbolic ideas

Brandon (1976, 2000) offered Zen ideas as a useful contribution to social work. His was an intense and personal vision in which workers should use all the elements of their personality to arrive at an authentic interrelationship with people in distress. Unlike many humanistic approaches to therapy, which have been criticised as therapies only for the mildly disturbed, seeking greater personal fulfilment, he sought to approach people in extreme difficulties. Work was directed towards self-understanding, enlightenment (the Zen concept is *satori*, a leap towards intuitive understanding) and self-growth for both worker and client. An important idea was 'hindering' people's movement towards self-development, and enabling them to avoid the many features of their environments which do so. Brandon's approach relied on personal charisma and sharing between clients and workers.

Several writers, for example England (1986), argue that we should see social work as an artistic endeavour rather than an application of social science. Walter (2003) argues for a sense of improvisation and seeing interactions with clients as provisional rather than contractual, which derives from theatrical ideas. Many writers use art and literature to aid an understanding of the world and assist in helping (Rose, 1992; Sanders, 1993). Black and Enos (1981) claim that phenomenological ideas validate this approach. This is because phenomenology argues that we can only understand human behaviour from the viewpoint of the people involved. Methods are required to explore and understand individual viewpoints. England extends this into a humanist theory of social work, based around the ideas of 'coping' (a concept important in ego psychology) and 'meaning' (also important in spirituality). As in personal construct theory (see Chapter 8), how social workers, clients and others around them attach meaning to events crucially affects how workers will deal with them. The idea of making sense is a way of humanising and interpreting clients as worthwhile contributors to society. Lantz and Greenlee (1990) show, in a discussion of working with war veterans, the importance of seeing a sense of meaning in distressing past situations.

Laing (1965, 1971) explicitly used existential ideas as well as psychoanalysis in his early work on theories of mental illness. These have had some influence in social work, particularly in the UK. In later work he became more radical and mystical (Sedgwick, 1972). His important work was on schizophrenia, and he argued that we can understand this major psychotic mental illness as a person's reaction to a bewildering or possibly damaging social environment. He gave great importance to the 'self' in his discussion of the 'false-self system' and self-consciousness. Later, he picked up the ideas of communication theories in the family, in particular the *double-bind* of Bateson et al. (1956). He proposed that disturbances in family communications lead to one family member being caught between conflicting demands from others, leading to disturbed reactions diagnosed as schizophrenia. Particularly in psychiatric settings, Laing's work taught social workers to be cautious about medical diagnoses which fail to consider social and family factors as possible elements in the cause of problems. More widely, symbolic interactional and phenomenological sociology has influenced work in settings where other people who are often regarded as deviant (such as offenders) are dealt with.

Symbolic interactionism is a sociological and social psychological perspective deriving from the work of George Herbert Mead (1934) and Blumer (1969). The basic idea is that people act according to symbols (ideas that stand in place) of the outside world which they hold in their minds. They create their symbols through interpreting interactions between themselves and the outside world, using language. Their self is similarly created because, to have interactions with the outside world, they must have an idea also of the being which is undertaking the interaction. To think about the world, therefore, people have to have interactions with themselves. Such ideas have links with personal construct theory, in which people's behaviour is seen as organised according to the internal constructs they hold about the external world, and social construction (Chapter 8). Ramon (1990) argues that symbolic interactionist ideas help people to understand the process of leaving a psychiatric hospital. This experience can be interpreted as a rite of passage in anthropological terms, a transition crisis and a process which threatens and requires the reinterpretation of self-identity.

Chaiklin (1979) argues that symbolic interactionism offers an alternative for social workers to a purely psychological mode of understanding human behaviour. Focusing on interactions and symbols may be less demanding emotionally for both client and worker than the traditional close relationship. Moreover, these ideas assume the basic normality and competence of most people, rather than assuming illness or maladaption and an inability to control their own destiny. One of the most important of these is the idea of labelling, which we met in Chapter 8.

Many of these ideas relate to role, social psychological and social construction theories explored in Chapter 8, for two reasons. First, symbolic interaction and related sociological ideas are concerned with social expectations and interpretations which are the meat of role theory, and accepting and interpreting roles are important aspects of the use of symbols in interaction. Second, as noted in Chapter 8, Goffman's ideas of role, in which people are seen as presenting themselves in different ways according to the social circumstances of the moment, are a significant variant of role theory, which stems from symbolic and phenomenological ideas.

Although broadly sociological, such ideas also offer important explanations for intense emotion. Smith (1975), for example, shows how the feelings associated with bereavement may be fully explained not by conventional explanations from psychoanalysis which rely on 'biological, instinctual and internal psychic processes' (p. 79), but by phenomenological explanations. On this basis, grief arises from the unique place allocated to certain relationships (such as marriage) within social expectations, and from the reorganisation of our social constructions of our world according to such expectations. When the relationship is lost, a social reconstruction must take place. Moreover, at the personal level, we construct ourselves including the lost person, and that internal reconstruction must also take place.

Wilkes (1981) argues, from a broadly humanist standpoint, that many 'undervalued groups' of clients, whose disability or problem we cannot cure immediately, would benefit from social work which was concerned with exploring meaning within their lives. The worker would share experiences in a liberating way, rather than make a fetish of method and achieving specific therapeutic aims, which is inappropriate with many clients.

Krill's work, formulated in articles in the 1960s (for example Krill, 1969) reached full expression in his book on existential social work (1978) and later work emphasising wisdom gained from practice experience as the basis for social work knowledge (1990). It is an eclectic model, taking insights from Rogers, gestalt psychology, Zen and similar philosophies, but its starting point is existential philosophy. Existentialism in his work is presented as about how we cope with the fact that our existence faces us with wanting to live a life which nonetheless has many unsatisfactory aspects. In the later work, Krill (1990) focuses on the importance of finding meaning within subjective understanding of the world. In finding subjective meaning, people should not be seen as the categories of their problems. Rather, they have personal freedom to be creative in dealing with the 'spirals of desire' that affect them. He argues that mere wishes become more intense as we experience them continually. This might lead to addiction, for example. To change, people need to broaden the range of their interests, but focus on particular interests. As a result, they can move from simply thinking about something, to seeing it as possible and then to being committed to it.

Spirituality

Spirituality as an element of practice has experienced a resurgence in the 2000s (Bullis, 1996; Canda, 1998, 2003; Nash and Stewart, 2002). Throughout the 1900s, the professionalisation of social work tended to emphasise its technical and rational elements in the importance given to rational knowledge bases. Evidence-based practice (Chapter 3), for example, encourages transparent sharing of evidence with clients in a process of rational decision-making, and incorporates spiritual elements, if at all, because clients would raise them. The concern for spirituality has arisen because of the growing impact in social work thinking of the following factors:

- social work is practised in societies where religion and spirituality are integral parts of living
- the need to respond to ethnic and cultural minorities in Western societies
- political interest in the possibility of faith communities and churches making a stronger contribution to organised care and community services, thus contributing to social stability, alongside evidence that spirituality and religious participation prevent some social difficulties from arising (for example Hodge et al., 2001)
- criticism of materialism and consumerist tendencies towards commodification in Western societies, that is, treating everything as though it was a good to be purchased in the economic system, and a perceived need to rebalance these tendencies with different ways of finding meaning in life.

Some of these trends are criticised because they seem to be rejecting the economic and social success of rational, technical development as part of economic development. Moreover, the interest in Eastern religions, such as Taoism and Buddhism, suggests an interest in the exotic rather than ideas that can be relevant and useful in contemporary societies.

A range of social work writing seeks to interpret religious or spiritual beliefs in particular cultures and ethnic groups to increase understanding by others, while others seek to extract useful ideas for practice from particular ethnic and cultural beliefs. For example, Ng (2003) examines the healing practices of Chinese shamans and argues for the value of seeking a feeling of harmony, consistency and integrity as a social work objective; Hurdle (2002) examines traditional Hawaiian healing; Voss et al. (1999) examine social work using tribal and shamanic traditions in the Lakota tribe; Lynn (2001) looks at helping in an Australian aborigine group; and Wolf (2003) explores Indian Vedic philosophy. More generally, Ng (2003) argues that it is not possible for workers to know about and understand the range of spiritual beliefs they meet, and these will often conflict with the worker's own beliefs.

An alternative approach is to identify principles that might inform a practice that has a greater concern with spiritual issues than many models of social work. This is a characteristic of more recent writings. For example, Consedine (2002) argues that spirituality requires four principles to inform practice:

- the idea of a *common good*, aiming for decentralisation, solidarity and connect-edness, protecting human rights and protecting and finding options for poor, oppressed and deprived people
- *sustainability*, that we should respect and work for economic and social systems that do not impose demands on resource-poor countries or future generations
- *wisdom*, the incorporation of carefully thought-out value judgements in our practice
- *holistic spirituality*, a concern for finding, developing, understanding and appreciating wholeness and integrity in our lives and actions.

Many of these ideas also connect to the growing concern for a practice that recognises ecological issues (see Chapter 7). Okundaye et al. (1999), for example, see non-Western spirituality as promoting people's natural authority through interconnectedness with the social and natural environment, rather than through the application of power in formal hierarchies. Wolf (2003) argues that Indian Vedic theory usefully focuses on the self as a non-material personal entity, separate from the body and the material world. Thus, our awareness that we are, for example, black or disabled is part of the material world that covers up our self and limits the free will that our self possesses. Social work practice seeks to get in touch with the self, covered up by all these material limitations, and stimulate and enable its free will to interact with the world and create personal and social change.

Stewart (2002) seeks to develop ideas for practice from many spiritual concerns:

- overcoming barriers to the development of spirituality, transcending materi-alism, fragmentation and linear and technical ways of understanding the world
- connecting beliefs and values to important cultural values, by being sensitive to cultural beliefs and values, aware of the importance of culture to people's spirituality and aware of and promoting the validity of cultural diversity
- developing a spiritual practice, by raising spiritual issues as part of cultural sensitivity, strengthening the importance of spirituality, integrity and wholeness, identifying and valuing differences in world views, being competent in working with diverse cultures, and finding and developing inclusive perspec-tives, rather than seeing spirituality and cultural issues as separate from social work practice.

Bullis (1996: Ch 3) suggests that spiritual issues can be incorporated into practice. For example, spiritual concerns may be assessed and addressed in work with clients.

Graham: African-centred world views

Graham (2002) provides a particularly well-worked out example of the applica-bility of non-Western spiritual ideas to social work in her account of African-centred world views, based on classical African intellectual traditions. They are also influenced by the civil rights and Pan-African movements, which seek unification of African world views following the social fragmentation caused by the experience of slavery and colonialism. The approach used in relation to Africans is applicable also to other minority ethnic groups. *Liberation* philosophies fall into three groups:

- redressing the political, social and cultural oppression under colonialism, imperialism and racism
- analysing the constraints on African societies through traditional African philosophy and ideals
- critical analysis of Western concepts of science and philosophy in its disparagement of African peoples.

The emphasis is on identifying, analysing and celebrating what is special about being African through cultural symbols, rituals, art, music and literature, so as to revise the commonplace disparagement of Africa and its peoples. This would identify and affirm a distinctive African place within wider social theories and practices. The principles of an *African-centred world view* are:

- All things are interconnected, for example people, animals and inanimate objects.
- Human beings are spiritual, that is, connected to others and their creator.
- Individuals cannot be understood separately from their collective identity, particularly their twinlineal (that is, taking account of both father's and mother's parentage) family trees. People's lives and experiences are integral with their family and community histories and connections, and commonalities are more important than individuality.
- Mind, body and spirit are one, equal and interrelated; each should be equally developed towards *maat*, a balanced sense of truth, right, harmony and order.

Maat is expressed in four areas of life:

- the universality of seeking harmony and place in our lives
- justice as the centre of practice
- duty as part of our community
- personhood making concrete the universal order in ourselves.

Rightness in the natural order of things connects to righteousness in social justice. There is a reciprocity between people; good begets good in exchange. Reciprocity in justice is obligatory, putting our ideology into action, and brings good in others. Self-realisation is achieved by having an ethic of caring for others and doing things that benefit the community. Womanhood is sacred in African communities as part of spiritual life in the community; women contributing to moral knowledge is part of their contribution to the community. The caring ideal is represented by women through mothering, and through the female god; it is a spiritual ideal and knowledge that is a crucial social skill.

Graham comments that these cultural ideals, while they emphasise that holistic spirituality is an important ideal, tend to provide a 'totalising discourse', that is, they try to provide one consistent account of the culture and beliefs of a large and diverse continent. However, the Pan-African movement can be seen as a political expression of the struggle for recognition and valuation, in a world where African culture and ideals have been disparaged. Such cultural ideals are a part of that struggle.

Gandhian social work

Gandhi was an Indian leader who formulated a philosophy of social development that has influenced social work in India, particularly because of its impact on the welfare of untouchables (people of the lowest social caste), women and rural areas (Muzumdar, 1964; Howard, 1971). Kumar (1995) summarises the main points of Gandhi's philosophy as follows:

- Reliance on Vedic philosophy
- People are both interdependent and self-reliant
- The spiritual is important in all worldly affairs
- Faith in purity of means rather than achieving ends is important
- Totality or holistic ideas are important especially in relation to political independence; social development, self-reliance and education should go with political independence – such ideas are important in social development (Chapter 10)
- Formal legal authority is disapproved, interdependence and self-reliance are, as the previous point suggests, more important.

The ideal society would contain:

- *Ram rajya:* a morally based social system; both justice and social justice are entwined in a democratic state. Simplicity and sustainable development would be the aim in a minimal state that would connect with a society in which people focused on their duties rather than their rights.
- *Sawraj:* independence, mainly of states from interferences but also of individuals from the state. Gandhi sees the state as an organised and centralised form of violence. He seeks a minimal state characterised by personal responsibility.
- *Swadeshi:* self-reliance in economic, political and social relationships. Production of the necessities of life should be close to consumption.
- *Village republics:* decentralisation and delegation of power to the lowest possible level.
- *Trusteeship:* in an attempt to marry socialism and capitalism, Gandhi proposes a system of considerable legal regulation of the economic system.

These ideas were important for social development (Chapter 10). He proposed rural development based on cottage industries, physical labour rather than the use of machinery, decentralisation of power and social justice and the equitable distribution of wealth. Kumar (1995) argues that these romantic philosophies nevertheless connect with social work values of promoting self-reliance, mutual help and personal and social development that rely on small, local groups rather than top-down direction. The process and means by which activities are carried out and the high value attached to collaboration and avoidance of compulsion are also shared philosophies.

Transactional analysis

Transactional analysis (TA) derives from the work of Eric Berne (1961, 1964) and has some obvious links with psychoanalytic personality structures, and some aspects of its terminology. It is, however, usually regarded as a form of humanistic therapy since its basic principles rely, unlike the more deterministic psychoanalytic theory, on the assumption that people are responsible, autonomous agents who have the energy and capacity to control their own lives and solve their own problems, but they are prevented from doing so only by left-over failings of early childhood behaviour patterns (Pitman, 1982). TA developed completely independently of psychoanalysis, with its own literature and training schemes. Pitman (1983) provides an introduction applying it to social work and Cooper and Turner (1996) a briefer account, which includes reference to some recent practice development, but it has not been widely integrated into social work with other techniques. It is, rather, a system of therapy which specially and separately trained people sometimes undertake within social work agencies. Some of the jargon, especially 'games' and 'strokes', is used without calling on the full system of thought.

There are four elements of TA: structural, transactional, games and script analyses. *Structural* analysis proposes that our personality has three 'ego states', ways of thinking about the world. These are associated with typical behaviour patterns. The parent state is a collection of attitudes typical of the sort of injunctions that a parent figure might give to a child, and the sort of perceptions that a child might have of such a figure. The child state contains feelings and attitudes left over from childhood, typically rather self-centred, but also uncontrolled and potentially creative. The adult state manages, mostly rationally, the relationships between the ego states and with the outside world. These concepts are like the psychoanalytic structures of superego, id and ego, but TA is less concerned with internal interactions among parts of the mind and drives and irrational responses. *Transactional* analysis is about how ego states in one person interact with those in another. Transactions are exchanges between people's ego states, which may be open or hidden. When open and hidden messages involve different ego states or transactions, problems arise. There are three kinds of transaction: 'complementary', where only two ego states are in play; 'crossed', where several are involved but verbal and non-verbal messages are consistent; and 'ulterior', where again several ego states are involved, but the open messages are different from the hidden ones. In practice, workers use transactional analysis to find out which ego states are involved in transactions, and help clients to use communication more constructively.

Games analysis is concerned with patterns of interaction and behaviour. People have three groups of emotional needs:

- stimulation, which they fulfil by artistic, leisure and work activities
- recognition, which is met by receiving 'strokes' either non-verbal or verbal, positive or negative from others (for example respectively, a smile and a thank you or a scowl and a criticism)
- structure in life, particularly of time.

The pattern of strokes and life experiences that we get used to in childhood sets up our life position, which is about how we feel about ourselves and others, and our general attitude to the world. There are four life positions (Harris, 1973), set out in Table 9.1.

Games are typical patterns of ulterior transactions which recur, reflect and promote damaging life positions. Workers analyse games with clients, who can then understand and avoid them in favour of more satisfying interactions. *Script* analysis is concerned with seeing how transactions in the past have led to present life positions and games.

From this brief account, it will be seen that TA is an attractive formulation of behaviour, emphasising communication patterns, which relates closely to more conventional communication theory (see Chapter 8). Its evident links with psychoanalysis should not be overemphasised, since it has travelled a long way from instinctual drives and determinism. There are clear relationships with ego psychology and psychodynamic structures of the personality. As a method, it may be criticised in the same way as psychodynamic theory for relying on insight. Other criticisms are that the technique is largely psychotherapeutic and does not have much to say about clients' practical problems of poverty and oppression. At least, however, supporters of TA would say that they can be helped to avoid oppressing themselves. Finally, it can be argued that it is a shallow technique, giving superficial accounts of behaviour in a jargon which might make some people feel that they are not being treated with respect, rather than permitting a thoughtful analysis of behaviour.

Table 9.1 The four life positions in transactional analysis

Life position	Meaning
I'm OK – you're OK	You feel good about yourself and others
I'm OK – you're not OK	You feel good about yourself but not about others, so you tend to blame others for your own problems, and criticise them (rather like projection in psychoanalysis)
I'm not OK – you're OK	You feel bad about yourself and see others as more powerful and capable than yourself, so you tend to feel inferior and incompetent all the time
I'm not OK – you're not OK	You are critical of both yourself and others

Source: Harris (1973).

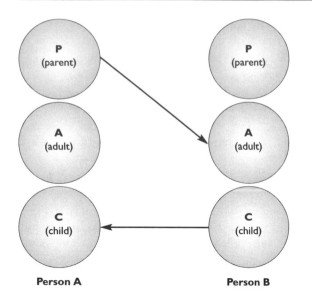

Person A   Person B

Figure 9.1 Diagrammatic representation of ego states in transactional analysis

For some people, on the other hand, its entertaining and unportentous terms can help them to look at their behaviour in a new, easily grasped way. This is enhanced by a diagrammatic technique, shown in Figure 9.1, which shows each personality in a transaction in terms of their parent-adult-child ego states and how these are interacting with one another. In this case, person A's parent is communicating with person B's adult, while person B's child is communicating with person A's child. Person A might be a man, tense at a dinner party and so communicating his hopes that his wife will support him in presenting a favourable impression to his boss. His wife, Person B, could respond as an adult to her husband's adult, by saying something like: 'I understand we have to be sensitive to keep your job, even though he doesn't fit with our way of life'. Alternatively, she could respond symmetrically, her child to her husband's parent, by complying with her husband's wishes. However, the diagram suggests that she responds to her husband's similar resistance to the imposition, by stimulating her husband to express their radical political views in the boss's presence.

Major statements

A wide range of texts are relevant to these areas, but few cover all of them, although where the main focus is spirituality many of the connections are made. On spirituality, Canda and Furman's *Spiritual Diversity in Social Work Practice* (1999) is the major text on spirituality in social work in general, following a series of publications in this area by Canda. However, its main focus is to bring together general social work practice with an understanding of a wide variety of religious traditions; it is also less concerned with the wider specific practices discussed here and spirituality as distinct from diverse religions. I therefore prefer to present the rather more focused texts by Glassman and Kates (*Group Work: a Humanistic Approach*, 1990) on humanistic principles applied to groupwork and Thompson (*Existentialism and Social Work*, 1992) on existential social work, because these demonstrate the application of ideas in this general area through application of specific theories to social work, rather than, as with Canda, an integrative model that does not deal with how specific theories are applied.

Glassman and Kates: humanistic groupwork

Groups have process, which here is 'democratic mutual aid' among group members, and purpose, which is the changes we want the process to bring about. This account of groupwork derives from democratic and humanistic values, stating that differences among group members enrich all and describes people's:

- inherent worth and capacity
- responsibility for and to one another in social life
- right to belong and be included
- right to participate and be heard
- right to freedom of speech and self-expression
- right to freedom of choice
- right to question and challenge professionals.

Groups develop in a series of stages. People's behaviour and the themes of group interaction are consistent within stages. Humanist theory allows members to use groups' development actively in pursuing their personal development. More authoritarian group theories mystify and limit behaviour to certain stages and stimulate particular behaviours in particular stages. The *stages* are as follows:

- *We're not in charge.* Group members approach the group with caution, uncertain about group norms. The worker helps them to explore possible ways of behaving in the group, and prevents any member imposing external assumptions.
- *We are in charge.* Some members attempt to impose their agenda or direction on the group. There is resistance to this and conflict. The worker helps them to explore the various consequences of proposals, and so the group begins to agree norms.
- *We're taking you on.* Group members struggle with how to use the worker or whether to reject their involvement. The worker helps them to explore various ways of using their contribution. This involves accepting and exploring the reasons for the occurrence and the viability of attitudes of hostility and rejection, or acquiescence and subjection.
- *Sanctuary.* Members feel that the group is more satisfying and less complicated than real life, and see it as an escape from their problems. The worker helps them to use the security they have created to work on real problems.

- *This isn't good any more.* Group members do not want to take the risk of struggling with their problems, but having had their security upset feel disenchanted with the group. The worker helps them to retain the valuable experience of the support of the group while seeing that they can work on their problems.

- *We're okay and able.* By working through their ambivalence about whether the group can help them, group members learn that they can work out difficult problems. This gives them confidence to work on their purpose. They choose from the various options available to them from the skills in the group. The

Table 9.2 Techniques and activities for achieving dual objectives in humanist groupwork

Actualising purpose		Developing the process	
Techniques	*Activities*	*Techniques*	*Activities*
Enable group members to use democratic norms, including rights to belong and be heard	Aid collective participation Scanning (pay attention to each group member in turn)	Identify themes for group's work Give experience of planning, role-playing and organising	Programming: plan and participate in a group programme: initiation, options, tasks and tools, experience, evaluation
Make decisions and develop rules of behaviour in the group	Engage group as a whole Check for opinions, weave consensus, compromise		Role rehearsal, plan future activities, try out useful behaviours
Develop leading/following skills Respect members' differences	Process 'here and now', point out important events and reaction patterns, get group to observe itself		Confrontation: challenge and require instant change in behaviour Dealing with unknown: discuss ideas about future changes
		Share feelings about each other's behaviour	Group mending: start discussion on hurtful issues
Express feelings about the worker, especially around power	Encourage expression; ask for reactions; point out avoidance; address expression of feeling	Help members to identify and express obstructive or helpful feelings	Self-disclosure: conveys humanness and fallibility
Develop and carry out goals together	Discuss how statements express changing needs; explore different needs and interests	Create activities for outside the group	Feedback Conflict resolution: define conflict, clarify themes, feelings, stakes, offer new perspectives
Express feelings to others helpfully	Control strong feelings; non-threatening atmosphere; limit personal details	Identify unhelpful thinking which interferes with group relationships	Group reflective discussion on details of particular events; sequences, feelings, interactions, choices
		Explain group process to help members be more self-aware	Data and facts: help study to avoid prejudice/bias
Develop emotional ties and better cohesion	Review the good and bad things about the meetings and how people feel	Reinforce successful change, so members repeat it	Interpretation; 'reading between the lines' helps individuals Taking stock: make achievements clear

Source: Glassman and Kates (1990).

worker helps them to make decisions and confronts attempts to jump into action thoughtlessly or avoid action on difficult issues.

■ *Just a little longer.* Group members want to keep on with the security of the group, since it has been successful in helping them with their problems. However, they can now use the experience to manage more effectively on their own. The worker helps them to separate from the group, valuing and confirming the helpful progress made.

The objective of groupwork is to develop the democratic mutual aid system and simultaneously help group members to express and carry out ('actualise') their purpose. These two main functions use various interactions, set out in Table 9.2. In this table, the columns for developing democratic mutual aid and actualising purpose are not necessarily aligned. I have presented them so as to make reasonable connections between the two purposes. In addition, workers use several techniques to achieve both purposes. These are as follows:

■ *Demanding work, directing, lending vision and support,* where workers use their own commitment to move members forward when they are stuck, by focusing their attention on acting and helping them to do so. All these techniques require workers to be active and positive, rather than being reflective and neutral.

■ *Staying with feelings,* where workers act as a model for expressing feelings positively, but also help members with expressing feelings when they are uncomfortable.

■ *Silence* conveys respect and support for members who are struggling with difficulties.

■ *Exploration* helps involve members in free-flowing activity. Open-ended questions, curiosity and interest stimulate involvement.

■ *Identification* involves pointing to repetitive patterns of behaviour and thinking in the group.

The humanist aspect of Glassman and Kates' (1990) account of groupwork lies in its two specific purposes and its personal development objectives, achieved through group experience.

Thompson: existentialism and social work

Thompson (1992) provides a comprehensive assessment of the value of existentialist thought to social work practice, based on Sartre's ideas. Because it is at the centre of existentialism, he focuses on *ontology*, the study of being. This means the way in which we think of what it is like to be human. However, he also examines the implications for practice of social work's *epistemology*, that is, its view of knowledge. Its view of the nature of society is equally important.

A central notion is '*being*'. 'Being-in-itself' is mere existence. 'Being-for-itself' is existence in which we are conscious and can therefore have potential, for example by making plans and decisions about how we want to be.

Existentialism rejects any prior expectations about how humans or society should live. People have *intentionality*, that is, they have the capacity to act bearing in mind goals about how they wish the future to be. This is different from the view of behaviourism or psychodynamic theory, which claim that the past is an important influence on the present. Blom (2002) discusses the difficulties of understanding what a therapeutic relationship is in this perspective. Neither the worker nor the client can know each other in advance from the perspective of the other or from the basis of formal knowledge because there are no prior expectations of how a human being can be. Thus, a therapeutic relationship is a struggle between two experiences of others outside themselves. It is through this struggle between different views of each other that we can take part with another person in social and personal transformation. But we cannot understand what is 'inside' them or how they would typically act, as psychological theories would propose. They have the free will to act, and our two conceptions of each other interact freely, allowing us to begin to gain external views of the other.

Existentialism emphasises that it is our interpretation of the past which is important. Therefore, how we interpret it and act towards the future gives meaning to our lives. Consequently, through their personal freedom humans are able to create or define themselves. Personality and social structures are the products of choices made by free human beings. However, others apply labels to our behaviour, and this gives us something to hang on to. So, we begin to accept the limitations of the social expectations which are applied to what we do and what we are. This is one way in which we cope with the feeling that life is 'absurd'. This feeling arises because existentialists accept that there is no purpose to life imposed by, for example, a belief in God as an ultimate director of personal and social development. There is a 'theatre of the absurd' demonstrating human attempts to come to terms with absurdity. An example is Ionesco's *Rhinoceros*, where humankind slowly turns into the eponymous creatures.

People are therefore completely responsible for their own actions. This is an important aspect of existential ethics. We are free *to* act, but not free *from* responsibility to respond to our environment and the pressures on us; these are the facts of existence. *Facticity*, the reality of external things, is different from *contingency*, the possibility of acting on and changing those conditions. Realising this can be empowering but also disturbing and frightening. This is because 'being-for-itself' implies *nothingness*, because it means that conscious decisions may create negative outcomes. That negativity can have no purpose, again because there is no assumed overall direction of existence. Therefore, we feel 'dread' or anguish about the unknown and uncertain contingencies that may affect us. Failing to accept or running away from our freedom is *bad faith*, and leads to a false stability from accepting rigid social boundaries. Equally, 'being-for-itself' implies constantly changing and developing, but human beings often want to arrive at some stable destination, to be certain who they are. This is also bad faith, since it also seeks stability and certainty. In one sense, it is a wish to 'be God' by having this unrealistic sense of certainty about the world. This may be an important motivator for many people. The absence of this possibility often leads to 'despair'. However, the motivation for certainty and stability leads people to seek ways of creating or defining themselves, and may lead to their empowerment and liberation. Thompson (1992: 47) connects the idea of absence of bad faith with 'authenticity', the idea that our behaviour does not conflict with our conception of ourselves as we present it to the world.

This approach has many connections with cognitive ideas where 'irrational' thoughts are considered to mislead us in our judgement of situations and therefore in our ability to respond appropriately. If we can accept and use our freedom, though, we can look forward optimistically to 'self-definition' or 'self-creation', as we generate or contribute to our constantly changing personality and social situation. Within freedom is responsibility for creating ourselves, and the anguish which comes from knowing that we have created the negative as well as the positives in our creation.

However, while this is possible at the personal level, we must see the ideas which limit individual freedom as ideologies, that is, shared conceptions of the world which have their own social power on behalf of particular social interests. This requires action at the political level for liberation. Otherwise, political and social constraints prevent people from using their personal freedom. These ideas have connections to Marxist dialectical materialism. There, however, economic forces are often seen as in control of the sweep of history, limiting human capacity to make history freely. Similarly, Marxian alienation is about cutting workers off from the tools they employ to do their work, which are owned and manipulated by capitalists. While this explains much human misery, existential ideas go further and argue that alienation comes from all kinds of oppression (for example because of race or gender). Existentialism seeks a complete social reorganisation, *resocialisation*, so that people can be free to take part in a process of continual reconstruction according to their needs and wishes. Such freedom would allow people to overcome alienation. Unlike some Marxist thought, there is no final ideal set of social relations – participants constantly reconstruct these. Such a view relates closely to postmodernist thought.

The 'other' plays an important part in these ideas. 'Being-for-itself' can only exist in relation to others. We can only experience many feelings (shame is the famous example) through the reaction of others to us.

The group is also important. Most groups are a 'series'. Here, people are individualised and competitive, even though a social situation links them. For example, several people may be neighbours and have a shared interest in sorting out arrangements not to interfere with one another's houses. Nevertheless, they do not have continual and complex social relations and would not necessarily help one another in difficulties. Some groups have *solidarity*, in which people are linked in multiple ways and share interests and activities in many different ways. They use their freedom to act in the interests of the group. Serial group relations is the most common state, and so we should nurture solidarity. Neighbours need to be encouraged and supported to help one another in difficulty and engage in a wide range of social activities. This would make the group stronger and more satisfying. Such ideas are related to ideas of network and community, where more links are seen as creating a 'better' set of social relations. Another important aspect of existential ethics is the value of *commitment* to solidarity with others. In this way, existential thought emphasises the humanist value of 'holism', treating individuals and social systems as wholes. 'Totalisation' implies trying to create a synthesis of our understanding of social situations and their histories. Such a synthesis appreciates that we form understanding from interplay and conflict among many different points of view. *Dialectical reason* is the process by which, through constant internal and existential debate, we try to develop our totalised concepts of the world. This interplay or (in Foucault's terms) discourse leads to constantly changing conceptions of the world.

Thompson argues that the strength of existentialism lies in its focus on ontology, the understanding of the fundamentals of human existence. This focus comes about through its ideas on being, nothingness and contingency. Most social work theories, he argues, are weak in considering these aspects of humanity, and this makes understanding social and personal relations unsatisfactory. He gives several examples relevant to commonplace social work practice.

For example, he examines several child care situations. Many problems in parent–child relationships stem from problems for children about managing their own freedom without bad faith. Thus, John has temper tantrums when he is told he cannot do something. He is seeking the freedom to act, without accepting the responsibility to take into account social conditions in which he may exercise that freedom. A more appropriate response might be to negotiate opportunities to do what he wants. To achieve such a response, however, he needs to have experience of working within a family group with solidarity where people behave in the interests of the group rather than in their own interests. A father who is distant might not give John the chance to learn to negotiate. A father who is overbearing might induce bad faith, that is, John can accept the constraints on him as given, instead of seeing them as a responsibility to be taken on and negotiated about. Thompson distinguishes this sort of situation from the common-sense assumption that consistency, discipline and love are needed from parents. Consistency might also lead to bad faith, because the environment seems rigid and certain instead of offering freedom for change. Love is an attempt to 'possess' the other person by controlling his or her freedom. It seeks to impose a concern for and solidarity with the person who loves above other possible concerns and solidarities. Discipline is an attempt to create excessive certainty through conformity. Psychodynamic theory assumes that we achieve self-discipline by internalising or embedding parental views about appropriate behaviour into a child's self. Behaviourism assumes that we learn and reinforce behaviour by social expectations of disciplined behaviour. To existentialism, self-discipline (which behaviourism would reject) is an essential idea, because it implies accepting responsibility for the social character of the situation in which we act. It also assumes, however, that our discipline comes from the acceptance of those responsibilities within our freedom to choose. Psychodynamic theory, on the other hand, assumes a choice determined by parental controls, which in their turn mediated and interpreted social expectations.

Existential thinking suggests that the different projects of members of a family need to interact within a group with solidarity. Social workers might seek to improve solidarity, that is, commitment to group interests. This would help mutual support in pursuing all individuals' projects, that is, the ways in which different people in the family see their interests as developing. Children and family relations are not best understood by general principles of behaviour.

Instead, we should consider their specific 'projects' and the constraints which restrict their freedom to carry them out with responsibility for reacting socially within their environment. General principles lead to bad faith because they lead to the expectation of an unreal consistency. Parents vary, and the important aspect of a successful relationship between parents and children is communication about the particular circumstances of parental reactions to children. For example, if the parent is worried and distracted, children can understand a distant or tense reaction to a request if they know the parent's position. However, they will be confused if they do not understand. They can only accept their responsibilities for acting freely if they do understand and therefore if communication is effective.

In very young children, parents see themselves in the child, because of the strength of their influence. The child similarly gains a sense of self-worth from the positive feelings experienced from the parents. This gives parents and child a view of themselves and their value in life and is the origin of parental or filial feelings and the 'maternal instinct'. This is a powerful motivator, and encourages group solidarity in a family and can promote it elsewhere, as people seek it in other relationships and social situations. However, it can also stifle independence and distort perceptions so that it reduces the capacity to accept freedom and responsibility.

In exploring existential work with older people, Thompson points out that social workers are involved with the social consequences of ageing, rather than a physical condition. He also distinguishes between services for older people and social work with them. Existential views of ageing point to the significance of contingency, that is, the freedom to act and change, and the fear of the uncertainty which arises from that freedom. Older people experience significant uncertainty: the ultimate uncertainty of approaching death, changes in life style through retirement, loss of companions and loss of community networks and familiar life styles on admission to residential care. Bad faith often leads to rigidity and sticking to unnecessary and conservative social rules. It is an avoidance of responsibility and therefore is bad faith to ignore the reality of approaching death and the social task of preparing for it. To existentialism, the problem may be that approaching death may cause people to accept restrictions on their freedom to choose various options in their lives: they may feel more restricted than they are. My mother, for example, decided that she was housebound after a fall, and thus restricted herself from a wider social life. However, in fact she could have gone out if she had not so readily accepted the restrictions on her. Existentialists would regard this as bad faith in accepting unrealistic restrictions on the freedom to choose. Social work would seek to remove that feeling of restriction to allow us to make more choices. Another issue may be the need to attribute 'meaning' to life. To the existentialist, this can only come from making and having made choices. Present problems can prevent people from making a realistic assessment of the value of the choices they have made and might still make. The sense of self which has been built up can be destroyed by the experiences of ageing, and, consistent with existentialist assumptions, may need reconstruction. It is important that work contributes to the maintenance and building up of clients' sense of self. Otherwise workers will contribute further to the sense of destruction coming from unwanted retirement, feeling devalued because older people are 'useless' in the labour market and being unvalued in the family.

Table 9.3 Thompson's practice principles of existential work

Principle	Practice implications
Freedom and responsibility are the main building blocks of human experience	Avoid thinking that clients' behaviour is determined or unchangeable. Seek areas of life where clients can make choices and help them to do so. Aim to recognise elements of clients' situations that constrain their choice and remove these
Freedom is both a liberation and a burden	Convert negative aspects of freedom such as anxiety, fear, 'bad faith' into positive ones such as self-control, confidence, self-esteem, authenticity
Authenticity is the key to liberation; 'bad faith' is a common unsuccessful strategy for dealing with problems	Workers must aim for authenticity; that is, accepting and using their own capacity to 'make a difference' to their lives and those of others. Clients must establish authenticity before other work can be done, otherwise they will rely on others or the straitjackets of rules and regulations to manage their lives
Existence is experienced as powerlessness; responsibility must be accepted by everyone	Clients struggle with immense problems. Workers must help them start to take responsibility in whatever limited areas are possible. As this is achieved, further progress in taking more collective responsibility (for example for solidarity in a family, or eventually for political action) can be achieved
Existentialism requires a shared subjective journey and a partnership approach	The starting point is accepting and recognising clients' feelings about their experiences and sharing a process of taking responsibility for acting
Recognise and manage the tension between authority/ control/legal duty and creative, non-directive work	Understanding and seeing complex conflicts between these two aspects of social work is integral to recognising the conflicts which create the totalised view of the client's freedom and responsibility
Existence is movement	Natural stability is impossible. Social work seeks development and progress rather than disintegration
Existential freedom and the process of self-creation are the basis of political liberation	The first has to be obtained before there is a possibility of achieving the latter

Source: Thompson (1992).

Workers should be politically informed in their work, by being aware of the general social and political issues which affect their clients. However, this is different from political work, that is, action to achieve political change. Thompson summarises his existential approach to social work in the practice principles set out in Table 9.3.

CRITICAL PRACTICE FOCUS

Kevin and his parents
The psychiatric unit social worker was asked to visit Kevin's parents to discuss arrangements with them for his discharge from the secure unit, where he had been treated for thirteen years after committing two violent sexual murders, one of them in a park near his parents house that they walked past nearly every day. Mrs and Mrs Burke were approaching retirement and had mixed feelings about Kevin's discharge. They had experienced his aggression at home and feared a recurrence; they also felt inadequate as parents of such a serious offender. They put a lot of

effort into being loving grandparents of Julia's three children, the nieces and nephews of Kevin who visited them often. Although Kevin would live in a hostel in a nearby town and be supervised by the social worker and psychiatrist, he would have contact with the family. Kevin was looking forward to resuming a less restricted life and had valued the support of his parents while he was at the unit.

What possible spiritual and existential issues might the social worker need to disentangle for the people involved in this situation? Are there emotional and practical issues to be explored, perhaps with psychodynamic, social construction or other psychological perspectives? Or perhaps, accepting realistic fears, careful planning in a task-centred way might help.

Commentary

The importance of considering humanism, existentialism and spirituality does not lie in their formal impact on social work theory in use within most agencies, which is slight, although increasing. They are important in two ways. First, social work values are humanist and spiritual. Thus, ideas of treating people as wholes, and as being in interaction with their environment, of respecting their understanding and interpretation of their experience, and seeing clients at the centre of what workers are doing all fit well with the central principles of social work. We see them in a wide range of social work theories discussed in this book, except particularly cognitive-behavioural theories.

The failure to import these potentially sympathetic ideas lies in the framework of social work in agencies which perform social control and bureaucratic functions. Spirituality raises a concern that workers might import their own values, which might be held more firmly or differ from those of others involved, into practice. This requires looking for connections with other relevant views, awareness of the worker's own spiritual beliefs and a commitment to avoid imposing it and promote inclusiveness in practice (Hodge, 2003a, b; Osmo and Landau, 2003). Research and development of assessment tools may also be helpful (Hodge and Williams, 2002). Also, the approach of humanism and spirituality already exists in social work and does not need explicit importation. Agency function and social control imply that a range of external objectives and targets have to be imposed on social work activities. These are inimical to the extremely free approach of humanist therapies, where clients are in control of the exploration and are facilitated, not directed, by workers.

Symbolic interaction and phenomenological ideas form the second area of great importance in present ideas in social work of the material discussed in this chapter. These provide a basis for understanding human beings which is more flexible, less deterministic and less judgemental than many psychological ideas that social work uses. The interaction of clients' perceptions and interpretations of the world and the reaction of the world to clients shows how situations arise in which clients' apparently bizarre or bad behaviour is established or amplified by social processes. These ideas can be a useful way of explaining clients' behaviour and problems without blaming clients who are victims of these social processes.

The problem with these ideas and approaches to therapy is, however, their lack of clarity and the difficulty of forming clear targets and agreed explanations about the behaviour. This means that, although these ideas have potential explanatory power in advocacy for clients, they may not be widely accepted among powerful groups in society that workers seek to influence on behalf of clients. Also, they may be criticised for their vagueness and lack of rigour by positivists, and for the lack of any evidence of effectiveness of the techniques proposed. Answering this, the work on the effectiveness of therapeutic relationships shows the importance of empathic, valuable and genuine relationships, and attempts were made to measure these elements. Although such relationships are not sufficient for therapy to be effective, they are necessary to therapeutic success. So, while they must be present for these techniques to be useful, they have to be part of other activities which intervene effectively in clients' behaviour or social circumstances. This material does not tell us, however, what we should do to intervene effectively in the client's situation within the relationship once we have achieved it.

OVERVIEW

- These theories emphasise that respect for whole persons and the common good are an essential part of effective practice and the value base of social work.

- Artistic and cultural understanding through metaphor, experience, revelation and faith are important parts of the lives of many people in all cultures and all social workers.

- Valuing spirituality and human fulfilment has always engaged commitment among clients and social work practice ideas.

- Understanding and accepting the role of spirituality and phenomenological social experience is essential to understanding many people and understanding the particular cultural experiences of minorities who may be oppressed or excluded in many societies.

- The technical, rational and secular elements in social work have often downplayed the importance of these elements of practice.

- Humanist, existential and spiritual elements of practice provide a useful balance to the main rationalist thrust of social work practice.

FURTHER READING

Canda, E. and Furman, L. (1999) *Spiritual Diversity in Social Work Practice: The Heart of Helping* (New York: Free Press).
A leading American text on spirituality in social work.

Glassman, U. and Kates, L. (1990) *Group Work: a Humanistic Approach* (Newbury Park, CA: Sage).
Excellent account of humanistic groupwork incorporating, fairly inexplicitly, humanist ideas.

Graham, M. (2002) *Social Work and African-Centred Worldviews* (Birmingham: Venture).
An outstanding account of African spirituality and its relevance to social work.

Martin, E. P. and Martin, J. M. (2002) *Spirituality and the Black Helping Tradition in Social Work* (Washington DC: NASW Press).
Interesting text covering the history of black contributions to social work and its relationships with spirituality.

Nash, M. and Stewart, B. (eds) (2002) *Spirituality and Social Care: Contributing to Personal and Community Well-being* (London: Jessica Kingsley).
A variable edited collection, with some useful introductory material.

Pitman, E. (1983) *Transactional Analysis for Social Workers* (London: Routledge & Kegan Paul).
The only extended analysis of application to social work, but its age reflects the way TA has remained a separate therapy.

Thompson, N. (1992) *Existentialism and Social Work* (Aldershot: Avebury).
An outstanding discussion of the theoretical and practical application of existentialist ideas to social work.

JOURNALS

Journal of Religion and Spirituality in Social Work (formerly *Social Thought*) Haworth Press.
Social Work and Christianity, North American Association of Christians in Social Work.

WEBSITE

http://www.nacsw.org/index.shtml
Website of the North American Association of Christians in Social Work – contains useful information and bibliographies.

CHAPTER 10

Social and Community Development

What this chapter is about

Social and community development are related but separable areas of practice. *Community development* is a form of community work (see Chapter 3), which seeks to engage people with shared interests usually in a particular locality to come together, identify shared concerns and work jointly to overcome them. *Social development* is the application of community development in resource-poor or developing countries as an aspect of overall economic and social development. Social development is the major form of social work in many resource-poor countries. Because many of the techniques are similar, community work and social development have influenced each other, particularly in colonial administrations until the 1960s, and through the social development work of the United Nations, which has often called upon community work expertise. The European concept of social pedagogy is also regarded as a tradition of social work, using informal education particularly in community facilities for children and young people. It therefore connects with community work and also with day and residential care for children. This chapter brings together these traditions, focusing on the implementation of them in social development. Although these methods focus on the social, rather than the individual, they are often reflexive-therapeutic in their objectives, since they seek the development of relatively small groups within the present social order, or reformist in seeking improvements in the present social order rather than its change.

MAIN POINTS

> ➤ Social development has a long history as a result of Eurocentric colonial and postcolonial approaches to developing resource-poor countries.

> ➤ Social development is the main form of social work in resource-poor countries and seeks to incorporate social progress with economic development.

> ➤ Community work is a practice helping people come together to identify issues of concern and take action to resolve them. Its development has been

influenced by community development in resource-poor countries, and social development has been influenced by community work methods.

➤ Social pedagogy is a European practice used particularly with children in residential and day care and in community work in which individual and collective self-development and education interact.

➤ Community social work is a largely British practice in which social work focuses on the needs of small communities, and, allied with a range of social care services, seeks to engage those communities in providing locally responsive services that meet identified needs.

➤ Poverty and social exclusion are important targets of social development in resource-poor and rich countries.

PRACTICE ISSUES AND CONCEPTS

➤ Developing *social capital,* increasing community and social infrastructure as an important resource in societies.

➤ *Social inclusion* and *exclusion* focus on ways in which stigmatised and disadvantaged individuals, and the stigmatised and disadvantaged communities in which they tend, or are forced, to congregate, should be helped to play a stronger role in society, by being provided with opportunities and resources for participation.

➤ *Capacity-building* seeks to build understanding and skills to enable excluded individuals, groups and communities to participate more effectively in their communities.

Wider theoretical perspectives

Social and community development is an aspect of the wider development of localities, areas, regions and countries. It is related to economic and industrial development. Ideas about development have a long history. European countries developed from the eighteenth century onwards, and many other countries in the nineteenth and twentieth centuries. Weber (1930) famously argued that non-European countries developed slowly because their cultural inheritance did not include the Protestant work ethic of northern European countries. Sinha and Kao (1988b) criticise this ethnocentric view, and argue that other Western concepts, such as individualism and achievement motivation, support it.

Economic and social development is now associated in many people's minds with former colonial countries, particularly in the southern hemisphere. A range of competing theories exist which take different views of the relationship between the market and economic development, and the role of the state in intervening to build markets or reduce oppression resulting from markets (Martinussen, 1997). Much of this debate is not relevant to the mainly social elements of development, although ideas from these theories are taken up in social development theory.

However, economic and social development also refer to areas or regions where economic development is sought in countries which are successful economically, for example northern Britain, southern Italy and Greece in the European Union. The need for development refers to widespread poverty among populations (Jones, 1990). Associated issues are health and disability, education, women's roles, industrialisation, and urbanisation with its related problems such as crime and family break-up. Governments seek to increase the amount of economic activity in a region or country to combat poverty and this has other economic, social and political consequences (Alexander, 1994). Sometimes, social or community development is a strategy for dealing with those consequences. Governments may also seek to reduce the economic and social demands on the wealth and income of a region or country. They might do this by, for example, trying to control population increase or social and health costs of the population.

In countries that are economically well developed, issues of social and economic development have been concerned with inner cities, declining industrial regions and planning of the environment. Dealing with the social consequences of these problems or the development process has sometimes led to a call for community development or organisation practice. Many ideas for such work originate from work undertaken in the colonies of the main European colonial powers from 1930–70.

The focus after the 1939–45 war was *Eurocentric*. The aim was to build nation states in former colonies, copying European models of statehood and welfare. This was emphasised by a political division (proposed by Horowitz, 1972) into the first world (the West), the second world (the Soviet bloc) and the third world (mainly economically underdeveloped nations, non-aligned in the political dispute between the first two 'worlds') (Spybey, 1992). The understanding of what a country was came from the European model of a centralised government, managing priorities for a country with defined boundaries. The understanding of development was also Eurocentric. The assumption was that, to be successful, states would need to create a developed market economy like those in Western countries. This led to the *modernisation theory* of development (see Hulme and Turner, 1990: 34–43). Resource-poor countries would be developed rapidly until they equated with Western countries. By the 1960s this approach was clearly not working, although particularly on the Pacific rim, the 'tiger' economies of Japan, Korea, Taiwan and their successors achieved this kind of development.

Marxist critical theory did not provide a satisfactory alternative to modernisation theory, because it assumed a single line of development to capitalist industrialised states. However, a neo-Marxist *dependency theory* developed in Latin America. This argued that a 'peripheral' group of underdeveloped nations was dependent for trade and investment on a 'core' of industrialised states. The core maintained terms of trade to their advantage. Integration into an increasingly globalised capitalist economy limited the possibilities for developing ways of life which were suited to the structure and culture of underdeveloped nations. Indian people, for example, are well integrated into a well-established culture. Economic and social problems arise from attempting to convert the largely rural, socially interdependent Hindu culture into one which can operate in an economic system which rewards industrialisation and individualist Western values. This led to a tradition of rural development (Singh, 1999). Focus moved from the nation state to changing the way the world economy worked to the disadvantage of underdeveloped or developing economies. Several countries sought to confront the issue of loan repayment.

By the 1980s, all these approaches were regarded as unsatisfactory (Midgley, 1984). An alternative response to the dependency theorists is termed *neo-populism* by Hulme and Turner (1990). This derives partly from the 'small is beautiful' philosophy of Schumacher and from politicians such as Nyerere, a Tanzanian political leader. Small-scale development could be created from cooperatives working as rural villages, using labour-intensive appropriate technologies, rather than seeking urban development through Western exploitation. These were often unsuccessful, due to inappropriate government interference, poor management and conflicts with other forms of production (Tenaw, 1995).

Related to these ideas are the theories of *ecodevelopment* and *ethnodevelopment* (Hettne, 1990). Ecodevelopment seeks 'sustainable' development which does not encroach upon natural resources (Estes, 1993; Jackson, 1994). Development should, in this view, be more people-centred and concerned with local needs (Else et al., 1986; Eziakor, 1989). Ethnodevelopment acknowledges that the focus of development cannot be the nation state or small groups. Ethnic groups within nation states often conflict over the use of resources and power in the nation. These factors must be acknowledged and worked with. An important related concept is the Latin American Catholic idea of *liberation theology* (Gutiérrez, 1973, 1992; Evans, 1992; Skeith, 1992). This focuses on movement from oppression to liberation within concrete issues in daily life, rather than accepting oppression as preparation for an afterlife. Both personal and 'social' sin (namely, structural oppression by social institutions) must be overcome by non-violent social change through personal empathy with others and their social situation, in the same way that Jesus Christ acted. This provides a religious basis for seeking social change.

The place of social development in these theoretical movements is uncertain, since the major focus of development work is at the policy and economic level. During the period when modernisation theory was influential, the development of welfare and other social provision continued, building on colonial progress, such as it was. Neo-populist policies place much of the concern for social provision within village and traditional social structures. This offers a role for social development in developing cooperatives or village structures (Burkey, 1993), but reduces the role of formal welfare. More recently, the focus on macroeconomic issues has sometimes excluded concern for social issues and disempowered local communities (Friedmann, 1992). For example, the World Bank's 'structural adjustment policies' in Africa involved ignoring the social consequences of creating economic recessions in order to create the economic conditions assumed to be necessary for the development of free-market economies (Messkoub, 1992; Adepoju, 1993; Hall, 1993b). Some countries attempted to develop welfare provision which reduced the impact of these economic rigours on the population.

Some of these more recent socially oriented approaches suggest a stronger role for social development. Also, movements for more indigenous and locally based development activities focused on local communities led to an emphasis on local development through education (Jones and Yogo, 1994). A strong focus on the role of voluntary or non-governmental organisations (NGOs) as leaders in this work (Thomas, 1992) led to an independence of external development efforts from centralised government control, overt political action (Booth, 1994a) and professional involvement (Chambers, 1993). However, many NGOs work with government, link with grassroots organisations, advocating and lobbying for poor communities (Edwards and Hulme, 1992). Local NGOs might be sought as useful partners in development (Salole, 1991a). However, effective management of their participation is needed, with a focus on ensuring consistency among cooperating organisations of values, ideology, practice approach and official or democratic mandates (Mwansa, 1995). NGOs create a diversity of activity and theoretical approaches. An example is indigenous community cultural theories in Thailand which focus on the idea of development of community as opposing the state (Nartsupha, 1991). Many of these have focused on women, partly because of their importance in local and family economies in many developing countries and also in response to worldwide feminist social movements aiming to achieve greater justice, independence and self-control for women and publicise issues of concern to them, especially child care (Yasas and Mehta, 1990; Johnson, 1992; Fisher, 1993; Harcourt, 1994; Wilson and Whitmore, 1994). Health and disability have also been important issues (Coleridge, 1993; Phillips and Verhasselt, 1994). Finally, important social movements responding to local ethnic and cultural needs in different countries also contest the significance of the centralised state (Wignaraja, 1993). Fisher and Kling (1994) argue that social movement theory connects community development ideas with wider forms of resistance among communities, by shifting the focus of socialist action from class-based to community-based action. Martin (2001) argues that feminist and other new social movements have achieved change in social policy by symbolic challenges to cultural assumptions. An example is the recognition that women's self-help movements are the only way to make a substantial difference in areas of postpartum depression, where interpersonal help from people with shared experiences can make a major difference. Thus, Western social policy becomes more responsive to a role for social work that is about organising self-help, rather than providing direct care.

Connections

The distinction made above between community development as a phenomenon of Western countries and social development as a method in developing countries is not universally agreed. Neither method is clearly associated only with social work. They might equally well be regarded as separate professional activities, part of wider development work, part of other professional responsibilities or, with social development, as a separate professional career for Western workers in international NGOs.

However, social development is related to participatory approaches in all kinds of social concerns and requires skills in interpersonal and group communication which relate closely to social work skills and connect to empowerment practice (Chapter 14) (White et al., 1994; Craig and Mayo, 1995). Self-help organisations can also be important mechanisms for social development by generating increased interpersonal skills (Abatena, 1995). In participating, individuals can be involved through local grassroots organisations, enabling education to take place, and avoiding general political influences or social assumptions such as gender oppression dominating local wishes, which create social injustice (Agere, 1986; Mulwa, 1988; Ukpong, 1990; David, 1993; Mararike, 1995). Effective participation requires partnership which offers ownership of activities and outcomes for local participants rather than simply imposing inconvenient consultative arrangements on them (Salole, 1991b). Midgley (1987) argues that views that participation is important do not deal adequately with the role of the state in modern life, relying on individualist, populist and anarchist views of the world. Nkunika (1987) argues that appropriate organisational bases for facilitating participation are needed.

Current approaches to development increasingly focus on issues of poverty, employment and enterprise, particularly social enterprise, issues of diversity, ethnicity and colonialism, and technology, sustainability, gender and urbanisation (Allen and Thomas, 2000). Many of the issues in social development concern poverty, gender and ethnicity and its consequences for identity, either gender or ethnic or national identity. Thus, social development increasingly connects to ideas from social construction, ethnic and cultural sensitivity and feminism (Chapters 8, 13 and 12 respectively).

Historically, community work thrived in the same American and British settings from which casework and groupwork emerged in the nineteenth and early twentieth centuries (Lappin, 1985). Settlements allowing middle-class university students to work in working-class areas were particularly important. General improvement to poor localities naturally went along with welfare work. In many countries, community work is regarded as a third aspect of social work, although even in the USA where this convention is well established, it is generally less strong than casework. Elsewhere, as in Britain, its role as part of social work is well accepted, although it is much less strong. There are also separate occupational groups deriving from the role of community work as part of informal education and sometimes leisure services and as part of public participation arrangements in official decision-making (Rothman and Zald, 1985). In the USA and Britain, various government projects designed to deal with inner-city problems had a base in community work practice in the 1960s and 70s (Brager and Purcell, 1967; Loney, 1983). During the 1980s, at a time of recession, many community projects were financed by insecure funding through temporary employment schemes, and this led to a period of short-term projects using low-paid unemployed people, but the best of these also provoked or recruited community activism. Inner-city development is now primarily economic, and there is little official sponsorship of community work. However, recent British projects require local participation strategies. They have focused on neighbourhood renewal and *capacity-building* among people without expertise to manage organisations and social developments in their locality. Some have been focused on health initiatives (Henderson et al., 2004). Increasingly, there has been government interest in invoking participation from formal voluntary sector organisations and faith groups (Gilchrist, 2000).

Western concern with the problems of inner cities is relevant to the third world concern about urbanisation, migration from rural to urban settings (Patel, 1988) and developing rural areas to reduce migration as well as for its intrinsic benefits (Muzaale, 1988). In some countries in mainland Europe, *social pedagogy*, *animation* and *agology* (a Dutch form of community work) form separate occupations whose focus varies in different countries. The Netherlands introduced a policy of *social renewal*, using community development to integrate action in deprived localities on employment, environment, welfare and education (Winkels, 1994). In some Nordic countries social pedagogy has a strong role in education and social welfare in informal group and community settings. Animation in France also has an informal education role through artistic work, concerned with social development and education through leisure activities (Lorenz, 1994: 99–103). A substantial literature on community work exists which overlaps these different aspects, although social pedagogy is not well established in the English-language literature. It developed from the work of German philosophers Diesterweg and Mager (Hämäläinen, 1989, 2003; Lorenz, 1994: 91–7), aiming at those social aspects of education which particularly focus on poor people in societies. The theory emphasises that education can make a major difference to the lives of poor people, using it to combat social exclusion and develop social identity, aiming at personal and social growth through problem-solving, rather than simply the resolution of personal problems (Hämäläinen, 2003).

Mathiesen (1999) defines social pedagogy as identifying how values, psychological, social and material resources may further or hinder a person's personality development or growth allied with that of a group and social institution (usually in residential or day care) of which they are part. In some conceptions social pedagogy is distinguished from individual pedagogy because the person becomes a part of the group; sometimes in an authoritarian and controlling way. However, other perspectives emphasise social pedagogy's role in social development, and focus on groups excluded from social development. Natorp's *transcendental philosophy* derives from an adaptation of the Kantian view that it is possible to arrive at an objective view of reality (see Mathiesen, 1999). Natorp starts from an idea about the world, and by constantly questioning experience of its reality, we arrive at a unified conception of it, which forms a new basis for hypothesis about how to achieve improvements. So, if we see that a child is hyperactive (our judgement and idea about the relationship of the child to the world), we question how this happened, how the behaviour developed, how others reacted to it and arrive at an overall view of the hyperactivity in relation to the personality of the child and the family and social environment around her. The next question is 'what should I do?' You should use the balance between the child and the collective around her: the child may only gain the will to develop her behaviour and grow in different ways by the response of the collective world around her responding to and joining with her to develop. Individual variation in the collective is a sign of its quality, because it contains the resources that allow and help its participants to develop. They may only do so by participation in and submission to the collective, but in turn the collective will need to respond to them and their needs. Experience within the collective is the only basis of knowledge; critical questioning allows all participants to learn from their experiences. People gain ideas about how it is possible to, or how they would like to, behave, and the collective gives them the will and also controls how they behave, so that they may perceive other ways of doing so. People educate themselves in interaction with others and in the interchange of perceptions about the world. Liberation is found in the mediation of one's views and behaviour through the collective, in which language plays an important part, since self-understanding comes through discussion and debate in the collective.

These ideas are an attractive basis of developmental work with children in residential and day care and in informal education and community work. They have many connections with self-realisation and personal growth of humanist ideas, and G. H. Mead's ideas about the interaction with the self and the other (Chapter 9). They also have some connections with critical and feminist thinking in the dialogical process and in the use of language and collective experience as the basis of both shared and personal experience, although, according to Mathiesen (1999), Natorp disputed several of Marx's theoretical positions.

Two aspects of the social work role lead to an emphasis on community work. First, social work in hospitals and other institutions works on the boundary of the institution and the wider community. This involves concern for issues in the community which lead to admission and arranging for discharge. Social workers are inevitably concerned for community factors or inadequacy in services which increase clients' problems and which prevent or might enable discharge (Taylor, 1985; Taylor and Roberts, 1985). Second, many countries decentralise welfare provision in local communities and may promote informal, or non-state-organised welfare provision. This is as true in China (Chan and Chow, 1992; Chan, 1993) as it is in Britain (Payne, 1995). Social workers therefore may become involved in stimulating or relating to local provision. Popple (1995) describes this as *community care work*, following the British terminology. One important model of action in Britain is *community social work* (Hadley and McGrath, 1980, 1984; Hadley et al., 1987). This grew up in the 1970s and 80s in Britain as part of a philosophy of decentralising and debureaucratising social work provision (Hadley and Hatch, 1981). Social workers work in a decentralised team including ancillary and indigenous staff. They are supposed to maintain close links with community organisations and stimulate welfare provision in the locality. Many such activities have links with networking (see Chapter 7).

Another important related area is *community* or *social action*. This involves local action by oppressed groups, traditionally working-class groups, in identifying local or sectional interests which are not adequately provided for and campaigning or negotiating, often from a conflict position, with powerful groups or institutions for change which makes appropriate provision (Grosser and Mondros, 1985; Popple, 1995). Often, the action seeks for such provision to be managed within the community. Professional work in this area involves stimulating the creation of such groups and assisting and supporting them in engaging with institutions (Alinsky, 1969, 1971; Piven and Cloward, 1977; Jones and Mayo, 1974, 1975; Craig et al., 1979, 1982; Smith and Jones, 1981). This is usually the province of specialist professionals. However, particularly in the USA, it is a social work specialism or involves social work agencies (Brager et al., 1987).

Also, work aimed at changing social policy from social work agencies is related to this. In the USA, systems theorists regard this as macro-level social work, and there is related literature (for example Brueggemann, 2002). Social workers occasionally become involved with self-help groups in social action roles, but these are generally less conflictual in their approach. This form of community work is an important aspect of critical social work and, particularly in relation to self-help, empowerment (see Chapters 11 and 13). Important areas of community action focus on the needs of women and minority ethnic groups (Ohri et al., 1982; Solomon, 1985; Dominelli, 1990), and it is an important aspect of anti-oppressive work (see Chapter 12).

The politics of social and community development

Social and community development is often peripheral to the main areas of social work practice in Western countries. In non-Western countries, however, if we exclude health and social security provision, it is often the main form of social intervention, although welfare provision is also sometimes needed and provided, especially in urban areas (Hardiman and Midgley, 1989: 237–57). *Social development* grew out of *community development* work in the later colonial period. The experience was reimported to Britain and the USA in the 1950s and 60s and formed the basis of an explosion of radical community action in the 1960s and 70s. Attempts were made to develop Western social work throughout the world, which has led to welfare services and social work education in casework and groupwork in many countries (Brigham, 1984). Walton and el Nasr (1988) call this the 'transmission' phase of interaction between Western and third world social work. This was widely seen as inappropriate to indigenous cultures and social needs (see Midgley, 1981; also the discussion in Chapter 1).

During the 1980s, social development therefore became the model of work considered most appropriate to most resource-poor countries (for example Midgley, 1989; Hall, 1993a) and has been most strongly extended there. Schools of social work shifted from teaching Western social work models to a stronger focus on social development, but seeing social work's human focus as valuable to counteract economic approaches to development (Osei-Hwedie, 1990). This is at least partly to maintain their credibility in a period when ethnic and cultural interests have achieved importance in many countries. However, a good deal of theoretical development has come from Western writers, also in schools of social work, with experience of, and calling on work from within, developing countries. Sustainability in social development proposes forms of economic and physical development that nurture human welfare through decentralisation and democratisation (Lusk and Hoff, 1994).

Elliott (1993), among others, argues that the experience of social development in developing countries is relevant for Western countries. This is because Western countries face wide disparities in poverty and economic development within their borders, making a social development approach relevant to them. Because of its emphasis on participation and self-construction of problems and issues, it may also be helpful where countries seek to deal with the needs of isolated or marginalised communities, for example where native populations have been oppressed by incomers (O'Brien and Pace, 1988). Social development theory is also a useful counterbalance to Western influence on global social work ideas, enabling a primarily non-Western model to gain wide relevance for practice.

Social development ideas

Social development has been variously defined, and the definitions are controversial. An important, often-quoted definition by Paiva (1977: 332) is: 'the development of the capacity of people to work continuously for their own and society's welfare'. This focuses on improving individual capacity. However, Paiva (1993) argues that this does not exclude four other important aspects of social development: structural change, socioeconomic integration, institutional development and renewal. Jones and Pandey (1981: v) focus on the element of institutional development, that is, making social institutions meet the needs of people more appropriately, when they say: 'Social development refers to the process of planned institutional change to bring about a better fit between human needs and aspirations on the one hand and social policies and programs on the other.'

An early official view is contained in the Preamble of the International Development Strategy for the Second United Nations Development Decade, quoted by Jones (1981: 2):

> As the ultimate purpose of development is to provide increasing opportunities to all people for a better life, it is essential to bring about a more equitable distribution of income and wealth for promoting both social justice and efficiency of production ... Thus qualitative and structural changes in society must go hand-in-hand with rapid economic growth and existing disparities ... should be substantially reduced.

This shift in thinking from an official concentration on economic planning led to an emphasis on social planning. As a result, institutions could be organised to support economic progress (Hardiman and Midgley, 1980).

A more recent official view, influenced by *ecodevelopmentalism* (UNDP, 1994: 4), 'puts people at the centre of development, regards economic growth as a means and not an end, protects the life opportunities of future generations as well as the present generations and respects the natural systems on which all life depends'. This approach leads to emphasis on the importance of 'sustainable' human development, which

> enables all individuals to enlarge their human capabilities to the full and to put those capabilities to best use in all fields – economic, social, cultural and political. It also protects the options of unborn generations. It does not run down the natural resource base for sustaining development in the future. (UNDP, 1994: 4)

Asian writers (for example Khandwalla, 1988; Sinha and Kao, 1988a) focus on understanding and aligning values represented in a society and in the development process. Booth (1994b), taking an ethnodevelopmental view, argues the importance of an increasing concern with diversity. By this he means exploring social differences which lie beneath geographical location and stage of development. At the national level, we should explore different historical and cultural bases for development, instead of looking just at economic indicators. Culturally, we should examine ethnic and gender differences, which affect how societies respond to social needs. At a local level, we need to respond to the particular needs and wishes of communities. The United Nations Centre for Regional Development local social development model (Jones and Yogo, 1994: 11–20) proposes a focus on people within their households, with the major interaction being between them and government and non-government development agencies. Each household has production, consumption and management activities. These refer, respectively, to facilities, labour and money for achieving things, housing, food, warmth, education and caring for living satisfactorily and the distribution of tasks, resources and welfare among members of the family.

We can thus identify moves in understanding social development which mirror ideas in wider development theory, discussed above. We have seen a shift from reactions to economic development alone, to seeing the need to balance economic and social objectives. This has progressed to a view that responding to detailed analysis of needs at the level of smallest living units is a crucial part of development which is empowering to people and self-sustaining.

Midgley (1993) divides social development ideologies into three types, as follows:

- *Individualist* strategies focus on self-actualisation, self-determination and self-improvement.
- *Collectivist* strategies emphasise building organisations as the basis for developing new approaches to action – institutional approaches.
- *Populist* strategies focus on small-scale activities based in local communities.

Pandey (1981) identifies three basic strategies, defined in terms of their purposes rather than, as with Midgley, as types of activity:

- *Distributive* strategies aim for improved social equity between groups nationally.
- *Participative* strategies aim to make structural and institutional reforms to involve people in development and social change.
- *Human development* strategies aim to increase the skills and capacity for people to act on their own behalf in improving the economy and institutional development of their area.

These distinctions may be compared with the models of community work reviewed in Table 3.3. Political, community action or planning strategies are not a focus of social development ideas, as presented here, but they might offer a methodology for distributive (Pandey) and collectivist (Midgley) strategies. Community development is aligned with participative and populist strategies. Feminist and anti-racist community work reflects the same ideological considerations as ethnodevelopmentalism and Booth's (1994b) diversities approach. Community work programme development, organisation, liaison and education all relate to individualist and human development strategies.

Major statements

Many important discussions of social development are texts primarily on practice in resource-poor countries, with more general features. For example, Singh (1999) provides an extensive account of Indian rural development, summarising various perspectives on social development, identifying approaches to rural development and providing many case studies. However, these are primarily about social development as an adjunct to economic development, rather than as a practice. Several American texts (for example Midgley, 1997; van Wormer, 1999) seek to meet the curriculum requirement for a global perspective in social work education and mainly focus on comparative welfare systems and policies, rather than practice. Midgley's *Social Development* (1995), however, focuses primarily on social development practice.

On community work, the pre-eminent British text is Henderson and Thomas (2002). A wide choice of American texts is available, all covering similar ground, presumably to comply with curricula requirements, of which Hardcastle et al. (1997) and Brueggemann (2002) are good and comprehensive examples.

Because of the emphasis of this chapter on social development as an element in the international understanding of social work, Midgley's (1995) text is given priority, with additional material from other writers. An abbreviated account of Henderson and Thomas (2002) is given to represent the focus of community work as an aspect of Western social provision.

Midgley: social development

Midgley's (1995) book offers a coherent account of modern social development ideas. Social development is 'a process of planned social change designed to promote the well-being of the population as a whole in conjunction with a dynamic process of economic development' (p. 25). It seeks to create resources for the community by linking social with economic developments, rather than seeing welfare as dependent on economic growth. Social development must be compatible with society's economic objectives. It transcends residualist approaches which target welfare on the most needy groups in a society and institutional approaches which seek wide state involvement in welfare. Development is distorted when social progress is not aligned with economic development. This may happen where one group, often a white or colonialist minority, achieves wealth at the expense of an impoverished majority, or where military expenditure diverts expenditure from promoting welfare towards other objectives.

Social development aims to promote people's well-being, through creating social changes so that social problems are managed, needs are met and opportunities for advancement are provided. In setting these objectives, Midgley sidesteps potential debate about how and by whom well-being, problems, needs and opportunities are defined. *Social philanthropy*, whereby individuals take social responsibility through ideals of charity in Christianity, or *zakat* in Islam, for helping other individuals, is one organised form of welfare. Social work, where educated professionals provide personal help, and the provision of social welfare services are institutional structures through which social well-being is promoted.

Social development is unlike these forms of welfare in that it does not deal with individuals by treating or rehabilitating them to existing structures. Rather, it aims to affect wider groups, such as communities or societies and the social relations which take place in those societies. It is universalistic rather than selective and seeks growth, rather than simply returning people to an existing level of well-being. It seeks to follow a process of social change through deliberate human action. A long history of ideals suggests that such change in various ideologically preferred directions can be achieved by social interventions. An important context for such ideas in the twentieth century is the creation of the welfare state and the development of social planning. These provided, respectively, for extensive social intervention for the general benefit of populations in industrialised societies and for organising the environment and social provision in support of those interventions. Latterly, attempts have been made to achieve such developments in underdeveloped countries, especially through the agency of the UN and similar international organisations.

Social development is a process. The meaning of process is not as in psychodynamic theory, where it concerns the interaction of communications, actions, perceptions of them and responses to them. In social development, process is more concerned with the idea that interventions are required in a connected and coherently planned series. Preconditions for social development mean removing obstacles. Modernisation views proposed that education and literacy work would overcome traditional attitudes. Also, population control would reduce the pressures on family and community resources of large families. Migration from rural to urban areas should be reduced so as to prevent pressure on urban infrastructure leading to squalid conditions. However, these controls on freedom of action are oppressive, and efforts to impose them have often not been successful. An alternative view about obstacles to social development suggests that government interventions and unrestrained capitalism (for example land or housing tenure, control of financial resources) have been just as significant as obstacles to development as modernisers' social factors. Other writers, particularly Marxists, have suggested the importance of apocalyptic events to get development moving.

Several elements are required for an adequate social development theory. These are as follows:

- Development implies an *ideological commitment to progress*. However, this concept implies accepting modernist ideas that knowledge and social institutions move forward to a social ideal. Critics of such ideas see the economically developed countries of the West as being part of a process of social, economic and moral decline. Midgley argues that social development theorists do not adequately respond to critics of the idea of progress.

- Development is also taken to require *intervention*. This concept, however, may also be criticised. Intervention can lead to distortions that harm social relations. New Right perspectives oppose intervention because it interferes with the market and freedom of choice. Marxist, neo-populist perspectives argue that planners cannot know and be all things. Small-scale developments responding to local wishes are likely to be more responsive and about real issues faced by disadvantaged groups.

- *Economic factors* must also be considered. Social intervention in the cause of well-being has a value in its own right, not merely as a promoter of economic efficiency. It should not be subsumed in economic objectives, nor made dependent on their achievement. It is difficult to see how to promote economic and social development as part of the same activity. This is needed, however. Many individuals, families and small communities that social workers and social development workers deal with need to find effective ways of promoting their economic well-being while also dealing with personal problems.

- *Ideological strategies* which inform social development need to be considered. These are the individualist, collectivist and populist strategies mentioned above.

- The *goals* of social development may be to seek complete reorganisation of society according to some overall plan, or more modest steady improvements through smaller-scale changes. Some goals also focus on material improvements, while others focus on personal and group self-fulfilment.

Strategies for social development categorised by Midgley under the three headings mentioned above, operate at three levels in societies, as follows:

- *Individualistic* strategies focus on helping people to become self-reliant and independent, although not necessarily self-interested. At the national and regional level, a creative enterprise culture does not put obstacles in people's way. Education and training, personal, financial and advisory support and transitional help from dependence on social security or relatives may all help people to achieve economic self-reliance. This may lead to greater personal independence and emotional security. We might take similar approaches with mentally ill people or people with learning disabilities in achieving independence from institutional care. It might also be used for young people leaving care. Social workers have often been too concerned with traditional welfare concerns and failed to ensure that needs for education and opportunities for work and housing have been met. Helping groups of young people to share skills and work together can also benefit them. In small communities, cooperative work or small enterprises using available skills, unpaid work exchange schemes with their own currency or a credit union can be participative ways of encouraging social development.

- *Collectivist* strategies are communitarian in focus. They assume that people in existing social groups can organise themselves to meet their needs and gain control over resources and issues which face them. This is the basis of community work and community development. The number of links between individuals in a locality are increased, and opportunities for coming together around issues of concern are created. For those who share a problem, such as mental illness, or a human condition, such as being a woman and suffering gender oppression, this can lead to personal support, but more importantly may also lead to efforts to gain control of their situation. In other cases, shared responsibility for caring for elderly mentally frail relatives or a shared wish for improvement to local facilities may lead to cooperative work. This kind of work has a long history in community work. Work with community groups may focus on education, by studying local or industrial history, literature or writing skills, artistic work, such as music, community photography, painting murals or graffiti, or acting.

■ *Government* also undertakes development work. Statist approaches argue that this should be so because the state embodies the interests and social aspirations of its people. Only the state can develop through large-scale social planning and mobilise considerable resources. At a more individual or group level, the statist approach would be to campaign for service improvements and effective and coherent plans. Movements for equality, social justice and countering oppression often rely on achieving legislative change. For example, attempts have been made to change the law to avoid discrimination against disabled people or promote the availability of services or protection for particular groups.

Midgley proposes an institutional perspective on social development pluralistically including elements of all three levels of work. This seeks to mobilise social institutions, including the market, the state and community organisations to promote people's well-being. Workers should accept and facilitate the involvement of diverse organisations in social development, through managed pluralism, working within the state, in local organisations and commercial and market enterprises. A degree of training and clearly identified professional roles are required to distinguish workers with different interests from activists and community members. Social development effort should be located at every level of social organisation, not merely locally, but also regionally and nationally, so that these efforts may be mutually supportive.

Three approaches are needed to align economic and social development. Formal organisations and social structures are needed to coordinate economic with social development efforts. This might be done by social planning forums. We should plan to ensure that economic development has a direct benefit for social well-being. This might include encouraging landscaping around new industrial developments benefiting householders, social facilities such as day nurseries associated with new factories, and mutual activities, such as charitable donations and programmes. Also, social development activities should be devised which have a benefit for economic development. The community centre should encourage work training in an area with high unemployment, for example. Efforts to reduce crime on housing estates or encourage community businesses with social and economic objectives are another possibility. This also serves to avoid those concerned with unemployment or dereliction in their area seeing social help as irrelevant or of a low priority.

Community work

Henderson and Thomas's (2002) account of community work starts from four contemporary concepts:

- *Social capital*, the idea of Puttnam's that developing social and community infrastructure provides an important resource for contemporary societies
- *Civil society*, groupings of ordinary people to form informal organisations to provide an alternative sector to government and business
- *Capacity-building*, the idea that we should seek to build up the human resources of communities
- *Social inclusion*, the idea that marginalised groups and communities need to be helped to play a stronger role in society.

To respond to these ideas, they argue that local communities need to be helped to escape from isolation and marginalisation, becoming connected with resources in wider society. This has direct connections with the ideas of social development discussed above. Their practice approach is summarised in Table 10.1. This indication of the practice elements of community work demonstrates that this would also be widely applicable in social development.

CRITICAL PRACTICE FOCUS

The Havenham Community Health Project

The Havenham Community Health Project has been set up to improve healthy eating in a deprived area of privately rented accommodation, with many multi-occupied houses, where migrants to the city have accumulated in overcrowded conditions. However, the majority of the population are still elderly people born in the locality, and now retired. The local community council has applied for special government finance. A requirement of the funding is that 50 per cent of the people involved should be from the local community. Although there is funding for three years, the project will have to be self-financing or be 'mainstreamed' into official funding after that.

At the inaugual meeting, groups of local people from Vietnam, India, Bangladesh and the Caribbean are present, and some community leaders from these groups argue for a project that focuses on support for meals for elderly people in their community. A social work manager from the local adult services team and an experienced social worker from a local coordinating group for voluntary organisations for elderly people are invited to join the committee.

Later local restuarants specialising in food from different parts of the world object to the idea, because meals services may reduce their custom and seek to change the food they produce on health grounds.

Looking at community and social development ideas, and possible implementation of social pedadgogy, what alternative ways of developing a healthy eating project might be devised? Looking back at Chapter 7, what ideas from systems theory might help? Looking at Chapters 3 and 5, what criticisms might be made of this approach to services for elderly people; what might be missing?

Table 10.1 Henderson and Thomas's neighbourhood work

Phase	Practice aims	Practice approach
Entering the neighbourhood	Think about going in	Orientation and information-gathering Identify values and roles for worker and relationship to community attitudes Plan approach and analyse evidence of community problems
	Negotiate entry	Establish relationships with existing groups Identify roles and establish appropriate relationships with agencies involved Identify and negotiate appropriate role for the worker's agency
Get to know the neighbourhood	Why collect data?	Justify to others and plan data collection
	Data requirements	Include history, environment, residents, organisations, communications, power and leadership
	Data collection	Specify the neighbourhood clearly Scan the area broadly, visit and travel round Use questionnaires and informal discussion, observation, written materials (eg local newspapers), local history sources, agency records
	Analyse, interpret and write up	Different types of report may be required
Identify needs, goals and roles	Assess problems	Describe, define, identify extent, origins and dynamic and present action around the problem
	Set goals/priorities	
	Decide role disposition	Will it be locality development, social planning or social action? Phasing, goals and preferences Agency constraints and opportunities
	Role arenas	Relations with local people, dealings between group and other groups, transaction about group in agencies
Making contacts and bringing people together	Reasons	Possible reasons are to allow people to assess the worker, provide information about the worker, motivate people to consider possibilities, increasing worker's knowledge
	Process of making contact	Prepare by selecting and sequencing people to talk to, selecting settings for meetings, decide aims, means of contact and how to present yourself Make contact: cross boundary, introduce yourself, agree aims of contact, see the contact through Afterwards: recall and write up, inform others, follow up
	Ways of making contact	Initiated by the worker: street work (perhaps using video), probing problems, surveys, petitions, public meetings, through third parties or existing events Initiated by community
Forming and building organisations	Context	Community condition: motivation, energy, barriers Community issues: concerns that engage support
	Form organisation	Check feasibility and desirability: existing groups, potential membership, timing, strategy Encourage leadership, give early help, surveys, groups members' motivation, wider community issues, clear goals Building: structure, tactics and strategies, group cohesion Public meetings

Source: Henderson and Thomas (2002).

Commentary

Midgley's (1995) attempt to create a theory of social development may be regarded as preliminary. So also is an attempt to import social development theory into wider social work usage. This is because Midgley's work contains very little development of models of action, and remains more a perspective promoting a particular form of action for incorporation more widely in social work. However, its relevance is shown by the examples of possible activities given in this chapter, and its links with community social work, community work and social pedagogy, all of which are widely used in Western countries. The community work illustrated by Henderson and Thomas's approach to community work shows wide applicability. So also does European social pedagogy, particularly with its application to work with children and in residential and day care. The community social work connection also demonstrates that this perspective on social work can contribute to delivering service as part of the social work role. Such a perspective sees the organisation and development of services as relevant to social development of a more general kind.

However, the weakness of both Midgley's approach to social development and community social work is their acceptance of working within existing social structures. Drucker (2003) argues that the claim of social work to be international reflects a continued attempt to indigenise a Western individual treatment model in resource-poor countries, when the appropriate approach would be for social workers to work for economic and social development. Individual methods would appropriately be used to identify personal consequences of poverty and economic underdevelopment. While they acknowledge critical perspectives, the response is even so to seek development within the accepted social order. Midgley makes much of the progressive, developmental approach of social development, as compared with the treatment perspective of much social work, but accepts formal institutional structures as a major part of social development work. Similarly, Hadley's community social work (in Hadley and McGrath, 1980) seeks to reform rather than transform the bureaucratic social work agency. His work also focuses community work onto welfare issues, rather than the priorities which people in the community might seek.

OVERVIEW

- Social and community development provide a wide social focus for workers' interventions to help oppressed people, much more so than systems theory, which focuses on the interpersonal.
- Social development and social pedagogy have developed outside the conventional Western social work literature and offer insights drawn from alternative theoretical and practice perspectives.
- They confirm and promote the existing social order.
- The detail of community work methods provides a useful codification of experience in dealing with community and social development.
- The perspectives considered in the next four chapters incorporate it into a more critical perspective of the adequacy of the present social order to meet the needs of oppressed groups within society.

FURTHER READING

Brueggeman, W. G. (2002) *The Practice of Macro Social Work*, 2nd edn (Belmont, CA: Brooks/Cole).

Hardcastle, D. A., Wenocur, S. and Powers, P. R. (1997) *Community Practice: Theories and Skills for Social Workers* (New York: Oxford University Press).

Henderson, P. and Thomas, D. (2002) *Skills in Neighbourhood Work*, 3rd edn (London: Routledge).

Comprehensive accounts of community work practice from the USA and (the last one) the UK.

Midgley, J. (1995) *Social Development: the Developmental Perspective in Social Welfare* (London: Sage).

Good account of social development theory and practice mainly in resource poor countries.

JOURNALS

Community Development Journal, Oxford University Press.
Indian Journal of Social Work, Tata Institute of Social Sciences, Mumbai.
Journal of Social Development in Africa, School of Social Work, Zimbabwe, Harare.
Social Development Issues, Inter University Consortium for International Social Development/Lyceum Books.

WEBSITE

http://www.infed.org/index.htm
Informal education website, with useful resources on the history and nature of community work.

CHAPTER 11

From Radical to Critical Perspectives

What this chapter is about

This chapter charts the movement from radical, structural social work practice theories to more contemporary critical theories. Radical perspectives on social work practice derive from Marxist social theories; there are many schools of thought. These have had influence on social work particularly at times of economic difficulty, such as the Depression of the 1930s, and at times of political commitment to social reform, such as the period of the 1960s and 70s. Existing radical practice theory originates mainly from this second period, but has been displaced by social movements concerned with women's rights (see Chapter 12 on feminist perspectives) and oppression of particular social groups on grounds of race, ethnicity and factors of concern to welfare services, such as disability, age and sexual orientation (see Chapter 13 on anti-discrimination and ethnic sensitivity). All these theories have been subjected to similar criticism for validity in social work practice on the basis of their lack of widely usable models for practice. This led to attempts in the 1990s to reformulate the basic Marxist theory using more recent forms of critical theory (considered in this chapter) and the practice of empowerment and advocacy (see Chapter 14). These ideas are primarily socialist-collectivist.

MAIN POINTS

> ➤ Radical and critical theory are transformational, proposing that social work should seek to change the way societies create social problems. In particular it rejects capitalist, economic liberal or economic rational approaches to managing economies either because of ideological objections or because they are inconsistent with a reasonable level of welfare provision.
>
> ➤ They are also emancipatory, being concerned with freeing people from the restrictions imposed by the existing social order.
>
> ➤ Radical social work of the 1970s has developed towards critical practice in the late 1990s, incorporating feminist and anti-discrimination perspectives and elements of empowerment theory alongside contemporary critical theory.

> ➤ Radical and critical social work reject elements of traditional social work practice that accept social policy based on economic liberalism or rationalism.
>
> ➤ The main elements of radical and critical theory include a focus on structural rather than personal explanations of social problems and a concern for inequality and oppression.
>
> ➤ Radical and critical practice seek to promote consciousness-raising about social inequalities, political action and social change because this helps to combat cultural hegemony, through which powerful people maintain a social order that benefits them by integrating social beliefs into people's cultural life through influence in the media and education.

PRACTICE ISSUES AND CONCEPTS

> ➤ Integrating *structural* explanations into practice, rather than relying on individual psychology and social networks as the basis for explanation.
>
> ➤ Aiming at social *transformation* building on and giving direction to individual and local change.
>
> ➤ Concern for responding to *inequalities*.
>
> ➤ *Praxis*, where working with people suffering from experience of injustice and inequality informs our ideological understanding of how society works and strengthens our capacity to pursue social transformation.
>
> ➤ Questioning assumptions about the present social order and those aspects of social work that lead to *social control*.
>
> ➤ *Dialogic* practice, that is, working with people in an equal relationship in which views of social situations are exchanged and discussed.
>
> ➤ *'Conscientisation'* – Freire's term – working to help people to understand and be able to criticise how social structures are implicated in their oppression and identify and take action about the practical consequences.
>
> ➤ *Animation*, techniques for engaging people's involvement in collective activity for community and cultural objectives.
>
> ➤ *Discourses*, language and practices through which people exercise power in cultural and social relations, may be understood and responded to.

Wider theoretical perspectives

This and the following three chapters deal with theories that take a socialist-collectivist or transformational perspective on social work. They reject or criticise the assumptions of economic liberalism or economic rationalism, and argue that societies should be transformed to accord with socialist assumptions. Liberal or rational philosophies, associated with Conservative, Republican and Christian Democratic political parties, propose that economic markets in which individuals compete to accumulate wealth are the most effective organisation for societies. This is because rational individuals will seek to benefit their own economic position and in doing so will contribute to economic growth and social development. Socialist philosophies, in contrast, associated with communist political parties, argue that competition and individualism are not necessary to economic development and have the disadvantage that they lead to economic inequalities between people, which lead to oppression by powerful social groups, elites, of less economically powerful people. Planned development would, socialists say, be as effective and could avoid the inequalities. Liberalism or rationalism argues that inequalities are an incentive for individuals to develop their economic power. There are many shades of radical opinion, and an important middle view is social democracy, associated with Labour and Social Democratic political parties. This view accepts the argument that markets in which individuals compete are the best form of organisation, but that a democratic system representing all social groups allows for social planning and provision which mitigates the most serious problems of markets.

Economic liberalism is different from social liberalism. Social liberals are open-minded about social freedoms and are questioning about traditional sources of authority, such as government, church, police, teachers and parents (and perhaps social workers). Conflicts are often associated with gender and sexuality. One important area is the right of women to equality in social status and independence, employment and income. Sexual freedom is also important, for example to permit sexual intercourse before or outside marriage, to deal flexibly with the consequences, in particular abortion, and to pursue gay and lesbian life styles. Social conservatives see the maintenance of systems of social status and associated authority as important for stability and order, and consider conventional gender divisions and sexual behaviour as an important element of stability in societies. In this view, social liberalism is destabilising. Social conservatism is often (but need not be) associated with fundamentalism in religion, that is, the view that the social and moral guidance in holy books such as the Bible for Christians and the Koran for Muslims should be taken literally. Such religious guidance is often interpreted in socially conservative ways (but need not be).

Radical social work emerged in the later 1960s. 'Radical' can mean anything which involves major changes, but is usually associated with politically radical ideas which are socialist or left-wing. The term 'left-wing' originates in the semi-circular physical layout of the French national assembly during the French Revolution, where people with socialist views sat on the left. Ideas of 'the left' were incorporated in a range of political movements since the late 1700s. There are many competing ideas within this tradition of thought. However, some typical ways of viewing the world arising from socialist thought affect social work:

■ Radical and critical theories are *materialist* (Burghardt, 1996). This means that how the materials of life, such as manufactured goods, are produced through the economic system is the crucial determinant of the social system in which we live.

- Social *structure* explains where social problems and issues come from rather than individual *agency*. In this sense, agency means the capacity to have an impact on what is going on around us. Structural explanations are *determinist*, that is, they emphasise how the social order – how society is arranged around us – has a strong influence on or determines our social relations, and we have very little influence on those social arrangements. Consequently, individual relationships and problems are the product of the social relations in a capitalist society. Capitalism is an economic system in which a few people accumulate capital to invest in producing goods and others 'sell' labour to them for wages. It is difficult for workers to accumulate capital from their wages and consequently they permanently lose control of the means by which goods are produced in society. Not all accounts of social work called 'structural' have this implication, for example Wood and Middleman's (1989) 'structural approach', is a systems approach.

- *Inequality* and *injustice* to particular groups in society come from their working-class position. Removing inequality and injustice is a major aim for social action. Accepting the economic liberal view that inequality and injustice are a necessary part of society to provide incentives for workers is inconsistent with being socialist. Analysing injustices affecting various groups is a significant part of socialist concern. This has led to the development of perspectives that broaden the range of factors that lead to inequality and injustice beyond the significance given to social class in traditional radical thought. Important among these have been feminist thought (Chapter 12) and anti-discriminatory or anti-oppressive theory (Chapter 13), which focus on the oppression affecting particular groups in society.

- *Cooperation* and *sharing* in social structures that encourage equality rather than inequality are the best ways of organising society.

- The focus of change is *political action* and broad *social change* rather than personal help. Since inequality and injustice is a product of the structure of society, a final resolution of problems cannot be achieved in a capitalist society. Only significant social change will resolve the problems arising from capitalism. This requires a revolution in at least social and political thought.

- The idea of *praxis* means that we must implement theories in practice, so that practice reflects on and alters the theory. As we act, the ideas used in acting find meaning in and are therefore expressed by what we do, and change our view of ourselves as we experience the idea in practice (Ronnby, 1992). Theory must come partly from ideas outside daily practice, otherwise it would only be a simple reflection of that practice, but it must not be totally outside recognisable practice.

Allied to the radical critique of social work methods, there is criticism of social work's system of service. Because agencies are part of the social system which supports capitalism, they have inherent failings in helping the working class (Ryant, 1969). Issues which are of central concern are as follows:

- *Social control* and the extent to which social work exercises it through the state on behalf of the ruling class. Critical theory is cautious of controlling activities.

- *Professionalisation* and the extent to which it is promoted by social work education to the disadvantage of the interests of oppressed communities and individuals. Critical workers seek alliances with working-class and community organisations rather than professional groups.

- Is *critical practice* possible in view of social and agency constraints on workers and the individual focus of much social work? The focus on collective and political work has led to the suggestion that critical practice is not possible in state agencies and charities, which are controlled on behalf of ruling elites, either through the political system or the management bodies that represent socially the ruling elites.

This account is designed to pull out of socialist theory some aspects which show where critical social work comes from. An example of such principles in action is Swartz's (1995) account of an urban job-training programme. The work promotes political education, tries to demystify services, partly by involving participants in making choices about the planning of service, and focuses on understanding how resources are inadequate to meet needs, and ways of dealing with this in a political context.

Rojek (1986) distinguishes three Marxist views of social work:

- The *progressive* position (Bailey and Brake, 1975a, 1980; Galper, 1980; Burghardt, 1996). Social work is a positive agent of change. It connects more general bourgeois society (that is, a society in which capitalism has created a system which exploits the working class) with representatives of the working class. Social workers are significant in promoting collective action and consciousness-raising, so helping to achieve change.

- The *reproductive* position (Skenridge and Lennie, 1971). Social workers are agents of class control enhancing the oppression by capitalist societies of the working class. They simply enable the capitalist system to reproduce itself in the next generation by helping people to cope with the difficulties of the system.

- The *contradictory* position (Corrigan and Leonard, 1978). Social workers are agents of capitalist control and undermine (at least potentially) class society. But while acting as agents of social control, they also increase working-class capacities to function, and offer some of the knowledge and power of the state to working-class people. The existence of this contradiction in their role leads to other contradictions which eventually contribute to the overthrow of capitalist society. Contemporary structural and critical theory is mainly a development of the contradictory position.

Radical ideas in social work migrated towards later practice theories, which are more social democratic in perspective, of which the most important are empowerment and advocacy theories (see Chapter 14). However, this has been resisted by radical social workers and some continued to espouse radical theory (for example Langan and Lee, 1989; Fook 1993) Alternatively, writers such as Langan (2002) have bemoaned its loss of influence, which was particularly associated with the discrediting of Marxism with the collapse of communist regimes in

Eastern Europe and Asia in the early 1990s and the success of neoliberal and economic rationalist regimes such as those led by Margaret Thatcher and Ronald Reagan, in Western countries (de Maria, 1993).

However, during the later 1990s, the idea of critical social work began to emerge. This has two meanings:

- To use *reflection* (see Chapter 2) in a questioning way, seeing that the consequences of reflection are not always comfortable and easily incorporated into current practice. This is perhaps better referred to as *critical thinking* or *critical reflection*, rather than critical practice.

- To incorporate more contemporary critical theories which go beyond Marxism, in particular those of the Frankfurt school of social thought, Habermas and Beck, and, for community workers, Gramsci (Ledwith, 1997). An important contribution of these writers is to emphasise how cultural, political and moral beliefs and structures are essential aspects of the way social orders are maintained through *hegemony*. This is important for social workers since, as we have seen, much of their work is concerned with trying to influence people's beliefs and perceptions about society.

Among the reasons for this development is the impact of postmodernism and social construction during the 1990s. These ideas are critical in the sense that they focus on the social origins of behaviour and social institutions, and do not take the present social order for granted. However, their objection to 'grand narratives' and practice that sets social objectives is contrary to the social activism and analysis of materialism and social structure in critical theory. Marxists see poverty and inequality as important, and criticise the concern with language and identity (Ferguson and Lavalette, 1999). Therefore, although welcoming the doubt and questioning inherent in postmodern perspectives, critical social workers sought alternative perspectives from contemporary critical theorists, to add to the perspectives derived from anti-discrimination and feminist perspectives. Allan's (2003) analysis of the relationship between modernist and postmodern critical theories in particular emphasises the importance to contemporary critical theory of analysing discourses through cultural and social relations, seeing power as available to be used, rather than just oppressive, and being open to self-reflection and reflexive creation of theory with clients. Although using empowerment and advocacy techniques, critical theorists also attack the use of these practice methods unless they are used within a structural and critical perspective (see Chapter 14).

Connections

Radical social work criticised 'traditional' (psychodynamic) social work, and other theories relying on psychological explanations of social problems, and functionalist theories which tend to take for granted the present social order. The radical view of traditional social work, largely maintained in critical practice, was as follows (partly from McIntyre, 1982):

- Explanations in traditional social work reduce complex social problems to individual psychological ones. They 'blame the victim', making clients responsible for problems which have social origins. In doing so, they deflect attention from social circumstances.

- Related to this, ideas such as adaptation and 'fit' in ecological theory assume that it is desirable for people to adjust to the present social order, rather than question and fight against the undesirable features of contemporary society.

- It 'privatises' people with social problems, for example by seeing them as confidential. This cuts them off from others who would share that experience and possibly deal jointly with it.

- It strengthens and follows the oppressive social order of capitalism.

In spite of this critique, there are links between many radical (now critical) theories and traditional social work. Webb (1981) identifies four main ones:

- Both accept that society contributes to generating personal problems. However, traditional social work accounts of the process by which this happens and interventions within it are inadequate, as we saw in the case of psychodynamic and systems theory.

- In both, the relationship between people and society is transactional, reflexive or interactive, so that we can affect our social circumstances as they affect us.

- Both seek client autonomy. Traditional social work criticised radical social work for ignoring it in pursuit of general social objectives which may conflict with individual needs and autonomy. Radicalism criticised traditional social work for ignoring the social constraints to conform.

- Both value insight so that clients can understand their circumstances in order to act on them. However, the purposes and means of action are different, and each perspective would deny the value of each other's forms of action.

The politics of the radical shift to critical theory

Radical views of social work gained significance in the 1970s. Their influence waned for a while in the 1980s One reason for this may be that general political developments in many Western countries moved against them and they seemed defeated, particularly with the collapse of communist regimes in Russia and Eastern Europe. Within social work, they were attacked, and as a general approach it seemed impossible to sustain in practice. Their resurgence in the late 1980s and 1990s may reflect a number of factors. Increasing criticism of the failings of and inequalities generated by the conservative governments in power in many Western countries during the 1980s led to a re-examination and recasting of radical ideas. Simpkin (1989) argues that the need to respond to the marginalisation of many social groups served by social workers remains, but more diverse critical responses could replace attempts to create a coherent radical theory.

Such recasting also took place within social work, first influenced by feminist thought then by concern about racism and discrimination and finally by critical theory. Some radical ideas remain embedded in social work thought from their period of influence in the 1970s. An element of social criticism deriving from radical thought is now more essential to social work theory than it was before this period of influence. These approaches also created a theoretical environment in which the development of forms of social work such as empowerment, advocacy and consciousness-raising grew up and became acceptable.

There is wide agreement that social work has a social control function, in that one of its tasks is to promote conformity with what Pearson (1975: 129) calls 'the binding obligations of civil society'. However, if we accept that such functions are always legitimate, we fail to question whether that control is always exercised for the benefit of clients or the social groups to which clients belong. Satyamurti (1979) argues that care and control are mixed together as part of public policy in British social work agencies, and their functions are hard to separate. This is probably true for many of those countries in which social work is primarily managed by state agencies. Goroff (1974) suggests that the activities of many agencies in the USA reflect coercive social control. Critical social workers argue that this is often on behalf of the state, representing the dominant interests of capitalist society.

Radical social work was concerned with how the professionalisation of social work disadvantages clients' interests, and leads social workers to become part of the state and social interests which oppress clients, and seeks their profession's development even where this is contrary to clients' interests. Moreover, professionalisation encourages an emphasis on the technical rather than moral and political aspects of helping, separates social work from other related professions by emphasising qualification and promotes professional hierarchies and so incorporates inequalities (Mullaly and Keating, 1991). The work of Illich et al. (1977), proposing that professions are often established to act in their own interests rather than (as they would themselves suggest) in the interests of those they serve, has generated a great deal of interest. The role of social work education is an example of this process. Radicals argued that it trains students for 'traditional' social work, reinforcing social control, individual explanations of clients' problems and conventional rather than radical interpretations of society (Cannan, 1972).

Radical practice is presented by Bailey and Brake (1975, 1980) as 'essentially understanding the position of the oppressed in the context of the social and economic structure they live in' (Bailey and Brake, 1975: 9). Casework is not rejected, only that which supports 'ruling-class hegemony', the use of ideology by ruling classes to maintain control of working classes. Generally, critical theory argues that residential care as at present offered may be damaging, but that communal living should in principle offer opportunities for unselfish self-actualisation that are not present in ordinary capitalist society or other therapies. Lee and Pithers (1980), for example, claimed that radical social work has had little impact on residential work. They propose that residential care could be a significant alternative model for living in a collective community environment, which provides a counterbalance to family socialisation. Residential care practice could combat, in their view, the deleterious effects of socialisation into dominant ideologies.

De Maria (1992) sets out radical practice methods. These are as follows:

- social work action should be sensitive to relevant social causes
- practice must be constantly tailored to the situation in which workers practise
- workers should be alert to contradictions between claimed low-level gains (such as client empowerment) and concomitant high-level losses (such as service disempowerment)
- social work is concerned with inherent humanity, and no single political or theoretical position has a monopoly of values which support such objectives
- critical thinking should lead to action
- it is important to preserve narratives about real life that explain and point up injustices
- we should focus on things which are marginalised by conventional thinking.

Radical social work also, significantly, argued that social work emphasises the traditional conceptions of the family, which led to the oppression of women. Women were often clients of social work when many of the problems should involve and may have been caused by men. Such approaches became allied with the developing women's movement of the 1960s and 70s. A distinctively feminist form of social work practice grew up (see Chapter 12).

A particularly important radical perspective, based on the work of Freire (1972; Brigham, 1977), developed in Latin America during the 1960s and 70s. Rather than a form of social action stemming from reform which maintains society in a steady state, liberation from the struggle to subsist requires revolutionary change (Lusk, 1981). A related set of ideas came from 'liberation theology' (see Chapter 10). These views led to a 'reconceptualisation' of social work in Latin America. Costa (1987) reviews a range of writing on these developments, emphasising the social worker as a wage earner in alliance with the working class, and political practice as part of social work. Among the techniques used is to seek the democratisation of social institutions so that clients may have influence within them, create space and services especially appropriate for working-class people (such as welfare and civil rights), become engaged with social movements and use professional associations and trade unions to seek change. Costa (1987) quotes Faleiros's four strategic alternatives:

- *conservative* – social work works professionally without political engagement
- *denial* – workers become involved in popular political work, but do not try to change social institutions for clients' benefit
- *counter-institutional* – workers seek deprofessionalisation, remove professional control and ask clients to make decisions (for example anti-psychiatry, which rejects medical and social help for mental illness in favour of self-help)
- *transformation* – workers seek the transformation of social institutions through support of clients, professional activity and political action. This concept is increasingly a focus of critical writing and teaching, see, for example, Coates and McKay (1995), Fook (2002), Mullaly (2003) and Pease (2002).

By implication, work in one sphere without accepting responsibility for other types of activity is likely to be ineffective.

Freire's (1972) approach focuses on education with people whose communities are oppressed by poverty and powerlessness. Such people are 'objects' who are acted upon, rather than having the freedom to act that people who are 'subjects' have. However, there is a 'fear of freedom', which must be disposed of. People develop an awareness of themselves within their environment, particularly their own culture (Poertner, 1994). This is done by education through involvement in a critical *dialogue* in which pure activism (trying to act without reflection and analysis) and pure verbalism (constantly talking about what to do without action) are merged together in *praxis*. This involves acting on analyses of social situations, and influencing the analysis by the experience and effects of the action.

One of the important aspects of this is *conscientisation*, which requires helping oppressed people to gain a *critical consciousness* of the social structures that are implicated in their oppression, including the impact of cultural hegemony. By this process they become aware of their oppression, rather than accepting it as inevitable. Through participation in dialogue and praxis, they can take action to lose their fear of freedom and some of their powerlessness. A Zimbabwean application of Freire (Moyana, 1989) shows how, by using education in creative work, it is possible to develop such consciousness without explicit participation in political action. Conscientisation has been connected to ideas of *animation* and *agology* (see Chapter 10), which have their influence in Continental Europe (Resnick, 1976). These are concerned with promoting collective activity, particularly artistic and leisure, as an expression of community experience and a medium of education. Agology is a service in which the worker guides and enables the intentional planning of social and personal change. The same radical roots have also given rise to the idea of consciousness-raising as part of the woman's movement, and it has many of the same objectives in freeing women's perceptions, understanding their oppressed state and taking collaborative action.

Major statements

There has been considerable activity in this area since the 1990s, particularly originating in Australia. Mullaly's (2003) second edition of *Structural Social Work* is now the major statement of Marxist social work (see below) based in a Canadian theoretical tradition of which Moreau (1979, 1990) was a founder.

Two influential texts focusing on critical practice are Healy's (2000) *Social Work Practices* and Fook's (2002: see below)) *Social Work: Critical Theory and Practice*, this latter book updating the same author's *Radical Social Work* (1993). Characteristic of these texts is the incorporation of ideas from Marxist structural perspectives, heavily modified by ideas from feminist, postmodern and the Frankfurt school of thought. Less comprehensive writings from this influential group are Pease and Fook's (1999) *Transforming Social Work Practice* and Allan's (2003) edited collection *Critical Social Work*; both have a broad compass.

Mullaly: structural social work

Structural social work is so called because social problems are inherent in our present social order and therefore the focus of change should be mainly on social structures and not individuals. Structural social work is inclusive because it is concerned with all forms of oppression; one is not more important than another. It uses a dialectical analysis, seeing both sides of social problems, the personal and the political. Because it is a critical theory, therefore, it includes both interpersonal and political action, which cannot be separated.

As with Corrigan and Leonard (1978), Mullaly (2003) starts from the position that the welfare state and social work are in crisis. This supposition of critical writers over the decades is so consistent that, as an analysis, it loses credibility. Marxist thought often seeks for the 'crisis' that will cause the downfall of capitalism. Mullaly argues that this is because social work has failed to clarify its ideology so that it has a clear paradigm to underlie all forms of practice. Debate about and prescriptions for practice should be rooted in an understanding of the political perspectives that underlie different views of policy and social structure. Workers should have a clear understanding of the comparisons between the present social order and the alternative views of the possibilities. Social work also needs a clear understanding of fundamental change. He contrasts a conventional view of social work, which accepts, participates in and seeks to reform the present social order with a progressive view which should be the basis of radical social work.

Progressive views include the following:

- a commitment to humanitarianism (which he incorrectly elides with humanism, so I have corrected his terminology – see Chapter 9), community and equality
- economic beliefs favouring government intervention, giving priority to social over economic goals and seeking an equitable distribution of society's resources
- participatory democracy and self-determination in government and non-government organisations
- seeing social welfare as an instrument to promote equality, solidarity and community
- seeking a social welfare state or structural model of practice
- seeking social work that treats people with respect, enhances dignity and integrity, enables clients to be self-determining, accepts difference and promotes social justice (Finn and Jacobson, 2003).

Mullaly compares the above views with four paradigms of political social thought which might underlie social work:

- *neoconservatism* sees welfare as having a residual role in the current social order
- *liberalism* has an individualistic view of welfare
- *social democracy* seeks a participative and humanitarian social system

- *Marxism* has a class analysis which seeks a planned economy based on the collective effort of everyone.

He argues that a progressive view of social work has much in common with Marxism and social democracy. They seek many of the same objectives. However, Mullaly calls the model of social work which emerges from this analysis 'structural social work' (based on Moreau's 1979, 1990, terminology). It is a critical theory in that it seeks to provide alternatives to and dispute mainstream social ideas. The starting point for structural theory is that it is a conflict rather than an order perspective, that is, it sees society as a struggle between social groups with competing interests, rather than being ordered and stable. A dialectical way of analysing issues seeks to identify opposing and contradictory forces that affect the relations between different groups. We must not see the interests of different groups as crudely opposed; this would be to see false dichotomies. Instead, we identify tensions, conflicts and areas of agreement and seek to include all areas of oppression. Mullaly's analysis is, then, very much in the contradictory tradition (see above). Thus, it is not a choice to work inside or outside the system; the benefits of social work and other welfare services are helpful to many different groups. However, we should expect to take appropriate actions to connect internal and external work.

The structural view of society focuses on economic and political institutions that influence and are influenced by welfare institutions. These, together with other social institutions, are the site of social relations, which are supported by a dominant ideology. Transformation means shifting social relations based on classes and divisions among social groups based on ideologies of inequality and individualism towards a society based on equality and grounded in an ideology of collectivism, planning, participation and solidarity.

Structural social work focuses on oppression, which arises around social groupings. The dominant social groups accept that their having more resources and power is justified by their effort, hard work and risk-taking in the market economy. There is a consistent, continuous and systematic bias in social relations towards the interests of the dominant groups. Distributional systems of social justice focus on the inequalities of resources and seek to redistribute them, but this ignores the social processes that maintain the assumption that inequality is right and ignores the difficulties of redistributing rights and opportunities when attitudes do not change. Particular social identities become associated with having resources and power. For example, being white and male is associated with wealth and power, while being black and female is associated with poverty. Hence, the police believe that an African Caribbean person driving an expensive car must have stolen it, because black people are typically poor. Oppression works not through coercion but through systematic constraints on subordinate groups. Forms of oppression include:

- *Exploitation*; for example women's caring is exploited by low pay and a low valuation of their effort

- *Marginalisation*; for example poor people from minority ethnic groups are often accommodated in poor-quality housing
- *Powerlessness*; for example workplaces are organised hierarchically excluding women and people from minorities, who therefore have less influence on policy and work practices
- *Cultural imperialism*; for example the experiences of minorities are not represented in the dominant cultural forms of expression, so that history appears to be made by powerful men and the white Florence Nightingale's work in creating nursing during the Crimean War is better remembered than the contribution of the black Mary Seacole
- *Violence*; for example violence and theft is more likely to affect people living in poor housing than people in more secure neighbourhoods.

Oppressed people respond to these experiences in ways typical of accepting their inferiority:

- *Minesis*, imitating the oppressors; for example poor young men idolise and copy successful sportsmen or actors
- *Escape from identity*, by denying the important aspects of the identity that creates the separation, for example women in business may become aggressive and dismissive of colleagues, following an exaggeration of male 'macho' behaviour
- *Psychological withdrawal*, for example people from ethnic minorities with outgoing personalities may moderate their behaviour when with people from dominant ethnic groups
- *Guilt-expiation rituals*, for example people of African origin may wear their hair to de-emphasise their difference, and minorities often have a higher level of self-destructive behaviour, such as self-harm and suicide
- *Magical ideologies* such as superstition, gambling or fantasies that lead to mental illnesses
- *In-group hostility*, where marginalised groups turn against each other
- *Social withdrawal* leads people to have different ways of behaving with different groups, and not show themselves to officials or other people from dominant groups.

Structural ideologies see creating a politics of difference as important, helping people to identify different social groups and how they are oppressed. Attempts at assimilation to the dominant group reject the culture of marginalised groups and deny the social mechanisms that create oppression. Understanding the structure of difference helps to prevent groups from being excluded.

Practice strategies for structural social work are set out in Table 11.1.

Table 11.1 Mullaly's structural social work practice

Issues	Limitations of distributional justice	Attend to social processes creating oppression
Humanitarian practice[1]	Oppression and dominance are socially constructed	Identify how victim-blaming and construction of oppression work
	Oppression is reproduced in everyday social processes	Examine poor 'adaptation' to identify moral and political oppression
	A variety of forms of oppression exist	Through dialogue, identify ways of consciousness-raising and normalising life experience
	Oppression is internalised	Dialogue to identify alternative ways of managing oppression
	Macro-level work is integral to practice	Identify groups and organisations that can promote collective responses
	The personal is political	Identify the political ends within your practice, how it may work towards transformation *and* raise consciousness about the processes that created social difference
	Empowerment	Increase the service user's control of personal and physical resources, aim organisational policies to support user control rather than conformity *and* seek user involvement in policy-making
		Engage in dialogue on problem solution rather than acting as an expert consultant to the user
		Avoid reinforcing victim status of user
	Consciousness-raising	Promote understanding of dehumanising structures and how to overcome their effects *and* join with user in changing social relations that cause oppression
	Normalisation	Help users to see that their problems are not unique, *especially* by linking them with others who share the problem
	Collectivisation	Forms groups of people who share the same problems *and* help to identify less obvious shared issues and allies
	Redefining	Expose the relationship between social conditions and personal response to and experience of them
	Dialogical relations	Maintain a dialogue of equals with user, demystifying your activities and providing inside information
	Survive in and change the workplace	Identify contradictions in agency practice to managers, radicalise and democratise processes within the agency especially by maximising users' benefits from the agency's work and protect yourself by having effective trade union and other representation
Radical structuralism	Alternative services and organisations	Assit in the creation of alternative and more radical services and organisations to provide user choice
	Social movements and coalition-building	Encourage and participate in social movements for change (for example environmental change, women's groups) and promote coalitions between groups that could form alliances for change
	Progressive unionism	Participate in trade unionism for the benefit of services and social change rather than personal benefit
	Professional associations	Engage professional associations in collective action for social transformation
	Electoral politics	Promote social transformation through participation in electoral politics
	Make the political personal	Seek to promote a vision of a transformed society in the way you live

Source: Mullaly (2001).
Note: 1. Mullaly calls this 'radical humanism', treating humanism as the same as humanitarianism.

Fook: critical theory and practice

Fook argues that a radical tradition in social work connects with a concern with the social rather than the personal, extended by the radical critique. This is a more cautious interpretation of the tradition than Simon's (1995) argument of the centrality of empowerment in American social work. Fook's structural perspective leads her to view Simon's empowerment as social democratic rather than transformational. However, the problems with radical social work led to a search for alternatives, of which postmodern and poststructural ideas were important. Critical social theory connected to these permit a more useful form of radical social work: *critical social work*, and Fook's analysis is set out in Figure 11.1.

The main points of critical social theory that are incorporated into critical social work are as follows:

- *Domination* is created structurally but experienced personally. Because powerful people may directly exploit people but also deceive themselves that oppression and inequality are unavoidable, these cultural beliefs lead people into self-defeating behaviour.

- *False consciousness*, therefore, means that people are not aware that social orders are created historically and might therefore be changed. They assume that inequalities are natural in society.

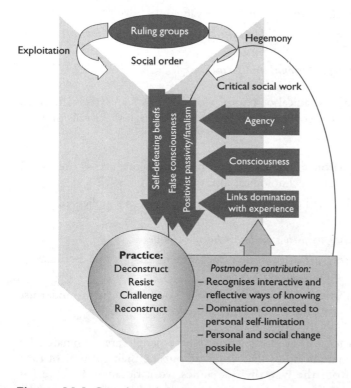

Figure 11.1 Critical social work process
Source: Fook (2002).

- *Positivism* as an ideology about how knowledge is created leads to passivity and fatalism, because people believe that social facts cannot be changed. Critical social theory emphasises people's *agency* – the capacity to achieve social change.

- Therefore, progress is possible, because the *awareness* of the possibility of change means that people have voluntary control over social arrangements, rather than the social order being determined by forces outside our control.

- Knowledge is not a reflection of external reality but actively *constructed* by researchers. Causal analysis differs from knowledge produced by self-reflection and interaction with others. Therefore, communication and reflection are essential to creating social change because they make possible the voluntary control of social issues in people's lives.

These points about positivism and reflection link the epistemological points discussed in Chapter 3 to the critical emphasis on awareness and agency. In this way, critical theory explains why discussion, reflection, analysis and insight are important in leading to a capacity to take action about problems in our lives. This explains why critical social work rejects evidence-based and other positivist views of social work knowledge.

Postmodern ideas that influence critical social work are:

- *Interactive and reflective ways of knowing* are valued
- *Connections between structural dominance and personal self-limitation* are acknowledged
- There are *possibilities for personal and social change.*

As with Mullaly and all radical or critical writers, Fook's analysis starts from the impact of current social contexts on social work, although she avoids the idea of crisis:

- *Globalisation* arises from the compression of connections across the world because of economic and technological innovation
- *Economic changes* have led to greater competition between suppliers of goods and services
- This leads to the *disaggregation and devaluing* of skills
- More rapid and *centralised provision* becomes more possible because of improvements in communications
- Welfare states and *progress* towards the public good are seen as modernist structures that will break down in postmodern globalised societies.

These trends lead to cultural domination, where people are dominated by cultural ideas and communications that originate outside their culture. In turn this excludes them from the way their societies work because the external cultural domination seems alien and their own culture becomes devalued by public stereotyping.

As a consequence, social work skills and knowledge are devalued, disaggregated into skills sets and boundaries between professions are broken down as services focus on skills and targeted programmes of social action, rather than holistic professional interventions. Managerialism means that general management skills are more valued than professional skills, and a focus on management separates professionals from policy change.

Critical possibilities that arise from these changes are as follows:

- *Professionalism* should be seen as a process of producing knowledge applicable to and transferable between a range of different situations
- *Practice* must deal with high levels of *complexity* and complicated contexts
- The need to aim for an increased *inclusivity* of ideas and people
- Complexity implies a need for *constant revision* in our critical analysis.

Fook's approach to social work concentrates on rethinking our ideas about practice in four different ways:

- *Knowing*

This is important because critical practice questions where knowledge comes from and how it is used, especially by professionals. Often it comes from dominant groups and professional knowledge takes for granted those groups' views of the world. Fook proposes a critical reflective approach to practice, challenging domination in external structures, social relations and personal constructions and recognising multiple and diverse constructions. When we do this, it disrupts dominant constructions. We should then try to reconstruct knowledge in an inclusive, sharing process with service users through communication and dialogue.

- *Power:* who has power and how they use it

This is important because power is often seen as a commodity, something someone or some group has, instead of the possibility of power being shared. Following from this, we tend to see groups as opposed to one another: if we think one thing, then someone who thinks something different is an enemy. However, we should allow that differences exist and try to account for contradictions in our thinking, and get other people to see contradictions in the way they are behaving. We must also recognise that there can be no assumptions about what is empowering to individuals: their reactions may vary. Critical social work tries to reconstruct power relations by analysing and reflecting on the power that exists in people's situations and then trying to reconceptualise it. Communication and dialogue helps people to see how power is being used in the situation they are in, and we must then try to negotiate experiences of new power relations, new structures that are less disempowering for people.

- *Discourse, language and narrative*

The Marxist concept of ideology sees it as a system of beliefs that has been institutionalised as part of the way in which a society or part of a society operates. This system interacts with the theories, explanations, behaviour and practical consequences related to the beliefs. The beliefs, behaviour and theories all affect and support one another. However, this way of seeing ideology leads to a number of problems. Different explanations are, according to your ideology, seen as true or false, and the split between your interests and awareness. Your behaviour is directional, that is, it always works in favour of one point of view rather than another. There is also a rational superstructure of ideas and a lack of plurality or contradiction in thinking, so that inconsistencies are ironed out. Postmodern discourse views about understanding run counter to these views. They suggest, calling particularly on Foucault's work, that understanding is constructed by social practices, particular forms of subjectivity and the power relations inherent in knowledge. Language is not seen as neutral but as colouring how we think and what we know. The narrative that we tell about something chooses between possible alternatives so that our communications convince others that what we say is true. If we can rethink it, a different interpretation may become true.

■ *Identity and difference*
Critical theories question the idea of a set, continuous self and identity. Part of this has to do with language. For example, we tend to think of things as dichotomies: what we are and what we are not. If I say that I am a quiet studious person, it excludes the possibility of being a lively, socially active person. However, critical ideas suggest that we can change, be contradictory and multiple: many things at once. We should see ourselves as whole people, who can develop more complexity and diversity.

The practice (see Table 11.2) that derives from these ways of thinking has some connections with the social construction approaches discussed in Chapter 8, since they emphasise the possibilities that might arise from reconceptualising our experience. The deconstruction elements of the main sequence of practice action that the theory proposes emphasise this:

■ Deconstruction

■ Resistance

■ Challenge

■ Reconstruction.

However, the ideas of resistance and challenge derive much more strongly from radical theory. Critical practice also has similarities with cognitive practice (Chapter 6) because it suggests that we should not be misled by irrational ways of thinking. Critical practice differs, however, because it emphasises particular areas of irrational thinking (misunderstanding about discourses of dominance) and flexibility and focuses on change in a particular direction (towards reconstructing relationships to enhance clients' understanding and use of power). These again connect more closely to radical thinking. It also rejects the authoritative 'therapist' practitioner implied by these theories in favour of a more complex relationship between worker and client that reflects the ambiguities of their relationships.

Table 11.2 Fook's critical social work

Process	Main strategies	Practice approaches
Critical reconstruction and deconstruction	Unsettle dominant discourses	Discourse analysis: identify possibilities for resistance, challenge and change
	Critical reconstruction process	Deconstruction: ■ Identify main themes, patterns, players and their perspectives, explanations ■ Create different interpretations/representations ■ Identify knowledges/assumptions, their origins and gaps in the narratives Resistance: refuse to accept the implications of dominant discourse Challenge Reconstruction: ■ Invent: new terms, languages, conversational devices, categories ■ Model new practices ■ Create structures, climates for new discourses to work
	Critical reflection and reconstruction	Critical incident – describe, analyse and create/adapt practice theory
Empowerment	Common constructions of power: ■ Workers' self-constructions ■ Opposition constructed as enemies ■ Power is not all structural ■ Small changes are valuable ■ Avoid participating in disempowerment ■ Responsibility goes with power to change ■ Reconstruct different kinds/uses of power	Deconstruct and reconstruct power: ■ Deconstruct power/power relations ■ Resist ■ Challenge ■ Reconstruct – negotiate, revaluation Construct your own theories of power
Problem conceptualisation and assessment	Criticisms of traditional notions of 'assessment' and 'problems' include: assumptions that problems have causes, there is a rational linear cause-problem-cure process, that workers are objective collectors of facts and that problems fit into preconceived categories. Note that labels and so on reflect discourses of powerful groups and that assessment often has a static view of problems/causes that 'blames' service users	Construction of professional narratives: ■ Problematise ■ Establish appropriate climate/process ■ 'We are investigating' orientation/strategy ■ Identify politics/contexts ■ Mutual dialogue/exchange leads to integrated, changing narrative ■ Reframe major concepts and language
Narrative strategies	Narrative reconstruction: ■ Identity reconstruction/politics ■ Action research ■ Narrative therapy	Uncover and challenge unhelpful assumptions: ■ Externalise problem narratives ■ Shift to enabling/empowering narratives ■ Create an audience
Contextual practices	Contextual practice: ■ Nature of contexts ■ Positionality – see different positions ■ Holistic approach to contexts – work with and also within contexts ■ Transferability – of knowledge and understanding ■ Reframe skills – contextual/cultural competence	Bureaucratic practice: ■ Reconstruct roles and identities ■ Challenge dichotomies and impossible dilemmas ■ Critical case management – complex user-focused practice ■ Advocacy ■ Construct enemies and allies – avoid dichotomising opposition ■ Supervision, management, education, organisational change
Ongoing learning	■ Work critically in uncertainty ■ Critical reflection – link reflection, evaluation, research ■ Ground action in local, immediate context, but: ■ Transcend everyday practice ■ Unity comes from marginalisation of diverse peoples	Critical practice in hostile environment: ■ Reframe practice as contextual ■ Challenge and resist ■ Expropriate and translate discourses ■ Identify contradictions, complexities, alliances

Source: Fook (2002).

Thus, as White (1995) shows in relation to women, we may seek equality and shared experience with clients, while realising that this is not always possible or helpful. In these ways critical practice picks up and uses feminist and empowerment theory (Chapters 12 and 14) directly, but it has a different view of them. Fook (2002) picks up Adams' (3rd edn, 2003) critique of empowerment theory, discussed in Chapter 14, that it is not possible to empower people; they must empower themselves. Also, empowering one person or group may disempower others. Empowerment may be diluted to mere enablement, particularly where, as in anti-oppressive theory (Chapter 13), there are too many target groups for empowerment so that in addressing all of them, none of them are addressed adequately. An ambiguous relationship between empowerment and self-help illustrates the problem. It is empowering to help yourself, but it is not empowering to be forced to do so when you do not have the resources. Consequently, Fook emphasises the importance of not trying to empower people unrealistically.

CRITICAL PRACTICE FOCUS

The Knightleys and the Karims

Mr Knightley was arrested for assaulting his neighbours, Mr Karim and his teenage son, in a street fight in their rundown area of town, released on bail, then reoffended. The Knightley family has been in a feud with the Karims about their recently established Indian takeaway restaurant, which has taken trade away from Mr Knightley's brother's fish and chip shop. Moreover, the three teenage Knightley children have been in constant trouble with the police for offences with motor vehicles; one has also been excluded from school for bullying the younger Karim children. Mrs Knightley is receiving medication for depression, and has recently had a hysterectomy, when cancerous cells were found on a routine scan. Mrs Karim is rarely seen, since she stays in the kitchen and does most of the cooking at the shop, but her two daughters help in the takeaway, taking orders and chatting with local youths, sometimes missing school to do so. The Knightley children have been on the at-risk register of children requiring child protection; there is also concern at school about the Karim children.

As a new social worker takes over the child protection case, what might different critical and radical views suggest to help to analyse this situation? In what ways would they help to take action, compared with the various psychological and systems approaches discussed in previous chapters?

Commentary

Critical social work has moved a long way from radical social work, particularly with the inclusion of postmodern and construction ideas, and the influence of feminism. However, critical social work practice still contains important elements of the radical approach, and therefore raises some of the same problems. Some of the criticisms are as follows:

- A tension exists between social work treating people as individuals, while also seeking collective social justice (Scourfield, 2002). Critical theory leans towards collective action, and this tends to neglect the immediate personal needs of clients. This sometimes seems unethical, uncaring or impractical because it is not what the social services are set up to do, or it provides only a partial explanation for the behaviour and events which are met by social workers. Leonard's (1984) Marxist individual psychology tries to connect broad general explanations from social theory with an understanding of individual responses.

- Critical theory is weak in dealing with emotional problems, although the impact of feminism has led to important developments. However, the concentration on material and social issues and the promotion of services like welfare rights advice ignore, to humanist and psychodynamic critics, clients' humanity and emotional and personal problems. Instead, critical prescriptions come from the theory rather than being a response to the problems that at least some clients present. So, it risks failing in the opposite way to traditional social work, by working from its own assumptions rather than those of the people served. It is one of the criticisms of evidence-based practice commentators that critical theories arise from workers' assumptions about people's positions, rather than their own views. The critical response is that people's consciousness should be raised.

- Radical theory was weak in offering practice guidelines. However critical theory has attempted to repair this deficit, particularly by relying on techniques from social construction that allow clients' voices to be heard and responded to, especially marginalised and excluded voices. Also, a perspective that offers a coherent and engaging view of the world is useful in itself, even without detailed practice help. Fook (2002) argues that a wide range of elements, including giving a name to things, making analyses and promoting broad social ideas can be useful in practice.

- Conscientisation relies on insight, without making it clear how this will lead to change. A similar criticism is raised about psychodynamic theories, but we saw with cognitive-behavioural theories that insight can speed people's responses to problems.

- Its accumulation of information critical of the treatment of many different groups identifies many problems. However, it fails to provide a coherent statement of what this means and a coordinated view of appropriate action (Rojek et al., 1989), so that it can seem negative and demotivating.

- It has a limited view of power and equates it with control. This allies social workers excessively with oppression, and does not fully identify the complexity of power relations among people at the personal level. As existentialists would argue, even victimised clients have a good deal of power (Rojek et al., 1989).

- Although it claims to seek social change, it is impossible to ally all the interests of the groups involved, which often conflict, and in practice seems to move towards achieving only more from existing services for those that it claims are oppressed (Rojek et al., 1989).

- Critical social work does not focus on religious oppression and human rights abuses, including torture and lack of political freedom to express views and vote accordingly. This may be because the texts come from Western countries where such rights are well established and their lack does not need to be strongly challenged. However, this cannot be assumed in many countries. Also, many Western countries suffer from some degree of abuses of this kind. Critical theory can thus seem to lack a sense of priority. In one way, however, traditional radical theory has the advantage over contemporary concern for inequalities, in that it focuses on structural inequalities, in particular of class and wealth. Concern with gender, race and other 'isms' can be criticised for focusing on what are to many people less fundamental issues.

- Conscientisation is claimed to avoid the problems of conventional insight therapies, because the aim is not just understanding, but action and understanding interacting with each other. However, failure to act on insight represents poor social work practice in psychological models, and similar poor practice might affect the link between insight and action in structural social work theory. The criticism here may be of bad practice in conventional social work and seeking to replace it with good critical practice. However, critical practitioners might also work ineffectively. Critical theory, in answer to this, argues that much insight in psychological models of practice is concerned with encouraging action to change attitudes and achieve alignment with expectations in the accepted social order. In critical theory, insight is concerned with achieving outward-going action to change the social order. The latter might be more successful because there can be alliances and mutual support. On the other hand, psychological change in desired directions through insight is inherently supported by the social system.

- It is an ideology, rather than a theory, that is, it does not offer an explanation which can be tested empirically. Marxists would answer that their method of investigation by historical analysis and debate is a legitimate form of study. Also, more broadly, critical theory argues that positivist science maintains the ruling hegemony by accepting and promoting the present social order, and is an inappropriate form of investigation for a radical theory. In this view, all theory represents ideological positions, often in support of the ruling class.

- Like many ideologies, critical theories define objections in their own terms and explain them away (objections are often taken to be representations of oppressive ideologies). The same is said of other theories (for instance, in psychodynamic theory, objections or the inability to accept the theory are sometimes claimed to arise from unconscious fears or conflicts in the objector).

- Some critical theories emphasise inadequate and oppressive environments and services as a better basis for the explanation of clients' problems than individual psychology. At its worst, this can substitute blame for local environments and their occupants in general rather than blame for the individual victim as an explanation (Galper, 1975; Webb, 1981). This might lead social workers' support for clients to be seen in opposition to the needs and interests of others in the same environment, since the needs and wishes of the poorest cannot always be aligned with those of all the working class. Clarke (1976) gives an example of this in a conflict over facilities on a public housing scheme where workers, by supporting one working-class group, raised opposition from others.

It is important not to go too far with these criticisms. Many agencies and clients welcome critical and community-oriented approaches, and opposition does not mean that a perspective should be ignored. It may offer a useful view to contribute to work using other theories or organise social workers' ideas, while not conflicting unreasonably with what they do in agencies. Over time, as with radical theory, it digs away at some of the weaknesses of conventional practice, improving it, and leading step by step to progress. In this regard, it is important to read carefully the more sophisticated analyses of the contradictory position, rather than assuming that all critical social work will necessarily require a conflictual approach to practice. More modern accounts of critical social work also contain much more sophisticated practice prescriptions which are easier to put into operation. It is also important to accept working in stages and not trying to achieve major social changes in every piece of work.

Some practice prescriptions of critical social work, however, concern collective action focused on structural change, rather than individual help, or helping people to achieve insight and therefore a critical analysis of their personal circumstances. Both clients and workers might find this difficult. Clients might find that their options are only acceptance or long-term resistance. Also they might not want their views of the world reformed. On the other hand, this kind of work can be affirming because it brings to the surface an understanding that explains and confirms feelings and attitudes that were otherwise unclear. Similarly, it is questionable whether it is the task of professionals and public officials to change the political or social views of their clients as part of their job, and this may not help workers to deal with matters such as child protection. Workers might have difficulties in official agencies that represent ruling ideologies in trying to promote critical approaches, and are likely to be either excluded or become frustrated in their inability to take action. On the other hand, a critical analysis of many ideas may be useful, for example the critical analysis of risk, which follows Beck (1992) in identifying how risk-averse contemporary societies may help workers to gain perspective on their work, and consider whether they are acting ethically or appropriately. Such views indicate that too much emphasis on risk oppresses people through child protection or putting elderly people into homes unnecessarily to protect agencies' reputations.

OVERVIEW

- Radical social work, historically the forerunner of critical social work, incorporated a useful critical perspective of the present social order and the social control and surveillance activities of social workers, the unfortunate consequences of social work professionalisation and the impact of agency power.

- Contemporary critical practice offers a distinctive analysis of social issues that helps social workers to think creatively about their practice and respond to concerns about oppressive practice.

- It highlights certain aspects of life, including the importance of power, ideological hegemony, class and status, professionalisation, gender and oppression. Critical theory makes these ideas available to social work in an understandable form, and has led to a substantial development of practice around these ideas.

- In particular, its emphasis on power draws perspectives into social work theory which have direct relevance to sexism and racism in ways which few other theories adequately achieve. We can see such developments more clearly in Chapter 12 on anti-discrimination/oppression.

FURTHER READING

Allan, J., Pease, B. and Briskman, L. (2003) *Critical Social Work: An Introduction to Theories and Practices* (Crows Nest, NSW: Allen & Unwin).

Fook, J. (2002) *Social Work: Critical Theory and Practice* (London: Sage).

Healy, K. (2000) *Social Work Practices: Contemporary Perspectives on Change* (London: Sage).

Mullaly, R. P. (Bob) (2003) *Structural Social Work: Ideology, Theory and Practice*, 2nd edn (Ontario: Oxford University Press).

Recent critical practice texts and collections, all deriving from Australia.

JOURNAL

Journal of Progressive Human Services, Haworth Press.

WEBSITES

http://www.criticalsocialwork.com/units/socialwork/critical.nsf/inToc/ 3E6C8461836592EF85256EC100669B75
The internet journal *Critical Social Work*.

http://www.radical.org.uk/barefoot/
Barefoot Social Work website, produced by an individual, with useful information.

http://www.geocities.com/rswsg/
Website of the Twin Cities Radical Social Work Group, a group based in Minneapolis, which also has useful practice ideas.

CHAPTER 12

Feminist Perspectives

What this chapter is about

Feminist perspectives on social work focus on explaining and responding to the oppressed position of women in most societies. This is important in social work because in most societies much of the work is done with women, and feminist perspectives help to understand their social roles and position. Methods of practice focus on collaborative and group work to achieve consciousness of issues that affect women in their social relations within societies. Also, in most agencies, a majority of workers are women, but they do not attain positions of seniority proportionate to their numbers. Feminist ideas have engaged the commitment of social workers in understanding such issues. While these ideas often seek radical change in societies, equality and mutual help, they are also often concerned with personal and social growth and development. Therefore, they lie between socialist-collectivist and reflexive-therapeutic views of social work, depending on the emphasis of the particular practice.

MAIN POINTS

> ➤ Feminist thinking has a long history, with many differentiated perspectives. It concerns the political, social, cultural and other forms of domination of women and their social relations by patriarchy, a system of thought and social relations that privileges and empowers men, and creates relationships between the genders that disfranchise, disempower and devalue women's experience.

> ➤ Liberal feminism focuses on inequalities in opportunity, radical feminism on patriarchy, socialist feminism on women's oppression as part of social inequalities in a class-based social structure, black feminism on the diversity and value of women's experience and postmodern feminism on cultural and social discourses in society that limit conceptions of women and the possibilities for development.

> ➤ In social work, feminist thinking has raised concern about power relations that disadvantage women in the profession and reject women's competence, experience and values, the need to understand and value women's experiences and lives as separate and different from those of men and the

role men should play where gender issues arise, as in issues around caring, prostitution and domestic and sexual violence and exploitation.

▶ Feminist social work focuses on the division and relationship between private experience and public problems, and how social workers intervene on behalf of the public within the domestic area, potentially oppressively.

▶ Feminist practice takes place in a dialogic, egalitarian relationship, within which women's experience and diversity can be shared and valued.

PRACTICE ISSUES AND CONCEPTS

▶ *Consciousness-raising* (connected to the critical practice conscientisation) as a strategy for stimulating awareness and change.

▶ *Reflexivity* as a research tool and its subsequent adaptation as an element of practice.

▶ *Dialogic, egalitarian relationships* as the vehicle of practice that values and empowers women.

▶ *Social and personal identity* and the social processes by which it is formed and by which it changes is an important aspect of creating and intervening in diverse relationships.

Wider theoretical perspectives

Feminism has a history stretching back for more than a hundred years. The first wave of feminist activism during the late 1800s was concerned with gaining political and legal property rights. From the 1960s onwards, the second wave was concerned with how the continued inequality of opportunity in work, political influence and the public sphere generally connected with attitudes towards women in the private sphere in interpersonal relationships. McLaughlin (2003) identifies debates between social theories and feminist thinking. In particular, standpoint theory derives from a Marxist perspective and examines the different interests represented in the perspectives on society held by different groups. Contemporary postmodern perspectives emphasise the cultural and linguistic aspects of power relations between the women and men. Gilligan's work (1982) has been influential. She shows that women and men have different modes of reasoning about moral questions (Rhodes, 1985), and Davis (1985) argues that female 'voices' have been suppressed in favour of a male positivist perspective. Gilligan (1986) argues that this means that men and women have different ways of understanding and valuing the self and defining what is moral. Alternative ways of defining social work, particularly ensuring that agencies are not managed to exclude women and their perspectives, are required.

Since the 1960s feminism has developed perspectives to explain inequalities between men and women:

- *Liberal feminism* (Reynolds, 1993; Dominelli, 2002a) or *gradualism* (Rojek et al., 1989) seeks equality between men and women, particularly in workplaces and caring and family responsibilities. This view focuses on how sex differences between women and men are translated by cultural assumptions into gender differences, which then affect social relations. The answer to inequalities is to reduce inequality and promote equal opportunities by legislation, changing social conventions and altering the socialisation process so that children do not grow up accepting gender inequalities.

- *Radical feminism* (Reynolds, 1993; Dominelli, 2002a) or *separatism* (Rojek et al., 1989) focuses concern on *patriarchy*, a social system characterised by men's power and privilege. This view values and celebrates the differences between men and women. It seeks to promote separate women's structures within existing organisations and women's own social structures.

- *Socialist* or *Marxist feminism* (Reynolds, 1993; Dominelli, 2002a) or *activism* (Rojek et al., 1989) emphasises women's oppression as part of structured inequality within a class-based social system. Because women are an important part of reproducing the workforce for the benefit of capitalism by carrying out domestic tasks and child care, this view particularly analyses this area. Women's oppression interacts with other forms of oppression (such as race, disability). Oppressive social relations should be analysed and understood, so that diverse interests can be met in various different ways.

- *Black feminsm* (Dominelli, 2002a; Collins, 2000) starts from racism and points to the diversity of women and the different kinds and combinations of oppression by which they are affected. Collins (2000) suggests that because black women are oppressed in many areas of social and domestic life, their experience of oppression is heightened compared with white women. There are diverse responses to such oppression depending on the particular experience, and because of the connection with different areas of oppression, connections are made with other campaigns for social justice. Important connections are made to family experience in slavery and historic family and social patterns derived from African and other originating countries.

- *Postmodern feminism* (Sands and Nuccio, 1992; Dominelli, 2002a) identifies the complexity and sophistication of social relations that involve women by focusing on how discourse in society creates social assumptions about how women are and should be treated. One of the important features of postmodern feminism is the concern to interrogate categories, rather than accepting them, and, deriving from Foucault's (1972) work, examine social relations of surveillance and discipline, which involve social workers.

Liberal feminism is criticised for ignoring real differences in interest and experience between men and women, and promoting equal *opportunities*, which may be ineffective in furthering women's equality since having an opportunity does not necessarily lead to fair *outcomes* if other aspects of inequality do not allow women to make good use of the opportunity. Radical feminism is criticised for focusing on gender differences and the common experiences of women, since this leads them to ignore the diversity of interests among different groups of women. Emphasising gender difference may play down women's capacity to achieve social change and trap them in a 'victimised' role. Socialist feminism is criticised by radical feminists for its limited view of the different forms of power relations between men and women (for example it does not strongly emphasise violence or sexuality). Focusing on class and economic oppression offers inadequate explanations of patriarchy. As with all postmodern perspectives, postmodern feminism may be criticised for emphasising relativity of social understanding. While this is integral to feminist thought, since it sees gender as a socially constructed category, rather than depending on the sexual identity of women, postmodern ideas emphasise how language creates different social perspectives and categories. Therefore, it implies that 'woman' is not a single category and diffuses focus on women's exploitation and oppression (Forcey and Nash, 1998). Some feminists, therefore, have been concerned that the influence of post-modernism has damagingly reduced the feminist focus on oppressive power relations (Fawcett and Featherstone, 2000).

Connections

A well-developed feminist social work analysis exists. Sands and Nuccio (1992) emphasise the importance of problematising social and gender categories, that is, avoiding taking for granted assumptions about social categories and the character- istics of people who are categorised in various ways. For example, we should not assume that women are natural carers for children and men not natural carers merely because biologically women have babies. Why should there be a simple either/or distinction? Taylor and Daly's (1995) collection considers the historical development of women's role as subservient to men in general social conventions, the law, medical practice and religion, which have had a considerable influence on the development of social work. This identifies many areas in which gender categories are taken for granted. Van den Bergh's (1995a) collection examines issues important to women that have influenced feminist practice, including peace, social justice and violence against women. Mills (1996) argues that taking control of decision-making in their own case is a crucial element of postmodern feminist thinking, leading to greater social justice for women suffering domestic violence. There has been concern about the way in which women's socialisation is inconsis- tent with male definitions of management, therefore they do not attain senior roles in agencies consistent with their representation among social workers generally, and are sometimes unhappy about the way in which authority and power are exercised within social work (Hallett, 1989; Grimwood and Popplestone, 1993; Taylor, 1995). Some writers (Grimwood and Popplestone, 1993; Chernesky, 1995; Coulshed et al., 2000) develop distinctively feminist approaches to social work management as a consequence.

Feminists seek to understand the lives and experience of women from their own perspectives and values, which are different from men's, and thus avoid being looked at from the point of view of men (androcentrism) (Hudson, 1985). Psychological understanding in social work, for example of child development, reflects study of males, rather than women (Walter and Peterson, 2002). An important method is *consciousness-raising*, by forming groups to share experiences and provide mutual support. Longres and McCleod (1980) relate consciousness-raising to the conscientisation of Freire (1972), which connects directly to critical theory. We saw in Chapter 11 that feminist thinking has had a strong influence on the shift from radical to critical theory. In social work, it is argued that goal and task-oriented practice, and positivist demands for scientific practice, are male-defined priorities, using a male language and way of thinking (Collins, 1986; Fawcett et al., 2000). Walker (1994), however, points to the gains achieved by the scientific method and argues that the criticism should be of the uses to which it has been put. Moreover, the 'ethics of care' position argues that caring is devalued by patriarchal societies because it is associated with women. Parton (2003) argues that the focus of construction theory on plurality of knowledge and voice by accepting alternative narratives and possibilities in practice connects to this view.

Many complexities are presented by work with men, since gender relationships are unlike many other forms of oppression and discrimination. This is because men and women are in close relationships, rather than separated out, as many oppressed groups are (Milner, 2004). Thus, feminist practice may give low priority to working with men, for example working with the victims of domestic violence rather than the perpetrators, who are usually men. Also, feminist views may seek to exclude men from contentious areas, such as working with the victims of male violence. Pro-feminist ideas on working with men have developed aimed at reducing violence and sexual exploitation and, particularly in social work education, combating sexual stereotypes (Cavanagh and Cree, 1996). Work with men and boys seeks to remove the damaging effects of their socialisation into conventional male behaviour, and enable them to manage personal relationships more successfully. In particular, this should reduce their tendency to be isolated because of the expectation that men do not need help or support and their tendency towards aggression and violence (van Elst, 1994). Men should take part in combating the problems of gender stereotyping, which they, as well as women, suffer from (Thompson, 1995). Conflict over masculinity exists – for example young men are the main clients of prisons and the care system, there is often conflict over fathers' involvement in families when they break up and men and women play different roles in family or informal caring (Pringle, 1995). Such social conflicts justify special attention to working with men so as to resolve issues of masculinity which cause problems for the men involved, or more widely. However, such work may be criticised if it leads to working with men for reasons other than their own needs only in order to achieve improvements for women.

The politics of feminist social work

Feminist theory emerged out of women social workers' commitment to wider feminist movements in Western societies in the 1970s. It became associated with radical social work movements of the 1960s and early 70s, but the earliest writings were from a broader, more liberal tradition, responding to general movements to improve civil and human rights. During the 1970s, academic work and radical theory on women's caring roles influenced professional thinking. Conversely, feminist movements affected counselling approaches on women's well-being and health. There was also campaigning around issues affecting women, particularly violence, rape and prostitution. Orme (2002) identifies four main areas of feminist social work:

- Women's conditions – with women sharing experience of oppression and discrimination in many areas of life and professionals being disadvantaged in pursuing their work and professional advancement
- Women-centred practice – where the focus is on identifying women's particular needs and responding to them
- Women's different voice – women experience the world differently, and have views different from men, particularly in matters of social and moral concern
- Working with diversity – because of their shared experience of oppression, women were able to identify, value and respond to many different sorts of social diversity.

Feminist approaches achieved major texts in the mid to late 1980s (for example Brook and Davis, 1985; Burden and Gottlieb, 1987; Hanmer and Statham, [1988] 1999; Dominelli and McCleod, 1989). Many of these texts sought to raise the relevance of feminist thinking on many of the issues that social work dealt with. For example, the fact that social workers did not, like many state services, act strongly enough to deal with battered women or rape reflected a weakness in social work theory (Orme, 2003). They were also included in major reviews of theory (Turner, 1986; Howe, 1987), even though during this period race issues did not appear. In the 1990s, a stream of publications reflected more detailed and specific analysis, for example Bricker-Jenkins et al. (1991) on feminist practice in clinical (that is, casework) settings, Langan and Day (1992) on a variety of feminist practice issues and Orme (2000) on community care. Their focus is often on situations where women suffered domestic violence or sexual assault or are part of social categories where women are strongly represented as a result of gender difference, such as mental health, caregivers and older people (Valentich, 1996). There is also a focus on reconsidering child care practice. Scourfield (2002), for example, notes that since social work operates individualistically, and child care is, in a patriarchal society, carried out by women, child protection work will inevitably involve a scrutiny of mothering, rather than issues of child poverty and poor nutrition. To give an example of the kinds of proposals that feminists make for such reconsideration, Callahan (1996) focuses on the following:

- women's experience of child care is a central aspect of understanding work with children
- families and the female role within them are crucial elements of child care
- reproduction as an element of society is as important as economic production
- relationships need to be reconstructed to see the connection between private relationships, between spouses and between women and children, interact with public definitions of what is considered appropriate and then enforced in family relationships.

There has been no coherent and extensive theoretical critique of feminist ideas in social work; their incorporation in social work ideas has been largely uncontroversial. However, there have been questions about the focus on working with women's issues. This may be seen as ghettoising the ideas into areas of special interest, rather than gaining credence for the feminist analysis more widely, or accepting that these are a minority interest. The analysis that places women as the main clients of social work may also be a characteristic of particular welfare systems. Some of the Nordic welfare systems, where social work is associated with the social security system, generate social work with men more easily, since they are referred for social work when seeking financial benefits. It is also, arguably, a product of preference or comfort among women workers in working with female members of families, rather than men, and the organisation of social services in the daytime, involving domestic visiting and child care issues. In spite of feminist analysis, there has been no concerted attempt to engage men in family and social care. But there is evidence that if a caring role is required of them, particularly in intimate relationships, they do perform it, for example Parker's (1993) study of men's care for wives affected by severe disability and Fisher's (1994) discussion of men's caring role in community care services generally.

While incorporation of feminist ideas has been uncontested, they are resisted. It is widely accepted that the history of social work and its role in surveillance on behalf of a patriarchal welfare state means that women remain socially oppressed and social work does not do much to alter that. Orme (2003) argues that feminist caution about pursing the path of creating extensive feminist models of general practice renders feminism invisible. This is true of the present book, since my criteria for covering a theory include the availability of an extensive account of the theory applied to create a practice model for general social work, and in previous editions, I have incorporated feminist ideas into anti-discriminatory and radical theory. I have always thought that this undervalues the impact of feminist ideas within social work generally and the richness of the ideas.

The resistance to feminism seems to lie in the refusal of male institutions, including marriage, employment and social work agencies, to give up power. This is the corollary of seeing feminist ideas as a matter of special interest, rather than a general critique of social ideas and practice. Thus, there is little change in social relationships, while the ideas are not directly contested. There have been continuing criticisms of the lack of women in senior positions in social work organisations, proportionate to the numbers of women in the organisation, and, in universities, of women's influence on academic work. Reactions have often been defensive, rather than making a theoretical analysis. Discrimination against women continues to be commonplace in the workplace and in welfare provision and they are disadvantaged economically and socially everywhere, especially in resource-poor countries.

Major statements

A major contemporary account of feminist social work is the edited collection of van den Bergh (1995a), which has the advantage of reflecting a range of perspectives on practice issues. Dominelli's *Feminist Social Work Theory and Practice*

(2002a) offers a coherent account of a structural perspective on feminist theory with some application to practice. Hanmer and Statham's *Women and Social Work* (1999) presents an account of issues important to feminists, also covering other social divisions as they relate to feminist practice. Earlier statements from Dominelli and McCleod (1989) and the edited text of Bricker-Jenkins et al. (1991) still give extended theoretical analyses and very useful accounts of practice respectively, but do not incorporate more recent developments in postmodern feminist thinking, although in some respects, Dominelli (2002a) is critical of this trend and does not incorporate it into her practice model. There is no comprehensive account of postmodern feminism applied to social work, and feminist texts do not present a general practice model. Hence, Dominelli's (2002a) primarily socialist text meets the criteria best for being used here as an example text, although it is by no means comprehensive in its coverage of client groups. Other broader accounts of feminist practice are briefly reviewed following discussion of her text.

Dominelli: feminist social work

Dominelli (2002a: 7) defines feminist social work as practice that starts from an analysis of women's experience of the world and focuses on the links between women's position in society and their individual predicaments to create egalitarian client–worker relationships and address structural inequalities. Since it works with women's lives and social relationships in a holistic manner, it also addresses the needs of people in social relationships with women, men, children and other women. Feminist social work emerged from activism by women working with women in their communities, linking their personal and local predicaments with public issues. The implication of this is a relocation of social work to recognise that gender neutrality ignores the substantial discrimination against women; structural change would address this by readjusting personal and professional relationships. The complex of different views in feminism, outlined above, requires, in Dominelli's view, a reconceptualisation of feminist social work theory and practice, as follows:

- Feminist social work usefully focuses on the division between public and private, because social workers often intervene on behalf of the public arena in the private and need to examine how the private is made public, and the public disciplines and controls women, for example through eligibility criteria for services. Public policy often oppresses women through social work practice. Domestic violence and other abuses of women can be isolating, and helping women to understand how they share these experiences with other women can be affirming.

- Concepts of discourse, looking at how language is used, deconstructing women's positions and social relations to identify power relations can help women to gain confidence and understanding of their position.

- Valuing women's capacities and skills also empowers women.

- Focusing on connectedness with others, reciprocity, mutual help and experience, power and citizenship can build links and support. However, it may sometimes overemphasise connectedness through caring, where responsibilities may be isolating and oppressive, for example the burden of isolated caring for an elderly relative or young child with very little other social contact or support.

- Creating an egalitarian process by which empowerment may be achieved is important.
- Loyalties to clients rather than agencies or systems can be supported by maintaining clients' participation in practice.

Among key contextual issues for feminists is the way contemporary welfare and social systems make people, but especially women, dependent on the state for services, because of patriarchy and such things as their low income. Globalisation has changed welfare regimes by focusing attention on budgetary control rather than needs and promoting privatisation within a mixed economy of care. The consequences for services are complex, including the costs of competition that cause reductions in wages for caring work that push women into poorly paid secondary labour markets. People are not citizens receiving services as a right, but services are commodified, that is, they become like products and clients become individual consumers, rather than supporting each other. Social work becomes deprofessionalised because rather than seeing services as a whole, provided consistently by one organisation, services are broken up into little pieces delivered by competing organisations. Instead of social concerns being looked at in the round, they become private troubles. Public regulation of social relations supports heterosexual marriages in which men have a dominant position, disadvantaging women in pension provision, and this may lead to conflicts over the responsibility for children if the marriage breaks up. Thus, postmodern welfare regimes individualise problems, rather than seeing them as the product of complex interactions and social relationships.

Social work's professionalisation has helpfully shifted welfare concerns into the public arena, but brings welfare services into the private situation of clients' home lives. Shifts towards the protection and controlling elements of social work have added to the oppression of women and have negated the potentially equalising aspects of social work values. Social work has tended to be 'oppression-blind' and has embraced roles that are concerned with promoting uniformity. Because feminism highlights and values difference, feminists have argued that difference should not be seen as a deficit and raised issues about how 'the family' is seen. Black feminists have also raised issues about the differentiated relationships between the state and welfare regimes and black women which promote inequality, for example through differential treatment of black people and in particular black women in immigration procedures and legislation. Feminist social work seeks to promote dialogue about oppressions and inequalities, and avoid 'false equality traps', where all women are seen as the same.

Dominelli (2002a) identifies a number of principles of feminist practice:

- Recognise women's diversity
- Value women's strengths

- Eliminate the privileging of some groups of women, so that it does not become the basis of unequal power relations
- Consider women as active agents, able to make their own decisions
- Identify social context and interconnectedness of individual women
- Give women space to voice their own needs and solutions
- Acknowledge that 'the personal is political' and all levels of practice interweave
- Redefine private problems as public issues
- Ensure that women's needs are addressed in such a way that they are treated holistically – each area of life interacts with all others
- Realise that human relations are interdependent and everyone affects all others who they interact with
- Address both the social and individual causes of women's problems
- Look for collective solutions to personal problems.

She also identifies a number of principles of practice for working with men:

- Gendered power relations have implications for men
- Masculinity is based on imposing power on others who are weaker
- Men are privileged over women because of social organisation (by implication, not because of how they individually behave, although they reflect the social organisation in their behaviour)
- Diversity exists among men
- Diversity among men reflects different levels of privileging (so that, for example, black men may be less privileged because of racism)
- Ensure than men take responsibility for oppressing others
- Make a connection between men who oppress women by violent crime and those who do not challenge oppressive social relations
- Celebrate the redefinition of masculinity towards nurturing and egalitarian relations
- Acknowledge the connection between structural constraints and personal behaviour and lack of emotional growth.

Dominelli's (2002a) book seeks to give evidence of the way in which feminist social work works by looking at various (but limited) categories of work, showing how distinctive feminist practice may work critically in these different areas. Table 12.1 sets out her practice proposals in each of these areas – men, children and families, adults (entirely focused on work with elders) and offenders. The most extensively developed accounts are on work with men. Material on work with elders and offenders is restricted to a few issues. I have emphasised in this tabulation her suggestions for workers' responses in practice, since these best give the flavour on the implementation of the principles she discusses.

Table 12.1 Dominelli's feminist social work practice

Client groups	Explanation	Practice
Men: Sexual politics	Unequal power	Identify and analyse privileging of men
Men in social work	Men dominate a woman's profession, by managing, not practising	Avoid gender dichotomies Use teams for affirmation Avoid bringing into practice workplace gender oppression Avoid focusing on men as breadwinners
Working with men	Model better ways of behaving or focus resources on women's needs	Debate role of men where women and children have been oppressed Protect women/children from male involvement
Men's movement	Use of myths, rituals, history to recreate traditional masculinity	Combat 'women-blaming' exaggeration of feminist gains Understand range of views on gender roles
Feminist theory for men	Social workers able to work with men in anti-sexist/pro-feminist ways	Commitment to avoiding gender stereotypes Engage men in caring Fulfilment for women Combat privileging of men
Children and families: Patriarchal families	Traditional families with man as leading partner still commonplace	Child welfare as positive and preventive, rather than protection Avoid seeing alternative family structures as inadequate Combat male employers' domination of caring/domestic workers
Contested families	Policy affirms the white male-dominated family, but women lone carers expected to be self-sufficient	Affirm alternative child care practices Avoid women-blaming for child care problems Support women resisting oppressive family/caring arrangements
Children's rights	Adultism leads to adults defining childrens' best interests	Support children's independence in making decisions Avoid excessive investigations in child protection
Fathering as economic relation	Fathers seen as primarily 'breadwinners', rather than full participants in family	Work for men accepting financial responsibilities Engage men in other personal support
Patriarchal control of reproduction	Men/the state control women's decisions on reproduction through new technologies (eg *in vitro* fertilisation, early abortion)	Work in partnership with women to achieve their aims Engage women in decisions on reproduction Avoid blaming women for difficulties eg disabled women having children
Focus on women's mothering	Much social work concentrates on women's mothering	Avoid crisis interventions Emphasise long-term support Address poverty/structural issues
Adults: Institutionalised ageism	Services affected by institutionalised ageism that women will care	Challenge old age as a state of decline Value contributions of elders Encourage education and self-development Promote intergenerational solidarity
Redefine community	Community assumptions define the kind of life elders can live	Encourage diverse responses to elders' needs Overcome problems of women's financial disadvantages
Deprofessionalisation	Elder care has been redefined as budget-led activity	Promote services that see women's needs as a whole Promote care for carers Combat elder abuse
Offenders: Rehabilitation or punishment	State redefines offender work as social control, with reduced elements of helping/support	Differentiate needs of women, men, ethnic groups Promote citizenship and responsibility
Masculinity and crime	Feminism links masculinity and crime	Challenge assumptions of men's violent natures Power relations explain men's sexual crimes Get men to take responsibility for violent behaviour
Women offenders	Criminal system focuses on male criminals	Concern for women victims of male violence
Young offenders criminalised	Young offenders are treated as criminals	Identify young offenders' needs for personal help

Source: Dominelli (2002a).

Feminist and critical practice theory

Feminism is a significant contributor to critical practice theory. Fook (2002) states that it has been a major influence on her. However, feminist ideas are woven within her work, rather than being explicitly identified. Healy (2000) deals more generally with feminism as part of critical practice: she sees feminism as going beyond critical practice. This is because it is open to a wider range of explanations of oppression than class and racial divisions and gives priority to interpersonal and personal experience as an expression of oppression and contributor to social change. Feminism is prepared to look at the interactions between different forms of oppression, rather than giving priority to one system of social oppression. On the other hand, she also sees feminism as part of critical practice because it refuses to take the present social order for granted.

Much of her material on feminist social work particularly emphasises the way in which difference and power are linked. Social and physical difference may become associated with the use of power in complex ways. For example, people may too readily give up elements of their own choice by accepting and valuing professional expertise or the help they receive, rather than entering a dialogue in which they may question particular things that do not suit them. For example, I recently worked with an elderly woman in a residential care home who valued the care given her, and appreciated her sister's frequent visits to take her out. However, the sister also managed the resident's money and was parsimonious. In one incident among many, the sister was slow to replace expensive batteries in the resident's hearing aid, thus isolating her socially. The resident would not question this, because she did not want to upset her main support. I engaged in a negotiation to get them to discuss this on the basis that small things were important when life is restricted by being in residential care. More broadly, having this particular incident questioned might mean that the sister would be more thoughtful about different attitudes to money in the future. It is also necessary to be aware that this behaviour may have been financial abuse of a vulnerable person, and action might have been needed to protect the resident from misuse of her money. One of the important aspects of postmodern feminism, to which we now turn, is an awareness of the diversity of behaviour, that 'woman are always oppressed, never the oppressor' is not always true.

Feminism and postmodernism

Sands and Nuccio (1992) and Healy (2000: 46–55) discuss some of the ideas that postmodern feminism contributes to social work, both focusing on poststructural theory. Poststructuralism, a set of theories of French origin, contests 'logocentrism', the idea that there is a single, fixed, logical social order that can be identified as reality. This connects with other postmodern ideas that question the possibility of understanding the world according to linear explanations of cause and effect (Chapter 3). Consequently, there will be a wide diversity of social forms and behaviours. One of the important areas of postmodern feminism that structural perspectives sometimes underplay is its recognition of diversity in women's and other people's social experience, in favour of one uncomplicated account of patriarchal oppression (Healy, 2000: 42; Orme, 2003: 137). Orme's (2001, 2003) example is the way a simple application of feminism argues that patriarchy has defined women's roles as caring, and has claimed the naturalness of women accepting caring roles. Thus, criticism of community care because it sets up a 'male' system for assessing need and allocating care services relying on routinisation and checklists only partially represents the possibilities in the situation. There would be opportunities to use this system more flexibly, as originally envisaged (Payne, 1995), and aspects of the formalisation of decision-making permit greater equity and social justice in provision of services (Payne, 2000; Orme, 2003). Also, caring continues, and there is evidence of both men and women accepting and negotiating caring roles in a complex interplay of relationships. Postmodern feminist theory acknowledges and seeks to understand this diversity and the multiple discourses that exist. However, it is criticised by structuralist writers such as Dominelli, because this emphasis on diversity makes it less easy to gain solidarity for political and social action; Sands and Nuccio (1992) identify feminist thought that emphasises 'positionality or 'both/and'. Here, while engaging in social action, workers would emphasise the universal experience of women, and promote men's support for the need for social change, while in other situations valuing and recognising diversity.

An important concept is *identity*. People's sense of themselves derives from myriad social relationships and institutional and personal influences upon them (Jenkins, 1996). It is, thus, constructed in the social and historical period that they experience. Exploring the factors that create someone's identity and how this relates to group membership is an essential part of postmodern feminism (Sands, 1996). It is also relevant to ethnic and cultural sensitivity (Chapter 13) because an important aspect of social identity is national identity and the factors that create it or may be assumed because of it.

Postmodern feminism particularly focuses on the deconstruction of discourses about women in society. The approach tries to destabilise conventional behaviour and provide openings for alternative and diverse interpretations. For example, it contests language that, by moderating and managing the impression of behaviour, denies domestic and sexual violence against women and children (Healy, 2000: 40). For example, I interviewed a man to question his violence towards his wife. He started by describing the event as 'I tapped her one' (hit or slapped her lightly once), whereas the police account that had led him to be imprisoned was of an extensive, public argument in the front garden of their house. Getting him to describe what happened in detail, I eventually got him to describe injuries such as grazes, cuts, bleeding, and aggression such as shouting, knocking her down and pushing her over a fence. Other examples of language use in particular discourses that need to be questioned to achieve destabilisation include describing sexual abuse of children as expressions of affection.

Another important area is reassessing the cultural characteristics of the 'feminine body' (Healy, 2000: 49–51), and the French writer Cixous has been influential on social work writing (Sands and Nuccio, 1992; Healy 2000). Women's bodies are not simply physical objects but their physical character and differences from male bodies are interwoven with cultural assumptions and expectations. Social assumptions about what is a good or attractive woman's body vary between cultures, and different presentations of a body incur social assumptions. For example, a rounded, fleshy female body might be regarded as maternal, warm and comforting or as representing gross overindulgence or lack of control in eating. In another culture or class, the rounded fleshy body might be regarded as an ideal of sexuality. Postmodern feminism attaches high valuation to diversity and women's individual choice. Social workers might be concerned about obesity leading to ill-health or early death in clients, for example, without recognising the emotional needs met by eating, or the consequences of poverty and assumptions about the role of women in families, which may lead a woman to eat poor food leading to obesity, giving better quality food to children and male partners.

Healy (2000: 51–5) identifies important principles of postmodern feminst practice:

- Focusing on detailed understanding of the complexity of how social and cultural factors interact to create discourses that affect how people behave
- Questioning and reworking explanations that rely on linear models of understanding human behaviour
- Focusing on social practices rather than social identities, so that we do not assume one single identity associated with a range of factors, but seek the complexities of the different factors that affect people's identities
- Promoting provisional coalitions between different interests, rather than assuming and trying to create collective identities to support political solidarity
- Promote an open-ended dialogue, rather than trying to define required outcomes too closely.

Van den Bergh (1995b), in an important American text, identifies similar practice principles of a more postmodern approach to feminist practice, which nonetheless emphasises standpoint theory:

- Question claims that particular social relations, especially gendered relations, are essential truths and underlying structures
- Promote partnerships rather than domination
- Focus on local contexts and truths, rather than seeking universal claims
- Establish meanings relevant to particular communities and stakeholders
- Deconstruct and reconstruct knowledge
- See knowledge as socially constructed
- See knowledge and power as inextricably linked.

She argues that feminist social workers achieve objectives by developing knowledge and understanding, emphasising connectivity, caring, mutuality and a multiplicity of perspectives. Knowledge should be used for helping to respond to social issues and inequalities, rather than for its own sake. Land (1995) in the same text, identifies practice approaches in individual work as follows:

- Validate social context as an important aspect of understanding
- Revalue the positions that women enact
- Recognise differences between male and female experience
- Rebalance perceptions of what is normal and deviant
- Be inclusive
- Attend to power dynamics in practice relationships
- Recognise that the personal is political
- Take a deconstructive stance
- See yourself and the client as partners
- Use knowledge inclusively, by explaining to the client where your understanding comes from, and using all appropriate sources of knowledge
- Challenge reductionist methods, that is, understanding that treats behaviour as made up of simple elements, rather than reflecting complex humanity
- Pursue empowerment practice.

Commentary

Feminist and non-sexist work has become important to many women. It also offers lessons to men in understanding and approaching their women clients, leading to new and less judgemental approaches to women's sexuality and lives. Wise (1995) claims that feminist practice is often exemplified by work outside the mainstream (for example in women's refuges) and its impact on conventional social work is uncertain. However, the availability of feminist theory has given greater priority to women's issues and makes it clear that there would be social value in replacing patriarchy in social relations. But, although there is much to be learned from feminist theory, a practice that is focused mainly on women's needs seems to ignore establishing and responding to the needs and role of men. While in most social relations, women's concerns are relevant, giving them a high priority in relation to other social issues may not be justified. There has been little independent research evidence of the effectiveness of feminist methods, although some approaches in empowerment have used similar ideas successfully (Chapter 14).

Feminism has also raised the policy context of welfare as it affects women, in its concern for the effects of gender on expectations of caring and services for women who suffer violence. This continues with the incorporation of therapeutic techniques within feminist theories. Peled et al. (2000), for example, recognising that many women choose to stay in situations where they suffer domestic violence, examine ways in which they may manage the situation using constructivist techniques to create social and emotional distance and by focusing on changes in their experiences and needs over time. McNay (1992) argues in relation to feminist practice that the analysis of power relations at individual and societal levels can lead to an approach to helping oppressed clients and groups gain experience of the use of power, so it can have broader application too. We saw in Chapter 11 that feminist thinking has had a significant impact, influencing particularly critical theory and enabling it to move forward towards a practice that focuses on structural issues, but contains a personal, valuing content. The next chapter notes the impact of black feminist ideas on anti-discrimination theory.

Feminist analysis is that consciousness-raising aims to encourage reflection so as to understand dehumanising social structures and action to change such social conditions. It involves dialogue between equals, concern for ideology and how dominant ideologies in society may create misfortune and social problems. However, at the same time, it creates mutual and shared exploration and respect for each other's views, making connections between private troubles and public issues and individual and class interests. Consciousness-raising is best done in groups for mutual support and broader exploration. It may be harder to find the time and commitment in individual work, and harder to empathise where the relationship between an individual client and worker is usually unequal. There needs to be a commitment to action to change situations that are identified in groups, otherwise complaining about the 'system' simply leads to a complaining acceptance of it. However, these difficulties are considerable, and one criticism of feminist social work is whether the dialogic, equal relationship is attainable or brings the results desired by both agencies and women themselves.

There has been criticism of the essentialism of treating women as a category and not recognising the diversity of women, their communities and relationships. Forcey and Nash (1998) argue that feminist practitioners need to both universalise and recognise the diversity in women's experience. Practice, in their view, must universalise women's experience as the basis for solidarity to achieve change. However, at the same time, they must recognise the danger in suppressing difference among women. Therefore, Sands and Nuccio (1992) note that postmodern feminists argue for an awareness of diversity, but when engaged in political or social action they focus on solidarity. Orme (2003) argues that standpoint theory does not adequately reflect the reality of social work with many women suffering oppression, since women cannot always be given priority, or always believed, where they may be neglecting children, for example. Therefore, it is important for women's views to be seen as situated in their social context, and for valuation of them to respect also their need for social and personal change and growth. However, this is consistent with more general social work values.

Although there are many examples of feminist practice, using groups to empower and develop women's sharing and mutual support, and protecting women against violence, much feminist theory does not have an explicit practice programme. Attending to gender issues, group consciousness-raising and dialogical, egalitarian relations between worker and client are the major distinctive practice contributions. Clifford (2002) argues that postmodernist feminism also usefully identifies the importance of using ethical commitments to equality and dialogical relationships in dealing with the inadequacies of postmodern ideas that uncertainty is a major aspect of the human condition.

CRITICAL PRACTICE FOCUS

The Cherries family centre

The Cherries family centre provides day care for preschool children, and groups for mothers to improve child care and child development skills. A new group of refugees from a Middle Eastern country has begun to move into the area and an English class has been provided for them at the local college. Social workers propose a parenting group to help women from this refugee group; there have been some concerns about standards of child care. Male members of the community management committee from the same minority ethnic community object that this is not necessary and individual help could be provided if the centre appointed a female visitor from their community. Some members of existing women's groups do not want their existing work disrupted by people who face different issues and have a language problem, and suggest forming a new group away from the centre at the college.

In considering how to act in this situation, the social workers may need to resolve alternatives proposed by different feminist positions. Empowerment and critical theory propose the value of dialogue and shared group experience; attachment and systems theories might support the value of individual help with child care problems. What approaches might be preferred? What approaches might be combined?

OVERVIEW

- Feminist theory has had a major impact in changing thinking about gender roles and relationships, particularly in relation to social policy and welfare services.

- It has raised awareness of the importance of women's leadership in working with other women, particularly those in oppressed situations.

- Feminist theory has been criticised as a perspective for more general application for its limited focus and priority to women's issues, its marginalised position in specialised agencies and its limited research base.

- It has contributed a practice of dialogical, egalitarian relations and group empowerment that has had a significant impact on critical and empowerment practice.

FURTHER READING

Dominelli, L. (2002) *Feminist Social Work Theory and Practice* (Basingstoke: Palgrave – now Palgrave Macmillan).

Fawcett, B., Featherstone, B., Fook, J. and Rossiter, A. (eds) (2000) *Practice and Research in Social Work: Postmodern Feminist Perspectives* (London: Routledge).

Hanmer, J. and Statham, D. (1999) *Women and Social Work: Towards a More Woman-centred Practice*, 2nd edn (Basingstoke: Macmillan – now Palgrave Macmillan).

Van den Bergh, N. (ed.) (1995) *Feminist Practice in the 21st Century* (Washington, DC: NASW Press).

All useful introductions to feminist social work from different perspectives: Dominelli's approach is socialist and structural, Hanmer and Statham more liberal, Fawcett et al. postmodernist and van den Bergh fairly eclectic.

JOURNAL

Affilia: Journal of Women and Social Work, Sage.

CHAPTER 13

Anti-discrimination and Cultural and Ethnic Sensitivity

What this chapter is about

From the 1980s onwards, growing concern about ethnic conflict in many Western societies and in global conflicts and social movements has raised the need and possibility of a social work practice that responds to ethnic and cultural division. Two related approaches try to deal with such issues: anti-discrimination and cultural and ethnic sensitivity. These originate from a concern about racism and ethnic conflict, but have broadened to incorporate discrimination against other social groups and wider forms of social exclusion. These approaches have distinct emphases, and social workers need to arrive at an understanding of how these issues may be incorporated into practice and a view about their own position in the theoretical debate, since this has direct consequences for how they practise and implement social work values. Anti-discrimination theories take a primarily socialist-collectivist view, while sensitivity approaches, although incorporating some structural perspectives that are socialist, apply these in a more reflexive-therapeutic way, rather than seeking broad social change. They aim to make the present social order more responsive to the problems these issues raise.

MAIN POINTS

> ➤ Anti-discriminatory, anti-oppressive and anti-racist perspectives focus on combating institutionalised discrimination in society, which represents the interests of powerful groups.

> ➤ Cultural and ethnic sensitivity promote responses to cultural and ethnic diversity in societies.

> ➤ Anti-discriminatory practice emerges from concern in many societies about racism and ethnic conflict.

> ➤ Multiculturalism affirms ethnic diversity and seeks to incorporate it into societies by valuing cultural contributions to the whole.

269

> ➤ Racism comprises ideologies and social processes that discriminate on grounds of assumed different racial membership, increasingly focusing on cultural factors.

> ➤ Alternative anti-racist perspectives are assimilation, liberal and cultural pluralism, structuralism and black perspectives.

> ➤ Anti-discrimination covers discrimination on grounds of race, gender, disability, sexuality and ageing; bringing such issues together incorporates an overarching structural explanation, but may not reflect the views of those involved or help to set practice priorities.

> ➤ Personal, cultural and social factors are all relevant to discrimination. The focus on language and culture as a basis for social change has led to accusations of political correctness.

> ➤ Dalrymple and Burke's (1995) anti-oppressive practice proposes working on the connections between feelings, ideas and action to respond to powerlessness, using the resources of the agency and professional help.

> ➤ Devore and Schlesinger's (1999) ethnic-sensitive practice focuses on awareness of the experience of minorities as part of every aspect of practice.

> ➤ Anti-discrimination incorporates structural explanations of discrimination and sensitivity incorporates cultural and social relationships into social work practice.

PRACTICE ISSUES AND CONCEPTS

> ➤ A focus on *discrimination* and *oppression* as important aspects of people's experience of social relations.

> ➤ A focus on *ethnicity* and *cultural issues* as crucial to people's identity.

> ➤ The idea of *sensitivity* to social and cultural difference as an important part of practice.

> ➤ Taking a *black and oppressed peoples'* perspectives as a guiding factor in practice.

Wider theoretical perspectives

There are two important areas of anti-discrimination and sensitivity practice. One derives from sociological and psychological study of how difference leads to social divisions; the focus on divisions is characteristic mainly of anti-discrimination and anti-oppressive practice. Dominelli (2002b) emphasises that the way in which divisions create social identities that generate oppression is central to anti-oppressive theory. The other important area is the study of cultures and their interaction with behaviour and relationships in societies. Much of the wider theory and research related to this area of social work theory lie in sociological and, to a lesser extent, psychological writing; the focus on ethnicity and culture is characteristic mainly of sensitivity practice. The two practices overlap but have different primary aims: anti-discrimination and anti-oppressive practice intends to transform social attitudes, sensitivity practice intends to modify wider social work practice and theory.

Anti-oppressive approaches to social work take in a variety of perspectives and models of work which have developed in the late 1980s and 90s. There have been policy concerns in Western democratic states. These have partly arisen from examples of serious social conflict, such as inner-city riots in the UK in the early 1980s, which were largely ascribed to alienation of young black people, similar riots and a high level of crime among black people in the USA, conflict in Germany and Italy over refugees from Eastern Europe and in France over refugees from North Africa. Official responses to this were largely socially liberal. That is, they focused on reducing inequalities and marginalisation by policies and practice that promotes social inclusion (Barry and Hallett, 1998). Anti-discriminatory practice also springs from concerns within radical thought for groups of people within societies who suffer from inequality and injustice. Since radical theory questions the existing social order, it sees the problem as one of social order and structures rather than one of individual or group problems or disadvantages.

Many countries face problems of conflict between different ethnic and cultural groups in their own way. In some, there are indigenous peoples, such as native Americans in Canada and the USA, Inuit people in Canada, Sami people in Nordic countries, gypsies or Romanies in Southern Europe and Aborigines and Maoris in Australia and New Zealand (Dixon and Scheurell, 1995). Often difficulties have arisen because of inward migration during a long history by other powerful ethnic groups and a long record of oppression and conflict, as in O'Hagan's (2001) example of Northern Ireland; another example might be Israel/Palestine.

Responding to such situations often led to an emphasis on respect for ethnic diversity or multiculturalism (Isajiw, 1997b), and in social work to cultural and ethnic sensitivity. There is no overall theory of multiculturalism (Rex, 1997). However, it refers to attempts to incorporate groups different from a dominant population into a nation or community by valuing their cultural contribution to the whole and emphasising the value of diversity and pluralism. In particular, it opposes separatism, and this idea was particularly influential at the time of socially liberal campaigns opposing social policies based on separation of ethnic and cultural groups in, for example, the American civil rights movement, South African apartheid and Australia and New Zealand, where there was concern to maintain the cultural identity of Aboriginal and Maori populations. Sanders (1978) defines multiculturalism as affirming the reality of cultural diversity, allowing individuals to keep much that is distinctive about their cultural traditions and integrating diverse cultural traditions into society, thus opposing a single, dominant culture. Such knowledge makes services more appropriate and responsive. Much of the literature focuses on culture, but a significant element of cultural diversity arises from religious and spiritual diversity. There has been growing interest in understanding different religious and spiritual experience as a result (see Chapter 9).

An important source of ideas is research and commentary on social issues concerned with race and ethnicity, but feminist theory and work on disability and sexuality have also been important. Anti-discriminatory and anti-oppressive practice seeks to bring together these areas of concern into an overarching theory and practice covering any area where people are inappropriately discriminated against or oppressed. Sensitivity focuses strongly on ethnicity and race, although it is potentially applicable to other social divisions where sensitivity is required. However, Devore and Schlesinger (1999) point out that many minority ethnic groups do not accept the association with wider oppressions, since there are particular factors involved in oppression of black and minority ethnic groups. Other groups usually included in anti-discrimination and anti-oppression theory often feel similarly. However, anti-discrimination and anti-oppression theory derives from a general critical social science analysis that oppression comes from inequalities arising from the power of ruling elites and sees various excluded groups as affected by similar social processes.

Anti-discrimination

Thompson (2003a: 19) asserts that a crucial aspect of much discrimination is a history of studies that incorporated widely held assumptions of the inferiority of particular biological categories. Contemporary social science seeks to question the false biological assumptions that underlie discrimination against various social categories and understand the social constructions that lead to those assumptions and the discriminatory behaviour that results. There is a literature on ideas of 'race' and ethnicity as factors in social relations and social structure. Reviewing the history of such ideas, Banton (1987) shows how 'race' in Europe was at one time associated with lineage. In colonial times, attempts were made to distinguish between different racial types, often associated with skin colour. Types became connected in the nineteenth century with the development of evolutionary ideas in biology, so that the different types were seen as related to different evolutionary lines of development. Thus they came to be associated with social status, the more successful and dominant societies claiming superiority over others. As 'races' came in contact with one another, superiority and inferiority became associated with class positions in societies where there were different 'races' in contact. There was a movement away from assumptions that biological differences between 'races' (which do not in fact exist, hence 'race' is often enclosed in inverted commas to indicate its lack of validity as a descriptive and analytical term) justified superiority to a concern about cultural and social differences.

Discrimination means identifying individuals and groups with certain characteristics and treating them less well than people or groups with conventionally valued characteristics. An important aspect of much anti-discriminatory theory is the analysis of the origins of discrimination. There is an extensive history of discrimination and oppression on the grounds of race and ethnicity across the world. However, changes from 1980 onwards accentuated this (Pilkington, 2003). As global travel and communication became quicker and more comprehensive, migration as a result of disasters and wars became more widespread, and cultures and ethnic groups came into contact more extensively. Significant minority groups with different physical appearances and cultures formed in many countries. Concern about discrimination first focused on inequalities in housing and employment markets, but has become associated with the idea of institutional racism. This proposes that much indirect discrimination arises because patterns of social relations privilege majority ethnic groups. Such privilege is part of the structure of organisations, such as the police, health and social care agencies, schools and government bodies in societies, and the assumptions of their workforces, managers and political leadership. Minority groups may become excluded from the main economic and social systems, and become centred in economically and socially deprived geographical communities that become associated with the ethnic minority. Consequently, minority ethnic groups become associated with the economic and social problems of deprived communities. Cultural representations, through the media, literature and films, connect deprivation with minorities.

Among modern theories of race (Rex and Mason, 1986), many sociological, psychological and biological perspectives are represented. Some theories of relations between races are pluralist in character, that is, they presume the possibility of equal and valid relations between races and ethnic groups. Such theories often focus on cultural and social difference and diversity rather than social inequality. The corollary is a social work practice concerned with awareness of, respect for and sensitivity to cultural and ethnic diversity. It values the rich stimulation to social relations from the range of cultures represented in countries with many different ethnic groups.

An alternative position is Marxist or class-based. It assumes that relations are likely to be conflictual and concerned with one superior social group oppressing others. Such concerns have driven a literature on conflict among races and the phenomenon of racism. Sociological analysis of race relations focused on class and status distinctions, these being the major factors in Marxist and more conventional analyses of social relations. Racism is a range of ideologies and social processes that discriminate against others on the basis of assumptions of different racial membership (Solomos, 2003: 11). Dominelli (1997) identifies personal, institutional and cultural racism as elements of such processes and ideologies, and Solomos comments that increasingly there is a shift from assumptions of biological superiority towards cultural superiority. This is a worldwide phenomenon throughout history (Bowser, 1995), and affects different societies differently.

Anti-racist perspectives

Table 13.1 identifies a number of perspectives in anti-racism, which may be extended to apply to most oppressed groups. Inevitably there are debates about the interaction and role of each.

Assimilation assumes that migrants to a new country will assimilate to the culture and life style of that country. Where there is a native population and dominant incomers, assimilation will be to the incomers (for example, in Australia, see LeSueur, 1970). This demonstrates that it is the power of the dominant culture which is at issue, and not who was present first. Small (1989) suggests that immigrants start by identifying with the culture and life style of their country of origin and then *substitute* the new country's culture and way of life. Herberg (1993) refers to this as *acculturation*. Isajiw (1997a) comments that

Table 13.1 Anti-racist perspectives

Perspective	Explanation	Practice consequences
Assimilation: Migrants or minorities will assimilate to the majority culture and life style	Migrants identify with the culture and life style of their country of origin and *substitute* or *acculturate* to the new country's culture and way of life *Social incorporation* (Isajiw, 1997a) refers to interweaving minority and majority social structures, cultures and identities, with reciprocity between minority group and majority society, which gains economically and culturally A *cultural deficit* model assumes the culture of origin did not provide necessary skills for the new culture (for example language, child care), so *pathologising* minorities	Social and personal difficulties, which social workers often deal with, are often interpreted pathologically as failures in substitution, acculturation or incorporation, or assumed to be the result of cultural deficit
Liberal pluralism: All groups should coexist and equal opportunities should be assured by legal and administrative means	Immigrants and oppressed black groups suffer multiple deprivations arising from their inferior position in the labour market and poor wage-earning capacity Often leads to a *colour-blind* approach (Dominelli, 1997: 37–40), where minority groups are treated in the same way as all others. This is partly designed to avoid a 'white backlash' against perceived unfairness of policies for special provision for black or other groups (Ely and Denney, 1987: 77)	Social work should provide equal access to services and special help to improve social conditions in compensation for multiple deprivations
Cultural pluralism: All groups should coexist, maintaining cultural traditions	Developing and valuing diverse cultural patterns should be encouraged. Knowledge, experience and understanding of different cultures should be spread	Multiculturalism, the study of diverse cultures, and ethnic and cultural sensitivity is essential to practice
Structuralist: Ethnic and cultural divisions are strengthened by economic and cultural domination by elite groups	Ethnic and gender divisions are the basis for economic and social domination of oppressed groups by economically and socially dominant groups in society Power is exercised by elites so that society is organised to avoid recognition of oppression of minorities, leading to institutional racism and discrimination Racism and other discrimination pervades society and therefore affects social work ideology, practice and training and requires anti-racist practice (Dominelli, 1997)	Workers explore their own racism and who holds power in particular situations Work with black families should accept families' own social values and expectations Change agency and other organisations' racism Move away from controlling towards supportive mechanisms Change social work practice and values by advocating anti-racist practice Confront and make explicit racism Work in alliance with black communities and organisations, following their priorities
Black perspectives: Black and minority ethnic groups develop particular perspectives on societies because of their history and experience	Black perspectives should be valued and guide social development and service provision Minority groups have an 'epistemic' privilege – understanding more directly the lived experience of oppression. Other groups must struggle to achieve this understanding (Narayan, 1994) Power is revealed in language and discourses which support oppressive assumptions	Help black people and communities participate in service and practice development Black perspectives should be dominant factor in policy, decision-making and practice Disclose black contributions to society and social work

Source: Denney (1983, 1991); Ely and Denney (1987); Jenkins (1988); Gould (1994); Dominelli (1997).

the idea of assimilation is too narrow, and *social incorporation* would be a more appropriate term. He refers to an interweaving of minority and majority social structures, cultures and identities, leading to reciprocity between the minority group and majority society, which gains economically and culturally.

An important issue with assimilation perspectives is that they assume a *cultural deficit*, that the original culture does not develop the skills and knowledge to cope with the new environment. This pathologises difference and assumes that the minority culture is deficient. For example, people might think that child care skills are lacking, or that oppression of female members of Muslim families is inappropriate in a Western society. This leads to *pathologising* black people (Singh, 1992), an example of 'blaming the victim'. Power here is used to remove oppression from the agenda, so that agencies do not recognise the problem. Herberg's (1993) approach to acculturation proposes that workers should understand the cultural origins of problems and work to change and develop the ability to manage in the new society. With offenders, workers should provide training and social control mechanisms to support acculturation.

Most anti-racist approaches are structuralist, like Dominelli's (1997) anti-racist work, from which the practice implications in Table 13.1 are drawn. Jenkins (1988) regards this as a *conflict* approach, since it assumes that the central issue will be increasing conflict between groups for resources and power. These lead to criticisms like those discussed in Chapter 10 in relation to structuralist perspectives. Ethnic and cultural sensitivity perspectives and black perspectives often include elements of explanation from structural perspectives but focus on cultural and social domination, rather than economic and class analysis. Consequently, structural theorists often regard them as providing inadequate accounts of racism. One aspect of sensitivity is to emphasise black people's contribution to the history of social work (Carlton-LaNey, 1994, 2001; Martin and Martin, 1995). These may have been hidden by racist assumptions which devalue such contributions. Ahmad's (1990: 3) view of black perspectives proposes that workers should explore black people's experience and writing. We should focus on those which express and clarify the history of black people's subordination to white people, the experience of racism and powerlessness and those which focus on attaining the goal of racial equality and justice. Practice should emphasise black people's own understanding of their experience, particularly during the assessment phases of social work. This should be interpreted to agencies and more widely within social work. Practice is 'empowering' (see Chapter 13). Resources offered by black workers, the black community and black organisations are relevant sources of change to black people. Workers should also explore and build on legislative provision and policy developments. In this way, the needs of black people and communities can be included in developments, systems and practice. Workers should be sensitive to black perspectives and experiences of the world, and in its attempts to adapt the skills of conventional practice to this perspective. Practice methods can contribute to this. For example, Martin (1995) shows how a process of exploring the 'oral history' of an individual in family and community contexts can include black and community perspectives in professional assessment. Efforts should be made to develop and make use of social science information about black people, which responds to the understandings which black people have about the world (Robinson, 1995). We should avoid assuming that there is only one minority culture, or that each group has a single culture, but explore the range of views in each case (Gross, 1995).

Wider discrimination and oppression

Another important strand in thinking about anti-discriminatory work comes from the influence of feminist thinking (see Chapter 12). The oppression of black women whose problems may combine racism and sexism has led to a distinctive approach from black feminist perspectives. An important wider debate which has relevance to social work is the issue of the role of psychoanalysis and its approach to women (see Chapter 4). Other influences on anti-discriminatory thought have been lesbian and gay rights work and ideas on disability, mental illness and learning disabilities and the political economy of ageing (Phillipson, 1982; Laczko and Phillipson, 1991; Bytheway, 1995). Many of these factors interrelate (for example, age and ethnicity, Blakemore and Boneham, 1994; age and gender, Arber and Ginn, 1991), so that problems where two or more aspects of identity lead to social oppression may be magnified, or may lead to conflicts in response and attitude.

Theoretical approaches in relation to other oppressed groups are less well developed, but it is possible to position them within these perspectives. *Normalisation* (Wolfensberger, 1972, 1984; Race, 2003) takes, in many ways, an assimilationist position. This is because it seeks to include people with learning disabilities as far as possible into 'ordinary life' (Towell, 1988), so that their social roles can, as far as possible, be equivalent to widely valued social roles. However, it also has elements of a perspectives position, because it seeks to take up and promote disabled people's own perspectives on their situation. A *social model of disability* view (Oliver, 1990, 1996) is a pluralist position with structural elements arguing that medical models concentrate on disabled people's impairment. Instead, we must recognise that social definitions of what is normal lead to society being organised in ways which create disability. For example, if there were no steps in buildings, a person with a walking impairment would not be disabled. Society should be changed so that all groups can coexist on an equal basis. Recognition of 'communities' among disabled people (such as a deaf community of people born deaf whose language and culture derives from sign language) suggests the possibility of a perspectives position as well. A *political economy of ageing* view (Laczko and Phillipson, 1991) is mainly structuralist. It argues that assumptions about ageing derive from the exclusion of older people from the labour market, making them economically and socially dependent. A *disabled living* view (Morris, 1993) is related to perspectives positions. It argues that disabled individuals and communities should direct and manage services designed to support them towards independence.

Connections

From radical social work to anti-discrimination

Concerns about social conflict led to attempts to frame an approach to combat racism within social work and to a lesser extent other related occupational groups. Radical social work texts in the 1970s often included items on what would now be called oppressed groups, for example Milligan (1975) on 'homosexuality'; Hart (1980) on gay and lesbian issues; Husband (1980) on racism. Feminism as a class-based analysis also made its appearance in the early 1980s (see Chapter 12). Major texts on work with minority ethnic groups appeared in the USA throughout the 1980s, for example the first edition of Devore and Schlesinger (1999) appeared in 1981, Jacobs and Bowles in 1988 and Pinderhughes in 1989, and in Britain in the mid to late 1980s, for instance Coombe and Little in 1986, Ely and Denney in 1987 and the first edition of Dominelli (1997) in 1988.

Impetus was given to many of these developments by the curriculum development activities of the UK and US education authorities for social work (for example Norton, 1978; CD Project Steering Group, 1991; CCETSW, 1991; Patel, 1994, all on race). Accounts of practice of this period include material on anti-racism or black perspectives (for instance Hanvey and Philpot, 1994) and virtually all American texts include it as a major area of knowledge and practice expertise. Some reviews of theory do not refer to anti-discrimination or feminism (for example Lishman, 1991; Stepney and Ford, 2000). This may reflect uncertainty about whether anti-discrimination is a separable theory of practice, since it does not refer to many social problems faced by social workers, and might be better regarded as a value principle which should 'permeate' all approaches to social work.

Social work in India interprets conflict between existing social groups as a problem of *communalism*. Chandra (1987) defines this as the belief that people following a particular religion consequently have common social, political and economic interests. This belief leads to conflict between different language, religious and caste communities (Miri, 1993; Kumar, 1994). Five conflict strategies have been identified (by Oomen, quoted by Kumar, 1994: 65–6):

- *assimilationist communalism*, where particular interests try to recruit others to their cause
- *welfarist communalism*, where social services and benefits are limited to one community
- *retreatist communalism*, where groups withdraw from interaction with others
- *retaliatory communalism*, where communities act violently against others when they perceive threats or acts against them
- *separatist communalism*, where language or culture is used to create enclaves away from others.

Here, the issue is constructed to define the issue as excessive separation or conflict. The social work role might be conflict reduction and achieving fair distribution of resources. Applying this to some Western countries might raise a concern for anti-discriminatory strategies which focus on extreme separatism, and suggest that it is important to understand and respond to the specific perspectives and needs of minority groups.

Analyses of anti-discrimination practice

A creation of the 1990s is an approach which includes all forms of oppression in a generic anti-discriminatory (Thompson, 1993) or anti-oppressive (Dalrymple and Burke, 1995) approach. Both make an analysis of discrimination – in Dalrymple and Burke's case drawing on the earlier work of Norton (1978) – which takes a concentric view of the relevant social forces. Figure 13.1 compares the terminology and approach of each. Norton's position sees the individual and their family and immediate community as 'embedded' (1978: 4) in a wider social system. The individual's primary identification is to the nurturing or immediate system. The wider or sustaining system is seen as 'taking on the attitude of the wider society in regard to oneself' (1978: 4). Thompson's (2003a) anti-discriminatory theory links the personal/psychological, cultural and social/structural levels of analysis of social issues. His view has presumably been developed without reference to Norton (whom he does not cite), but is similar. Here, the personal (P) level is about interpersonal relationships, and personal or psychological feelings, attitudes and actions between people, including social work practice, which is mainly carried out at this level. This takes place within a cultural context (C), which influences and forms individual thought and action, that is, the C level refers to shared ways of thinking, feeling and acting. Thus, it is about commonalities between people within different groups, an assumed consensus about normality and the assumption that people conform to social norms created within particular cultures. We internalise these cultural norms. These levels are in turn embedded in a structural

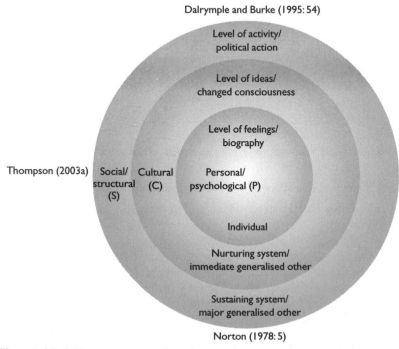

Dalrymple and Burke (1995: 54)

Level of activity/
political action

Level of ideas/
changed consciousness

Level of feelings/
biography

Thompson (2003a)   Social/   Cultural   Personal/
structural   (C)   psychological (P)
(S)

Individual

Nurturing system/
immediate generalised other

Sustaining system/
major generalised other

Norton (1978: 5)

Figure 13.1 Three concentric formulations of anti-oppressive practice

level (S), which is an established social order and a set of accepted social divisions. This established social order and its structures, and the cultural norms and assumptions and personal behaviour that results, come from acceptance of the social order and its divisions. Workers have a good deal of influence over the personal level, but decreasing influence over matters at the cultural and then structural levels.

Dalrymple and Burke's (1995) analysis, reflecting an awareness of Norton and earlier editions of Thompson's book, develops a practice model involving the worker and client in a partnership committed to change in order to achieve greater equality in society. This operates at the level of feelings, reflecting the client's and worker's biographies, at the level of ideas, working to achieve a changed consciousness of both feelings and society and at the level of political action in wider society.

There are problems with a concentric view, because it may assume that wider social ideas and structures are always mediated by a more immediate culture in their effect on the ideas and feelings of individuals. Against this, the immediate culture may be in conflict with the wider society, and support individuals against wider ideas and structures. Alternatively, individuals may be in conflict with their culture and more in touch with wider ideas.

Anti-discrimination, ethnic sensitivity and other social work practices

Anti-discrimination and anti-oppression seek to incorporate into social work practice a concern for combating discrimination against all groups. Thompson's (1993, 1997, 2003a) analysis of anti-discriminatory practice is important as the first account to attempt to provide a theoretical rationale for practice across a range of discriminatory behaviour; the theoretical account has changed little in later editions. It emphasises the importance of social divisions of class, gender and race and ethnicity in creating social structures in which people experience discrimination. He includes gender, ethnicity, ageing, disability and, less comprehensively, sexual orientation, religion, language, nation, region, and mental illness and impairment. This avoids separating different forms of discrimination into a hierarchy in which one is more important than another. All forms of discrimination are seen as important. They have a potentiating effect on one another so that one form of discrimination strengthens the adverse effects of others. Being female, elderly and from an ethnic minority, for example, has been described as triple jeopardy (Norman, 1985), although there is not yet clear evidence that black elderly people in Britain are more disadvantaged than equivalent white people (Blakemore and Boneham, 1994: 55).

Ideas of cultural pluralism accentuate the cultural element of ethnic difference, for example different dress, social customs, artistic and musical contributions and diet and cuisine. Education of children in religious and social customs is an important strategy and multiculturalism influenced education in the 1980s. A similar approach was also applied to social work and similar professions to encourage sensitivity to needs and choices among different ethnic groups. Developing from this is the idea of workers having 'cultural competence' (Lum, 1999; O'Hagan, 2001) to carry out their work with respect for maintaining diversity and understanding the main cultures they would have contact with. Forte (1999) proposes that social workers develop 'toolkits' of information about values associated with different cultures. A characteristic of the American literature (for instance Jacobs and Bowles, 1988; Ryan, 1992; Kim, 1995) is the exploration of detailed information about different minority groups. This appears to be at least partly because of the presence in the USA of large groups of recent migrants, raising specific language, cultural and practical issues, and the indigenous 'Indian' (native American) ethnic groups. Dungee-Anderson and Beckett (1995) argue that we need to understand other cultures with which we work to avoid mistakes in intervention caused by misunderstanding our own or clients' reactions.

Placing an emphasis on culture presents practical difficulties. Culture may imply a relatively unchanging, dominating collection of social values, and assumes that members of an identified group will always accept all of these. Against this assumption, the source of influences on an individual or a social or ethnic group may be variable. Multiculturalism in education is criticised for encouraging people to gain a smattering of other cultures, without an in-depth appreciation of the origins and reasons for difference. Applied to social work, anti-discrimination theorists argue that it may encourage a surface appreciation of visible diversities, without dealing with substantial social inequalities and discrimination. This risks ignoring diversity within categories, subordinating alternative cultures to Western interpretations of them, or simplifying them and denying real philosophical and practical differences in cultural views (Gross, 1995). In this way, multiculturalism does not address inequality, discrimination and the depth of cultural diversity. My own experience is that it is more respectful to ask about any culturally specific requirements that clients may have, rather than making assumptions from the broad generalisations in texts. Fellin (2000) argues that multiculturalism also fails to address diversity within white communities, focusing instead on difference within minority ethnic groups and between minority ethnic and white groups.

Taking a rather different approach to diversity, Cox and Ephross (1998), like Lee (2001, Chapter 13), emphasising the lens through which workers see clients and their social situations, argue that we must identify aspects of homogeneity and heterogeneity in the ethnic groups we deal with. So, faced with a situation in which ethnicity is an issue, we should assess where there are connections with wider issues of inequality and structural racism, but also identify issues that particularly affect the group, including diversities such as gender and sexuality. We would identify that an African Caribbean man suffers structural inequality in Western societies, for example, but also work on the specific issues raised by his oppressive gender relations with his wife and the personal and social issues raised by his increasing awareness that he is gay. Seeley (2004) suggests that in short-term work with people from cultural minorities, it is important to focus on their own interpretations of their cultural experience, to grasp issues that are important to the client.

Practical benefits come from multiculturalism where workers from a dominant population group are dealing with clients from other ethnic and cultural groups. Their practice will be more respectful and sensitive by responding to different dietary needs and child-rearing practices, and agencies may be organised to take account of cultural expectations, such as religious festivals and rituals, and language differences by providing interpretation and information in appropriate languages. O'Hagan (2001) refers to the 'primacy of effort over knowledge', the high value that minority groups put on workers who ask how they would choose to be dealt with rather than assuming the majority conventions or some overgeneralised stereotype of the minority. Thus, the worker who asks how someone from a different culture would like to be addressed or the residential care worker who asks how a child would like to dress to respect her religion demonstrate respect, even though they are not able to assess these needs accurately from their own knowledge. This would deal with the criticism of multiculturalism applied to social work that it encourages cultural assumptions and surface appreciation of cultural difference. Houston (2002) incorporates ideas from Bourdieu's sociology to propose that culturally sensitive work tries to identify links between culture, power and the reproduction of social structures. Cultural ideas and assumptions persist, influenced by the power of particular social groups, and contribute to the reproduction of social structures that advantage powerful groups and disadvantage those with less power. We can see, in this way, how culture connects with class and political power to maintain social divisions and discrimination.

The practice benefits for workers in diverse societies have ensured the continued use and development of ethnic and cultural sensitivity and competence approaches. However, their pragmatism and their emphasis on the contested concept of culture means that the ideological and theoretical elements of anti-discrimination theory have in many respects become a competing theoretical position to ethnic sensitivity.

The politics of anti-oppression and cultural and ethnic sensitivity

Anti-discrimination and sensitivity as alternative perspectives

The competition between anti-discrimination and sensitivity approaches derives from:

- the emphasis on structural explanation in anti-discrimination theory
- the emphasis on the cultural and social inclusion in sensitivity theory.

While both perspectives include both elements, structural explanations would logically obstruct the inclusion and empowerment strategies that sensitivity theory focuses on. Anti-racist practices, as opposed to multicultural perspectives, according to Naik (1991: 51, emphasis original) 'attend to *structural inequalities in society*, ... [including] the dynamics of race, economics and political power'. The British anti-racist structuralist emphasis on power derives from the structuralist position, considered in Chapter 10. Sensitivity practice encourages awareness and acceptance of structural explanations leading towards an empowerment approach, but not prioritising them to adapt practice towards social transformation. Several British writers (for example Sivanandan,

1991; Husband, 1991; Mullard, 1991) explicitly reject pluralist perspectives, and relate anti-racism to socialist political objectives. Others (such as Ahmed, 1991) comment on the failure of class-based radical structuralist theory to respond to black perspectives, particularly women's perspectives. Singh (1992), in seeing a black pathology view as moving towards a black perspectives view, and Ely and Denney (1987), in proposing a basically historical account, imply that theoretical development is leading towards structuralist and possibly black perspectives positions.

Sensitivity and multicultural perspectives see themselves as a legitimate alternative. They may also be taken up as an aspect of relational social work in complex therapeutic work, since cultural and ethnic issues are often important aspects of the issues faced by such clients (Ganzer and Ornstein, 2002). American accounts of anti-racism (for example Pinderhughes, 1988, 1989) similarly attach great significance to power, but see this in relation to its interpersonal effects and consequences for behaviour and experience. Dietz (2000) argues for a clinical practice that assesses the impact of oppression, but works on strengths and personal social and political contexts. The increasing emphasis on different cultural expressions of spirituality is another aspect of this approach (Chapter 9). Gould (1995) argues that we should develop multiculturalism to offer a framework for all groups to integrate thinking across cultures.

Black perspectives propose a more experiential and political understanding of the black experience. We should focus on understanding and working with power differentials and value opportunities to achieve power for black perspectives, black participation and black influence and control in services and attitudes. They connect with the approach of the disabled living perspective and some aspects of normalisation and ordinary life perspectives. This leads us to the possibility of an oppressed groups' perspective, with a detailed analysis and understanding of the views and experience of oppressed groups. This is the basis for social work action, and for promoting the involvement of members of those groups in the management and development of services.

Several writers, including Dalrymple and Burke (1995), whose work is discussed more fully below, move on to propose forms of anti-oppressive practice that rely on structuralist analyses of power, while proposing an empowering anti-oppressive practice. Such an approach to power argues that power does not need to be equated with control, but may be spread widely in society, and may be taken up by apparently powerless groups. Structuralists regard such views as failing to focus primarily on inequalities of power. Fook (1993: 17), for example, criticises empowerment for not necessarily being informed by or actively opposing structural oppression.

Problems with anti-discrimination

O'Hagan (2001) presents a multicultural critique of anti-discrimination as follows:

- It focuses on racism, while ignoring important cultural aspects of discrimination, such as religion.

■ It focuses on 'black/white' distinctions, referring to such ideas as 'black tradition', 'black experience' and 'black perspectives' contrary to the wishes of many people within the groups so labelled, who prefer to distinguish different histories, cultures and religions as aspects of personal and social identity.

■ It uses terms such as 'ethnicity', with a meaning in historical derivation implying 'not us', which are associated with pejorative terms such as 'ethnic cleansing', and have come to be used offensively, as in referring to people from minority groups as 'ethnics'. Since O'Hagan was writing, the rise of the abbreviation BME (black and minority ethnic group) and reference to BMEs in daily practice is similarly offensive. Such changes have led to accusations of linguistic 'political correctness' (see below).

In addition, Clarke (2003) proposes that structural origins of racism interact with emotional responses to create a complex mixture of factors; neither the internal and emotional nor the external can be ignored. Robinson (1999) argues that the stage that a person has reached in the development of racial identity is more important that the mere fact of their race. Thus, in general, the picture is of a more complex set of social interactions than simple discrimination. Even so, Robinson (2001) argues that there is a shared experience of discrimination and racism.

Attempts to create an overall theoretical model of anti-discriminatory and anti-oppressive practice sought to subsume anti-racist and other special concerns with feminism. However, the strong ideological and theoretical roots of feminism in wider political, social and cultural ideology and many distinctive features lead me to treat it separately in Chapter 12.

Anti-discrimination sees the interaction between various oppressions as complex and requiring analysis. However, this presents practical and ideological problems. Macey and Moxon (1996) criticise anti-racism because it emphasises racism as an explanation of discrimination in the context of high levels of poverty and poor environments. Poor education, crime and disorder, unemployment and inequality are due to many other factors, and anti-discrimination exaggerates the importance of racism in its interaction with other sources of inequality. An agency or workers may specialise in ways which make it impossible for them to accord equal weight to all the oppressions. The needs of clients may present in one area, and they may resist dealing with other areas. Both workers and clients may, at the level of ideas, have difficulty in accepting the equivalence of oppression of, say, ageism or lesbians and gays with that of, say, race. This may be due to their own prejudice or their reasonable assessment that ageism, say, has far less serious consequences for particular clients or in general than racism.

Hegemony, language and political correctness

The structural elements of anti-discriminatory practice connect to the conventional radical criticism of the failings of traditional social work theory (see Chapter 10). Since structure and commonalities arising from cultural assumptions are such an important part of personal behaviour, discrimination does not wholly or even mainly arise from personal prejudice, although in a particular instance this may be so. It arises first from the fact that powerful groups in society maintain discrimination in society as a way of preserving their power. They do so using their hegemony, that is, through their social control of beliefs about the nature of society which creates an ideology. Thus discrimination is created and maintained by personal beliefs and behaviour reinforced by ideologies that develop from the power exerted by groups in order to sustain and strengthen their dominant position within social structures. This is an increasingly important concept in critical theory, as we saw in Fook's account of critical practice in Chapter 11. Wilson and Beresford (2000) go further to argue that the way in which social work has given importance to anti-oppressive practice allows workers to appropriate the ideas of oppressed service users while retaining the power to define what it oppressive. Service users still lose control of how their lives are defined, and this is in itself oppressive.

One of the ways in which discrimination is maintained through cultural means is by the use of language and social assumptions to support conventions which are discriminatory. This makes important connections with social construction theory. Denney (1992) argues that poststructuralist theory provides a method for exploring, through the analysis of court or agency reports, how people have moved from assumptions to making discriminatory decisions. Another example is using the words 'spastic' and 'idiot' as terms of abuse, when originally they were technical terms referring to a particular form or severity (respectively) of physical and learning (respectively) disabilities. Now, I am white and grew up without meeting any black people until my late teens, so I find it hard not to think of being white as normal and being black as out of the ordinary. We tend to take for granted such assumptions about ourselves and others. As a result, Owusu-Bempah (1994) shows, workers assume that self-identity in black children will be problematic, when they do not make the same assumptions about white children. This suggests that we need to be open and flexible in our views about all ethnic groups and listen carefully to their own perspective, rather than taking any issue for granted in relation to ethnic identity.

Connected to this concern to achieve language and cultural change away from discriminatory assumptions is the issue of 'political correctness'. This concept implies excessive concern with the form of anti-discriminatory practice and particularly the overcareful use of language. Philpot (1999) points out 'political correctness' is often used indiscriminately as a term of abuse, with very little meaning, or in jokes that criticise overconcern with anti-discrimination. Pinker's (1999) main example of the consequences is that for a period social workers were concerned to pursue same-race adoption and foster care, when there is little evidence that this is such an overriding factor. As a result, he argues, both children and adopters missed out on opportunities. Dent (1999) argues that the effective provision of services is a more important focus of anti-discrimination than language use or procedural caution, which are often used to disguise inadequacies. It is widely agreed that sensitive language is an appropriate courtesy. Fairclough (2003), reviewing the issue extensively, points out that the demands that led to accusations of political correctness sought social and political change through a new approach: by changing cultural attitudes and language rather than seeking to change social institutions, law or policy. Trying to change social behaviour and structure by changing language use was new to most people and was experienced as an arrogant personal attack, rather than a valid way of achieving social change. Moreover, Fairclough argues, unlike many campaigns for social change, the campaigners did not work in a strategic way, seeing the changes sought as a matter of justice requiring immediate and practicable changes, and this meant that they did not establish the case fully, before the backlash emerged.

In summary, anti-discriminatory/oppressive perspectives are critical of all social work practice and organisation in their failure to incorporate major social change to achieve equality and social justice for minority and oppressed groups. Cultural and sensitivity approaches question the structuralist focus on inequalities and social transformation. The choice presented for practitioners is to embrace the structural critique completely (a socialist-collectivist strategy), or focus on cultural and black or oppressed groups' perspectives as a way of being committed to meeting oppressed minorities' needs within interpersonal and therapeutic practice (a reflexive-therapeutic strategy). To avoid this 'either/or' dichotomy, workers would need an individualist-reformist strategy incorporating a structuralist awareness with sensitivity. However, this compromises the views particularly of the structuralist perspective.

Major statements

The major anti-discrimination statements build upon Thompson's (2003a) introductory *Anti-discriminatory Practice*, now in its third edition. Dalrymple and Burke's (1995) *Anti-Oppressive Practice* offers a practical account of practice related to social work responsibilities in welfare states, focusing on legal and professional responsibilities. Dominelli's *Anti-Oppressive Social Work Theory and Practice* (2002b) provides a practice guide, although not as well informed as Dalrymple and Burke by interpersonal practice. Dominelli's text is more theoretically comprehensive than Thompson, more internationally focused and builds on her work in anti-racism, where her introductory text (1997) remains well used. Dominelli's *Social Work* (2004) is a more general social work practice text, covering major British client groups and is informed by anti-oppressive perspectives.

The major statement of ethnic-sensitive practice remains Devore and Schlesinger's (1999) *Ethnic-Sensitive Social Work Practice*, now in its fifth edition. Dhooper and Moore (2001) provide a useful introduction, but focused on minority ethnic groups most often encountered in the USA. Martin and Martin's (1995) and Carlton-LaNey's (2001) books are accounts of the impact of black people on American social work. O'Hagan (2001) is a research-based discussion of cultural competency, with a British perspective, but does not provide, except by implication, comprehensive practice guidance.

Dalrymple and Burke: anti-oppressive practice

Dalrymple and Burke (1995) place many of the ideas discussed here in a comprehensive account of anti-oppressive practice. Their focus is how the legal and professional responsibilities of social workers may be implemented oppressively or in an empowering way. They have thus developed their model in an extremely difficult area for social work – the use of power and authority – in search of protection for both public and clients. It makes their formulation all the more powerful for focusing on an area of social work which seems to conflict with attacking discrimination and developing empowerment for clients.

Their starting point is an assertion that effective anti-oppressive practice requires a clear theoretical perspective to inform a value base which will permit anti-oppressive work. A clear understanding of power and oppression must also inform the values of practice. Power is seen as concerned with personal and social relationships where one person or group consistently prevents others, who are seen as powerless, from achieving their needs or aspirations. Oppression is understood to be characterised by personal and social relationships based upon the assumption of inequalities of power, so that people internalise acceptance of their own lack of power in their lives. Dalrymple and Burke argue that a clear connection must be seen between an individual's personal social environment which may render them powerless and the wider social system which reinforces and takes for granted the powerlessness of certain groups. Workers must also be aware of agency contexts so that they do not just accept policy issues about service provision as routine constraints, and they must build reflection, involvement and evaluation into everything they do.

Such principles must be applied in practice to enable workers to understand where they are applying values and legal rights and duties in a liberal rather than radical way. Thus, for Dalrymple and Burke, anti-oppressive practice requires:

- an empowering approach
- working in partnership with clients
- minimal intervention.

Workers can use these practices to inform their use of the conventional powers of social work practice and avoid acting oppressively. For example, a worker should not arrange for a carer to assist an elderly lady with the covert aim of checking up on the client's capacity to manage alone. Instead, the worker should openly discuss the risks of managing alone, working with her on a plan to prevent problems arising. This avoids trying to set up a system which takes away too much responsibility for action from the client. Such an approach would mean that she has even less practice in taking responsibility for her own safety.

An empowering approach requires focusing on helping clients to gain more control over their lives, become aware of and use their own personal resources, overcome obstacles in meeting their needs and aspirations, have their voice heard in decision-making and be able to challenge situations where they experience inequality and oppression. Empowerment requires making links between clients' personal positions and structural inequalities. This involves helping people to understand how things have happened to them and trying to find ways in which they can gain control over at least some aspects of their lives. This reduces their confusion and helps them to feel more in touch with their lives.

For example, Mrs Wilkins is an elderly lady who has saved for most of her life, but now finds she cannot manage on her small pension. This makes her feel incompetent and confused about priorities. The worker helped her to understand that she was affected by poor mobility, so that she could not use cheaper superstores but had to rely on expensive local shops, and historically poor pension provision, which she had saved to compensate for. She could set priorities for daily expenditure such as food, rent, heating and lighting. This could be made from her pension and then she could feel that she was managing efficiently with that. She could draw from her savings for more major expenditure on clothes and equipment purchases. In this way, she could feel in control of the expenditure from her savings, seeing it as appropriate to what she had saved for, instead of leaking away on everyday necessities. The worker was also able to get advice for her on ways in which she could invest her money to gain a better income. In this case the worker was operating at the interpersonal level to harness the client's own resources and using the agency's knowledge and information resources at the organisational level. In the long run, information from situations such as this can be accumulated to work at a policy level to improve the way pension provision is made.

Dalrymple and Burke work at several different levels:

- *Feelings*, where they try to reduce the effect of the personal experiences which have led to the client feeling powerless. They emphasise, as does Rees (1991 – see Chapter 12), the importance of exploring biography in understanding such personal experiences.
- *Ideas*, where they concentrate on clients' feelings of self-worth and try to strengthen their ability to control their lives, feelings and ability to act. This is similar to ego-supportive work in psychodynamic social work and much of the focus of cognitive theory. The aim here is to lead to a changed consciousness within the client of their capacity.
- *Action*, which is concerned with seeking changes in the agency, social welfare or wider systems which adversely affects clients.

The next aspect of Dalrymple and Burke's anti-oppressive practice involves partnership. One formulation of partnership, identified by Stevenson and Parsloe (1993) from a community care project, requires the following policies:

- only investigating problems with the client's explicit consent
- only acting where there is clear agreement by the client or an explicit legal requirement
- basing action on the views and needs of all relevant family members
- basing action on negotiated agreement rather than assumptions or prejudices about clients' needs and wishes
- giving clients the greatest possible degree of choice, even when they must be legally compelled.

Dalrymple and Burke recommend the use of written agreements, produced in circumstances where there is effective communication between worker and client. Also, clients should have access to independent advocates who can represent their views effectively. Written charters or standards of service and explanations of clients' rights create a clear focus for them to be able to understand their entitlement. Partnership involves effective inter-agency work and careful planning of services, so that clients have the widest degree of choice with the minimum of professional and agency barriers to exercise that choice.

Minimal intervention requires workers to be aware of their potential power. This may oppress clients, either leading to excessive or non-participative intervention or failure to intervene when their use of appropriate powers might assist and protect clients. Workers should prefer to intervene at various levels:

- *The primary level*, to prevent problems arising. Services might be adapted to be appropriate and helpful to clients, community resources mobilised to help them, and the public and people involved given information and education to enable them to manage themselves.
- *The secondary level*, to catch problems and try to deal with them early, before they become serious. This reduces the amount of interference in clients' lives.
- *The tertiary level*, to reduce the consequences for people when something has gone wrong or action has been forced on the agency.

This approach stresses not waiting until the last possible moment, and then being forced into excessive or oppressive action. It is better to intervene at an earlier stage to prevent greater incursions into clients' lives.

A crucial element of Dalrymple and Burke's approach is to link strategies for wider change to everyday action. This avoids oppressing clients by the worker's actions and the agency's policies and services. A strategic approach to issues involves the following:

- clearly identifying the issue and goals which would resolve it
- breaking down the issue and goals so that they are manageable
- setting a time limit or target
- reviewing and evaluating achievement against the definition and the target
- making links with others who are working on the same or similar issues.

Devore and Schlesinger: ethnic-sensitive practice

As with many accounts of practice with minority ethnic groups, Devore and Schlesinger (1999) start with an understanding of the historical position of black and minority ethnic groups and demographic and cultural understanding of their life experience. Their starting point is the historical experience of both slavery and migration and the acquisition of citizenship in the USA. Similar, but different historical material would be relevant in other countries. For example, in Australia, Canada, New Zealand and the USA, the experience of the indigenous population before white settlement during the colonial period and the aftermath of relations between ethnic groups would be crucial.

The next important basis for ethnic-sensitive practice is understanding the position of different ethnic groups in particular societies. Devore and Schlesinger call this 'ethnic reality', the word 'reality' recognising that this position is often worse than the ideal presented by official agencies, rather than claiming to privilege one perception of reality. Important issues are what different groups prefer to be called (for example black or white) and how issues are described. For example, some people dislike being called minority or oppressed groups, or being associated with any groups at all, sometimes because it might imply being seen as a victim of some categorisation, which the person does not accept. Different countries have arrived at terminologies appropriate for their history and demography, for example the commonly used American term 'people of colour' has not yet travelled elsewhere. Views on these issues change as different views emerge, and vary between countries, so the requirement is to be aware of the debates and be sensitive to the views of particular people we deal with.

Related to such issues, Devore and Schlesinger also deal with policies and ideologies about social relations between ethnic groups. Particular points are:

- *assimilationism*, in the USA the ideology of the 'melting pot' is relevant, in which it was assumed that different cultures and groups would integrate together to become one shared culture; many societies contain ideologies that have similar assumptions that assimilation is either desirable or undesirable
- *ethnic conflict*, which may connect with ideas of ethnic competition in which ethnic groups compete with each other for dominance or influence
- *ethnic pluralism*, the idea that many different ethnic groups can coexist in a diverse society
- *ethnic identity*, in which language, rituals and celebrations, separate schools and reference groups are thought to maintain or develop identifiable ethnic groups.

Since 'race' is itself a social construction, all these ideas, which assume that different ethnic groups have some meaning in their own view of their identity and in others' views, are ideologies that people hold about what should or might happen, rather than an appropriate representation of the complexities of social relationships. For example, in the UK during the period of new Commonwealth immigration in the 1950s and 60s, there was an initial assumption of integration. However, minority ethnic groups often preferred or came to live in the same areas as people from the same group. Therefore, there was acceptance of people living where they preferred and forming ethnic communities. More recently, the consequent separation in education and social experience has led to suggestions that a more integrating policy is required.

Devore and Schlesinger also consider the importance of the life course and the differing and shared experiences of different stages of the life course and transitions between them. The historical, social and psychological understandings of all this material is important to effective ethnic-sensitive practice. They then identify

Table 13.2 Devore and Schlesinger's ethnic-sensitive practice

Element of practice	Practice principle	Commentary
Assumptions and principles	Individual and collective history bears on problems and solutions	Group history Individual history Interaction between individual and group history
	The present is most important	Focus on the present problem Recognise how the past affects the present problem
	Ethnicity is a source of cohesion, identity and strength and a source of strain, discordance and strife	Families Rituals and celebrations Ethnic schools Language
	Social context and resources needed to enhance life make the major contribution to human functioning	Simultaneous attention to micro- and macro-issues
	Non-conscious phenomena affect individual functioning	Culture important
Generic practice: layers of understanding: 1 Social work values	Values as: ■ preferred conceptions of people ■ preferred outcomes for people ■ preferred ways of dealing with people	Uniqueness important Self-realisation and equality of opportunity important Maximise self-direction
2 Basic knowledge of human behaviour	Individual and family life course Social role theory Social systems theory Sociological theory Psychological theories Domain specific theories	Refers to theories of the client world relevant to client's problems
3 Knowledge and skill in agency policy and services		Understand community and organisation and its adaptation to 'ethnic reality' Provide private, comfortable spaces adapted to ethnic reality; tune in to ethnic experiences
4 Self-awareness, including insight into the impact of one's own ethnicity	Who am I? Who do others think I am? Who would I like to be? Dual ethnicity	Childhood and family experience are particularly relevant Refers to situations where worker has hidden knowledge of other ethnicities, eg through marriage to someone from another ethnic background Attend to client, nature of your questioning, source and locus of problem, and adapt these to ethnic reality
5 The impact of ethnic reality	Refers to the economic and social consequences of discrimination	Incorporate ethnic reality in contracting, working on the problem, sharing information, identifying obstacles, termination
6 Understanding route to the social worker	Routes to the social work might vary from the highly coercive to the completely voluntary	Identify all possible information before meeting client; consider its relevance to ethnic reality

Source: Devore and Schlesinger (1999).

six layers of understanding to build upon this foundation, set out in Table 13.2. These also form the basis of the account of practice. An analysis of various social work theories follows, covering some of those considered in this book, considering the extent to which they are congruent with ethnic-sensitive practice. Many are considered to be weak in their attention to the 'ethnic reality'.

Devore and Schlesinger's account of practice summarised in Table 13.2 starts from a range of assumptions and principles, some ideas about generalist practice and adaptation of social work procedures and strategies to incorporate ethnic-sensitive practice. This is important, since they criticise the failure of many practice theories to respond adequately to the need for ethnic-sensitive practice. Workers may therefore use their suggestions to adapt other practice guidelines. The remainder of their book explores detailed prescriptions according to the model of different client groups. A crucial element of their practice is that workers adapt their thinking by focusing on the 'ethnic reality' as an important element for the assessment and practice decisions that they make. Thus, the model does not propose specific actions which are ethnic-sensitive. Instead, it requires workers to be aware of evidence and information about ethnic issues in their community and affecting individuals from minority ethnic groups, and incorporate that understanding into all their practice.

CRITICAL PRACTICE FOCUS

Reflection
Looking back at the critical practice focus cases raised in previous chapters, examine how anti-discriminatory and cultural and ethnic sensitivity might offer a different view of them. Do issues of ethnicity and racism conflict with other anti-discrimination actions that might be required? How might they be dealt with jointly? This focus is presented in this way to emphasise the importance of applying a sensitive or anti-discrimination approach across a wide range of theories of practice. How might anti-discrimination or sensitivity approaches be applied alongside other social work interventions?

Commentary

Anti-discriminatory and anti-oppressive theories in social work have had a significant influence in the 1980s and 90s. This is for practical and theoretical reasons. In practice, many societies and agencies have faced pressures from the consequences of population migration through an increasingly global economy and refugee movements. Moreover, attitudes among groups such as disabled people and women have become less deferential, and less accepting of present patterns of power, particularly patriarchal power. These theoretical perspectives have helped to analyse and respond to these new social issues. Perspectives from black and other oppressed groups and multicultural approaches have also helped workers to put into action new knowledge about various minority ethnic groups and women, disabled and older people in social relations.

Anti-discriminatory and anti-oppressive theories also offer theoretical advantages over other approaches to social work. They develop radical approaches to take into account the range of different bases for oppression of groups and inequalities and divisions in society, and thus provide a more effective account of issues that social work must face. This has also permitted a new and increasingly relevant lease of life for radical approaches within social work. A new focus on oppression has emerged, which has made possible more directed accounts of radical social work, which have in turn contributed to the development of critical theory. They draw attention to the weaknesses of many psychological and individualistic theories of social work in dealing with discrimination and the issues facing minority groups and women in present-day society, and offer a way of understanding these issues. They thus strengthen the sociological basis of social work.

Criticisms of anti-discriminatory and anti-oppressive theories depend on the particular perspective taken. Liberal feminist and anti-racist views, and pluralist multicultural and sensitivity theories, are criticised because they accept the present social order and do not adequately recognise differences in interest and power in society which lead to the oppression of particular groups. If we accept this kind of criticism, we are led towards a structuralist perspective. Radical feminist views and oppressed groups' perspectives may be criticised for failing to take account of institutionalised structural oppression, although they do take account of inequalities of power as they affect and are experienced by individuals and groups.

Structural analysis of issues of discrimination and oppression has been more successful than the economic and class-based analysis of Marxist perspectives in social work. It has been more relevant to the issues faced daily by many social workers in practice. These views have been criticised because they lead professionals to prescribe 'correct' behaviour and attitudes, and this, in itself, is experienced as oppressive. Anti-oppressive theory takes control of understanding about oppression from oppressed groups themselves. Oppressed groups' perspectives and those of black people do not permit a wholly structural response. They require careful attention to be paid to the wishes and needs of the groups affected, in all their variety, and do not accept just one structural explanation of oppression. Nonetheless, there is a shared experience of oppression that requires a response from services and workers.

Cultural and sensitivity and black and oppressed peoples' approaches reject the alignment of all members of a group together as victims of oppression, and seek a more diversified, complex analysis of their needs. Sensitive plural responses will be required, while acknowledging the importance of structural analyses of power as partly conditioning the appropriate response. As a result, a variety of services involving and fitting the needs of particular minorities and oppressed groups would grow up. Sensitivity approaches focus on building up a range of workers with detailed and specialised understanding. All workers would take responsibility for a sensitive response to the expressed needs and wishes of people they worked with. If these required specialised understanding, there would be referral to someone with appropriate knowledge and experience.

The remaining weakness of these approaches, if an oppressed groups' and black perspectives approach is taken, is in prescribing practice responses. We have seen that some feminist, anti-oppressive and sensitivity theories have recruited empowerment approaches to respond to this lacuna, and developments in this area of theory are the subject of Chapter 14.

OVERVIEW

- Anti-discrimination/oppression and sensitivity approaches underline the importance of responding to discrimination and oppression, especially on grounds of ethnicity and race, as part of all social work.

- While they represent values that should permeate social work, it is not clear that they can form the basis of a distinctive approach in themselves, since other service and therapeutic objectives will usually also be required.

- They often call for an empowerment approach, which, however, may not be consonant with the structural focus of anti-discrimination.

- Criticism of anti-oppressive practice focuses on its claims to prescribe correct behaviour and attitudes, appropriating to professionals control of what is considered oppressive or discriminatory.

- Structural explanations of oppression are central to anti-discrimination/oppression and offer a clear view of the social objectives of such a theory.

- Sensitivity approaches focus on cultural and social relationships as a way of incorporating these issues into other approaches to practice.

- Both approaches seek to influence all forms of social work, rather than create specific models of practice.

FURTHER READING

Cox, C. B. and Ephross, P. H. (1998) *Ethnicity and Social Work Practice* (New York: Oxford University Press).
Useful text, focusing on responding to needs arising from diverse ethnicities in social work practice.

Dalrymple, J. and Burke, B. (1995) *Anti-oppressive Practice: Social Care and the Law* (Buckingham, Open University Press).
Influential text with a strong practice element.

Devore, W. and Schlesinger, E. G. (1999) *Ethnic-Sensitive Social Work Practice* (Boston, MA: Allyn & Bacon).
Comprehensive text presenting a sensitivity approach.

Dominelli. L. (1997) *Anti-Racist Social Work*, 2nd edn (Basingstoke: Palgrave – now Palgrave Macmillan).
Dominelli, L. (2002) *Anti-Oppressive Social Work Theory and Practice*, (Basingstoke: Palgrave – now Palgrave Macmillan).
Two examples of Dominelli's many ideologically informed books in this area.

O'Hagan, K. (2001) *Cultural Competence in the Caring Professions* (London: Jessica Kingsley).
A good account of the cultural competence approach to responding to diverse ethnicities.

Thompson, N. (2003) *Anti-discriminatory Practice*, 3rd edn (Basingstoke: Palgrave – now Palgrave Macmillan).
The latest edition of Thompson's important introductory text.

CHAPTER 14

Empowerment and Advocacy

What this chapter is about

Empowerment seeks to help clients to gain power of decision and action over their own lives by reducing the effect of social or personal blocks to exercising existing power, increasing capacity and self-confidence to use power and transferring power from the groups and individuals. Advocacy seeks to represent the interests of powerless clients to powerful individuals and social structures. Critical social workers argue that empowerment and advocacy are not always structural in their implied explanations of social and psychological issues. This is partly because these ideas have wider use in non-radical contexts. They are also increasingly being used as a terminology to reflect self-determination and openness in other theories of social work, rather than implementing critical practices, as in Simon's (1995) claims that social work has demonstrated commitment to empowerment throughout its history. Therefore, these approaches, as with sensitivity theories, lie between socialist-collectivist, individualist-reformist and reflexive-therapeutic, with the emphasis on social change as against personal and group development creating different approaches within practice.

MAIN POINTS

> ➤ Empowerment and advocacy relate to critical, feminist and anti-discrimination theories, but originate from social democratic practice aiming to enable people to overcome barriers in achieving life objectives and gain access to services.
>
> ➤ Advocacy originates in legal skills and is a role for many caring professions.
>
> ➤ Self-help particularly through groupwork connects with self-advocacy.
>
> ➤ Advocacy represents people in two different ways: speaking for them, and interpreting and presenting them to those with power.
>
> ➤ Cause advocacy promotes social change for groups and their causes, while case advocacy seeks individuals' and families' welfare rights.
>
> ➤ Advocacy on behalf of people with disabilities, particularly learning disabilities, mental illness and physical disabilities, was an important source of impetus for an advocacy movement.
>
> ➤ Advocacy and empowerment are connected with self-help and the participation of individuals and communities in decisions that affect them.

> ▶ Empowerment aims to achieve the social justice objectives of social work, both in the way it is practised and its aims.

> ▶ Mullender and Ward's self-directed groupwork is an important practice exemplar of empowerment and participative practice.

> ▶ Normalisation and social role valorisation seek positive environments for people living in institutions, originating in and related to advocacy movements for people with learning disabilities.

> ▶ Empowerment theory, deriving from Solomon's ground-breaking work and recently developed by Lee, is closely related to the history of the struggle for equality by black people in America.

> ▶ Power may not be given to people; they must be helped to take it for themselves.

> ▶ There is evidence that group empowerment work with people from deprived communities can increase later citizen participation.

PRACTICE ISSUES AND CONCEPTS

> ▶ *Barriers* or *blocks* to achieving social objectives.

> ▶ Being *sharing and open in practice* and helping clients to be self-directing, while recognising the impossibility of changing, through welfare interventions, the barriers to empowerment that derive from capitalism.

> ▶ *Normalisation* to create environments for people in residential and other care institutions that ordinary people would value.

> ▶ Sharing and appreciating *commonalities* among people.

> ▶ *Validation* of people's feelings and experiences.

Wider theoretical perspectives

Related contexts for empowerment and advocacy include management theory and practice and conservative political ideology. The management view of empowerment (for example Stewart, 1994) is concerned with motivating individuals and teams to achieve more within organisational objectives by granting them independence from managerial controls. Political empowerment ideology often seeks to place responsibility on individuals for providing for their own needs, with the covert aim of limiting state services. We need to be cautious about social work implementation of empowerment to avoid similar impositions.

Advocacy has its origins particularly in the legal field. Here, 'advocacy' is the term applied to lawyers' practice in the courts and elsewhere in representing their clients. In addition, it is an explicit group of skills, with a literature that forms an important element in legal training (for example Boon, 1993). Social workers might gain useful skills by pursuing similar skills training, but this is rarely actively done in social work courses. It is used as a skill and value objective in other professions. For example, UK professional codes enjoin nurses to undertake advocacy in the sense of raising problems in the resourcing or management of services which might lead to detriment to their patients.

Furlong (1987) expresses the social democratic emphasis of empowerment by arguing that it avoids a crude polarisation of social action and individualised perspectives, placing work with individuals and families in a context of concern for social objectives. Rojek (1986) argues that, although closely related to critical and Marxist perspectives, empowerment and advocacy have different objectives, being rationalist in nature, and assuming that changing the environment in clients' favour is possible. Critical approaches are materialist and claim that the social system needs broad change before true empowerment is possible. Critical social workers would seek empowerment to create social contradictions leading to eventual change, rather than, as the rationalist would, expecting to change society directly.

Connections

Empowerment and advocacy theories

Empowerment and advocacy are aspects of the social work role that have generated practice theories to incorporate into social work practice aspects of radical and critical theories. They try to achieve this without drawing on the Marxist roots of radical and critical theory (see Chapter 11). From the 1970s onwards, advocacy has been incorporated into general social work practice, particularly in rights work aimed at achieving the maximum welfare and other benefits for users. In the USA, the term is also used to refer to 'cause advocacy', seeking change in legislation or policy on behalf of user groups. Empowerment theory has been developed to offer ways of implementing radical objectives, sometimes without allegiance to the ideological objectives of radical and critical work. Ramcharan et al. (1997) draw attention to the importance of focusing empowerment and advocacy in informal settings, such as family relationships, formal settings such as agency decision-making processes, and legal settings where courts or tribunals give access to powers to reassess existing decisions.

Sources of empowerment theories

Empowerment theories arise from the difficulties of radical practice in economically liberal societies (see Chapters 11–13). Empowerment practice helps individuals and groups to overcome social barriers to self-fulfilment within existing social structures, thus rejecting the transformational aims of radical and critical theory and the emancipatory aims of feminist and anti-discrimination theory. Lee (2001: 34) for example talks about 'interventions to deal with personal pain by taking social forces into account'. However, its methods might achieve some social progress through individual and group learning and encourage participation in broader social movements later. Empowerment and advocacy practice might be included in community and social development and macro-social work (see

Chapter 10) thus achieving their objectives. For example, a group of women from a minority ethnic group may be helped in getting better resources for their families through a women's group – a classic piece of empowerment practice. This may give some of them the confidence to play a more active part in campaigning organisations for women's rights – an emancipatory outcome. The work may also give the agency information to seek changes in policy or welfare systems that disadvantage women – a transformational outcome. To carry out empowerment and advocacy work without planning for these further outcomes fails to extend the possibilities towards critical social work, but may be more acceptable to agencies established for personal help. For example, John Carpenter (1996) argues that family therapy practice is sometimes not empowering, and that development of a partnership approach through contracting and planning the process jointly with the family may benefit family therapy practice.

Empowerment ideas have gained importance in social development (de Graaf, 1986; Chapter 10). Anderson et al. (1994) present a model of empowerment for social development in Africa concerned with five dimensions of practice: personal, social, educational, economic and political. Seeing these dimensions as interlocking allows people to meet individual needs (personal power), improves their capacity to influence others (interpersonal power), and in turn this creates an ability to influence the distribution of power more widely (political power). Ntebe (1994) argues that the social work profession must develop an advocacy role for oppressed communities as part of empowerment within a radical model of practice.

Different forms of advocacy

A difficult aspect of advocacy is the dual but related meanings of 'representation'. Advocates 'represent', in the sense of acting and arguing for the interests of their clients. But Philp (1979) uses advocacy to imply the aspect of social work that 'represents' in the sense of interpreting or displaying the value of clients to powerful groups in society. So, advocacy can mean a service that argues clients' views and needs, a set of skills or techniques for doing so and the interpretation of powerless people to powerful groups.

Early in its development, advocacy was seen as a service to clients. Freddolino et al. (2004) distinguish four types of advocacy service to clients:

- Protecting vulnerable people
- Creating support that enhances functioning
- Protecting and advancing claims or appeals
- Fostering identity and control.

The third area developed during the 1970s in two ways. *Case advocacy* is provided by professionals to enhance people's access to provisions designed to benefit them. *Cause advocacy* sought to promote social change for the benefit of social groups from which clients came. An important strand of practice lies in *welfare rights*, which is concerned with ensuring that clients benefiting from other welfare services receive their entitlement to other welfare provision. Initially, this term focused on social security benefits, but now has wider application. It is concerned with rights because, unlike many welfare services, such benefits are often founded on legal entitlements. There has been controversy (see Fimister, 1986; Burgess, 1994) about whether such work is integral to social work. This is because it relies on the analysis of legal rights and espousal of them in official tribunals rather than using interpersonal relationship skills with therapeutic aims. However, the boundaries are blurred, since we need relationship skills to work with people to understand their rights and help them to understand. Also, we need advocacy skills to act on behalf of people in other forms of social work. Ensuring that people receive all their entitlements to other services is an important part of social work (Payne, 2001; 2002a). Poverty and economic welfare are important aspects of many clients' problems. An effective response to these issues is integral to most social work, although specialised social security assessment and advocacy may require referral elsewhere by the non-specialist worker. Bateman (2000) develops an account of the skills needed for such work in ways which are widely applicable in social work. He calls it 'principled advocacy', a policy of getting as much from the social security system as possible, without colluding with its oppressive aspects. This includes a focus on particular kinds of interviewing, value principles similar to those of social work, except that advocates work only following clients' wishes and instructions. Skills such as assertiveness and negotiation are crucial.

A different form of advocacy work, incorporating the other elements of advocacy service, grew up during the 1980s. It started as a process of increasing the capacity of people with mental illness and learning disabilities to manage their own lives. A movement grew up to give them assistance in achieving their civil rights within institutions, and in leaving institutions where they may have been held by compulsion (Brandon et al., 1995; Brandon, 1995). This movement started in Scandinavia, grew up in the USA and has moved to the UK. It has been particularly important in promoting the independence of people with all kinds of disabilities. One area of work lies in helping families of people with disabilities to present the difficulties both of disabled people and the families caring for them. Empowerment here is not just about arguing for particular services to be provided or needs met. Bayley (1997) discusses, for example, how many people with learning disabilities suffer from a relationship 'vacuum', and need help in developing relationships in the main settings in which they live: in their home, work and leisure settings. Barnes (1997) shows how families can be important sites of personal and social development for people with learning disabilities, if workers can help to make or remake connections with them. Self-advocacy, mainly for people with learning disabilities, involves helping people to speak for themselves. This takes place particularly in official planning processes, such as case conferences or individual programme planning meetings. It is a group activity, where people meet together to discuss their situation, and use this support to present their personal difficulties and wishes within this context. An important organisation is People First, an international advocacy group. Citizen advocacy involves volunteers in developing relationships with potentially isolated clients, understanding and representing their needs. Peer advocacy derives from self-help organisations, in which people recovering from difficulties in their lives work together to represent individual needs. It is a short step from all these approaches to more general campaigning in the interests of the group represented.

Self-help and participation

An important area of practice has been to assist self-help groups to develop (Jack, 1995; Wilson, 1995a, b; Thursz et al., 1995; Adams, 2003). Here, workers have supported groups of people sharing the same problems to come together to support one another. New responses to and ideas about appropriate services often arise from these groups. The groups either create the services themselves, or pressurise agencies to change their practices. Mondros and Wilson (1994: 2–5) classify the theoretical work on these activities into four groups, as follows:

- theoretical debate about the origins of social discontent
- classifications of community organisations
- descriptions of poor people's campaigns for power
- practice wisdom about organising to help such groups.

Much of this connects to the discussion in Chapter 10 about social and community development.

Jack (1995) argues that empowerment is paradoxical, because if power is given by an organisation or individual, they must give it from a powerful position. Self-help groups must take power, since there is little mandate in legislation or management of services for empowerment. It should not be confused with enablement, which is what workers do when they help organisations to develop to take power. Oliver (1996) argues that social and political rights drawn from citizenship should form the basis of taking power by groups of disabled people. An important aspect of working in this context is to make the operation of services more participatory (Croft and Beresford, 1994; Shemmings and Shemmings, 1995), thus leading to shared ownership of provision, cultural appropriateness and sensitivity (O'Brien and Pace, 1988). A movement to this effect is connected to the idea of consumerism. This is concerned to promote opportunities for consumers of services to criticise and complain about services which do not suit their needs. Beresford and Croft (1993) take this further, to promote it for seeking changes in services through group activity and campaigning. Such approaches are closely allied both to supporting self-help and social and community development. This is possible even in areas where the law (in the UK, at any rate) is very restrictive, such as child protection (Cloke and Davies, 1995). In child protection, according to Katz (1995), participation and empowerment can be enhanced by giving access to information, involvement in decision-making processes and paying careful attention to alternative views of social work processes. Hegar (1989) argues that empowerment practice with children benefits from children being able to identify with empowered adults, being part of traditions that value empowerment, having involvement in decisions and experiencing supported independence in various activities.

Croft and Beresford (1994) argue that a participative approach is valuable because people want and have a right to be involved in decisions and actions taken in relation to them. Their involvement reflects the democratic value base of social work; it increases accountability, makes for more efficient services and helps to achieve social work goals. It also helps to challenge institutionalised discrimination. Their view of participatory practice has four elements:

- *Empowerment* involves challenging oppression and making it possible for people to take charge of matters which affect them.
- *Control* for people in defining their own needs and having a say in decision-making and planning.
- *Equipping people with personal resources* to take power, by developing their confidence, self-esteem, assertiveness, expectations, knowledge and skills.
- Organising the agency to be open to *participation*.

The practice approach to this, in Shemmings and Shemmings' (1995) view, is to foster mutuality through reciprocity, directness and sensitivity to people's wishes and needs. Workers must also show their trustworthiness, by being even-handed and acting in ways that clients define as trustworthy.

The philosophy of self-direction, personal responsibility and self-actualisation through empowerment has relationships with cognitive and particularly humanist approaches. They emphasise the process of recognising and building on people's strengths or competence. Maluccio (1981) regards this as related to ecological systems theory, since it requires working on the people's ability to interact effectively with their environment. However, this is equally cognitive, since, as we saw in Chapter 6, it involves working on attribution, that is, how people perceive and interpret information about the environment (Fleming, 1981). The strengths perspective is humanist or constructionist, in that it focuses on people's own ability to define their interaction with the environment, although accounts of it focus on its capacity for empowerment, as opposed to problem-based or deficit models of practice (Saleebey, 1992, 1996). However, empowerment and advocacy give more importance to power differentials, class and oppression as aspects of society which obstruct self-actualisation and actively need to be overcome.

The politics of empowerment and advocacy

Empowerment and advocacy are relatively new concepts. Although they have been available in social work, they have not been at the centre of thinking. Simon (1995) argues that empowerment is a long-standing ideal of American social work. Ezell (1994) claims this for advocacy. However, this seems to reinterpret in modern terminology related historical ideas which do not imply the same objective of political and social change. Nevertheless, Ezell's (1994) study found that most American social workers undertook some advocacy, mainly case-based and internal to their own agencies. Cause advocacy was done on a voluntary basis. Cnaan (1996) argues that American society is multilayered and incorporates both ruthless capitalism and complex systems for promoting welfare and independence through voluntary and community endeavour.

In the 1990s, as we have seen, empowerment and advocacy were attached to many different kinds of work. In particular, individualised work has been seen as empowering, although many original uses of the word in social work were applied to oppressed groups rather than individuals. Parsloe (1996a) suggests that empowerment is used to mean giving people a greater say in how services for themselves and their family are organised, allowing people to take part in planning services through representative consultations and join with others in organising services in the way they want through self-help. The use of empowerment as a fashionable concept creates an idealistic and perhaps misleading objective for practice in a period when the role of social work agencies is increasingly limited to protection or service provision. Equally, it may be used as an objective because providing comprehensive services is difficult in a restricted financial environment. This is a misuse of the term, since the assumption of empowerment practice is that workers lend their power to a client for a period to assist them to take power permanently through helping them attain control over their lives. Workers need resources to do this. Moreover, we should not mistake empowerment for enablement. Empowerment is not limited, as enablement is, to allowing or assisting people to take actions, but is aimed at relinquishing and transferring to them the power to control their lives permanently. Miley and DuBois (1999) propose a more community-oriented practice involving phases of dialogue, in which partnerships are formed and directions for activities identified, discovery, where strengths, resources and alliances are identified or created, and development, where progress is made using the resources discovered towards the objectives. They focus particularly on the practice of activating resources, creating alliances and expanding opportunities for people in groups and communities.

However, Jack's (1995) criticism that giving power from a powerful position is impossible seems to go too far. Increasing the total amount of power in use is possible, since not all capacity for power is taken up. Clients often have power which they are unable to use or do not believe they have. Therefore, empowerment is a more positive approach to social work than the traditional radical or anti-oppressive approaches which argue that oppressed groups are completely powerless in the face of structural oppression (Pease, 2002). Macdonald and Macdonald (1999) argue for the power of information and transparency of practice and objectives as important aspects of empowerment practice. Imbrogno (1999) argues for a 'dialectic discourse' in which empowerment is experienced through interaction with those who have power. Hence the worker empowers people by the processes of engaging in discourse over important issues with them. Sherraden et al. (2002) argue that 'collaborative policy advocacy' can helpfully engage alliances of clients, community organisations and professionals in policy advocacy, particularly as devolution in many countries permits greater local influence of policy initiatives. However, Barry and Sidaway (1999) argue that work on community participation and empowerment is often focused on 'how to do it' issues and analysis of barriers, rather than analysis of what kinds of changes are desired and might be achieved; objectives, in their view, are not well enough defined.

Advocacy is in part an aspect of empowerment, since it can be used to argue for resources, in general in this way, or change the interpretation which powerful groups make of clients. It also has a long history as an aspect of welfare rights work, and as an integral aspect of workers' activities on behalf of clients within their own agencies or arguing on their behalf with other agencies. Recent advocacy movements have sometimes led workers to deny their involvement in advocacy, because they believe it can only be practised by client groups themselves, through peer- or self-advocacy. However, as well as taking the traditional professional role of working on behalf of clients, workers can act as formal advocates, by following clients' instructions.

Rees (1991) also focuses on the political role of empowerment in social work. He identifies five essential practice ideas within empowerment:

- *Biography* analyses clients' experience and understanding about the world, allowing us to draw in a wide range of ideas. It places the present struggle in context, allows us to understand the continuity and coherence in people's experience and helps to identify what prevents people from acting. Exploring a biography raises the potential of changing the way someone participates in future events.

- *Power* needs to be understood as potentially liberating as well as oppressive. Empowerment ideas view power as something that might be used positively; it is not, as in radical theory, always oppressive. Rees values understanding power as it affects those subject to it. He focuses on politics as a process of getting resources and settling conflicts using influence through power struggles. He emphasises how the use of language expresses power relations.

- *Political understanding* needs to inform practice, in observing both constraints and opportunities. Social work acts always involve either accepting or seeking to change an existing way of organising power relations. Belief in economic liberalism as the best way of understanding human life is allied to managerial control of agencies and social systems in the cause of 'efficiency and effectiveness'. Setting this against the ideal of social justice shows how managerial purposes express different and more oppressive goals than the justice purposes of social work.

- *Skills* can empower. Gaining and using skills can be an important way of experiencing liberation.

- *Interdependence of policy and practice* must be established. This is contrary to convention, which regards the development of policy as outside the role of practitioners and their work with clients.

The basic objective of empowerment, in Rees's view, is social justice, giving people greater security and political and social equality, through mutual support and shared learning, building up small steps towards wider goals. Kondrat (1995) argues that empowerment requires us to consider whose knowledge is valuable. We should focus on local knowledge, particularly that gained from clients. Also practice should reject insight and self-awareness as professional, treatment objectives and instead focus on critical discernment through dialogical processes of power differences and changes. Holmes and Saleebey (1993) argue that only a collaborative approach will remove the power aspects of the traditional medical model in social work. Similarly, Kieffer (1984) argues that empowerment contains elements of achieving a better self-concept and self-confidence, gaining a more critical capacity in relation to our environment and cultivating personal and collective resources for social and political action. Parsloe (1996b) proposes that workers may be empowering by achieving a positive relationship with clients, being determined to understand the client and their point of view, being self-aware and skilful in their practice, using language carefully and being sharing in work and use of records.

Mullender and Ward's (1991) self-directed groupwork reflects an important development in groupwork in the 1980s. Recent trends are much more towards self-help and client participation through groups, rather than the therapeutic approaches of many other theories. However, all groupwork can be seen as empowering because of its democratic, participative and humanist values (Pernell, 1985) and the experience it gives in affecting others in a protected environment (Hirayama and Hirayama, 1985). It can also help to overcome the dependency-creating effects of residential care (Coppola and Rivas, 1985). Pinderhughes (1995) usefully points out that dependency is not a preferred option, but is a way of seeking power by being close to the powerful.

Gutiérrez et al. (1995) studied workers' views of empowerment in the USA. Their concepts included control over our lives, confidence in our ability to act over issues which are important to us, ability to recognise or develop our own power to act, being aware of and having access to choices and independence from others in making decisions and acting. In another study, Gutiérrez (1995) found that consciousness-raising groups increased the ethnic awareness of people from a minority group; this led them to change their way of understanding their problems and the way they might change their situation. This is likely to make them more politically active in ethnic minority issues. This research gives some support to the assumption that raising consciousness can lead to empowerment. Speer and Peterson (2000) created a scale to measure individuals' analysis of changes in their empowerment, covering cognitive factors, such as beliefs about how power was exercised, emotional factors, such as whether they felt they had influence in various situations, and behavioural factors, such as whether they had taken part in various forms of political influence. All this research demonstrates a movement towards providing empirical support for empowerment practice, and raising its professional rather than ideological stance.

Empowerment may be particularly appropriate with adults such as elderly people (Thursz et al., 1995; Stevenson, 1996). This is because mutual support in adulthood allows people to share experiences of stigmatisation and reduce isolation. Cox (1989), for example, used groupwork to empower elderly people to respond to issues such as income maintenance, elder abuse and health care.

Barber (1986) proposes that *learned helplessness theory* may be a useful perspective for social work. These ideas are closely related to and offer some research support for ideas of empowerment. Seligman's (1975) theory is based on experiments with animals and humans. If people have important experiences which show that what they do does not affect what happens to them, they form the expectation that their actions will generally not produce any useful results. Their capacity to learn useful behaviour in other situations becomes impaired. People may lose motivation, become anxious and depressed and poor at thinking and learning. This evidence clearly supports some of Solomon's (1976) ideas about powerlessness. People who are powerless throughout their lives would carry a sizeable burden of learned helplessness. The response should be, according to Barber (1986), *environmental enrichment,* by giving such people experience of situations in which they are in control and achieve successful results.

Normalisation or *social role valorisation* (Wolfensberger, 1972, 1984; Race, 2003) is related to this form of advocacy (Towell, 1988; Ramon, 1991; Brown and Smith, 1992). This form of policy and practice seeks to offer people in institutions an environment which gives them valued social roles and a life style as close as possible to those valued by people outside institutions. This is an influential development in the residential care field (Sinclair, 1988). It is also used as a philosophy for people being reintegrated into the community from hospital or residential care. Ramon (1989) argues that it involves attempts at changing attitudes among the general public and the professionals providing services, and at changing the attitudes of people with handicaps and organisations involved with them.

Many of these developments are brought together in the work on advocacy of Rose and Black (1985), describing a project promoting independent living for mentally ill people in the community. They base their approach explicitly on the work of Freire (1972), in that they seek to empower people to become subjects rather than objects in their lives, by involving them in the process of advocacy. *Critical debate* with clients enters their present subjective reality and explores objective reality with them. As a result, they can see various situations where their subjective reality limits their control of the environment. Clients are engaged in a *transformation* from dependence to interdependence, with collective networks of social support. Total autonomy is not desirable (or attainable for many people): we are all interdependent with others to some extent.

The work is broadly educational, following Freire's perspective. All social exchanges have a political content, in that they either accept or deny the present social order. By *dialogue* in a situation of trust, with people who behave authentically (in humanist terms), clients engage in a *praxis,* acting and experiencing the reality that results from their actions which then affects later actions. Praxis is reflexive in this way. Workers try to get inside and understand clients' reality. Their history in mental hospitals has oppressed them through institutionalisation, poverty and material deprivation. They have taken these experiences into their own view of the world. Self-expression is encouraged, helping them to gain vitality and acceptance of their own capacity and worth. *Validation* is the main treatment process, aimed at reconnecting clients to their capacity for self-expression. This is done by trying to understand the reality of their own life history, and rejecting internalised judgements that they are incompetent. Clients become 'producer-participants' in their lives rather than passively consuming services.

In a later formulation, Rose (1990) gives three principles of advocacy and empowerment practice:

- *Contextualisation* involves focusing on clients' own understanding of their 'social being' rather than workers' assumptions or policies. This allows a dialogue to develop based on clients' reality. In the dialogue, clients are enabled to express, elaborate and reflect upon their feelings and understandings about life.

- *Empowerment* is a process through which workers support clients to identify the full range of possibilities which might meet clients' needs. The work centres on helping clients to make decisions which affect their lives.

- *Collectivity* focuses on reducing feelings of isolation and connecting clients to relationships. The experience of this form of socialisation produces stronger feelings of self-worth among clients. Similarly, an important principle of Moreau's (1990) structural approach to social work is to collectivise rather than personalise experience.

Empowerment: major statements

Full-blown empowerment and advocacy perspectives are products of the 1980s and 90s. In the USA, they derive particularly from work with minority ethnic groups, but extend beyond ethnic and cultural sensitivity in interpersonal practice (see Chapter 12) by incorporating social change and transformation (see Chapter 11), especially using group and community work. In the UK, writers on empowerment try to incorporate a transformational perspective within the administrative and political constraints of state social work. Critical theorists (see, for example, Humphries, 1996) argue that such attempts to incorporate social change within practice aimed at social cohesion will always be unsuccessful because they attenuate the impact of the social change sought by critical perspectives.

An important early statement of the US approach based on emancipatory work with minority ethnic groups is Solomon's (1976) ground-breaking book *Black Empowerment*, which is still valuable, but has not been updated, and so has been displaced by other accounts of practice, particularly Lee's *The Empowerment Approach to Social Work Practice* (2001 – see below), and Gutiérrez et al.'s *Empowerment in Social Work Practice* (1998). Important statements outside the American tradition include the policy-related discussion, discussed above, by Rees (1991) who has worked in the UK and Australia and a Canadian edited collection by Shera and Wells (1999) which has an international focus and contributors. All these works also include a feminist element of empowerment for women, since they are important objects of social work activity. There are also two important British statements, each with a different focus. Adams (2003) provides a general account of empowerment, particularly related to a community and groupwork approach to promoting self-help; this connects with the advocacy tradition through the idea of self-advocacy. Braye and Preston-Shoot (1995) present a more comprehensive practice perspective. However, Mullender and Ward's (1991) *Self-Directed Groupwork* provides one of the best practice accounts of empowerment groupwork and offers a more radical/critical account of empowerment practice.

Advocacy: major statements

One source of advocacy practice may be identified in the major statements about work deriving from transformational participative practice, particularly in the fields of community mental health and learning disabilities of Rose (1990; Rose and Black, 1985) and the Brandons (1995). Bateman's (2000) skills-based handbook and Fimister's (1986) practice book represent the British welfare rights advocacy approach. A broader perspective on advocacy is offered by American texts on advocacy, of which Schneider and Lester (2001) is a good example, whose approach is briefly considered below. It incorporates general social work skills into a practice aimed at preserving various legal and social rights. The related area of macro-social work (for example Brueggemann, 2002) reflects the American focus on systems theory in incorporating cause advocacy with broad approaches to community and social change.

Lee: empowerment approach

Lee's (2001) starting point is social work's aspiration to social justice and caring communities engendering hope and power among people. Although emerging from work with ethnic minorities, empowerment practice listens to the voices and dreams of powerless groups such as children and women. Lee focuses particularly on the international economic system as a contributor to poverty. Although clinical and dealing with individuals and families, empowerment also seeks to be community-oriented. Three concepts are central:

- Developing a more positive and potent sense of self
- Constructing the knowledge and capacity to achieve a critical perspective on social and political realities
- Cultivating resources, strategies and competences to attain personal and collective goals.

Workers should try to create a sense of community with clients so that they may jointly challenge contradictions that arise from vulnerability and oppression within a society of the affluent and powerful. Having a critical consciousness, in the Freirean sense, and a knowledge of structural inequalities and oppression gives people power. Transformation occurs when people can see alternatives to their present predicament as a result of consciousness-raising. This allows people to avoid self-blame for their problems, accept personal responsibility for trying to achieve change and work to enhance their effectiveness in making changes. Working to achieve as sense of community within a group is the central practice method.

Aspects of empowerment that connect with other perspectives on social work are as follows:

- Empowerment is a biopsychosocial theory, employing ideas such as ego functioning from psychodynamic practice and adaptation and coping from ecological practice

- Construction and narrative approaches make it clear that how people construe their situation is important, rather than the Marxist focus on 'either/or' (Lee, 2001: 40) explanations, and promote the idea that people can be co-constructors of their environment

- Cognitive theory focuses on helping people to remove false perceptions and beliefs

- Feminist, interactionist and integrated approaches emphasise how workers may mediate between different social groups

- Groupwork and community work approaches are central to empowerment practice.

Social work has a dual emphasis on individuals and their environments removing both direct and indirect blocks to power. Its ethical basis requires action to respond to discrimination and a special focus on people suffering from oppression. Therefore mere understanding of oppression and treating all people the same is not sufficient; oppression must be acted upon, and oppressed peoples should identified for action. The perspective and approach to action is outlined in Table 14.1. An essential requirement is to maintain a *multifocal vision* of the world, described in the first three columns, which provides a 'lens' with which to inform practice principles, which then guides the selection of practice methods. The multifocus is considered important so that the complexity of the factors affecting oppression is incorporated into practice.

While Lee's account specifically rejects the structural perspective of critical practice, she usefully emphasises the importance of understanding the effect of global economic and social developments as an important element in people's oppression, a wider perspective than many social work practice theories. Her account of working jointly provides a helpful analysis of workers' skills and approach and her 'leaving' task of *reunification* with the community, to which might be added family and other social networks, is a useful reminder of the need to connect the personal gains made with the experience of the people who surround the client. Her suggestions about focusing on measures of oppression in evaluation are also creative.

The book goes on to discuss group and community empowerment, using similar techniques, but Mullender and Ward's (1991) account of self-directed groupwork provides a fuller and more structural and critical account of groupwork. It offers, therefore, a different perspective on empowerment practice from a more critical point of view.

Mullender and Ward: self-directed groupwork

Mullender and Ward's (1991) account of self-directed groupwork offers a clear view of empowerment theory focused on groupwork settings and processes. They also offer it (1991: 2) as a basis for wider forms of social action. They argue that empowering action must be 'self-directed' (that is, by services users) but must also oppose oppression. This is defined as the state of affairs whereby a presumption in favour of dominant groups arises and skews relationships in society so that

Table 14.1 Lee's empowerment practice

Multifocal vision	Description	Acting on multifocal vision	Empowerment principles	Empowerment practice
Historical view of oppression	Understanding of history and policy affecting oppressed groups	Awareness of oppressed groups' history	All oppression destroys life and should be challenged	*Prepare to enter client world:* 'tune in' to client's world think what it might feel like
Ecological view	Understanding of individual adaptation/coping, ego functioning, cognitive-behavioural learning and power	Active problem-solving, regulate negative feelings Collective action, human relatedness/family, attachment Competence, self-direction, self-esteem, identity Cultural solutions, physical/social environments Ego/cognitive functions; stigma	Maintain a holistic vision of situations of oppression Assist people to empower themselves	*Enter and join forces:* ask for client's story show worker's commitment mutual role definition *Mutual assessment:* share knowledge of community resources/issues assess family, ego, narrative assess empowerment: basic information, life transitions, physical/mental health, interpersonal patterns, socioeconomic and physical environment, oppression, power and powerlessness, strengths
Ethclass perspective [connecting claims with ethnicity issues]	Appreciate relationships between class, poverty, power and oppression	Life chances and conditions; poverty and self-esteem	People who share commonalities need each other to attain empowerment	*Problem definition, contracting:* identify client and worker tasks include multiple oppression in contract
Cultural/multicultural perspective	Attend to norms, nuances and expectations of client's culture and potential diversity	Maintain culture, feeling of liberation, parity, unique personhood	Establish reciprocal relationships with clients	*Work jointly on problems:* client takes responsibility for empowerment worker empathy assists show awareness of threats of oppression
Feminist perspective	Identifies and conceptualises women's different 'voice' and limitless power	Shared consciousness-raising, unity, praxis, power for action not domination, personal is political, validate the non-rational	Encourage clients to use their own word	share reflection/consciousness of problem interactions, socioeconomic stresses critical praxis on problems of oppression identify personal/communal strengths *Leaving:* deal with feelings about ending consider/consolidate gains reunification with community identify power gains
Global perspective	Awareness of global interdependence and social exclusion	Comparative and cross-national research and study, shared problems and solutions, going beyond local boundaries	Focus on the person as victor, not victim	
Critical perspective	Critique of oppression and link individual and social change	Abuse of power, withdrawal of resources, identify direct and indirect power blocks, social solutions inadequate to respond to inequalities, identify powerful organisations, critical perspective connects analysis to action	Focus on social change	*Evaluation:* ethno- and gender-sensitive, evaluation research impact of oppression, strengths, language styles and concerns of minority experience include data from reflection, participation do not overvalue simple and measurable aims

Lens between multifocal vision and practice

Source: Lee (2001).

all social institutions are affected. This includes the processes by which this occurs, thus limiting the life opportunities and experiences of people not in dominant groups. Such a definition implies that empowering work must confront the nature of power. It must do so in both its direct exercise and the way it subsists and persists in social structures, benefiting dominant groups whether or not they have sanctions to back up their influence. This is more important and more generally applicable than radical theories of the state and class. However, many ideas from feminist and anti-racist work are relevant to self-directed work. It must include analysis of the situation and action to deal with it. This is better done in groups, because in individual and family work, individualisation of private troubles is too powerful to promote shared, social responses. Groups allow people to share resources and initiate and experiment with action jointly.

The model of practice has five stages.

- *Pre-planning:* find a compatible co-working team, consultancy support and agree on empowering principles.
- *Taking off:* engage with users as partners and plan the group jointly through 'open planning'.
- *Group preparation* for action: help the group to explore what issues are to be tackled, why these issues exist and how we can produce change.
- *Taking action:* group members carry out agreed actions.
- *Taking over:* workers begin to withdraw, and the group reviews what it has achieved, seeing connections between what, why and how. It then identifies new issues, sees links between the issues and again decides what actions to take. This process then continues throughout the group's life.

Co-working is preferred because it offers a richer experience to service users and provides more support for them. Consultancy is needed to question and challenge the workers in helping them to an anti-oppressive perspective. Five important empowering practice principles are:

- All people have skills, understanding and ability. We must recognise these rather than negative labels.
- People have rights, especially to be heard, control their own lives, choose to participate or not and define issues and take action.
- People's problems always reflect issues of oppression, policy, economy and power as well as personal inadequacies.
- People acting collectively can be powerful, and practice should build on this.
- Practising what you preach involves facilitating, not 'leading' and challenging oppression.

The empowering approach to starting a group involves workers in the following. Workers must acknowledge and contract to work with an existing group on members' issues. Alternatively, they should get the idea from one or more members and check whether others might join, arranging for members to set the goals. Self-directed groups are not there to meet agency objectives or as workers' pet projects. Membership should not be selected, but should come from a wide dispersal of invitations. We should take specific steps to signal to potentially oppressed people, such as black, disabled or elderly people or women, that they will not be oppressed in the group. Workers should accept that voluntary and open-ended membership will lead to fluctuating membership and no minimum or maximum size. The venue should be accessible to people with physical and communication disabilities and those who have caring responsibilities which might prevent attendance. It should be on members' own territory or neutral ground, and members should make their own way there rather than relying on agency transport. Agreement and mutual convenience of members should decide timing frequency and number of meetings. Members should agree and maintain rules for conduct and recording systems in the group. Worker roles should be clear and distinguished from any other roles that workers have in relation to the service users. The group works on agreed problems, not the individual problems of service users.

In the preparation for the action stage, workers facilitate participants' views of what the problem is. This might include brainstorming, creating an art gallery of individuals' responses to the issue, using films and videos as discussion starters, and using statements on display cards devised by members as discussion starters. The 'why' stage might involve consciousness-raising (see Chapter 12). Workers should help with problem-posing. This involves taking participants through the following stages:

- *Description* – what do you see happening?
- *Analysis* – why is it happening?
- *Related problems* – what problems does it lead to?
- *Root causes* – what leads to these problems?
- *Action planning* – what can we do about it?

Workers will often have to help participants to find ways of feeding in information. The group can then move on to a cycle of reflecting (looking, thinking and planning), taking action, seeing the results and then taking in new information to restart the cycle. The 'how' stage involves breaking down issues into component parts, rather like task-centred work. The group can work on grids on blackboards or large sheets of paper. One axis can set out possible actors, another various time-scales for action (now-soon-later). A force-field analysis allows people to evaluate the various pressures for and against particular solutions.

The 'taking action' stage may involve public campaigns, setting up representative systems such as advocacy schemes or promoting influence and action by creating linkages and alliance with other agencies. Communication with and involvement in other groups may be an important strategy. Workers should help groups to dig deeper for the answers to 'why' questions, especially if their first moves are unsuccessful. This often reveals further action to take. Community arts and other techniques for allowing a community's voice (Payne, 1988) to be heard more widely can often be effective. Throughout this stage, as elsewhere, an approach which challenges oppression enables participants to see issues more clearly, particularly where they are obstructed from action. It also helps participants themselves to act less oppressively, rather than learning manipulative power tactics from the process of resolving their problems.

In the final 'taking over' stage, workers help group members to take on some facilitating roles they themselves have fulfilled. Thus, group members learn to challenge and work unoppressively. They gain confidence in working with the media and public and official bodies. Using the experience of the group, they also work on gaining access to information which they can use in future themselves. They can also be helped to learn how to evaluate their own activities, their own performance and the contribution that the workers have made to the group.

Schneider and Lester: social work advocacy

Schneider and Lester (2001) distinguish two different aspects of social work advocacy: representation and influence.

Representation involves exclusivity, that is, the worker acts only for the client, not in the client's best interests or while affected by other responsibilities to an agency, and mutuality, an equal and open relationship between worked and client. Communication in writing or speaking may be involved, with careful attention in both cases to structuring, purpose, timing and strategic considerations. *Influence* is concerned with trying to change decisions or policies about issues that affect the client. This does not necessarily involve exclusivity and mutuality, since an advocate may be acting on behalf of more than one client, or raising concerns about an issue that affects several clients. For example, some colleagues were concerned with a change in government policy that forced clients to attend for job interviews before they could receive social security benefits, when this was stressful and unrealistic in their circumstances. They used representation to get decisions changed in particular cases. Then they used case examples from their experience to complain to the regional social security office and eventually to their MP to try to get the policy changed. The clients were anonymous and not involved in this process, which was 'influence'. Both processes can be used in client advocacy, cause advocacy, legislative advocacy, that is, seeking changes in legislation, and administrative advocacy, that is, seeking change in administrative procedures and policies.

CRITICAL PRACTICE FOCUS

Celia

Celia is a fifteen-year-old girl looked after in a children's home after her alcoholic mother separated from her father, a violent and abusive man, mainly employed on sea-based oil platforms around the world. Celia would like to live with her elder sister, Joan, who is married; her husband has convictions for dealing in drugs some time ago. However, the home appears stable and warm, and Celia enjoys visiting there. At a case review, managers refuse to accept the risk of criticism if Celia lives with Joan and her husband. Celia asks her social worker to advocate on her behalf at the meeting; the worker is aware that this request for advocacy would prevent her from acting in Celia's 'best interests', which may be contrary to her wishes. However, there is little alternative.

What barriers exist for Celia, Joan and Joan's husband to achieve what they want? What approaches might the social worker use to be effective and appropriate as Celia's advocate and in empowering other members of the family?

Commentary

Advocacy and empowerment strategies have proved attractive in recent years as a development and implementation of critical social work and as an aspect of anti-discriminatory work. Advocacy has evolved strongly as part of the movement to discharge many people from long-stay institutions in which they would previously have been cared for, and as part of welfare rights work. These approaches are idealistic, but it is a practical idealism, which can be carried out. Self-help groups, however, are sometimes criticised because they lack public accountability, avoid social change and may attach victimising labels to clients as part of stigmatised groups (Yip, 2003). Some forms of therapy can, if used incautiously, make people dependent on the expertise of the worker. Therefore, it may be argued that advocacy and empowerment represent an ideology of treatment which is different, or at least is experienced differently by client and, perhaps, worker. However, power given by a worker leaves the power with the worker. Moreover, state employees may use empowerment for the wrong reasons, as a subtle way of manipulating people to comply with official and social requirements (Parsloe, 1996a). People must *take* power, and it is the role of social work to organise the institutional response which makes this possible and accept it when it occurs (Gomm, 1993). Dominelli (2000) argues that useful benefits in the way practice is implemented can be achieved through such means, while recognising that this cannot change the structural problems of capitalism.

Like insight therapies, empowerment concentrates on developing people's capacities and does not seek direct change in oppressive social structures, except by the effects of individual cases through advocacy. Thus it might place responsibility for social change upon clients, who may be strengthened, but still face formidable social obstacles, which according to the structural analysis are immovable by personal and group change. The account of empowerment practice given by Lee (2001), in its rejection of structural explanations of oppression, illustrates this inconsistency in empowerment ideas. While Lee seeks to include explanations of oppression and activity around it in her practice model, the change effort is directed only at clients and their surrounding networks. Thus, consciousness-raising in her model of practice raises the same problems as insight in psychodynamic practice: the client understands better, but is enabled, by the practice model, to act only upon the personal and local consequences of that understanding.

Also related to this point, empowerment practice prescriptions do not address powerless people whose own capacities are inadequate for the assumption of full power over their lives. There is a danger that workers will act as though all clients can achieve a high degree of empowerment. Boehm and Staples (2002) found in focus groups with clients that different kinds of clients expected different forms of empowerment and argue that one generalised theory of empowerment for all clients is insufficient. This might particularly be so since modern developments of the theory derive from work with intellectually and socially able minority ethnic groups. Very damaged, oppressed and institutionalised clients can achieve much greater degrees of self-control and power through such techniques, but this should not exclude therapeutic work for their benefit as well. Freddolino et al. (2004) make a similar argument about advocacy, that it should be used differently in different situations.

Similarly, the role of empowerment is unclear where protection for clients or security for the public is at issue. Ideas such as normalisation and self-advocacy have often become associated with civil liberties perspectives which focus on the need to free people oppressed by assumptions about their dependence on care. However, it is not empowerment to fail to provide services that clients need. For example, a young man was discharged from a mental hospital, and hostel accommodation was arranged. This was set up to offer a great deal of freedom of action, but there was security through a system where a worker was 'on call'. This was explained to the client, who missed the point of the explanation because he did not understand what 'on call' meant. Then the worker arranged to show him how to use local shops, but failed to check that his social security allowance had arrived or that he had some provisions until it did so. He did not feel that he could raise these problems because the worker had already been so helpful, so a later visitor found him completely unable to make a hot drink. It is, therefore, important not to use the idea of empowerment to avoid responsibility for assessing and providing for appropriate care and support. Gray and Bernstein (1994), describing a South African project to help 'pavement people', argue that practical help is an essential part of responding to serious difficulties, but becomes part of empowerment strategies where this develops towards responses to structural oppression.

Another difficulty, where workers deal with individuals, is that empowering individuals may not extend to their wider community or networks. So empowered individuals may be taking power and resources from others in their oppressed environment, to their disadvantage, rather than taking it from wider society. Where social and political resources are limited, empowerment may set oppressed or deprived groups against others, rather than uniting them.

OVERVIEW

- Empowerment and advocacy are supported by some evidence of the effectiveness of group methods that promote solidarity and consciousness-raising.
- They draw attention to the possibility of seeing power positively as available within society for people to use.
- Empowerment and advocacy offer workers useful ideas for including issues of oppression, critical thinking and joint working with clients into their practice.

- They are inconsistent in helping clients understand but not act on structural explanations of oppression in their lives, which is only empowering in the sense of reducing the tendency to mystify the effects and sources of oppression on their lives.

- Empowerment and advocacy fail to deal adequately with clients who are incapable of achieving power and control over their lives or who need protection, since they may disappoint or mislead them about the possibility of their own empowerment.

FURTHER READING

Adams, R. (2003) *Social Work and Empowerment*, 3rd edn (Basingstoke: Palgrave – now Palgrave Macmillan).
Good conceptual text on empowerment.

Bateman, N. (2000) *Advocacy Skills for Health and Social Care Professionals* (London: Jessica Kingsley).
British text on advocacy, focusing on skills.

Braye, S. and Preston-Shoot, M. (1995) *Empowering Practice in Social Care* (Buckingham, Open University Press).
Good general text on empowerment.

Gutiérrez, L. M., Parsons, R. J. and Cox, E. O. (1998) *Empowerment in Social Work Practice: A Sourcebook*, (Pacific Grove, CA: Brooks/Cole).
Lee, J. A. B. (2001) *The Empowerment Approach to Social Work Practice: Building the Beloved Community*, 2nd edn (New York: Columbia University Press).
Well-established American texts.

Mullender, A. and Ward, D. (1991) *Self-Directed Groupwork: Users Take Action for Empowerment* (London, Whiting and Birch).
Ground-breaking practical text on empowering groupwork.

Race, D. G. (ed.) (2003) *Leadership and Change in Human Services: Selected Readings from Wolf Wolfensberger* (London: Routledge).
Useful selection of writings from an important contributor to ideas about normalisation.

Schneider, R. L. and Lester, L. (2001) *Social Work Advocacy: A New Framewokr for Action* (Belmont CA: Brooks/Cole).
Good American text on advocacy.

Shera, W. and Wells, L. M. (eds) (1999) *Empowerment Practice in Social Work: Developing Richer Conceptual Foundations* (Toronto: Canadian Scholars Press).
An interesting collections of papers covering a wide conceptual and practical landscape.

Bibliography

Abatena, H. (1995) 'The significance of community self-help activities in promoting social development', *Journal of Social Development in Africa* **10**(1): 5–24.

Abrams, P. (1984) 'Social change, social networks and neighbourhood care', *Social Work Service* **22**: 12–23.

Adams, R. (2003) *Social Work and Empowerment* (3rd edn) (Basingstoke: Palgrave).

Adepoju, A. (ed.) (1993) *The Impact of Structural Adjustment on the Population of Africa: the Implications for Education, Health and Employment* (Portsmouth, NH: Heinemann/UNFPA).

Agere, S. (1986) 'Participation in social development and integration in sub-Saharan Africa', *Journal of Social Development in Africa* **1**(1): 93–110.

Ahmad, B. (1990) *Black Perspectives in Social Work* (Birmingham: Venture).

Ahmed, S. (1991) 'Developing anti-racist social work education practice', in CD Project Steering Group (1991) *Setting the Context for Change* (London: CCETSW): 166–82.

Ainsworth, F. and Fulcher, L. C. (eds) (1981) *Group Care for Children: Concepts and Issues* (London: Tavistock).

Ainsworth, M. D., Blehar, M. C., Waters, E. and Wall, S. (1978) *Patterns of Attachment*, (New Jersey: Erlbaum).

Aldgate, J. (1991) 'Attachment theory and its application to child care social work – an introduction', in Lishman, J. (ed.) *Handbook of Theory for Practice Teachers in Social Work* (London: Jessica Kingsley): 11–35.

Alexander, K. C. (1994) *The Process of Development of Societies* (New Delhi: Sage).

Alexander, L. B. (1972) 'Social work's Freudian deluge: myth or reality?', *Social Service Review* **46**(4): 517–38.

Alinsky, S. D. (1969) *Reveille for Radicals* (New York: Vintage).

Alinsky, S. D. (1971) *Rules for Radicals* (New York: Random House).

Allan, G. (1983) 'Informal networks of care: issues raised by Barclay', *British Journal of Social Work* **13**(4): 417–34.

Allan, J. (2003) 'Theorising critical social work', in Allan, J., Pease, B. and Briskman, L. *Critical Social Work: An Introduction to Theories and Practices* (Crows Nest, NSW: Allen & Unwin): 52–72.

Allan, J., Pease, B. and Briskman, L. (2003) *Critical Social Work: An Introduction to Theories and Practices* (Crows Nest, NSW: Allen & Unwin).

Allen, J. A. (1993) 'The constructivist paradigm: values and ethics', *Journal of Teaching in Social Work* **8**(1/2): 31–54.

Allen, T. and Thomas, A. (eds) (2000) *Poverty and Development into the 21st Century* (Oxford: Oxford University Press).

Anderson, R. E., Carter, I. with Lowe, G. R. (1999) *Human Behaviour in the Social Environment* (New York: Aldine de Gruyter).

Anderson, S. C., Wilson, M. K. Mwansa. L-K. and Osei-Hwedie, K. (1994) 'Empowerment and social work education and practice in Africa', *Journal of Social Development in Africa* **9**(2): 71–86.

Angell, G. B. (1996) 'Neurolinguistic programming theory and social work treatment', in Turner, F. J. (ed.) *Social Work Treatment: Interlocking Theoretical Perspectives* (4th edn) (New York: Free Press): 480–502.

Applegate, J. S. (2000) 'Theory as story: a postmodern tale', *Clinical Social Work Journal* 29(2): 141–53.

Arber, S. and Ginn, J. (1991) *Gender and Later Life: a Sociological Analysis of Resources and Constraints* (London: Sage).

Archer, M. S. (1995) *Realist Social Theory: The Morphogenetic Approach* (Cambridge: Cambridge University Press).

Archer, M. S. (1996) *Culture and Agency: The Place of Culture in Social Theory* (rev. edn) (Cambridge: Cambridge University Press).

Archer, M. S. (2000) *Being Human: the Problem of Agency* (Cambridge: Cambridge University Press).

Argyris, C. and Schön, D. A. (1974) *Theory in Practice: Increasing Professional Effectiveness* (San Francisco: Jossey-Bass).

Atherton, J. S. (1989) *Interpreting Residential Life: Values to Practise* (London: Tavistock/Routledge).

Bailey, R. and Brake, M. (1975) 'Introduction: social work in the welfare state', in Bailey, R. and Brake, M. (eds) *Radical Social Work* (London: Edward Arnold): 1–12.

Bailey, R. and Brake, M. (1980) 'Contributions to a radical practice in social work', in Brake, M. and Bailey, R. (eds) *Radical Social Work and Practice* (London: Edward Arnold): 7–25.

Balgopal, P. R. and Vassil, T. (1983) *Groups in Social Work: an Ecological Perspective* (New York: Macmillan).

Bandura, A. (1977) *Social Learning Theory* (Englewood Cliffs, NJ: Prentice-Hall).

Banton, M. (1987) *Racial Theories* (Cambridge: Cambridge University Press).

Barber, J. G. (1991) *Beyond Casework* (Basingstoke: Macmillan – now Palgrave Macmillan).

Barbour, R. S. (1984) 'Social work education: tackling the theory-practice dilemma', *British Journal of Social Work* 14(6):557–78.

Barker, M. and Hardiker, P. (eds) (1981) *Theories of Practice in Social Work* (London: Academic Press)

Barnes, M. (1997) 'Families and empowerment', in Ramcharan, P., Roberets, G., Grant, G. and Borland, J. (eds) *Empowerment in Everyday Life: Learning Disabilities*, (London: Jessica Kingsley): 70–87.

Barry, M. and Hallett, C. (eds) (1998) *Social Exclusion and Social Work: Issues of Theory, Policy and Practice* (Lyme Regis: Russell House).

Barry, M. and Sidaway, R. (1999) 'Empowering through partnership – the relevance of theories of participation to social work practice', in Shera, W. and Wells, L. M. (eds) *Empowerment Practice in Social Work: Developing Richer Conceptual Foundations* (Toronto: Canadian Scholars Press): 13–37.

Bateman, N. (2000) *Advocacy Skills for Health and Social Care Professionals* (London: Jessica Kingsley).

Bateson, G., Jackson, D. Haley, J. and Weakland, J. (1956) 'Toward a theory of schizophrenia', *Behavioral Science* 1: 251–64.

Batten, T. R. with Batten, M. (1967) *The Non-directive Approach in Group and Community Work* (London: Oxford University Press).

Bayley, M. (1997) 'Empowering and relationships', in Ramcharan, P., Roberets, G., Grant, G. and Borland, J. (eds) *Empowerment in Everyday Life: Learning Disabilities* (London: Jessica Kingsley): 15–34.

Beck, A. T. (1989) *Cognitive Therapy and the Emotional Disorders* (Harmondsworth: Penguin).

Beck, U. (1992) *Risk Society: Towards a New Modernity* (London: Sage).

Becker, H. (1963) *Outsiders: Studies in the Sociology of Deviance* (New York: Free Press).

Beresford, P. and Croft, S. (1986) *Whose Welfare? Private Care of Public Services* (Brighton: Lewis Cohen Centre for Urban Studies).

Beresford, P. and Croft, S. (1993) *Citizen Involvement: a Practical Guide for Change* (Basingstoke: Macmillan – now Palgrave Macmillan).

Beresford, P. and Croft, S. (2001) 'Service users' knowledges and the social construction of social work', *Journal of Social Work* **1**(3): 295–316.

Berger, P. L. and Luckmann, T. (1971) *The Social Construction of Reality* (Harmondsworth: Penguin) (original American publication, 1966).

Berglind, H. (1992) 'Action theory: a tool for understanding in social work', *Scandinavian Journal of Social Welfare* **1**(1): 28–35.

Berlin, S. B. (1990) 'Dichotomous and complex thinking', *Social Service Review* **1**: 46–59.

Berne, E. (1961) *Transactional Analysis in Psychotherapy* (New York: Grove Press).

Berne, E. (1964) *Games People Play* (Harmondsworth: Penguin).

Berzoff, J. (2003) 'Psychodynamic theories in grief and bereavement', *Smith College Studies in Social Work* **73**(3): 273–98.

Best, J. (1989) 'Debates about constructionism', in Rubington, E. and Weinberg, M. S. (eds) *The Study of Social Problems: Seven Perspectives* (New York: Oxford University Press): 341–52.

Besthorn, F. H. and McMillen, D. P. (2002) 'The oppression of women and nature: ecofeminism as a framework for an expanded ecological social work', *Families in Society* **83**(3): 221–32.

Bettelheim, B. (1950) *Love is Not Enough* (Glencoe: IC Free Press).

Bhaskar, R. (1979) *A Realist Theory of Science* (2nd edn) (Brighton: Harvester).

Bhaskar, R. (1989) *Reclaiming Reality* (London: Verso).

Biddle, B. J. and Thomas, E. J. (eds) (1979) *Role Theory: Concepts and Research* (Huntington, NY: Robert S. Krieger).

Biegel, D. E., Tracey, E. M. and Corvo, K. N. (1994) 'Strengthening social networks: intervention strategies for mental health case managers', *Health and Social Work* **19**(3): 206–16.

Bion, W. R. (1961) *Experiences in Groups and Other Papers* (London: Tavistock).

Birchwood, M., Hallett, S. and Preston, M. (1988) *Schizophrenia: an Integrated Approach to Research and Treatment* (London: Longman).

Birdwhistell, R. L. (1973) *Kinesics and Context: Essays on Body-motion Communications* (Harmondsworth: Penguin).

Black, C. and Enos, R. (1981) 'Using phenomenology in clinical social work: a poetic pilgrimage', *Clinical Social Work Journal* **9**(1): 34–43.

Blakemore, K. and Boneham, M. (1994) *Age, Race and Ethnicity: A Comparative Approach* (Buckingham: Open University Press).

Blom, B. (1994) 'Relationem socialarbetare – klient ur ett Sartre anskt perspektiv', *Nordisk Sosialt Arbeid* **4**: 265–76.

Blom, B. (2002) 'The social worker-client relationship – a Sartrean approach', *European Journal of Social Work* **5**(3): 277–85.

Blumer, H. (1969) *Symbolic Interactionism: Perspective and Method* (Englewood Cliffs, NJ: Prentice-Hall).

Bocock, R. (1988) 'Psychoanalysis and social theory', in Pearson, G., Treseder, J. and Yelloly, M. (eds) *Social Work and the Legacy of Freud: Psychoanalysis and its Uses* (Basingstoke: Macmillan – now Palgrave Macmillan): 61–81.

Boeck, T., McCullogh, P. and Ward, D. (2001) 'Increasing social capital to combat social exclusion', in Matthies, A.-L., Närhi, K and Ward, D. (eds) (2001) *The Eco-Social Approach in Social Work* (Jyväskylä: SoPhi): 4–107.

Boehm, A. and Staples, L. H. (2002) 'The functions of the social worker in empowering: the voices of consumers and professionals', *Social Work* **47**(14): 449–60.

Bonner, C. E. (2002) 'Psychoanalytic theory and diverse populations: reflections of old practices and new understandings', *Psychoanalytic Social Work* **9**(2): 61–70.

Boon, A. (1993) *Advocacy* (London: Cavendish)

Booth, D. (ed.) (1994a) *Rethinking Social Development: Theory, Research and Practice* (London: Longman).

Booth, D. (1994b) 'Rethinking social development: an overview, in Booth, D. (ed.) *Rethinking Social Development: Theory, Research and Practice* (London: Longman).

Borensweig, H. (1980) 'Jungian theory and social work practice', *Journal of Sociology and Social Welfare* 7(4): 571–85.

Borton, T. (1970) *Reach, Touch, Teach* (London: Hutchinson).

Boud, D. and Knights, S. (1996) 'Course design for reflective practice', in Gould, N. and Taylor, I. (eds) *Reflective Learning for Social Work* (Aldershot: Arena).

Bowell, T. and Kemp, G. (2002) *Critical Thinking: A Concise Guide* (London: Routledge).

Bowlby, J. (1951) *Maternal Care and Mental Health* (Geneva: World Health Organisation).

Bowlby, J. (1969) *Attachment and Loss,* vol. I: *Attachment* (London: Hogarth Press).

Bowlby, J. (1973) *Attachment and Loss,* vol. II: *Separation* (London: Hogarth Press).

Bowlby, J. (1980) *Attachment and Loss,* vol. III: *Loss* (London: Hogarth Press).

Bowser, B. P. (ed.) (1995) *Racism and Anti-racism in World Perspective* (Thousand Oaks, CA: Sage).

Bradford, K. A. (1969) *Existentialism and Casework: the Relationships between Social Casework Theory and the Philosophy and Psychology of Existentialism* (Jericho, NY: Exposition Press).

Brager, G. and Purcell, F. (1967) *Community Action against Poverty: Readings from the Mobilization for Youth Experience* (New Haven, CT: College and University Press).

Brager, G., Specht, H. and Torczyner, J. L. (1987) *Community Organizing* (2nd edn) (New York: Columbia University Press).

Brake, M. and Bailey, R. (eds) (1980) *Radical Social Work and Practice* (London: Edward Arnold).

Brandell, J. (2002) 'The marginalization of psychoanalysis in academic social work', *Psychoanalytic Social Work* 9(2): 41–50.

Brandon, D. (1976) *Zen and the Art of Helping* (London: Routledge & Kegan Paul).

Brandon, D. (1995) 'Peer support and advocacy – international comparisons and developments', in Jack, R. (ed.) *Empowerment in Community Care* (London: Chapman & Hall): 108–33.

Brandon, D., Brandon, A. and Brandon, T. (1995) *Advocacy: Power to People with Disabilities* (Birmingham: Venture).

Brandon, D. (2000) *Tao of Survival: Spirituality in Social Care and Counselling* (Birmingham: Venture).

Brawley, E. A. and Martinez-Brawley, E. E. (1988) 'Social programme evaluation in the USA: trends and issues', *British Journal of Social Work* 18(4): 391–414.

Braye, S. and Preston-Shoot, M. (1995) *Empowering Practice in Social Care* (Buckingham: Open University Press).

Breakwell, G. M. and Rowett, C. (1982) *Social Work: the Social Psychological Approach* (Wokingham: Van Nostrand Reinhold).

Brearley, J. (1991) 'A psychodynamic approach to social work', in Lishman, J. (ed.) *Handbook of Theory for Practice Teachers in Social Work* (London: Jessica Kingsley): 48–63.

Brechin, A. (2000) 'Introducing critical practice', in Brechin, A., Brown, H. and Eby, M. A. (eds) *Critical Practice in Health and Social Care* (London: Sage): 25–47.

Brechin, A. and Sidell, M. (2000) 'Ways of knowing' in Gomm, R. and Davies, C. (eds) *Using Evidence in Health and Social Care* (London: Sage): 3–25.

Brennan, W. C. (1973) 'The practitioner as theoretician', *Journal of Education for Social Work* 9(1): 5–12.

Bricker-Jenkins, M., Hooyman, N. R. and Gottlieb, N. (eds) (1991) *Feminist Social Work Practice in Clinical Settings* (Newbury Park, CA: Sage).

Brigham, T. M. (1977) 'Liberation in social work education: applications from Paulo Freire', *Journal of Education for Social Work* 13(3): 5–11.

Brigham, T. M. (1984) 'Social work education in five developing countries', in Guzzetta, C., Katz, A. J. and English, R. A. (eds) *Education for Social Work Practice: Selected International Models* (New York: Council on Social Work Education): 59–70.

Brook, E. and Davis, A. (1985) *Women, the Family and Social Work* (London: Tavistock).

Brown, A. (1992) *Groupwork* (3rd edn) (Aldershot: Arena).

Brown, A., Caddick, B., Gardiner, M. and Sleeman, S. (1982) 'Towards a British model of groupwork', *British Journal of Social Work* 12(6): 587–603.

Brown, C. (1994) 'Feminist postmodernism and the challenge of diversity', in Chambon, A. S. and Irving, A. (eds) *Essays in Postmodernism and Social Work* (Toronto: Canadian Scholars' Press): 35–48.

Brown, H. and Smith, H. (1992) (eds) *Normalisation: a Reader for the Nineties* (London: Routledge).

Brown, L. N. (1993) 'Groupwork and the environment: a systems approach', *Social Work in Groups* 16(1/2): 83–95.

Browne, E. (1978) 'Social work activities', in DHSS *Social Service Teams: the Practitioner's View* (London: HMSO).

Brueggeman, W. G. (2002) *The Practice of Macro Social Work* (2nd edn) (Belmont, CA: Brooks/Cole).

Bullis, R. K. (1996) *Spirituality in Social Work Practice* (Washington, DC: Taylor & Francis).

Bulmer, M. (1987) *The Social Basis of Community Care* (London: Allen & Unwin).

Bundey, C. (1976) 'Developments in social group work, 1965–1975', in Boas. P. J. and Crawley, J. (eds) *Social Work in Australia: Responses to a Changing Context* (Melbourne: Australia International): 142–55.

Burden, D. S. and Gottlieb, N. (eds) (1987) *The Woman Client: Providing Services in a Changing World* (New York: Tavistock).

Burgess, P. (1994) 'Welfare rights', in Hanvey, C. and Philpot, T. (eds) *Practising Social Work* (London: Routledge): 173–84.

Burgess, R., Jewitt, R., Sandham, J. and Hudson, B. L. (1980) 'Working with sex offenders: a social skills training group', *British Journal of Social Work* 10(2): 133–42.

Burghardt, S. (1996) 'A materialist framework for social work theory and practice' in F. J. Turner (ed.) *Social Work Treatment: Interlocking Theoretical Approaches* (New York: Free Press): 409–33.

Burkey, S. (1993) *People First: a Guide to Self-Reliant, Participatory Rural Development* (London: Zed Books).

Burn, M. (1956) *Mr Lyward's Answer: a Successful Experiment in Education* (London: Hamish Hamilton).

Burr, V. (2003) *Social Constructionism* (2nd edn) (London: Routledge).

Burrell, G. and Morgan, G. (1979) *Sociological Paradigms and Organisational Analysis* (London: Heinemann).

Bytheway, B. (1995) *Ageism* (Buckingham: Open University Press).

Callahan, M. (1996) 'A feminist perspective on child welfare', in Kirwin, B. (ed.) *Ideology, Development and Social Welfare: Canadian Perspectives* (Toronto: Canadian Scholars Press): 111–126.

Canda, E. R. (ed.)(1998) *Spirituality in Social Work: New Directions* (New York: Haworth Press).

Canda, E. R. (2003) 'Heed your calling and follow it far: suggestions for authors who write about spirituality or other innovations for social work', *Families in Society* 84(1): 80–5.

Canda, E. R. and Furman, L. (1999) *Spiritual Diversity in Social Work Practice: The Heart of Helping* (New York: Free Press).

Cannan, C. (1972) 'Social workers: training and professionalism', in Pateman, T. (ed.) *Counter Course: a Handbook for Course Criticism* (Harmondsworth: Penguin): 247–63.

Caplan, G. (1965) *Principles of Preventive Psychiatry* (London: Tavistock).

Caplan, G. (1974) *Support Systems and Community Mental Health: Lectures on Concept Development* (New York: Behavioral Publications).

Caplan, G. and Killilea, M. (eds) (1976) *Support Systems and Mutual Help: Multidisciplinary Explorations* (New York: Grune & Stratton).

Carew, R. (1979) 'The place of knowledge in social work activity', *British Journal of Social Work* 9(3): 349–64.

Carkhuff, R. R. and Berenson, B. C. (1977) *Beyond Counseling and Therapy* (2nd edn) (New York: Holt, Rinehart & Winston).

Carlton-LaNey, I. (ed.) (1994) *The Legacy of African-American Leadership in Social Welfare*. Special issue of *Journal of Sociology and Social Welfare* 21(1).

Carlton-LaNey, I. P. (ed.)(2001) *African American Leadership: An Empowerment Tradition in Social Welfare History* (Washington DC: NASW Press).

Carpenter, D. (1996) 'Constructivism and social work treatment' in Turner, F. J. (ed.) *Social Work Treatment: Interlocking Theoretical Perspectives* (4th edn) (New York: Free Press): 146–67.

Carpenter, J. (1996) 'Family therapy and empowerment', in Parsloe, P. (ed.) *Pathways to Empowerment* (Birmingham: Venture): 157–71.

Case, L. P. and Lingerfelt, N. B. (1974) 'Name-calling: the labeling process in the social work interview', *Social Service Review* 18(2): 75–86.

Cavanagh, K. and Cree, V. E. (eds) (1996) *Working with Men: Feminism and Social Work* (London: Routledge).

CCETSW (1991) *One Small Step Towards Racial Justice: the Teaching of Antiracism in Diploma in Social Work Programmes* (London: CCETSW).

CD Project Steering Group (1991) *Setting the Context for Change* (London: CCETSW).

Cecil, R., Offer, J. and St Leger, F. (1987) *Informal Welfare: a Sociological Study of Care in Northern Ireland* (Aldershot: Gower).

Chaiklin, H. (1979) 'Symbolic interaction and social practice', *Journal of Sociology and Social Welfare* 6(1): 3–7.

Chambers, R. (1993) *Challenging the Professions: Frontiers for Rural Development* (London: Intermediate Technology Publications).

Chambon, A. S. and Irving, A. (eds) (1994) *Essays on Postmodernism and Social Work* (Toronto: Canadian Scholars' Press).

Chambon, A. S., Irving, A. and Epstein, L. (eds) (1999) *Reading Foucault for Social Work* (New York: Columbia University Press).

Chan, C. L. W. (1993) *The Myth of Neighbourhood Mutual Help: the Contemporary Chinese Community-based Welfare System in Guangzhou* (Hong Kong: Hong Kong University Press).

Chan, C. L. W. and Chow. N. W. S. (1992) *More Welfare after Economic Reform? Welfare Development in the People's Republic of China* (Hong Kong: Department of Social Administration, University of Hong Kong).

Chandra, B. (1987) *Communalism in Modern India* (2nd edn) (New Delhi: Vikas).

Chernesky, R. H. (1995) 'Feminist administration: style, structure, purpose', in Van den Bergh, N. (ed.) *Feminist Practice in the 21st Century* (Washington, DC: NASW Press): 70–88.

Chiu, T. L. and Primeau, C. (1991) 'A psychiatric mobile crisis unit in New York City: description and assessment, with implications for mental health care in the 1990s', *International Journal of Social Psychiatry* 37(4): 251–8.

Cigno, K. (1998) 'Intervention in group care for older people', in Cigno, K. and Bourn, D. (eds) *Cognitive-behavioural Social Work in Practice* (Aldershot: Ashgate): 221–35.

Cigno, K. (2002) 'Cognitive-behavioural practice', in Adams, R., Dominelli, L. and Payne, M. (eds) *Social Work: Themes, Issues and Critical Debates* (2nd edn) (Basingstoke: Palgrave): 180–90.

Cigno, K. and Bourn, D. (eds) (1998) *Cognitive-behavioural Social Work in Practice* (Aldershot: Ashgate).

Clark, D. H. (1974) *Social Therapy in Psychiatry* (Harmondsworth: Penguin).

Clarke, M. (1976) 'The limits of radical social work', *British Journal of Social Work* 6(4): 501–6.

Clarke, S. (2003) *Social Theory, Psychoanalysis and Racism* (Basingstoke: Palgrave).

Claxton, G. (ed.) (1986) *Beyond Therapy: the Impact of Eastern Religions on Psychological Theory and Practice* (London: Wisdom).

Clifford, D. (2002) 'Resolving uncertainties? The contribution of some recent feminist ethical theory to the social professions', *European Journal of Social Work* 5(1): 31–41.

Cloke, C. and Davies, M. (eds) (1995) *Participation and Empowerment in Child Protection* (London: Pitman).

Clough, R. (2000) *The Practice of Residential Work* (Basingstoke: Macmillan – now Palgrave Macmillan).

Cnaan, R. A. (1996) 'Empowerment under capitalism: the case of the United States', in Parsloe, P. (ed.) *Pathways to Empowerment* (Birmingham: Venture): 27–39.

Coates, J. (2003) *Ecology and Social Work: Towards a New Paradigm*' (Halifax, NS: Fernwood).

Coates, J. and McKay, M. (1995) 'Toward a new pedagogy for social transformation', *Journal of Progressive Human Services* 6(1): 27–43.

Cohen, S. (1972) *Folk Devils and Moral Panics* (London: Paladin).

Coleridge, P. (1993) *Disability, Liberation and Development* (Oxford: Oxfam).

Collins, B. G. (1986) 'Defining feminist social work', *Social Work* 31(3): 214–19.

Collins, P. H. (2000) *Black Feminist Thought: Knowledge, Consciousness, and the Politics of Empowerment* (2nd edn) (New York: Routledge).

Compton, B. R. and Galaway, B. (eds) (1999) *Social Work Processes* (6th edn) (Pacific Grove, CA: Brooks/Cole).

Consedine, J. (2002) 'Spirituality and social justice', in Nash, M. and Stewart, B. (eds) *Spirituality and Social Care: Contributing to Personal and Community Well-being* (London: Jessica Kingsley): 31–48.

Coombe, V. and Little, A. (eds) (1986) *Race and Social Work: a Guide to Training* (London: Tavistock).

Cooper, M. and Turner, S. (1996) 'Transactional analysis theory and social work treatment', in Turner, F. J. (ed.) *Social Work Treatment: Interlocking Theoretical Approaches* (New York: Free Press): 641–62.

Cooper, M. G. and Lesser, J. G. (2002) *Clinical Social Work Practice: An Integrated Approach* (Boston, MA: Allyn & Bacon).

Coppola, M. and Rivas, R. (1985) 'The task-action group technique: a case study of empowering the elderly', in Parries, M. (ed.) *Innovations in Social Group Work: Feedback from Practice to Theory* (New York: Haworth): 133–47.

Corden, J. and Preston-Shoot, M. (1987a) *Contracts in Social Work* (Aldershot: Gower).

Corden, J. and Preston-Shoot, M. (1987b) 'Contract or con trick? a reply to Rojek and Collins', *British Journal of Social Work* 17(5): 535–43.

Corden, J. and Preston-Shoot, M. (1988) 'Contract or con trick? a postscript', *British Journal of Social Work* 18(6): 623–34.

Corrigan, P. and Leonard, P. (1978) *Social Work Practice under Capitalism: a Marxist Approach* (London: Macmillan – now Palgrave Macmillan).

Costa, M. das Dores (1987) 'Current influences on social work in Brazil: practice and education', *International Social Work* 30(2): 115–28.

Coulshed, V., Mullender, A. and Malahlekha, B. (2000) *Management in Social Work* (2nd edn) (Basingstoke: Palgrave).

Cox, C. B. (2003) 'Designing interventions for grandparent caregivers: the need for an ecological perspective for practice', *Families in Society* 84(1) 127–34.

Cox, C. B. and Ephross, P. H. (1998) *Ethnicity and Social Work Practice* (New York: Oxford University Press).

Cox, E. O. (1989) 'Empowerment of low income elderly through group work', *Social Work with Groups* 11(4): 111–25.

Craig, G., and Mayo, M. (eds) (1995) *Community Empowerment: a Reader in Participation and Development* (London: Zed Books).

Craig, G., Derricourt, N. and Loney, M. (eds) (1982) *Community Work and the State: Towards a Radical Practice* (London: Routledge & Kegan Paul).

Craig, G., Mayo, M. and Sharman, N. (eds) (1979) *Jobs and Community Action* (London: Routledge & Kegan Paul).

Crawford, F., Dickinson, J. and Leitmann, S. (2002) 'Mirroring meaning making: narrative ways of reflecting on practice for action', *Qualitative Social Work* 1(2): 170–90.

Cree, V. E. and Macaulay, C. (eds) (2000) *Transfer of Learning in Professional and Vocational Education* (London: Routledge).

Croft, S. and Beresford, P. (1994) 'A participatory approach to social work', in Hanvey, C. and Philpot, T. (eds) *Practising Social Work* (London: Routledge): 49–66.

Curnock, K. and Hardiker, P. (1979) *Towards Practice Theory: Skills and Methods in Social Assessments* (London: Routledge & Kegan Paul).

Curry, J. F (1995) 'The current status of research into residential treatment', *Residential Treatment for Children and Youth* 12(3): 1–17.

Dalrymple, J. and Burke. B. (1995) *Anti-oppressive Practice: Social Care and the Law* (Buckingham: Open University Press).

Darlington, Y., Osmond, J. and Peile, C. (2002) 'Child welfare workers' use of theory in working with physical child abuse: implications for professional supervision', *Families in Society* 83(1): 54–63.

David, G. (1993) 'Strategies for grass roots human development', *Social Development Issues* 15(2): 1–13.

Davies, M. (1994) *The Essential Social Worker: a Guide to Positive Practice* (3rd edn) (Aldershot: Arena).

Davis, A., Newton, S. and Smith, D. (1985) 'Coventry crisis intervention: the consumer's view', *Social Services Research* 14(1): 7–32.

Davis, D. L. and Broster, L. H. (1993) 'Cognitive-behavioral-expressive interventions with aggressive and resistant youth', *Residential Treatment for Children and Youth* 10(4): 55–68.

Davis, L. V. (1985) 'Female and male voices in social work', *Social Work* 30(2): 106–13.

Davis, L. V. (1996) 'Role theory', in Francis J. Turner (ed.) *Social Work Treatment: Interlocking Theoretical Approaches* (4th edn) (New York: Free Press): 581–600.

de Graaf, M. (1986) 'Catching fish or liberating man: social development in Zimbabwe', *Journal of Social Development in Africa* 1(1): 7–26.

de Lange, J. M., Barton, J. A. and Lanham, S. L. (1981) 'The WISER way: a cognitive-behavioral model for group social skills training with juvenile delinquents', *Social Work with Groups* 4(3/4): 37–48.

de Maria, W. (1992) 'On the trail of a radical pedagogy for social work education', *British Journal of Social Work* 22(3): 231–52.

de Maria, W. (1993) 'Exploring radical social work teaching in Australia', *Journal of Progressive Human Services* 4(2): 45–63.

de Shazer, S. (1985) *Keys to Solution in Brief Therapy* (New York: Norton).

de Shazer, S. (1988) *Clues: Investigating Solutions in Brief Therapy* (New York: Norton).

de Shazer, S. (1991) *Putting Difference to Work* (New York: Gardner).

de Shazer, S. and Berg, I. K. (1997) 'What works?', *Journal of Family Therapy* 19(2): 1221–5.

Dean, R. G. (1993) 'Teaching a constructivist approach to clinical practice', in Laird, J. (ed.) *Revisioning Social Work Education: a Social Constructionist Approach* (New York: Haworth Press): 55–75.

Dean, R. G. (2002) 'Teaching contemporary psychodynamic theory for contemporary social work practice' *Smith College Studies in Social Work* 73(1): 11–27.

Denney, D. (1983) 'Some dominant perspectives in the literature relating to multi-racial social work', *British Journal of Social Work* 13(2): 149–74.

Denney, D. (1991) 'Antiracism, probation training and the criminal justice system', in CCETSW, *One Small Step Towards Racial Justice: the Teaching of Antiracism in Diploma in Social Work Programmes* (London: CCETSW): 58–80.

Denney, D. (1992) *Racism and Anti-Racism in Probation* (London: Routledge).

Dent, H. (1999) 'PC pathway to positive action', in Philpot, T. (ed.) *Political Correctness and Social Work* (London: IEA Health and Welfare Unit): 27–41.

DeVito, J. A. (2002) *Essentials of Human Communication* (4th edn) (Boston, MA: Allyn & Bacon).

Devore, W. (1983) 'Ethnic reality: the life model and work with black families', *Social Casework* 64(9): 525–31.

Devore, W. and Schlesinger, E. G. (1999) *Ethnic-sensitive Social Work Practice* (5th edn) (New York: Allyn & Bacon).

Dhooper, S. S. and Moore, S. E. (2001) *Social Work Practice with Culturally Diverse People* (Thousand Oaks, CA: Sage).

DHSS (1978) *Social Services Teams: the Practitioner's View* (London: HMSO).

Dietz, C. A. (2000) 'Reshaping clinical practice for the new millennium', *Journal of Social Work Education* **36**(3): 503–20

Dixon, J. and Scheurell, R. P. (eds) (1995) *Social Welfare with Indigenous Peoples* (London: Routledge).

Docl, M. (1994) 'Task centred work', in Hanvey, C. and Philpott, T. (eds) *Practical Social Work* (London: Routledge): 22–36.

Doel, M. (2002) 'Task-centred work', in Adams, R. , Dominelli, L. and Payne, M. (eds) *Social Work: Themes, Issues and Critical Debates* (Basingstoke: Palgrave Macmillan): 191–199.

Doel, M. and Marsh, P. (1992) *Task-centred Social Work* (Aldershot: Ashgate).

Dominelli, L. (1990) *Women and Community Action* (Birmingham: Venture).

Dominelli. L. (1997) *Anti-Racist Social Work* (2nd edn) (Basingstoke: Macmillan – now Palgrave Macmillan).

Dominelli, L. (2000) 'Empowerment: help or hindrance in professional relationships', in Stepney, P. and Ford, D. (eds) *Social Work Models, Methods and Theories: A Framework for Practice* (Lyme Regis: Russell House): 125–38.

Dominelli, L. (2002a) *Feminist Social Work Theory and Practice* (Basingstoke: Palgrave Macmillan).

Dominelli, L. (2002b) *Anti-Oppressive Social Work Theory and Practice* (Basingstoke: Palgrave Macmillan).

Dominelli, L. (2002c) 'Anti-oppressive practice in context' in Adams, R., Dominelli L. and Payne, M. (eds) *Social Work: Themes, Issues and Critical Debates* (2nd edn) (Basingstoke: Palgrave Macmillan): 3–19.

Dominelli, L. (2004) *Social Work: Theory and Practice for a Changing Profession* (Cambridge: Polity).

Dominelli, L. and McCleod, E. (1989) *Feminist Social Work* (Basingstoke: Macmillan – now Palgrave Macmillan).

Dore, M. M. (1990) 'Functional theory: its history and influence on contemporary social work', *Social Service Review:* 358–74.

Douglas, T. (1979) *Group Processes in Social Work: a Theoretical Synthesis* (Chichester: John Wiley).

Douglas, T. (1993) *A Theory of Groupwork Practice* (Basingstoke: Macmillan – now Palgrave Macmillan).

Dowrick, C. (1983) 'Strange meeting: Marxism, psychoanalysis and social work', *British Journal of Social Work* **13**(1): 1–18.

Drucker, D. (2003) 'Whither international social work? A reflection', *International Social Work* **46**(1): 53–81.

Dungee-Anderson, D. and Beckett, J. O. (1995) 'A process model for multicultural social work practice', *Families in Society* **76**(8): 459–66.

Dunlap, K. M. (1996) 'Functional theory and social work practice' in Turner, F. J. (ed.)*Social Work Treatment: Interlocking Theoretical Approaches* (4th edn) (New York: Free Press): 319–40 .

Edwards, M. and Hulme, D. (eds) (1992) *Making a Difference: NGOs and Development in a Changing World* (London: Earthscan).

Eisenhuth, E. (1981) 'The theories of Heinz Kohut and clinical social work practice', *Clinical Social Work Journal* **9**(2): 80–90.

Elliott, D. (1993) 'Social work and social development: towards an integrative model for social work practice', *International Social Work* **36**(1): 21–36.

Ellis, A. (1962) *Reason and Emotion in Psychotherapy* (Secaucus, NJ: Lyle Stuart).

Else, J. F., Gamanya, Z. M. and Jirira, K. O. (1986) 'Economic development in the African context: opportunities and constraints', *Journal of Social Development in Africa* **1**(2): 75–87.

Elson, M. (1986) *Self Psychology in Clinical Social Work* (New York: Norton).

Ely, P. and Denney, D. (1987) *Social Work in a Multi-Racial Society* (Aldershot: Gower).

England, H. (1986) *Social Work as Art* (London: Allen & Unwin).

Epstein, L. (1992) *Brief Treatment and a New Look at the Task-Centered Approach* (New York: Macmillan).

Erikson, E. (1965) *Childhood and Society* (2nd edn) (London: Hogarth Press).

Estes, R. J. (1993) 'Toward sustainable development: from theory to praxis', *Social Development Issues* 15(3): 1–29.

Evans, D. and Kearney, J. (1996) *Working in Social Care: A Systemic Approach* (Aldershot: Arena).

Evans, E. N. (1992) 'Liberation theology, empowerment theory and social work practice with the oppressed', *International Social Work* 35(2): 135–47.

Evans, R. (1976) 'Some implications of an integrated model of social work for theory and practice', *British Journal of Social Work* 6(2): 177–200.

Everitt, A., Hardiker, P., Littlewood, J. and Mullender, A. (1992) *Applied Research for Better Practice* (London: Macmillan).

Eyrich, K. M., Pollio, D. E. and North, C. S. (2003) 'An exploration of alienation and replacement theories of social support in homelessness', *Social Work Research* 27(4): 222–31.

Ezell, M. (1994) 'Advocacy practice of social workers', *Families in Society* 75(1): 36–46.

Eziakor, I. G. (1989) 'Rethinking Third World development: an analysis of contemporary paradigms', *Journal of Social Development in Africa* 4(2): 39–48.

Fairbairn, W. R. D. (1954) *An Object Relations Theory of Personality* (New York: Basic Books).

Fairclough, N. (2003) '"Political correctness": the politics of culture and language', *Discourse and Society* 14(1): 17–28.

Faul, A., Mc Murtry, S. L., Hudson, W. W. (2001) 'Can empirical clinical practice techniques improve social work outcomes?' *Research on Social Work Practice* 11(3): 277–99.

Fawcett, B. and Featherstone, B. (2000) 'Setting the scene: An appraisal of notions of postmodernism, postmodernity and postmodern feminism', in Fawcett, B., Featherstone, B., Fook, J. and Rossiter, A. (eds) *Practice and Research in Social Work: Postmodern Feminist Perspectives* (London: Routledge): 5–23.

Fawcett, B., Featherstone, B., Fook, J. and Rossiter, A. (eds) (2000) *Practice and Research in Social Work: Postmodern Feminist Perspectives* (London: Routledge).

Feldman, R. A. and Wodarski, J. S. (1975) *Contemporary Approaches to Group Treatment* (San Francisco: Jossey-Bass).

Fellin, P. (2000) 'Revisiting multicultural social work', *Journal of Social Work Education* 36(12): 261–75.

Ferguson, I. and Lavalette, M. (1999) 'Social work, postmodernism, and Marxism', *European Journal of Social Work* 2(1): 27–40.

Fimister, G. (1986) *Welfare Rights Work in Social Services* (London: Macmillan – now Palgrave Macmillan).

Finlay, L. (2003) 'The reflexive journey: mapping multiple routes', in Finlay, L. and Gough, B. (eds) *Reflexivity: A Practical Guide for Researchers in Health and Social Sciences* (Oxford: Blackwell): 3–20.

Finlay, L. and Gough, B. (eds) (2003) *Reflexivity: A Practical Guide for Researchers in Health and Social Sciences* (Oxford: Blackwell).

Finn, J. L. and Jacobson, M. (2003) 'Just justice: steps toward a new social work paradigm', *Journal of Social Work Education* 39(1): 57–78.

Fischer, J. (1973) 'Is casework effective? a review', *Social Work* 18(1): 5–20.

Fischer, J. (1976) *The Effectiveness of Social Casework* (Springfield, IL: Charles C. Thomas).

Fischer, J. (1981) 'The social work revolution', *Social Work* 26(3): 199–207.

Fischer, J. and Gochros, H. L. (1975) *Planned Behaviour Change: Behaviour Modification in Social Work* (New York: Free Press).

Fishbein, M. and Adzen, I. (1975) *Belief, Attitude and Intention: an Introduction to Theory and Research* (Reading, MA: Addison-Wesley).

Fisher, D. D. V. (1991) *An Introduction to Constructivism for Social Workers* (New York: Praeger).

Fisher, J. (1993) *Out of the Shadows: Women, Resistance and Politics in South America* (London: Latin America Bureau).

Fisher, M. (1994) 'Man-made care: community care and older male carers', *British Journal of Social Work* **24**(6): 659–680.

Fisher, R. and Kling, J. (1994) 'Community organization and new social movement theory', *Journal of Progressive Human Services* **5**(2): 5–23.

Fisher, W. H., Geller, J. L. and Wirth-Cauchon, J. (1990) 'Empirically assessing the impact of mobile crisis capacity on state hospital admissions', *Community Mental Health Journal* **26**(3): 245–53.

Fleming, R. C. (1981) 'Cognition and social work practice: some implications of attribution and concept attainment theories', in Maluccio, A. N. (ed.) *Promoting Competence in Clients: a New/Old Approach to Social Work Practice* (New York: Free Press): 55–73.

Folgheraiter, F. (2004) *Relational Social Work: Toward Networking and Societal Practices* (London: Jessica Kingsley).

Fook, J. (1993) *Radical Casework: A Theory of Practice* (St Leonards: Allen & Unwin).

Fook, J. (2002) *Social Work: Critical Theory and Practice* (London: Sage).

Forcey, L. R. and Nash, M. (1998) 'Rethinking feminist theory and social work therapy', *Women and Therapy* **21**(4): 85–99.

Ford, P. and Postle, K. (2000) 'Task-centred practice and care management', in Stepney, P. and Ford, D. (eds) *Social Work Models, Methods and Theories: A Framework for Practice* (Lyme Regis: Russell House): 52–64.

Forder, A. (1976) 'Social work and systems theory', *British Journal of Social Work* **6**(1): 24–41.

Forte, J. A. (1999) 'Culture: the tool-kit metaphor and multicultural social work', *Families in Society* **80**(1): 51–62.

Fortune, A. E. (1985) *Task-centered Practice with Families and Groups* (New York: Springer).

Foucault, M. (1972) *The Archaeology of Knowledge and the Discourse on Language* (New York: Pantheon).

Foucault, M. (1999) 'Social work, social control and normalization: roundtable discussion with Michel Foucault,' in Chambon, A. S., Irving, A. and Epstein, L. (eds) *Reading Foucault for Social Work* (New York: Columbia University Press): 83–97.

Foulkes, S. H. (1964) *Therapeutic Group Analysis* (London: Allen & Unwin)

Fraiberg, S. (1978) 'Psychoanalysis and social work: a re-examination of the issues', *Smith College Studies in Social Work* **48**(2): 87–106.

Frankl, V. F. (1964) *Man's Search for Meaning: An Introduction to Logotherapy* (rev. edn) (London: Hodder & Stoughton).

Franklin, C. and Nurius, P. S. (eds) (1998) *Constructivism in Practice Methods and Challenges* (Milwaukee, WI: Families International).

Franklin, C., Biever, J., Moore, K., Clemons, D. and Scamondo, M. (2001) 'The effectiveness of solution-focused therapy with children in a school setting', *Research on Social Work Practice* **11**(4): 411–34.

Franklin, M. E. (1968) 'The meaning of planned environment therapy', in Barron, A. T. (ed.) *Studies in Environment Therapy*, vol. 1 (Worthing: Planned Environment Therapy Trust).

Freddolino, P. O., Moxley, D. M. and Hyduk, C. A. (2004) 'A differential model of advocacy in social work practice' *Families in Society* **85**(1): 119–28.

Freire, P. (1972) *Pedagogy of the Oppressed* (Harmondsworth: Penguin).

Friedmann, J. (1992) *Empowerment: the Politics of Alternative Development* (Cambridge, MA: Blackwell).

Froggett, L. (2002) *Love, Hate and Welfare: Psychosocial Approaches to Policy and Practice* (Bristol: Policy Press).

Fulcher, L. C. and Ainsworth, F. (eds) (1985) *Group Care Practice with Children* (London: Tavistock).

Furlong, M. (1987) 'A rationale for the use of empowerment as a goal in casework', *Australian Social Work* **40**(3): 25–30.

Furlong, M. (1990) 'On being able to say what we mean: the language of hierarchy in social work practice', *British Journal of Social Work* **20**(6): 575–90.

Galper, J. (1975) *The Politics of Social Service* (Englewood Cliffs, NJ: Prentice-Hall).

Galper, J. (1980) *Social Work Practice: a Radical Approach* (Englewood Cliffs, NJ: Prentice-Hall).

Gambrill, E. (1977) *Behavior Modification: a Handbook of Assessment, Intervention and Evaluation* (San Francisco, CA: Jossey-Bass).

Gambrill, E. (1994) 'What's in a name? Task-centred, empirical, and behavioral practice', *Social Service Review* **68**(4): 578–99.

Gambrill, E. (1995) 'Behavioral social work: past, present and future', *Research on Social Work Practice* **5**(4): 460–84.

Gambrill, E. (2001) 'Social work: an authority-based profession', *Research on Social Work Practice* **11**(2): 166–75.

Ganzer, C. and Ornstein, E. D. (2002) 'A sea of trouble: a relational approach to the culturally sensitive treatment of a severely disturbed client', *Clinical Social Work Journal* **30**(2): 127–44.

Garber, B. (1992) 'Countertransference reactions in death and divorce: comparison and contrast', *Residential Treatment for Children and Youth* **9**(4): 43–60.

Gardner, F. (2003) 'Critical reflection in community-based evaluation' *Qualitative Social Work* **2**(2): 197–212.

Garfinkel, H. (1970) ' "Good" organizational reasons for "bad" clinic records,' in Turner, R. (ed.) *Ethnomethodology* (Harmondsworth: Penguin): 109–27.

George, V. and Wilding, P. (1994) *Welfare and Ideology* (London: Harvester Wheatsheaf).

Gergen, K. J. (1994) *Realities and Relationships: Soundings in Social Construction* (Cambridge, MA: Harvard University Press).

Gergen, K. J. (1999) *An Invitation to Social Construction* (London: Sage).

Gergen, K. J. and Gergen, M. J. (1986) 'Narrative forms and the construction of psychological science', in Garbin, T. R. (ed.) *The Storied Nature of Human Conduct* (New York: Praeger).

Gergen, M. and Gergen, K. J. (2003) *Social Construction: A Reader* (London: Sage).

Germain, C. B. (1976) 'Time: an ecological variable in social work practice', *Social Casework* **57**(7): 419–26.

Germain, C. B. (1977) 'An ecological perspective on social work practice in health care', *Social Work in Health Care* **3**(4): 67–76.

Germain, C. B. (1978a) 'General-systems theory and ego psychology: an ecological perspective', *Social Service Review* **52**(4): 534–50.

Germain, C. B. (1978b) 'Space, an ecological variable in social work practice', *Social Casework* **59**(11): 15–22.

Germain, C. B. (ed.) (1979a) *Social Work Practice: People and Environments – an Ecological Perspective* (New York: Columbia University Press).

Germain, C. B. (1979b) 'Introduction: ecology and social work', in Germain, C. B. (ed.) *Social Work Practice: People and Environments – an Ecological Perspective* (New York: Columbia University Press): 1–22.

Germain, C. B. and Gitterman, A. (1980) *The Life Model of Social Work Practice* (New York: Columbia University Press).

Germain, C. B. and Gitterman, A. (1996) *The Life Model of Social Work Practice: Advances in Theory and Practice* (2nd edn) (New York: Columbia University Press).

Gibbons, J., Bow, I., Butler, J. and Powell, J. (1979) 'Clients' reactions to task-centred casework: a follow-up study', *British Journal of Social Work* **10**(2): 203–15.

Gibbs, G. (1988) *Learning by Doing: A Guide to Teaching and Learning Methods* (Oxford: Oxford Polytechnic).

Gibbs, L. and Gambrill, E. (2002) 'Evidence-based practice: counterarguments to objectives', *Research in Social Work Practice* 12(3): 452–76.

Giddens, A. (1984) *The Constitution of Society* (Oxford: Polity).

Gilchrist, A. (2000) 'Community work in the UK – an overview', *Talking Point* 191: 1–4.

Gilchrist, A. (2004) *The Well-Connected Community: A Networking Approach to Community Development* (Bristol: Policy Press).

Gilgun, J. F. (1994a) 'Hand in glove: The grounded theory approach and social work practice research', in Sherman, E. and Reid, W. J. (eds) *Qualitative Research in Social Work* (New York: Columbia University Press): 115–25.

Gilgun, J. F. (1994b) 'An ecosystemic approach to assessment', in Compton, B. R. and Galaway, B. *Social Work Processes* (5th edn) (Pacific Grove, CA: Brooks/Cole): 380–94.

Gilligan, C. (1982) *In a Different Voice: Psychological Theory and Women's Development* (Cambridge, MA: Harvard University Press).

Gilligan, C. (1986) 'Reply to critics', in Larrabee, M. J. (ed.) *An Ethic of Care: Feminist and Interdisciplinary Perspectives* (New York: Routledge): 207–14.

Gingerich, W. J. (1990) 'Re-thinking single-case designs', in Videka-Sherman, L. and Reid, W. J. (eds) *Advances in Clinical Social Work Research* (Silver Spring, MD: NASW Press): 11–24.

Gingerich, W. J., Kleczewski, M. and Kirk, S. A. (1982) 'Name-calling in social work', *Social Service Review* 56(3): 366–74.

Gitterman, A. (1983) 'Uses of resistance: a transactional view', *Social Work* 28(2): 127–31.

Glasser, W. (1965) *Reality Therapy: a New Approach to Psychiatry* (New York: Harper & Row).

Glassman, U. and Kates, L. (1990) *Group Work: a Humanistic Approach* (Newbury Park, CA: Sage).

Goffman, E. (1968a) *Stigma: Notes on the Management of Spoiled Identity* (Harmondsworth: Penguin).

Goffman, E. (1968b) *The Presentation of Self in Everyday Life* (Harmondsworth: Penguin).

Goffman, E. (1972a) *Relations in Public: Microstudies of the Public Order* (Harmondsworth: Penguin).

Goffman, E. (1972b) *Interaction Ritual: Essays on Face-to-face Behaviour* (Harmondsworth: Penguin).

Goffman, E. (1972c) *Encounters: Two Studies in the Sociology of Interaction* (Harmondsworth: Penguin).

Golan, N. (1978) *Treatment in Crisis Situations* (New York: Free Press).

Golan, N. (1986) 'Crisis theory', in Turner, F. J. (ed.) *Social Work Treatment: Interlocking Theoretical Approaches* (3rd edn) (New York: Free Press): 296–340.

Goldapple, G. C. and Montgomery, D. (1993) 'Evaluating a behaviorally based intervention to improve client retention in therapeutic community treatment for drug dependency', *Research on Social Work Practice* 3(1): 21–39.

Goldberg, E. M. (1987) 'The effectiveness of social care: a selective exploration', *British Journal of Social Work* 17(6): 595–614.

Goldstein, E. G. (1995) *Ego Psychology and Social Work Practice* (2nd edn) (New York: Free Press).

Goldstein, E. G. (2002) *Object Relations Theory and Self Psychology in Social Work Practice* (New York: Free Press).

Goldstein, H. (1973) *Social Work Practice: a Unitary Approach* (Columbia, SC: University of South Carolina Press).

Goldstein, H. (1981) *Social Learning and Change: a Cognitive Approach to Human Services* (Columbia, SC: University of South Carolina Press).

Goldstein, H. (ed.) (1984) *Creative Change: a Cognitive-humanistic Approach to Social Work Practice* (New York: Tavistock).

Gomm, R. (1993) 'Issues of power in health and welfare', in Walmsley, J., Reynolds, J.

Shakespeare, P. and Woolfe, R. (eds) *Health, Welfare and Practice: Reflecting on Roles and Relationships* (London: Sage): 131–8.

Gomm, R. (2000a) 'Understanding experimental design', in Gomm, R. and Davies, C. (eds) *Using Evidence in Health and Social Care* (London: Sage): 46–64.

Gomm, R. (2000b) 'Making sense of surveys', in Gomm, R. and Davies, C. (eds) *Using Evidence in Health and Social Care* (London: Sage): 26–45.

Goodman, J. (1984) 'Reflection and teacher education: a case study and theoretical analysis', *Interchange* **15**: 9–26.

Gorey, K. M. (1996) 'Social work intervention effectiveness research: comparison of the findings from internal versus external evaluations', *Social Work Research* **20**(2): 119–28.

Goroff, N. N. (1974) 'Social welfare as coercive social control', *Journal of Sociology and Social Welfare* **2**(1): 19–26.

Gould, K. H. (1995) 'The misconstruing of multiculturalism: the Stanford debate and social work', *Social Work* **40**(2): 198–205.

Gould, N. (1994) 'Anti-racist social work: a framework for teaching and action', *Issues in Social Work Education* **14**(1): 2–17.

Graham, M. (2002) *Social Work and African-Centred Worldviews* (Birmingham: Venture).

Gray, E. (1987) 'Brief task-centred casework in a crisis intervention team in a psychiatric setting', *Journal of Social Work Practice* **3**(1): 111–28.

Gray, M, (2002) 'Art, irony and ambiguity: Howard Goldstein ad his contributions to social work', *Qualitative Social Work* **1**(4): 413–33.

Gray, M. and Bernstein, A. (1994) 'Pavement people and informal communities: lessons for social work', *International Social Work* **37**(2): 149–63.

Greene, G. J. (1996) 'Communication theory and social work treatment', in Turner, F. J. (ed.) *Social Work Treatment: Interlocking Theoretical Approaches* (New York: Free Press): 116–45.

Greene, G. J., Jensen, C. and Jones, D. H. (1996) 'A constructivist perspective on clinical social work practice with ethnically diverse clients', *Social Work* **41**(2): 172–80.

Greene, G. J., Lee, M.-Y., Trask, R. and Rheinscheld, J. (eds) (2000) 'How to work with clients' strengths in crisis intervention: a solution-focused approach,' in Roberts, A. R. (ed.) *Crisis Intervention Handbook: Assessment, Treatment and Research* (2nd edn) (New York: Oxford University Press): 31–55.

Greif, G. L. and Lynch, A. A. (1983) 'The eco-systems perspective', in Meyer, C. H. (ed.) *Clinical Social Work in the Eco-Systems Perspective* (New York: Columbia University Press).

Grimwood, C. and Popplestone, R. (1993) *Women, Management and Care* (Basingstoke: Macmillan – now Palgrave Macmillan).

Gross, E. R. (1995) 'Deconstructing politically correct practice literature: the American Indian case', *Social Work* **40**(2): 206–13.

Grosser, C. F. and Mondros, J. (1985) 'Pluralism and participation: the political action approach', in Taylor, S. H. and Roberts, R. W. (eds) *Theory and Practice of Community Social Work* (New York: Columbia University Press): 154–78.

Guntrip, H. (1968) *Schizoid Phenomena, Object Relations and the Self* (London: Hogarth Press).

Gutiérrez, G. (1973) *A Theology of Liberation* (Maryknoll: Orbis Books).

Gutiérrez, G. (1992) 'Poverty from the perspective of liberation theology', in Campfens, H. (ed.) *New Reality of Poverty and Struggle for Social Transformation* (Vienna: International Association of Schools of Social Work): 19–24.

Gutiérrez, L. M. (1995) 'Understanding the empowerment process: does consciousness make a difference?', *Social Work Research* **19**(4): 229–37.

Gutiérrez, L. M., DeLois, K. A. and GlenMaye, L. (1995) 'Understanding empowerment practice: building on practitioner-based knowledge', *Families in Society* **76**(8): 534–42.

Gutiérrez, L. M., Parsons, R. J. and Cox, E. O. (1998) *Empowerment in Social Work Practice: A Sourcebook* (Pacific Grove, CA: Brooks/Cole).

Hadley, R. and Hatch, S. (1981) *Social Welfare and the Failure of the State: Centralised Social Services and Participatory Alternatives* (London: Allen & Unwin).

Hadley, R. and McGrath, M. (eds) (1980) *Going Local: Neighbourhood Social Services* (London: Bedford Square Press).

Hadley, R., and McGrath, M. (1984) *When Social Services are Local: the Normanton Experience* (London: Allen & Unwin)

Hadley, R., Cooper, M., Dale, P. and Stacy, G. (1987) *A Community Social Worker's Handbook* (London: Tavistock).

Hall, C. Juhila, K., Parton, N. and Pösö, T. (2003) *Constructing Clienthood in Social Work and Human Services: Interaction, Identities and Practices* (London: Jessica Kingsley).

Hall, E. T. (1966) *The Hidden Dimension* (Garden City, NY: Doubleday).

Hall, N. (1993a) 'The social workers of tomorrow and fieldwork today: poverty and urban social work in Africa in the 1990s', in Hall, N. (ed.) *Social Development and Urban Poverty* (Harare: School of Social Work): 7–14.

Hall, N. (ed.) (1993b) *Social Development and Urban Poverty* (Harare: School of Social Work).

Hallett, C. (ed.) (1989) *Women and Social Services Departments* (London: Harvester Wheatsheaf).

Halmi, A. (2003) 'Chaos and non-linear dynamics: new methodological approaches in the social sciences and social work practice', *International Social Work* **46**(1): 83–101.

Hämäläinen, J. (1989) 'Social pedagogy as a meta-theory of social work education', *International Social Work* **32**(2): 117–28.

Hämäläinen, J. (2003) 'The concept of social pedagogy in the field of social work', *Journal of Social Work* **3**(1): 69–80.

Hamilton, G. (1950) *Theory and Practice of Social Casework* (2nd edn) (New York, Columbia University Press).

Hanmer, J. and Statham, D. ([1988] 1999) *Women and Social Work: Towards a More Woman-centred Practice* (Basingstoke: Macmillan – now Palgrave Macmillan).

Hanson, B. G. (1995) *General Systems Theory: Beginning with Wholes* (Washington, DC: Taylor & Francis).

Hanvey, C. and Philpot, T. (eds) (1994) *Practising Social Work* (London: Routledge).

Harcourt, W. (ed.) (1994) *Feminist Perspectives on Sustainable Development* (London: Zed Books).

Hardcastle, D. A., Wenocur, S. and Powers, P. R. (1997) *Community Practice: Theories and Skills for Social Workers* (New York: Oxford University Press).

Hardiker, P. (1981) 'Heart or head – the function and role of knowledge in social work', *Issues in Social Work Education* **1**(2): 85–111.

Hardiman, M. and Midgley, J. (1980) 'Training social planners for social development', *International Social Work* **23**(3): 2–15.

Hardiman, M. and Midgley, J. (1989) *The Social Dimensions of Development: Social Policy and Planning in the Third World*, rev. edn (Aldershot: Gower).

Harris, T. A. (1973) *I'm OK – You're OK* (London: Pan).

Harrison, W. D. (1991) *Seeking Common Ground: a Theory of Social Work in Social Care* (Aldershot: Avebury).

Hart, J. (1980) 'It's just a stage we're going through: the sexual politics of casework', in Brake, M. and Bailey, R. (eds) *Radical Social Work and Practice* (London: Edward Arnold): 43–63.

Hartman, A. (1971) 'But what is social casework?', *Social Casework* **52**(7): 411–19.

Hazell, J. (1995) *Personal Relationships Therapy* (London: Jason Aronson).

Healy, K. (2000) *Social Work Practices: Contemporary Perspectives on Change* (London: Sage).

Heap, K. (1992) 'The European groupwork scene: where were we? where are we? where are we going?' *Groupwork* **5**(1): 9–23.

Heard, D. and Lake, B. (1997) *The Challenge of Attachment for Caregiving* (London: Routledge).

Hearn, G. (1958) *Theory-building in Social Work* (Toronto: University of Toronto Press).

Hearn, G. (ed.) (1969) *The General Systems Approach: Contributions toward an Holistic Conception of Social Work* (New York: Council on Social Work Education).

Hearn, J. (1982) 'The problem(s) of theory and practice in social work and social work education', *Issues in Social Work Education* 2(2): 95–118.

Hegar, R. L. (1989) 'Empowerment-based practice with children', *Social Service Review* 63(3): 372–83.

Heineman-Pieper, J., Tyson, K. and Pieper, M. H. (2002) 'Doing good science without sacrificing good values: why the heuristic paradigm is the best choice for social work', *Families in Society* 83(1): 15–28.

Heller, N. R. and Northcut, T. B. (2002) 'Constructivism: a meeting ground for evolving psychodynamic and cognitive-behavioral practice?' *Smith College Studies in Social Work* 72(2): 197–215.

Henderson, P. and Thomas, D. (2002) *Skills in Neighbourhood Work* (3rd edn) (London: Routledge).

Henderson, P., Summer, S. and Raj, T. (2004) *Developing Healthier Communities: An Introductory Course for People Using Community Development Approaches to Improve Health and Tackle Health Inequalities* (London: NHS Health Development Agency).

Herberg, D. C. (1993) *Frameworks for Cultural and Racial Diversity: Teaching and Learning for Practitioners* (Toronto: Canadian Scholars' Press).

Hettne, B. (1990) *Development Theory and the Three Worlds* (London: Longman).

Hindmarsh, J. H. (1992) *Social Work Oppositions: New Graduates' Experiences* (Aldershot: Avebury).

Hinshelwood, R. D. (1999) 'Psychoanalytic origins and today's work: The Cassel Heritage', in Campling, P. and Haigh, R. (eds) *Therapeutic Communities: Past, Present and Future* (London: Jessica Kingsley): 39–49.

Hirayama, H. and Hirayama, K. (1985) 'Empowerment through group participation: process and goal', in Parnes, M. (ed.) *Innovations in Social Group Work: Feedback from Practice to Theory* (New York: Haworth): 119–31.

Hodge, D. R. (2003a) 'Differences in worldviews between social workers and people of faith', *Families in Society* 82(2): 285–95.

Hodge, D. R. (2003b) 'The challenge of spiritual diversity: can social work facilitate an inclusive environment?' *Families in Society* 84(3): 348–58

Hodge, D. R. and Williams, T. R. (2002) 'Assessing African-American spirituality with spiritual ecomaps', *Families in Society* 83(5): 585–95.

Hodge, D. R., Cardenas, P. and Montoya, H. (2001) 'Substance use: spirituality and religious participation as protective factors among rural youths' *Social Work Research* 25(3): 153–61.

Hogg, M. A. and Abrams, D. (1988) *Social Identifications: a Social Psychology of Intergroup Relations and Group Processes* (London: Routledge).

Hogg, M. A. and Abrams, D. (eds)(2001) *Intergroup Relations* (Brighton: Psychology Press).

Hollin, C. R. (1990) 'Social skills training with delinquents: a look at the evidence and some recommendations for practice', *British Journal of Social Work* 20(5): 483–93.

Hollis, F. and Woods, M. E. (1981) *Casework: A Psychosocial Therapy* (3rd edn) (New York: Random House).

Holmes, G. E. and Saleebey, D. (1993) 'Empowerment, the medical model and the politics of clienthood', *Journal of Progressive Human Services* 4(1): 61–78.

Horowitz, J. (1998) 'Contemporary psychoanalysis and social work theory', *Clinical Social Work Journal* 26(4): 369–83.

Horowitz, L. I. (1972) *Three Worlds of Development: the Theory and Practice of International Stratification* (2nd edn) (New York: Oxford University Press).

Houston, S. (2001) 'Beyond social constructionism: critical realism and social work', *British Journal of Social Work* 31(6): 845–61.

Houston, S. (2002) 'Reflecting on habitus, field and capital: Towards a culturally sensitive social work', *Journal of Social Work* 2(2): 149–67.

Howard, J. (1971) 'Indian society, Indian social work: identifying Indian principles and methods for social work practice', *International Social Work* 14(4): 16–31.

Howard, M. O. and Jenson, J. M. (1999a) 'Clinical practice guidelines: should social work develop them?' *Research on Social Work Practice* 9(3): 283–301.

Howard, M. O. and Jenson, J. M. (1999b) 'Barriers to development, utilization, and evaluation of social work practice guidelines: toward an action plan for social work', *Research on Social Work Practice* 9(3): 347–64.

Howard, T. U. and Johnson, F. C. (1985) 'An ecological approach to practice with single-parent families', *Social Casework* 66(8): 482–9.

Howe, D. (1987) *An Introduction to Social Work Theory* (Aldershot: Wildwood House).

Howe, D. (1995) *Attachment Theory for Social Work Practice* (Basingstoke: Macmillan – now Palgrave Macmillan).

Howe, D., Brandon, M., Hinings, D. and Schofield, G. (1999) *Attachment Theory, Child Maltreatment and Family Support* (Basingstoke: Macmillan – now Palgrave Macmillan).

Hudson, A. (1985) 'Feminism and social work: resistance or dialogue?', *British Journal of Social Work* 15(6): 635–55.

Hudson, B. and McDonald, G. (1986) *Behavioural Social Work: an Introduction* (Basingstoke: Macmillan – now Palgrave Macmillan).

Hudson, B. L. (1982) *Social Work with Psychiatric Patients* (London: Macmillan – now Palgrave Macmillan).

Hugman, B. (1977) *Act Natural: a New Sensibility for the Professional Worker* (London: Bedford Square Press).

Hugman, R. (1987) 'The private and the public in personal models of social work: a response to O'Connor and Dalgleish', *British Journal of Social Work* 17(1): 71–6.

Hulme, D. and Turner, M. (1990) *Sociology and Development: Theories, Policies and Practices* (Hemel Hempstead: Harvester Wheatsheaf).

Humphries, B. (1996) 'Contradictions in the culture of empowerment', in Humphries, B. (ed.) *Critical Perspectives on Empowerment*, (Birmingham: Venture): 1–16.

Hurdle, D. E. (2002) 'Native Hawaiian traditional healing: culturally based interventions for social work practice, *Social Work* 47(2): 183–92.

Husband, C. (1980) 'Culture, context and practice: racism in social work', in Brake, M. and Bailey, R. (eds) *Radical Social Work and Practice* (London: Edward Arnold): 64–85.

Husband, C. (1991) '"Race", conflictual politics, and anti-racist social work: lessons from the past for action in the 90s', in CD Project Steering Group *Setting the Context for Change* (London: CCETSW): 46–73.

Hutten, J. M. (1977) *Short-term Contracts in Social Work* (London: Routledge & Kegan Paul).

Illich, I., Zola, I. K., McKnight, J., Caplan, J. and Shaiken, H. (1977) *Disabling Professions* (London: Marion Boyars).

Imbrogno, S. (1999) 'A dialectic discourse as a strategy for empowerment', in Shera, W. and Wells, L. M. (eds) *Empowerment Practice in Social Work: Developing Richer Conceptual Foundations*, (Toronto: Canadian Scholars Press): 79–99.

Irvine, E. E. (1956) 'Transference and reality in the casework relationship', *British Journal of Psychiatric Social Work* 3(4): 1–10.

Irving, A. (1999) 'Waiting for Foucault: social work and the multitudinous truth(s) of life' in Chambon, A. S., Irving, A. and Epstein, L. (eds) *Reading Foucault for Social Work* (New York: Columbia University Press): 27–50.

Isajiw, W.W (1997a) 'On the concept and theory of social incorporation', in Isajiw, W. W. (ed.) *Multiculturalism in North American and Europe: Comparative Perspectives on Interethnic Relations and Social Incorporation* (Toronto: Canadian Scholars' Press): 79–102.

Isajiw, W. W. (ed.)(1997b) *Multiculturalism in North American and Europe: Comparative Perspectives on Interethnic Relations and Social Incorporation* (Toronto: Canadian Scholars' Press).

Jack, R. (1995) 'Empowerment in community care', in Jack, R. (ed.) *Empowerment in Community Care* (London: Chapman & Hall).

Jackson, B. (1994) *Poverty and the Planet: a Question of Survival,* rev. edn (London: Penguin).

Jackson, H. J. and King, N. J. (1982) 'The conceptual basis of behavioural programming: a review with implications for social work', *Contemporary Social Work Education* 5(3): 227–38.

Jacobs, C. and Bowles, D. D. (eds) (1988) *Ethnicity and Race: Critical Concepts in Social Work* (Silver Spring, MD: National Association of Social Workers).

James, R. K. and Gilliland, B. E. (2001) *Crisis Intervention Strategies* (4th edn) (Belmont, CA: Wadsworth).

Jansen, E. (ed.) (1980) *The Therapeutic Community Outside the Hospital* (London: Croom Helm).

Jasper, M. (2003) *Beginning Reflective Practice* (Cheltenham: Nelson Thornes).

Jasper, M. (2004) 'Using journals and diaries within reflective practice', in Bulman, C. and Schutz, S. (eds) *Reflective Practice in Nursing* (3rd edn) (Oxford: Blackwell): 94–112.

Jayaratne, S. (1978) 'A study of clinical eclecticism', *Social Service Review* 52(4): 621–31.

Jehu, D. (1967) *Learning Theory and Social Work* (London: Routledge & Kegan Paul).

Jehu, D. (ed.) (1972) *Behaviour Modification in Social Work* (Chichester: John Wiley).

Jenkins, R. (1996) *Social Identity* (London: Routledge).

Jenkins, S. (1987) 'The limited domain of effectiveness research', *British Journal of Social Work* 17(6): 587–94.

Jenkins, S. (1988) 'Ethnicity: theory base and practice link', in Jacobs, C. and Bowles, D. D. (eds) *Ethnicity and Race: Critical Concepts in Social Work* (Silver Spring, MD: NASW).

Johnson, H. (1992) 'Women's empowerment and public action: experiences from Latin America', in Wuyts, M., Mackintosh, M. and Hewitt, T. (eds) *Development Policy and Public Action* (Oxford: Oxford University Press): 147–72.

Jokinen, A., Juhila, K. and Pösö, T. (1999) *Constructing Social Work Practices* (Aldershot: Ashgate).

Jones, D. and Mayo, M. (eds) (1974) *Community Work One* (London: Routledge & Kegan Paul).

Jones, D. and Mayo, M. (eds) (1975) *Community Work Two* (London: Routledge & Kegan Paul).

Jones, H. (1979) *The Residential Community* (London: Routledge & Kegan Paul).

Jones, H. (1990) *Social Welfare in Third World Development* (Basingstoke: Macmillan – now Palgrave Macmillan).

Jones, J. F. (1981) 'An introduction to social development: an international perspective', in Jones, J. F. and Pandey, R. S. (eds) *Social Development: Conceptual, Methodological and Policy Issues* (Delhi: Macmillan India).

Jones, J. F. and Pandey, R. S. (eds) (1981) *Social Development: Conceptual, Methodological and Policy Issues* (Delhi: Macmillan India).

Jones, J. F. and Yogo, T. (1994) *New Training Design for Local Social Development: the Single System Design in Competency-based Training* (Nagoya, Japan: United Nations Centre for Regional Development).

Jones, M. (1968) *Social Psychiatry in Practice: the Idea of the Therapeutic Community* (Harmondsworth: Penguin).

Juhila, K. (2003) 'Creating a "bad" client: disalignment of institutional identities in social work interaction', in Hall, C. Juhila, K., Parton, N. and Pösö, T. (2003) *Constructing Clienthood in Social Work and Human Services: Interaction, Identities and Practices* (London: Jessica Kingsley): 83–95.

Kabadaki, K. K. (1995) 'Exploration of social work practice: models for rural development in Uganda', *Journal of Social Development in Africa* 10(1): 77–88.

Kadushin, G. (1998) 'Adaptations of the traditional interview in the brief-treatment context' *Families in Society* 79(4): 346–57.

Kanel, K. (2003) *A Guide to Crisis Intervention* (2nd edn) (Pacific Grove, CA: Brooks/Cole)

Karls, J. M. and Wandrei, K. E. (eds)(1994) *Person In Environment System: The PIE Classification for Social Functioning Problems* (Silver Spring, MA: NASW Press).

Karvinen, S., Pösö, T. and Satka, M. (1999) *Reconstructing Social Work Research* (Jyväskylä: SoPhi).

Katz, I. (1995) 'Approaches to empowerment and participation in child protection', in Cloke, C. and Davies, M. (eds) *Participation and Empowerment in Child Protection* (London: Pitman): 154–69.

Kazi, M. A. F. (1998) *Single-case Evaluation by Social Workers* (Aldershot: Ashgate).

Kazi, M. A. F. (2003) *Realist Evaluation in Practice: Health and Social Work* (London: Sage).

Kazi, M. A. F. and Mir, S. (1998) 'Behavioural work in residential child care' in Cigno, K. and Bourn, D. (eds) *Cognitive-behavioural Social Work in Practice* (Aldershot: Ashgate): 115–25.

Keefe, T. (1996) 'Meditation and social work treatment', in Turner, F. J. (ed.) *Social Work Treatment: Interlocking Theoretical Approaches* (4th edn) (New York: Free Press): 434–60.

Keenan, C. (1991) 'Working within the life-space', in Lishman, J. (ed.) *Handbook of Theory for Practice Teachers in Social Work* (London: Jessica Kingsley): 220–32.

Kelley, P. (1994) 'Integrating systemic and postsystemic approaches to social work practice with refugee families', *Families in Society* 75: 541–9.

Kelly, G. (1955) *The Psychology of Personal Constructs* (2 vols) (New York: Norton).

Kennard, D. (1983) *An Introduction to Therapeutic Communities* (London: Routledge & Kegan Paul).

Kennard, D. (1998) *An Introduction to Therapeutic Communities* (2nd edn) (London: Jessica Kingsley).

Kennett, C. (2001) 'Psychosocial day care', in Hearn, J. and Myers, K. (eds) *Palliative Day Care in Practice* (Oxford: Oxford University Press): 59–78.

Kenny, L. and Kenny, B. (2000) 'Psychodynamic theory in social work: a view from practice', in Stepney, P. and Ford, D. *Social Work Models, Methods and Theories: A Framework for Practice* (Lyme Regis: Russell House): 30–9.

Khandwalla, P. N. (ed.) (1988) *Social Development: a New Role for the Organizational Sciences* (New Delhi: Sage).

Kieffer, C. H. (1984) 'Citizen empowerment: a developmental perspective', *Prevention in Human Services* 3(1): 9–36.

Kim, Y.-O. (1995) 'Cultural pluralism and Asian-Americans: culturally sensitive social work practice', *International Social Work* 38(1): 69–78.

Kirk, S. A. (1999) 'Good intentions are not enough: practice guidelines for social work', *Research on Social Work Practice* 9(3): 302–10.

Kirk, S. A. and Reid, W. J. (eds)(2002) *Science and Social Work: A Critical Appraisal* (New York: Columbia University Press).

Kitsuse, J. I. and Spector, M. (1973) 'The definition of social problems', *Social Problems* 20(4): 407–19.

Klein, M. (1959) 'Our adult world and its roots in infancy', in Segal, H. (ed.) (1988) *Envy and Gratitude* (London: Virago).

Klugman, D. (2002) 'The existential side of Kohut's tragic man' *Clinical Social Work Journal* 30(1): 9–21.

Kohlberg, L. (1984) *The Psychology of Moral Development: The Nature and Validity of Moral Stages* (San Francisco: Harper & Row).

Kohut, H. (1978) *The Search for the Self: Selected Writings of Heinz Kohut: 1950–1978,* 2 vols (New York: International Universities Press).

Kolevson, M. S. and Maykranz, J. (1982) 'Theoretical orientation and clinical practice: uniformity versus eclecticism?', *Social Service Review* 58(1): 120–9.

Kondrat, M. E. (1995) 'Concept, act, and interest in professional practice: implications of an empowerment perspective', *Social Service Review* 69(3): 405–28.

Kondrat, M. E. (2002) 'Actor-centred social work: re-visioning "person-in-environment" through a critical theory lens' *Social Work* 47(4): 435–48.

Krill, D. F. (1969) 'Existential psychotherapy and the problem of anomie', *Social Work* 14(2): 33–49.

Krill, D. F. (1978) *Existential Social Work* (New York: Free Press).

Krill, D. F (1990) *Practice Wisdom: a Guide for Helping Professionals* (Newbury Park, CA: Sage).

Krumer-Nevo, M. (2003) 'What helps in help? A new look at help for women in deep, long-term economic and social deprivation', *Families in Society* 84(2): 169–78.

Kuhn, T. S. (1970) *The Structure of Scientific Revolutions* (Chicago: University of Chicago Press).

Kumar, H. (1994) *Social Work: an Experience and Experiment in India* (New Delhi: Gitanjali).

Kumar, H. (1995) *Theories in Social Work Practice* (Delhi: Friends).

Lacan, J. (1979) *The Four Fundamental Concepts of Psychoanalysis* (Harmondsworth: Penguin).

Laczko, F. and Phillipson, C. (1991) *Changing Work and Retirement* (Buckingham: Open University Press).

Laing, R. D. (1965) *The Divided Self: an Existential Study in Sanity and Madness* (Harmondsworth: Penguin).

Laing, R. D. (1971) *Self and Others* (2nd edn) (Harmondsworth: Penguin).

Land, H. (1995) 'Feminist clinical social work in the 21st century' in Van den Bergh, N. (ed.) *Feminist Practice in the 21st Century* (Washington DC: NASW Press): 3–19.

Lane, H. J. (1984) 'Self-differentiation in symbolic interactionism and psychoanalysis', *Social Work* 29(3): 270–4.

Langan, M. (2002) 'The legacy of radical social work', in Adams, R., Dominelli, L. and Payne, M. (eds) *Social Work: Themes, Issues and Critical Debates* (2nd edn) (Basingstoke: Palgrave Macmillan): 209–17.

Langan, M. and Day, L. (eds) (1992) *Women, Oppression and Social Work: Issues in Anti-discriminatory Practice* (London: Routledge).

Langan, M. and Lee, P. (eds) (1989) *Radical Social Work Today* (London: Unwin Hyman).

Lantz, J. (1987) 'The use of Frankl's concepts in family therapy', *Journal of Independent Social Work* 2(2): 65–80.

Lantz, J. and Greenlee, R. (1990) 'Existential social work with Vietnam veterans', *Journal of Independent Social Work* 5(1): 39–52.

Lappin, B. (1985) 'Community development: beginnings in social work enabling', in Taylor, S. H. and Roberts, R. W. (eds) *Theory and Practice of Community Social Work* (New York: Columbia University Press): 59–94.

Ledwith, M. (1997) *Participating in Transition: Towards a Working Model of Community Empowerment* (Birmingham: Venture).

Lee, J. A. B. (2001) *The Empowerment Approach to Social Work Practice: Building the Beloved Community* (2nd edn) (New York: Columbia University Press).

Lee, M. Y. (2003) 'A solution-focused approach to cross-cultural clinical social work practice: utilizing cultural strengths', *Families in Society* 84(3): 385–95.

Lee, P. and Pithers, D. (1980) 'Radical residential child care: Trojan horse or non-runner?', in Brake, M. and Bailey, R. (eds) *Radical Social Work and Practice* (London: Edward Arnold): 86–122.

Leighninger, R. D. (1978) 'Systems theory', *Journal of Sociology and Social Welfare* 5: 446–66.

Lemert, E. (1972) *Human Deviance, Social Problems and Social Control* (2nd edn) (Englewood Cliffs, NJ: Prentice-Hall).

Leonard, P. (1975) 'Towards a paradigm for radical practice', in Bailey, R. and Brake, M. (eds) *Radical Social Work* (London: Edward Arnold): 46–61.

Leonard, P. (1984) *Personality and Ideology: Towards a Materialist Understanding of the Individual* (London: Macmillan – now Palgrave Macmillan).

LeSueur, E. (1970) 'Aboriginal assimilation: an evaluation of some ambiguities in policy and services', *Australian Journal of Social Work* **23**(2): 6–11.

Levinson, D. J. (1978) *The Seasons of a Man's Life* (New York: Knopf).

Levy, A. and Kahan, B. (1991) *The Pindown Experience and the Protection of Children: the Report of the Staffordshire Child Care Inquiry* (Stafford: Staffordshire County Council).

Levy, C. S. (1981) 'Labeling: the social worker's responsibility', *Social Casework* **62**(6): 332–42.

Lewin, K. (1951) *Field Theory in Social Science* (New York: Harper).

Lindemann, E. (1944) 'Symptomatology and management of acute grief', in Parad, H. J. (ed.) (1965) *Crisis Intervention: Selected Readings* (New York: Family Service Association of America): 7–21.

Lishman, J. (ed.) (1991) *Handbook of Theory for Practice Teachers in Social Work* (London: Jessica Kingsley).

Lishman, J. (1994) *Communication in Social Work* (Basingstoke: Macmillan – now Palgrave Macmillan).

Loney, M. (1983) *Community Against Government: the British Community Development Project 1968–1978: a Study of Government Incompetence* (London: Heinemann).

Longres, J. F. and McCleod, E. (1980) 'Consciousness raising and social work practice', *Social Casework* **61**(5): 267–76.

Lorenz, W. (1994) *Social Work in a Changing Europe* (London: Routledge).

Lowenstein, S. (1985) 'Freud's metapsychology revisited', *Social Casework* **66**(3): 139–51.

Lum, D. (1999) *Culturally Competent Practice: A Framework for Growth and Action* (Pacific Grove, CA: Brooks/Cole).

Lusk, M. W and Hoff, M. D. (1994) 'Sustainable social development', *Social Development Issues* **16**(3): 20–31.

Lusk, M. W. (1981) 'Philosophical changes in Latin American social work', *International Social Work* **24**(2): 14–21.

Lynn, E. and Muir, A. (1996) 'Empowerment in social work: the case of CCETSW's Welsh language policy, in Humphries, B. (ed.) *Critical Perspectives on Empowerment* (Birmingham: Venture): 131–44.

Lynn, R. (2001) 'Learning from a "Murri way"', *British Journal of Social Work* **31**(5)903–16.

Lyon, K. (1993) 'Why study roles and relationships?', in Walmsley, J., Reynolds, J., Shakespeare, P. and Woolfe, R. (eds) *Health Welfare and Practice: Reflecting on Roles and Relationships* (London: Sage): 231–9.

McAuley, P., Catherwood, M. L. and Quayle, E. (1988) 'Behavioural-cognitive groups for adult psychiatric patients: a pilot study', *British Journal of Social Work* **18**(5): 455–71.

McCleod, J. (1997) *Narrative and Psychotherapy* (London: Sage).

McCouat, M. (1969) 'Some implications of object relations theory for casework', *Australian Journal of Social Work* **22**(3): 34–42.

MacDonald, G. and Sheldon, B. with Gillespie, J. (1992) 'Contemporary studies of the effectiveness of social work', *British Journal of Social Work* **22**(6): 615–43.

Macdonald, K. and Macdonald, G. (1999) 'Empowerment: a critical view', in Shera, W. and Wells, L. M. (eds) *Empowerment Practice in Social Work: Developing Richer Conceptual Foundations* (Toronto: Canadian Scholars Press): 50–78.

Macey, M. and Moxon, E. (1996) 'An examination of anti-racist and anti-oppressive theory and practice in social work education', *British Journal of Social Work* **26**(3): 297–314.

McIntyre, D. (1982) 'On the possibility of "radical" casework: a "radical" dissent', *Contemporary Social Work Education* **5**(3): 191–208.

McLaughlin, J. (2003) *Feminist Social and Political Theory: Contemporary Debates and Dialogues* (Basingstoke: Palgrave Macmillan).

McNamee, S. and Gergen, K. J. (eds) (1992) *Therapy as Social Construction* (London: Sage).

McNay, M. (1992) 'Social work can improve relations: towards a framework for an integrated practice', in Langan, M. and Day, L. (eds) *Women, Oppression and Social Work: Issues in Anti-discriminatory Practice* (London: Routledge): 48–66.

MacNeil, G. and Stewart, C. (2000) 'Crisis intervention with school violence problems and volatile situations' in Roberts, A. R. (ed.) *Crisis Intervention Handbook* (New York: Oxford University Press): 229–49.

Maguire, L. (1991) *Social Support Systems in Practice* (Silver Spring, MD: NASW Press).

Mahler, M., Pine, F. and Bergman, A. (1975) *The Psychological Birth of the Human Infant* (New York: Basic Books).

Mahrer, A. R. (2004) *Theories of Truth: Models of Usefulness* (London: Whurr).

Major, D. A. (2003) 'Utilizing role theory to help employed parents cope with children's chronic illness', *Health Education Research* 18(1): 45–57.

Malkinson, R. (2001) 'Cognitive-behavioral therapy of grief: a review and application', *Research on Social Work Practice* 11(6): 671–98.

Maluccio, A. N. (1981) 'Competence-oriented social work practice: an ecological approach', in Maluccio. A. N. (ed.) *Promoting Competence in Clients: A New/Old Approach to Social Work Practice* (New York: Free Press): 1–26.

Mancoske, R. (1981) 'Sociological perspectives on the ecological model', *Journal of Sociology and Social Welfare* 8(4): 710–32.

Manning, N. (1989) *The Therapeutic Community Movement: Charisma and Routinisation* (London: Routledge).

Mararike, C. G. (1995) *Grassroots Leadership: the Process of Rural Development in Zimbabwe* (Harare: University of Zimbabwe).

Marsh, J. (2003) 'Chewing on cardboard and other pleasures of knowledge utilization', *Social Work* 48(3): 293–4.

Marsh, P. (1991) 'Task-centred practice', in Lishman, J. (ed.) *Handbook of Theory for Practice Teachers in Social Work* (London: Jessica Kingsley): 157–72.

Marshall, E. K. and Kurtz, P. D. (1982) *Interpersonal Helping Skills* (San Francisco: Jossey-Bass).

Marshall, M., Crowther, R., Almaraz-Serrano, A., Creed, F., Sledge, W. and Kluiter, H. et al; (2001) 'Systematic reviews of the effectiveness of day care for people with severe mental disorders: (1) Acute day hospital versus admission; (2) vocational rehabilitation; (3) day hospital versus outpatient care', *Health Technology Assessment* 5(21): i-iii.

Martin, E. P. and Martin, J. M. (1995) *Social Work and the Black Experience* (Washington, DC: NASW Press).

Martin, E. P. and Martin, J. M. (2002) *Spirituality and the Black Helping Tradition in Social Work* (Washington, DC: NASW Press).

Martin, G. (2001) 'Social movements, welfare and social policy: a critical analysis', *Critical Social Policy* 21(3): 361–83.

Martin, R. R. (1995) *Oral History in Social Work: Research, Assessment, and Intervention* (Thousand Oaks, CA: Sage).

Martyn, H. (ed.) (2000) *Developing Reflective Practice: Making Sense of Social Work in a World of Change* (Bristol: Policy Press).

Martinussen, J. (1997) *Society, State and Market: A Guide to Competing Theories of development* (London: Zed Books).

Maslow, A. (1970) *Motivation and Personality* (2nd edn) (New York: Harper & Row).

Mathiesen, R. (1999) 'An examination of the theoretical foundation of social pedagogy', *Journal of the European Association of Training Centres for Social Educational Care Work* 3: 3–28

Mattaini, M. A. (1993) 'Behavior analysis and community practice: a review', *Research on Social Work Practice* 3(4): 420–47.

Mattaini, M. A., Lowery, C. T. and Meyer, C. H. (eds) (2002) *Foundations of Social Work Practice: A Graduate Text* (Washington, DC: NASW).

Matthies, A.-L., Närhi, K and Ward, D. (eds) (2000a) *From Social Exclusion to Participation: Explorations across Three European Cities* (Jyväskylä: Working Papers in Social Policy 106, University of Jyväskylä).

Matthies, A.-L., Järvelä, M. and Ward, D. (2000b) 'An eco-social approach to tackling exclusion in European cities: a new comparative research project in progress', *European Journal of Social Work* 3(1): 43–51.

Matthies, A.-L., Närhi, K and Ward, D. (eds) (2001) *The Eco-Social Approach in Social Work* (Jyväskylä: SoPhi).

Mead, G. H. (1934) *Mind, Self and Society* (Chicago: University of Chicago Press).

Meichenbaum, D. (1977) *Cognitive Behaviour Modification: an Integrative Approach* (New York: Plenum).

Meichenbaum, D. (1985) *Stress Inoculation Training* (New York: Pergamon).

Menzies-Lyth, I. (1988) *Containing Anxiety in Institutions* (London: Free Association).

Messkoub, M. (1992) 'Deprivation and structural adjustment', in Wuyts, M., Mackintosh, M. and Hewitt, T. (eds) *Development Policy and Public Action* (Oxford: Oxford University Press): 175–98.

Meyer, C. H. (ed.) (1983) *Clinical Social Work in the Eco-Systems Perspective* (New York: Columbia University Press).

Meyer, W. S. (2000) 'The psychoanalytic social worker/the social work psychoanalyst: what shall be our message?' *Clinical Social Work Journal* 28(4): 355–67.

Midgley, J. (1981) *Professional Imperialism: Social Work in the Third World* (London: Heinemann).

Midgley, J. (1984) 'Social welfare implications of development paradigms', *Social Service Review* 58(2): 182–98.

Midgley, J. (1987) 'Popular participation, statism and development', *Journal of Social Development in Africa* 2(1): 5–15.

Midgley, J. (1989) 'Social work in the Third World: crisis and response', in Carter, P., Jeffs, T. and Smith, M. (eds) *Social Work and Social Welfare Yearbook 1, 1989* (Milton Keynes: Open University Press): 33–45.

Midgley, J. (1993) 'Ideological roots of social development strategies', *Social Development Issues* 15(1): 1–13.

Midgley, J. (1995) *Social Development: the Developmental Perspective in Social Welfare* (London: Sage).

Midgley, J. (1997) *Social Welfare in Global Context* (Thousand Oaks, CA: Sage).

Mikulas, W. L. (2002) *The Integrative Helper: Convergence of Eastern and Western Traditions* (Pacific Grove, CA: Brooks/Cole).

Miley, K., and DuBois, B. (1999) 'Empowering processes for social work practice', in Shera, W. and Wells, L. M. (eds) *Empowerment Practice in Social Work: Developing Richer Conceptual Foundations* (Toronto: Canadian Scholars Press): 2–12.

Milligan, D. (1975) 'Homosexuality: sexual needs and social problems', in Bailey, R. and Brake, M. (eds) *Radical Social Work* (London: Edward Arnold): 96–111.

Mills, L. (1996) 'Empowering battered women transnationally: the case of postmodern interventions' *Social Work* 41(3): 261–68.

Milner, J. (2004) 'From "disappearing" to "demonised": the effects on men and women of professional interventions based on challenging men who are violent', *Critical Social Policy* 24(1): 79–101.

Miri, S. (1993) *Communalism in Assam: a Civilisational Approach* (New Delhi: Har-Anand).

Mitchell, J. (1975) *Psychoanalysis and Feminism* (Harmondsworth: Penguin).

Mondros, J. B. and Wilson, S. M. (1994) *Organizing for Power and Empowerment* (New York: Columbia University Press).

Montgomery, A. (2002) 'Converging perspectives of dynamic theory and evolving neurobiological knowledge', *Smith College Studies in Social Work* 72(2): 177–96.

Mor-Barak, M. E. (1988) 'Support systems intervention in crisis situations: theory, strategies and a case discussion', *International Social Work* 31(4): 285–304.

Moreau, M. J. (1979) 'A structural approach to social work practice', *Canadian Journal of Social Work Education* 5(1): 78–94.

Moreau, M. J. (1990) 'Empowerment through advocacy and consciousness-raising: implications of a structural approach to social work', *Journal of Sociology and Social Welfare* 17(2): 53–68.

Morén, S. (1994) 'Social work is beautiful: on the characteristics of social work', *Scandinavian Journal of Social Welfare* 3(3): 158–66.

Morén, S. and Blom, B. (2003) 'Explaining human change: on generative mechanisms in social work practice', *Journal of Critical Realism* 2(1): 37–61.

Morgan, R. T. T. and Young, G. C. (1972) 'The conditioning treatment of childhood enuresis', *British Journal of Social Work* 2(4): 503–10.

Morris, J. (1993) *Disabled Lives: Community Care and Disabled People* (Basingstoke: Macmillan – now Palgrave Macmillan).

Moyana, T. T. (1989) *Education, Liberation and the Creative Act* (Harare: Zimbabwe Publishing House).

Mullaly, R. P. (2003) *Structural Social Work: Ideology, Theory and Practice* (2nd edn) (Ontario: Oxford University Press).

Mullaly, R. P. and Keating, E. F. (1991) 'Similarities, differences and dialectics of radical social work', *Journal of Progressive Human Services* 2(2): 49–78.

Mullard, C. (1991) 'Towards a model of anti-racist social work', in CCETSW *One Small Step Towards Racial Justice: the Teaching of Antiracism in Diploma in Social Work Programmes* (London: CCETSW): 10–19.

Mullen, E. J. and Dumpson, J. R. et al. (1972) *Evaluation of Social Intervention* (San Francisco: Jossey-Bass).

Mullender, A. and Ward, D. (1991) *Self-Directed Groupwork: Users Take Action for Empowerment* (London: Whiting and Birch).

Mulwa, F. W. (1988) 'Participation of the grassroots in rural development: the case of the Development Education Programme of the Catholic Dioceses of Machakos, Kenya', *Journal of Social Development in Africa* 3(2): 49–65.

Muzaale, P. J. (1988) 'The organisation and delivery of social services to rural areas', *Journal of Social Development in Africa* 3(2): 33–48.

Muzumdar, A. M. (1964) *Social Welfare in India: Mahatma Gandhi's Contributions* (London: Asia Publishing House).

Mwansa, L.-K. (1995) 'Participation of non-governmental organisations in social development process in Africa: implications', *Journal of Social Development in Africa* 10(1): 65–75.

Myer, R. A. (2001) *Assessment for Crisis Intervention: A Triage Assessment Model* (Belmont, CA: Brooks/Cole).

Naik, D. (1991) 'Towards an antiracist curriculum in social work training', in CCETSW *One Small Step Towards Racial Justice: the Teaching of Antiracism in Diploma in Social Work Programmes* (London: CCETSW): 50–7.

Narayan, U. (1994) 'Working together across differences', in Compton, B. R. and Galaway, B. (eds) *Social Work Processes* (Pacific Grove, CA: Brooks/Cole): 177–88.

Närhi, K (2002) 'Transferable and negotiated knowledge: constructing social work expertise for the cuture', *Journal of Social Work* 2(3): 317–36.

Närhi, K. (2004) *The Eco-social Approach in Social Work and the Challenges to Expertise in Social Work* (Jyväskylä Studies in Education Psychology and Social Research 243) (Jyväskylä: University of Jyväskylä) http://selene.lib.jyu.fi: 8080/vaitos/studies/studeduc/9513918343.pdf (accessed 30th August 2004).

Närhi, K. and Matthies, A.-L. (2001) 'What is the ecological (self-)consciousness of social work?' in Matthies, A.-L., Närhi, K and Ward, D. (eds) (2001) *The Eco-Social Approach in Social Work* (Jyväskylä: SoPhi): 16–53.

Nartsupha, C. (1991) 'The community culture school of thought', in Chitakasem, M. and Turton, A. (eds) *Thai Constructions of Knowledge* (London: School of Oriental and African Studies, University of London): 118–41.

Nash, M. and Stewart, B. (eds) (2002) *Spirituality and Social Care: Contributing to Personal and Community Well-being* (London: Jessica Kingsley).

Neary, M. (1992) 'Some academic freedom', *Probation Journal* 39(8): 200–2.

Neill, A. S. (1964) *Summerhill* (London: Victor Gollancz).

Neimeyer, G. J. and Neimeyer, R. A. (1993) 'Defining the boundaries of constructivist assessment', in Neimeyer, G. J. (ed.) *Constructivist Assessment: a Casebook* (Newbury Park, CA: Sage): 1–30.

Neimeyer, R. A. (1993) 'Approaches to the measurement of meaning', in Neimeyer, G. J. (ed.) *Constructivist Assessment: a Casebook* (Newbury Park, CA: Sage): 58–103.

Nelsen, J. C. (1980) *Communication Theory and Social Work Practice* (Chicago: University of Chicago Press).

Nelsen, J. C. (1986) 'Communication theory and social work treatment', in Turner, F. J. (ed.) *Social Work Treatment: Interlocking Theoretical Approaches* (3rd edn) (New York: Free Press): 219–44.

Nelsen, J. C. (1990) 'Single-case research and traditional practice: issues and possibilities', in Videka-Sherman, L. and Reid, W. J. (eds) *Advances in Clinical Social Work Research* (Silver Spring, MD: NASW Press): 37–47.

Ng, H.-Y. (2003) 'The "social" in social work practice: shamans and social workers', *International Social Work* 46(3): 289–301.

Nkunika, A. I. Z. (1987) 'The role of popular participation in programmes of social development', *Journal of Social Development in Africa* 2(1): 17–28.

Norman, A. (1985) *Triple Jeopardy: Growing Old in a Second Homeland* (London: Centre for Policy on Ageing).

Northcut, T. B. and Heller, N. R. (2002) 'The slippery slope of constructivism', *Smith College Studies in Social Work* 72(2): 217–29.

Norton, D. G. (1978) *The Dual Perspective: Inclusion of Ethnic Minority Content in the Social Work Curriculum* (Washington, DC: Council on Social Work Education).

Ntebe, A. (1994) 'Effective intervention roles of South African social workers in an appropriate, relevant and progressive social welfare model', *Journal of Social Development in Africa* 9(1): 41–50.

O'Brien, D. and Pace, J. (1988) 'The role of social work development theory in informing social work degree programs for indigenous native people: a critique of the Canadian experience', in Guzzetta, C. and Mittwoch, F. (eds) *Social Development and Social Rights* (Vienna: International Association of Schools of Social Work): 89–99.

O'Connor, I. and Dalgleish, L. (1986) 'Cautionary tales about beginning practitioners: the fate of personal models of social work in beginning practice', *British Journal of Social Work* 16(4): 431–47.

O'Connor, M. (1992) 'An Adlerian approach to casework in a hospital setting', *The Social Worker* 60(2): 121–2.

O'Hagan, K. (1986) *Crisis Intervention in Social Services* (Basingstoke: Macmillan – now Palgrave Macmillan).

O'Hagan, K. (1991) 'Crisis intervention in social work', in Lishman, J. (ed.) *Handbook of Theory for Practice Teachers in Social Work* (London: Jessica Kingsley): 138–56.

O'Hagan, K. (1994) 'Crisis intervention: changing perspectives', in Hanvey, C. and Philpot, T. (eds) *Practising Social Work* (London: Routledge): 134–45.

O'Hagan, K. (2001) *Cultural Competence in the Caring Professions* (London: Jessica Kingsley).

O'Melia, M. and Miley, K. K. (eds)(2002) *Pathways to Power: Readings in Contextual Social Work Practice* (Boston, MA: Allyn and Bacon).

Ohri, A., Manning, B. and Curno, P. (1982) *Community Work and Racism* (London: Routledge & Kegan Paul).

Okundaye, J. N. , Gray, C. and Gray, L. B. (1999) 'Reimaging field instruction from a spiritually sensitive perspective: an alternative approach', *Social Work* 44(4): 371–83.

Oldfield, M. (2002) 'What works and the conjunctural politics of probation: effectiveness, managerialism and neoliberalism', *British Journal of Community Justice* 1(1): 79–88.

Oliver, M. (1990) *The Politics of Disablement* (Basingstoke: Macmillan – now Palgrave Macmillan).

Oliver, M. (1996) *Understanding Disability: From Theory to Practice* (Basingstoke: Macmillan – now Palgrave Macmillan).

Olsen, M. R. (ed.) (1978) *The Unitary Model: Its Implications for Social Work Theory and Practice* (Birmingham: BASW Publications).

Olsson, E. (1993) ' "Naiv teori" i socialt behandlingsarbete', *Nordisk Socialt Arbete* 2(1): 3–17.

Olsson, E. and Ljunghill, J. (1997) 'The practitioner and 'naive theory' in social work intervention processes', *British Journal of Social Work* 27(6): 931–950.

Orcutt, B. A. (1990) *Science and Inquiry in Social Work Practice* (New York: Columbia University Press).

Orme, J. (2000) *Gender and Community Care: Social Work and Social Care Perspectives* (Basingstoke: Palgrave – now Palgrave Macmillan).

Orme, J. (2001) *Gender and Community Care: Social Work and Social Care* (Basingstoke: Palgrave Macmillan).

Orme, J. (2002) 'Feminist social work' in Adams, R., Dominelli, L. and Payne, M. (eds) *Social Work: Themes, Issues and Critical Debates* (2nd edn) (Basingstoke: Palgrave Macmillan): 218–26.

Orme, J. (2003) '"It's feminist because I say so!' Feminism, social work and critical practice in the UK', *Qualitative Social Work* 2(2): 131–53.

Osei-Hwedie, K. (1990) 'Social work and the question of social development in Africa', *Journal of Social Development in Africa* 5(2): 87–99.

Osei-Hwedie, K. (1993) 'The challenge of social work in Africa: starting the indigenisation process', *Journal of Social Development in Africa* 8(1): 19–30.

Osmo, R. and Landau, R. (2003) 'Religious and secular belief systems in social work: a survey of Israeli social work professionals', *Families in Society* 84(3): 359–66.

Osmo, R. and Rosen, A. (2002) 'Social workers' strategies for treatment hypothesis testing', *Social Work Research* 26(1): 9–18.

Owusu-Bempah, J. (1994) 'Race, self-identity and social work', *British Journal of Social Work* 24(2): 123–36.

Paiva, J. F. X. (1977) 'A conception of social development', *Social Service Review* 51(2): 327–36.

Paiva, J. F. X. (1993) 'Excuse me, I wish to be unboxed...', *Social Development Issues* 15(1): 22–3.

Pandey, R. S. (1981) 'Strategies for social development: an analytical approach', in Jones, J. F. and Pandey, R. S. (eds) *Social Development: Conceptual, Methodological and Policy Issues* (Delhi: Macmillan India): 33–49.

Papell, C. P and Rothman, B. (1966) 'Social group work models: possession and heritage', *Journal of Education for Social Work* 2(2): 66–73.

Parad, H. J. (ed.) (1965a) *Crisis Intervention: Selected Readings* (New York: Family Service Association of America).

Parad, H. J. (1965b) 'Introduction', in Parad, H. J. (ed.) *Crisis Intervention: Selected Readings* (New York: Family Service Association of America): 1–4.

Parad, H. J. and Parad, L. G. (1990) *Crisis Intervention Book 2: the Practitioner's Sourcebook for Brief Therapy* (Milwaukee, WI: Family Service America).

Parker, G. (1993) *With This Body: Caring and Disability in Marriage* (Buckingham: Open University Press).

Parker, I. (ed.) (1998) *Social Constructionism, Discourse and Realism* (London: Sage).

Parkes, C. M. (1972) *Bereavement: Studies of Grief in Adult Life* (Harmondsworth: Penguin).

Parkes, C. M., Stevenson-Hinde, J. and Marris, P. (eds) (1993) *Attachment Across the Life Cycle* (London: Routledge).

Parsloe, P. (1996a) 'Empowerment in social work practice', in Parsloe, P. (ed.) *Pathways to Empowerment* (Birmingham: Venture): 1–10.

Parsloe, P. (1996b) 'Helping individuals to take power', in Parsloe, P. (ed.) *Pathways to Empowerment* (Birmingham: Venture): 111–23.

Parton, N. (2003) 'Rethinking professional practice: the contributions of social constructionism and the feminist "ethics of care"', *British Journal of Social Work* 33(1): 1–16.

Parton, N. (ed.) (1996) *Social Theory, Social Change and Social Work* (London: Routledge).

Parton, N. and O'Byrne, P. (2000) *Constructive Social Work: Towards a New Practice* (Basingstoke: Macmillan – now Palgrave Macmillan).

Patel, D. (1988) 'Some issues of urbanisation and development in Zimbabwe', *Journal of Social Development in Africa* 3(2): 17–31.

Patel, N. (1994) 'Establishing a framework for anti-racist social work education in a multi-racial society – the UK experience from a statutory body, CCETSW', in Dominelli, L., Patel, N. and Bernard, W. T. *Anti-Racist Social Work Education: Models for Practice* (Sheffield: University of Sheffield Department of Sociological Studies): 7–21.

Pawson, R. and Tilley, N. (1997) *Realistic Evaluation* (London: Sage).

Payne, C. (1977) 'Residential social work', in Specht, H. and Vickery, A. (eds) *Integrating Social Work Methods* (London: Allen & Unwin): 195–216.

Payne, M. (1988) 'How can we hear the community voice? Responding to community participation at consumer feedback' *Practice* 2(1): 74–84.

Payne, M. (1992) 'Psychodynamic theory within the politics of social work theory', *Journal of Social Work Practice* 6(2): 141–9.

Payne, M. (1993) Routes to and through clienthood and their implications for practice', *Practice* 6(3): 169–80.

Payne, M. (1995) *Social Work and Community Care* (Basingstoke: Macmillan – now Palgrave Macmillan).

Payne, M. (1996a) *What is Professional Social Work?* (Birmingham: Venture).

Payne, M. (1996b) 'The politics of social work theory and values', in IASSW (ed.) *Proceedings of the 27th Congress* (Hong Kong: IASSW): 73–6.

Payne, M. (1997) 'Task-centred practice within the politics of social work theory', *Issues in Social Work Education* 17(2): 48–65.

Payne, M. (1999) 'Social construction in social work and social action' in Jokinen, A., Juhila, K. and Pösö, T. (eds) *Constructing Social Work Practices* (Aldershot: Ashgate): 25–65.

Payne, M. (2000) 'The politics of case management in social work', *International Journal of Social Welfare* 9(2): 82–91.

Payne, M. (2002a) 'Balancing the equation', *Professional Social Work*, January, 12–13.

Payne, M. (2002b) 'Social work theories and reflective practice', in Adams, R., Dominelli, L. and Payne, M. (eds) *Social Work: Themes, Issues and Critical Debates*, (2nd edn) (Basingstoke: Palgrave Macmillan): 123–38.

Payne, M. (2002c) 'The politics of systems theory within social work', *Journal of Social Work* 2(3): 269–92.

Payne, M. (2005) *Social Work Change and Continuity* (Basingstoke: Palgrave Macmillan).

Payne, M., Adams, R. and Dominelli, L. (2002) 'On being critical in social work', in Adams, R., Dominelli, L. and Payne, M. (eds) *Critical Practice in Social Work* (Basingstoke: Palgrave Macmillan): 1–12.

Pearson, G. (1975) *The Deviant Imagination: Psychiatry, Social Work and Social Change* (London: Macmillan – now Palgrave Macmillan).

Pearson, G., Treseder, J. and Yelloly, M. (eds) (1988) *Social Work and the Legacy of Freud* (London: Macmillan – now Palgrave Macmillan).

Pease, B. (2002) 'Rethinking empowerment: a postmodern reappraisal for emancipatory practice', *British Journal of Social Work* 32(2): 135–47.

Pease, B. and Fook, J. (1999) *Transforming Social Work Practice: Postmodern Critical Perspectives* (London: Routledge).

Peled, E., Eisikovets, Z., Enosh, G. and Winstok, Z. (2000) 'Choice and empowerment for battered women who stay: toward a constructivist model', *Social Work* 45(1): 9–25.

Pepper, D. (1991) *Communes and the Green Vision: Counterculture, Lifestyle and the New Age* (London: Green Print).

Perlman, H. H. (1957a) *Social Casework: a Problem-Solving Process* (Chicago: University of Chicago Press).

Perlman, H. H. (1957b) 'Freud's contribution to social welfare', *Social Service Review* 31(2): 192–202.

Perlman, H. H. (1968) *Persona: Social Role and Personality* (Chicago: University of Chicago Press).

Perlman, H. H. (1970) 'The problem-solving model in social casework', in Roberts, R. W. and Nee, R. W. (eds) *Theories of Social Casework* (Chicago: University of Chicago Press): 129–79.

Perlman, H. H. (1986) 'The problem-solving model', in Turner, F. J. (ed.) *Social Work Treatment: Interlocking Theoretical Approaches* (3rd edn) (New York: Free Press): 245–66.

Perls, F., Hefferline, R. F. and Goodman, P. (1973) *Gestalt Therapy: Excitement and Growth in the Human Personality* (Harmondsworth: Penguin) (original American edition, 1951).

Pernell, R. B. (1985) 'Empowerment and social group work', in Parnes, M. (ed.) *Innovations in Social Group Work: Feedback from Practice to Theory* (New York: Haworth): 107–17.

Phillips, D. R. and Verhasselt, Y. (eds) (1994) *Health and Development* (London: Routledge).

Phillipson, C. (1982) *Capitalism and the Construction of Old Age* (London: Macmillan – now Palgrave Macmillan).

Philp, M. (1979) 'Notes on the form of knowledge in social work', *Sociological Review* 27(1): 83–111.

Philpot, T. (1999) 'The modern mark of Cain', in Philpot, T. (ed.) *Political Correctness and Social Work* (London: IEA Health and Welfare Unit): 1–15.

Pilkington, A. (2003) *Racial Disadvantage and Ethnic Diversity in Britain* (Basingstoke: Palgrave Macmillan).

Pincus, A. and Minahan, A. (1973) *Social Work Practice: Model and Method* (Itasca, IL: Peacock).

Pincus, L. (1976) *Death and the Family* (London: Faber and Faber).

Pinderhughes, E. B. (1983) 'Empowerment for our clients and ourselves', *Social Casework* 64(6): 331–8.

Pinderhughes, E. B. (1989) *Understanding Race, Ethnicity and Power: the Key to Efficacy in Clinical Practice* (New York: Free Press).

Pinderhughes, E. B. (1995) 'Empowering diverse populations: family practice in the 21st century', *Families in Society* 76(3): 131–40.

Pinderhughes, E. B. (1988) 'Significance of culture and power in the human behavior curriculum', in Jacobs, C. and Bowles, D. D. (eds) *Ethnicity and Race: Critical Concepts in Social Work* (Silver Spring, MD: National Association of Social Workers): 152–66.

Pinker, R. (1999) 'Social work and adoption: a case of mistaken identities', in Philpot, T. (ed.) *Political Correctness and Social Work* (London: IEA Health and Welfare Unit): 16–26.

Pitman, E. (1982) 'Transactional analysis: an introduction to its theory and practice', *British Journal of Social Work* 12(1): 47–64.

Pitman, E. (1983) *Transactional Analysis for Social Workers* (London: Routledge & Kegan Paul).

Pitts, J. (1992) 'The end of an era', *Howard Journal of Criminal Justice* 31(2): 133–49.

Piven, F. and Cloward, R. O. (1977) *Poor People's Movements: Why They Succeed, How They Fail* (New York: Vintage).

Pizzat, F. J. (1973) *Behaviour Modification in Residential Treatment for Children: Model of a Program* (New York: Behavioral Publications).

Poertner, J. (1994) 'Popular education in Latin America: a technology for the North?', *International Social Work* 37(3): 265–76.

Polanyi, M. (1958) *Personal Knowledge* (Chicago: University of Chicago Press).

Polsky, H. (1968) *Cottage Six: the Social System of Delinquent Boys in Residential Treatment* (Chapel Hill, NC: University of North Carolina Press).

Popple, K. (1995) *Analysing Community Work: Its Theory and Practice* (Buckingham: Open University Press).

Preston-Shoot, M. and Agass, D. (1990) *Making Sense of Social Work: Psychodynamics, Systems and Sense* (Basingstoke: Macmillan – now Palgrave Macmillan).

Priestley, P. and McGuire, J. (1978) *Social Skills and Personal Problem-solving* (London: Tavistock).

Priestley, P. and McGuire, J. (1983) *Learning to Help: Basic Skills Exercises* (London: Tavistock).

Pringle, K. (1995) *Men, Masculinities and Social Welfare* (London: UCL Press).

Pugh, R. (1996) *Effective Language in Health and Social Work* (London: Chapman & Hall).

Race, D. G. (2003) *Leadership and Change in Human Services: Selected Readings from Wolf Wolfensberger* (London: Routledge).

Ramcharan, P., Roberts, G., Grant, G. and Borland, J. (eds)(1997) *Empowerment in Everyday Life: Learning Disabilities* (London: Jessica Kingsley).

Ramon, S. (1989) 'The value and knowledge bases of the normalization approach: implications for social work', *International Social Work* **32**(1): 11–23.

Ramon, S. (1990) 'The relevance of symbolic interaction perspectives to the conception and practice construction of leaving a psychiatric hospital', *Social Work and Social Sciences Review* **1**(3): 163–76.

Ramon, S. (ed.) (1991) *Beyond Community Care: Normalisation and Integration Work* (Basingstoke: Macmillan – now Palgrave Macmillan).

Rapoport, L. (1970) 'Crisis intervention as a mode of brief treatment', in Roberts, R. W. and Nee, R. H. (eds) *Theories of Social Casework* (Chicago: University of Chicago Press): 265–311.

Rasmussen, B. M. and Mishna, F. (2003) 'The relevance of contemporary psychodynamic theories to teaching social work', *Smith College Studies in Social Work* **74**(1): 31–47.

Rawlinson, D. (1999) 'Group analytic ideas: extending the group matrix into TC', in Campling, P. and Haigh, R. (eds) *Therapeutic Communities: Past, Present and Future* (London: Jessica Kingsley): 50–62.

Raynor, P. (2003) 'Evidence-based probation and its critics' *Probation Journal* **50**(4): 334–45.

Raynor, P. and Vanstone, M. (1994) 'Probation practice, effectiveness and the non-treatment paradigm', *British Journal of Social Work* **24**(4): 387–404.

Raynor, P. and Vanstone, M. (1998) 'Adult probationers and the STOP programme', in Cigno, K. and Bourn, D. (eds) *Cognitive-behavioural Social Work in Practice* (Aldershot: Ashgate): 143–62.

Raynor, P., Smith, D. and Vanstone, M. (1994) *Effective Probation Practice* (Basingstoke: Macmillan – now Palgrave Macmillan).

Reamer, F. G. (1994) *The Foundations of Social Work Knowledge* (New York: Columbia University Press).

Redl, F. (1959) 'Strategy and techniques of the life space interview', *American Journal of Orthopsychiatry* **29**: 1–18.

Rees, S. (1991) *Achieving Power* (Sydney: Allen & Unwin).

Reid, W. J. (1978) *The Task-Centered System* (New York: Columbia University Press).

Reid, W. J. (1985) *Family Problem-solving* (New York: Columbia University Press).

Reid, W. J. (1992) *Task Strategies: an Empirical Approach to Clinical Social Work* (New York: Columbia University Press).

Reid, W. J. (1996) 'Task-centered social work', in Turner, F. J. (ed.) *Social Work Treatment: Interlocking Theoretical Approaches* (New York: Free Press): 617–40.

Reid, W. J. (2000) *The Task Planner* (New York: Columbia University Press).

Reid, W. J. (2001) 'The role of science in social work: the perennial debate', *Journal of Social Work* **1**(3): 273–93.

Reid, W. J. and Epstein, L. (1972a) *Task-centered Casework* (New York: Columbia University Press).

Reid, W. J. and Epstein, L. (eds) (1972b) *Task-centered Practice* (New York: Columbia University Press).

Reid, W. J. and Hanrahan, P. (1982) 'Recent evaluations of social work: grounds for optimism', *Social Work* 27: 328–40.

Reid, W. J. and Shyne, A. W. (1969) *Brief and Extended Casework* (New York: Columbia University Press).

Resnick, R. P. (1976) 'Conscientization: an indigenous approach to international social work', *International Social Work* 19(1): 21–9.

Rex, J. (1997) 'Multiculturalism in Europe and North America', in Isajiw, W. W. (ed.) *Multiculturalism in North American and Europe: Comparative Perspectives on Interethnic Relations and Social Incorporation* (Toronto: Canadian Scholars' Press): 5–33.

Rex, J. and Mason, D. (eds) (1986) *Theories of Race and Ethnic Relations* (Cambridge: Cambridge University Press).

Reynolds, J. (1993) 'Feminist theory and strategy in social work', in Walmsley, J., Reynolds, J., Shakespeare, P. and Woolfe, R. (eds) *Health Welfare and Practice: Reflecting on Roles and Relationships* (London: Sage): 74–82.

Rhodes, M. L. (1985) 'Gilligan's theory of moral development as applied to social work', *Social Work* 30(2): 101–5.

Richey, C. A. and Roffman, R. A. (1999) 'On the sidelines of guidelines: further thoughts on the fit between clinical guidelines and social work practice', *Research on Social Work Practice* 9(3): 311–21.

Righton, P. (1975) 'Planned environment therapy: a reappraisal', *Association of Workers with Maladjusted Children Journal,* Spring 1975; reprinted in Righton, P. (ed.) *Studies in Environment Therapy,* vol. 3 (Teddington: Planned Environment Therapy Trust): 9–16.

Robbins, S. P., Chatterjee, P. and Canda, E. R. (1999) 'Ideology, scientific theory and social work practice', *Families in Society* 80(4): 374–58.

Roberts, A. R. (ed.) (1995) *Crisis Intervention and Time-Limited Cognitive Treatment* (Thousand Oaks, CA: Sage).

Roberts, A. R. (ed.) (2000) *Crisis Intervention Handbook* (2nd edn) (New York: Oxford University Press).

Roberts, A. R. (2000) 'An overview of crisis theory and crisis intervention', in Roberts, A. R. (ed.) *Crisis Intervention Handbook* (2nd edn) (New York: Oxford University Press): 3–30.

Roberts, A. R. and Dziegielewski, S. P. (1995) 'Foundation skills and applications of crisis intervention and cognitive therapy', in Roberts, A. R. (ed.) *Crisis Intervention and Time-Limited Cognitive Treatment* (Thousand Oaks, CA: Sage): 3–27.

Roberts, R. (1990) *Lessons from the Past: Issues for Social Work Theory* (London: Tavistock/Routledge).

Roberts, R. W. and Nee, R. H. (eds) (1970) *Theories of Social Casework* (Chicago: University of Chicago Press).

Roberts, R. W. and Northen, H. (eds) (1976) *Theories of Social Work with Groups* (New York: Columbia University Press).

Robinson, L. (1995) *Psychology for Social Workers: Black Perspectives* (London: Routledge).

Robinson, L. (1999) 'Racial identity attitudes and interracial communication: implications for social work practice in Britain', *European Journal of Social Work* 2(3): 315–26.

Robinson, L. (2001) 'A conceptual framework for social work practice with black children and adolescents in the United Kingdom: some first steps', *Journal of Social Work* 1(2): 165–85.

Rodger, J. J. (1991) 'Discourse analysis and social relationships in social work', *British Journal of Social Work* 21(1): 63–80.

Rogers, C. R. (1951) *Client-centered Therapy: Its Current Practice, Implications and Theory* (London: Constable).

Rogers, C. R. (1961) *On Becoming a Person: a Therapist's View of Psychotherapy* (London: Constable).

Rogers, C. R. (1977) *Carl Rogers on Personal Power* (London: Constable).

Rogers, C. R. and Strauss, M. (1967) *Person to Person: the Problem of Being Human* (London: Souvenir Press).

Rojek, C. (1986) 'The "Subject" in social work.' *British Journal of Social Work* 16(1): 65–77.

Rojek, C. and Collins, S. (1987) 'Contract or con trick?', *British Journal of Social Work* 17(2): 199–211.

Rojek, C., and Collins, S. (1988) 'Contract or con trick revisited: comments on the reply by Corden and Preston-Shoot', *British Journal of Social Work* 18(6): 611–22.

Rojek, C., Peacock, G. and Collins, S. (1989) *Social Work and Received Ideas* (London: Routledge).

Ronen, T. (1994) 'Cognitive-behavioural social work with children', *British Journal of Social Work* 24(3): 273–85.

Ronen, T. (1998) 'Direct clinical work with children' in Cigno, K. and Bourn, D. (eds) *Cognitive-behavioural Social Work in Practice* (Aldershot: Ashgate): 39–59.

Ronnby, A. (1992) 'Praxiology in social work', *International Social Work* 35(3): 317–26.

Rose, M. (1992) 'The design of atmosphere: ego nurture and psychic change in residential treatment', *Residential Treatment for Children and Youth* 10(1): 5–23.

Rose, S. (1991) 'Cognitive behavioural modification in groups', *International Journal of Behavioural Social Work and Abstracts* 1(1): 27–38.

Rose, S. M. (1990) 'Advocacy/empowerment: an approach to clinical practice for social work', *Journal of Sociology and Social Welfare* 17(2): 41–52.

Rose, S. M. and Black, B. L. (1985) *Advocacy and Empowerment: Mental Health Care in the Community* (Boston: Routledge & Kegan Paul).

Rosen, A. (2003) 'Evidence-based social work practice: challenge and promise', *Social Work Research* 27(4): 197–208.

Rosen, A., Proctor, E. K. and Staudt, M. (2003) 'Targets of change and interventions in social work: an empirically based prototype for developing practice guidelines', *Research on Social Work Practice* 113(2): 208–33.

Ross, R. R., Fabiano, E. A. and Ross, R. (1989) *Reasoning and Rehabilitation: a Handbook for Teaching Cognitive Skills* (Ottawa: The Cognitive Centre).

Ross, R. R., Fabiano, E. A. and Ewles, C. D. (1988) 'Reasoning and rehabilitation', *International Journal of Offender Therapy and Comparative Criminology* 32(1): 29–35.

Rothman, J. and Zald, M. N. (1985) 'Planning theory in social work community practice', in Taylor, S. H. and Roberts, R. W. (eds) *Theory and Practice of Community Social Work* (New York: Columbia University Press): 125–53.

Rubin, A. (1985) 'Practice effectiveness: more grounds for optimism', *Social Work* 30: 469–76.

Rutter, M. (1981) *Maternal Deprivation Reassessed* (Harmondsworth: Penguin).

Ryan, A. S. (ed.) (1992) *Social Work with Immigrants and Refugees* (New York: Haworth Press).

Ryan, P. (1979) 'Residential care for the mentally disabled', in Wing, J. K. and Olsen, R. (eds) *Community Care for the Mentally Disabled* (Oxford: Oxford University Press): 60–89.

Ryant, J. C. (1969) 'The revolutionary potential of social work', *Social Worker* 37(3): 151–6.

SCIE (Social Care Institute for Excellence) (2001) *Managing Practice* (London: SCIE) http://www.elsc-bestpracticeguides.org.uk/first_line/firstline.asp.

SCIE (Social Care Institute for Excellence) (2002) *Assessing Mental Health Needs of Older People*, (London: SCIE) http://www.elsc.org.uk/knowledge_floor/bpg2/older.htm.

Saari, C. (1999) 'Intersubjectivity, language and culture: bridging the person/environment gap', *Smith College Studies in Social Work* 69(2) 221–37.

Sainsbury, E. (1987) 'Client studies: their contribution, and limitations in influencing social work practice', *British Journal of Social Work* 17(6): 633–44.

Saleebey, D. (1992) *The Strengths Perspective in Social Work Practice* (New York: Longman).

Saleebey, D. (1994) 'Culture, theory and narrative: the intersection of meanings in practice', *Social Work* 39(4): 351–59.

Saleebey, D. (1996) 'The strengths perspective in social work practice: extensions and cautions', *Social Work* 41(3): 296–305.

Saleebey, D. (ed.) (2001) *The Strengths Perspective in Social Work Practice*, 3rd edn (Boston, MA: Allyn & Bacon).

Salole, G. (1991a) 'Not seeing the wood for the trees: searching for indigenous non-government organisations in the forest of voluntary self-help associations', *Journal of Social Development in Africa* 6(1): 5–17.

Salole, G. (1991b) 'Participatory development: the taxation of the beneficiary', *Journal of Social Development in Africa* 6(2): 5–16.

Salzberger-Wittenberg, I. (1970) *Psychoanalytic Insights and Relationships: a Kleinian Approach* (London: Routledge & Kegan Paul).

Sanders, D. S. (1978) 'Multiculturalism: implications for social work', in IFSW *Social Work and the Multi-cultural Society* (Geneva: International Federation of Social Workers): 33–41.

Sanders, J. (1993) 'Culture and residential treatment', *Residential Treatment for Children and Youth* 10(3): 337–48.

Sands, R. G. (1996) 'The elusiveness of identity in social work practice with women: A postmodern feminist perspective' *Clinical Social Work Journal* 24(2): 167–86.

Sands, R. G,. and Nuccio, K. (1992) 'Postmodern feminist theory and social work', *Social Work* 37(6): 489–94.

Satir, V. (1964) *Conjoint Family Therapy* (Palo Alto, CA: Science and Behavior Books).

Satir, V. (1972) *Peoplemaking* (Palo Alto, CA: Science and Behavior Books).

Satyamurti, C. (1979) 'Care and control in local authority social work', in Parry, N., Rustin, M. and Satyamurti, C. (eds) *Social Work, Welfare and the State* (London: Edward Arnold): 89–103.

Sayer, A. (2000) *Realism and Social Science* (London: Sage).

Sayers, J. (1986) *Sexual Contradictions: Psychology, Psychoanalysis and Feminism* (London: Tavistock).

Sayers, J. (1988) 'Feminism, social work and psychoanalysis', in Pearson, G., Treseder, J. and Yelloly, M. (eds) *Social Work and the Legacy of Freud: Psychoanalysis and its Uses* (Basingstoke: Macmillan – now Palgrave Macmillan): 97–113.

Scheflen, A. E. (1972) *Body Language and Social Order* (Englewood Cliffs, NJ: Prentice-Hall).

Scheflen, A. E. and Ashcraft, N. (1976) *Human Territories: How we Behave in Space-time* (Englewood Cliffs, NJ: Prentice-Hall).

Schneider, R. L. and Lester, L. (2001) *Social Work Advocacy: A New Framework for Action* (Belmont CA: Brooks/Cole).

Schön, D. A. (1983) *The Reflective Practitioner: How Professionals Think in Action* (New York: Basic Books).

Schön, D. A. (1987) *Educating the Reflective Practitioner* (San Francisco: Jossey-Bass).

Scott, J. J., Williams, M. G. and Beck, A. T. (1989) *Cognitive Therapy in Clinical Practice: an Illustrative Casebook* (London: Routledge).

Scott, M. (1989) *A Cognitive-behavioural Approach to Clients' Problems* (London: Tavistock/Routledge).

Scott, M. J. and Dryden, W. (1996) 'The cognitive-behavioural paradigm', in Woolfe, R. and Dryden, W. (eds) *Handbook of Counselling Psychology* (London: Sage).

Scott, M. J. and Stradling, S. G. (1991) 'The cognitive-behavioural approach with depressed clients', *British Journal of Social Work* 21(5): 533–44.

Scourfield, J. B. (2002) 'Reflections on gender, knowledge and values in social work', *British Journal of Social Work* 32(1): 1–15.

Secker, J. (1993) *From Theory to Practice in Social Work: the Development of Social Work Students' Practice* (Aldershot: Avebury).

Sedgwick, P. (1972) 'R. D. Laing: self, symptom and society', in Boyers, R. and Orrill, R. (eds) *Laing and Anti-psychiatry* (Harmondsworth: Penguin): 11–47.

Seed, P. (1990) *Introducing Network Analysis in Social Work* (London: Jessica Kingsley).

Seeley, K. M. (2004) 'Short-term intercultural psychotherapy: ethnographic inquiry' *Social Work* 49(1): 121–30.

Sefansky, S. (1990) 'Pediatric critical care social work: interventions with a special plane crash survivor', *Health and Social Work* 15(3): 215–20.

Seikkula, J., Arnkil, T. E. and Eriksson, E. (2003) 'Postmodern society and social networks: open and anticipation dialogues in network meetings', *Family Process* 42(2): 185–203.

Seligman, M. E. P (1975) *Helplessness: on Depression, Development and Death* (San Francisco: Freeman).

Sellick, M. M., Delaney, R. and Brownlee, K. (2002) 'The deconstruction of professional knowledge: accountability without authority', *Families in Society* 83(5): 493–8.

Sharry, J. (2001) *Solution-Focused Groupwork* (London: Sage).

Sheldon, B. (1987) 'Implementing findings from social work effectiveness research', *British Journal of Social Work* 17(6): 573–86.

Sheldon, B. (1995) *Cognitive-behavioural Therapy: Research, Practice and Philosophy* (London: Routledge).

Sheldon, B. (1998) 'Research and theory', in Cigno, K. and Bourn, D. (eds) *Cognitive-behavioural Social Work in Practice* (Aldershot: Ashgate): 1–38.

Sheldon, B. (2000) 'Cognitive-behavioural methods in social care: a look at the evidence' in Stepney, P and Ford, D. (eds) *Social Work Models, Methods and Theories: A Framework for Practice*, (Lyme Regis: Russell House): 65–83.

Shemmings, D. and Shemmings, Y. (1995) 'Defining participative practice in health and welfare', in Jack, R. (ed.) *Empowerment in Community Care* (London: Chapman & Hall): 43–58.

Sheppard, M. and Ryan, K. (2003) 'Practitioners as rule using analysts: a further development of process knowledge in social work', *British Journal of Social Work* 33(2): 157–76.

Sheppard, M., Newstead, S., di Caccavo, A. and Ryan, K. (2000) 'Reflexivity and the development of process knowledge in social work: a classification and empirical study', *British Journal of Social Work* 30(4): 465–88.

Shera, W. and Wells, L. M. (1999) *Empowerment Practice in Social Work: Developing Richer Conceptual Foundations* (Toronto: Canadian Scholars).

Sherraden, M. S., Sloar, B. and Sherraden, M. (2002) 'Innovation in social policy: collaborative policy advocacy', *Social Work* 47(3): 209–21.

Sibeon, R. (1990) 'Comments on the structure and forms of social work knowledge', *Social Work and Social Sciences Review* 1(1): 29–44.

Simon, B. L. (1995) *The Empowerment Tradition in American Social Work: A History* (New York: Columbia University Press).

Simpkin, M. (1989) 'Radical social work: lessons for the 1990s', in Carter, P., Jeffs, T. and Smith, M. (eds) *Social Work and Social Welfare Yearbook 1, 1989* (Milton Keynes: Open University Press): 159–74.

Sinclair, E. (1988) 'The formal evidence', in National Institute for Social Work *Residential Care: a Positive Choice* (London: HMSO).

Singh, G. (1992) *Race and Social Work from 'Black Pathology' to 'Black Perspectives'* (Bradford: Race Relations Research Unit, University of Bradford).

Singh, K. (1999) *Rural Development: Principles, Policies and Management* (New Delhi: Sage).

Sinha, D. and Kao, H. S. R. (eds) (1988a) *Social Values and Development: Asian Perspectives* (New Delhi: Sage).

Sinha, D. and Kao, H. S. R. (1988b) 'Introduction: values-development congruence', in Sinha, D. and Kao, H. S. R. (eds) *Social Values and Development: Asian Perspectives* (New Delhi: Sage).

Siporin, M. (1975) *Introduction to Social Work Practice* (New York: Macmillan).

Siporin, M. (1980) 'Ecological systems theory in social work', *Journal of Sociology and Social Welfare* 7(4): 507–32.

Sivanandan, A. (1991) 'Black struggles against racism', in CD Project Steering Group *Setting the Context for Change* (London: CCETSW): 28–45.

Skeith, P. (1992) 'Liberation theology and social development', in Estes, R. J. (ed.) *Internationalizing Social Work Education: a Guide to Resources for a New Century* (Philadelphia, PA: University of Pennsylvania School of Social Work): 262–6.

Skenridge, P. and Lennie, I. (1971) 'Social work: the wolf in sheep's clothing', *Arena* 5(1).

Small, J. (1989) 'Towards a black perspective in social work: a trans-cultural exploration', in Langan, M. and Lee, P. (eds) *Radical Social Work Today* (London: Unwin Hyman): 279–91.

Smalley, R. E. (1967) *Theory for Social Work Practice* (New York: Columbia University Press).

Smid, G. and van Krieken, R. (1984) 'Notes on theory and practice in social work: a comparative view', *British Journal of Social Work* 14(1): 11–22.

Smith, C. R. (1975) 'Bereavement: the contribution of phenomenological and existential analysis to a greater understanding of the problem', *British Journal of Social Work* 5(1): 75–94.

Smith, C. R. (1982) *Social Work with the Dying and Bereaved* (Basingstoke: Macmillan – now Palgrave Macmillan).

Smith, D. (2000) 'The limits of positivism revisited', *ESRC-funded Seminar series: Theorising Social Work Research* http://www.elsc.org.uk/socialcareresource/tswr/seminar5/smith.htm.

Smith, D. (ed.) (2004) *Social Work and Evidence-Based Practice* (London: Jessica Kingsley).

Smith, L. and Jones, D. (eds) (1981) *Deprivation, Participation and Community Action* (London: Routledge & Kegan Paul).

Solomon, B. B. (1976) *Black Empowerment: Social Work in Oppressed Communities* (New York: Columbia University Press).

Solomon, B. B. (1985) 'Community social work practice in oppressed minority communities', in Taylor, S. H. and Roberts, R. W. (eds) *Theory and Practice of Community Social Work* (New York: Columbia University Press): 217–57.

Solomos, J. (2003) *Race and Racism in Britain* (3rd edn) (Basingstoke: Palgrave Macmillan).

Specht, H. (1986) 'Social support, social networks, social exchange and social work practice', *Social Service Review* 60(2): 218–40.

Specht, H. and Vickery, A. (eds) (1977) *Integrating Social Work Methods* (London: Allen & Unwin).

Spector, M. and Kitsuse, J. I. (1977) *Constructing Social Problems* (Menlo Park, CA: Cummings).

Speer, P. W. and Peterson, N. A. (2000) 'Psychometric properties of an empowerment scale: testing cognitive, emotional, and behavioral domains', *Social Work Research* 24(2): 109–118.

Spybey, T. (1992) *Social Change, Development and Dependency: Modernity, Colonialism and the Development of the West* (Cambridge: Polity).

Stanworth, R. (2004) *Recognising Spiritual Needs in People who are Dying* (Oxford: Oxford University Press).

Stenson, K. and Gould, N. (1986) 'A comment on "A framework for theory in social work" by Whittington and Holland', *Issues in Social Work Education* 6(1): 41–5.

Stepney, P. and Ford, D. (eds) (2000) *Social Work Models, Methods and Theories: A Framework for Practice* (Lyme Regis: Russell House).

Stern, D. (1985) *The Interpersonal World of the Infant: A View from Psychoanalysis and Developmental Psychology* (New York: Basic Books).

Stern, R. and Drummond, L. (1991) *The Practice of Behavioural and Cognitive Psychotherapy* (Cambridge: Cambridge University Press).

Stevenson, O. (1996) 'Old people and empowerment: the position of old people in contemporary British society', in Parsloe, P. (ed.) *Pathways to Empowerment* (Birmingham: Venture): 81–91.

Stevenson, O. and Parsloe, P. (1993) *Community Care and Empowerment* (York: Joseph Rowntree Foundation).

Stewart, A. M. (1994) *Empowering People* (London: Pitman).

Stewart, B. (2002) 'Spirituality and culture: challenges for competent practice in social care', in Nash, M. and Stewart, B. (eds) (2002) *Spirituality and Social Care: Contributing to Personal and Community Well-being* (London: Jessica Kingsley): 49–68.

Strean, H. S. (1971) 'The application of role theory to social casework', in Strean, H. S. (ed.) *Social Casework: Theories in Action* (Metuchen, NJ: Scarecrow Press): 196–227.

Strean, H. S. (1979) *Psychoanalytic Theory and Social Work Practice* (New York: Free Press).

Sundel, M. and Sundel, S. S. (2004) *Behavior Change in the Human Services: Behavioral and Cognitive Principles and Applications* (5th edn) (Thousand Oaks, CA: Sage).

Sutton, C. (1994) *Social Work, Community Work and Psychology* (London: British Psychological Society).

Swartz, S. (1995) 'Community and risk in social service work', *Journal of Progressive Human Services* 6(1): 73–92.

Taylor, C. and White, S. (2000) *Practising Reflexivity in Health and Welfare: making Knowledge* (Buckingham: Open University Press).

Taylor, C. and White, S. (2001) 'Knowledge, truth and reflexivity', *Journal of Social Work* 1(1): 37–59.

Taylor, P. (1995) 'Power and authority in social work', in Taylor, P. and Daly, C. (eds) *Gender Dilemmas in Social Work: Issues Affecting Women in the Profession* (Toronto: Canadian Scholars' Press).

Taylor, P. and Daly, C. (eds) (1995) *Gender Dilemmas in Social Work: Issues Affecting Women in the Profession* (Toronto: Canadian Scholars' Press).

Taylor, S. H. (1985) 'Community work and social work: the community liaison approach', in Taylor, S. H. and Roberts, R. W. (eds) *Theory and Practice of Community Social Work* (New York: Columbia University Press): 179–216.

Taylor, S. H. and Roberts, R. W. (eds) (1985) *Theory and Practice of Community Social Work* (New York: Columbia University Press).

Tenaw, S. (1995) *Time is for All* (Helsinki: Institute for Cooperative Studies, University of Helsinki).

Tester, F. (1994) 'In an age of ecology: limits to voluntarism and traditional theory in social work practice', in Hoff, M. and McNutt, J. (eds) *The Global Environmental Crisis: Implications for Social Work and Social Welfare* (Aldershot: Avebury): 240–57.

Thomas, A. (1992) 'Non-governmental organizations and the limits to empowerment', Wuyts, M., Mackintosh, M. and Hewitt, T. (eds) *Development Policy and Public Action* (Oxford: Oxford University Press): 117–46.

Thomas, E. J. (1968) 'Selected sociobehavioural techniques and principles: an approach to interpersonal helping', *Social Work* 13(1): 12–26.

Thomas, E. J. (1971) 'The behaviour modification model and social casework', in Strean, H. S. (ed.) *Social Casework: Theories in Action* (Metuchen, NJ: Scarecrow Press): 267–96.

Thomlison, R. J. (1984) 'Something works: evidence from practice effectiveness studies', *Social Work* 29(1): 51–7.

Thompson, N. (1992) *Existentialism and Social Work* (Aldershot: Avebury).

Thompson, N. (1993) *Anti-Discriminatory Practice* (Basingstoke: Macmillan – now Palgrave Macmillan).

Thompson, N. (1995) 'Men and anti-sexism', *British Journal of Social Work* 25(4): 459–76.

Thompson, N. (1997) *Anti-discriminatory Practice* (2nd edn) (Basingstoke: Palgrave – now Palgrave Macmillan).

Thompson, N. (2003a) *Anti-discriminatory Practice* (3rd edn) (Basingstoke: Palgrave Macmillan).

Thompson, N. (2003b) *Communication and Language: A Handbook of Theory and Practice* (Basingstoke: Palgrave Macmillan).

Thursz, D., Nusberg, C. and Prather, J. (1995) *Empowering Older People: an International Approach* (London: Cassell).

Thyer, B. A. (1987) 'Contingency analysis: toward a unified theory for social work practice', *Social Work* **32**: 150–7.

Thyer, B. A. (ed.) (1989) *Behavioral Family Therapy* (Springfield, IL: Charles C. Thomas).

Thyer, B. A. and Hudson, W. W. (1987) 'Progress in behavioral social work: an introduction', *Journal of Social Services Research* **19**(2/3/4): 1–7.

Thyer, B. A. and Kazi, M. A. F. (eds) (2004) *International Perspectives on Evidence-Based Practice in Social Work* (Birmingham: Venture).

Timms, E. (1983) 'On the relevance of informal social networks to social work intervention', *British Journal of Social Work* **13**(4): 405–16.

Tolman, R. M. and Molidor, C. E. (1994) 'A decade of social group work research: trends in methodology, theory, and program development', *Research on Social Work Practice* **4**(2):142–59.

Tolson, E. R., Reid, W. and Garvin, C. D. (1994) *Generalist Practice: A Task-Centered Approach* (New York: Columbia University Press).

Towell, D. (ed.) (1988) *An Ordinary Life in Practice* (London: King Edward's Hospital Fund for London).

Trevillion, S. (1999) *Networking and Community Partnership* (2nd edn) (Aldershot: Arena).

Truax, C. B. and Carkhuff, R. J. (1967) *Toward Effective Counseling and Psychotherapy: Training and Practice* (Chicago: Aldine).

Tubbs, S. L. and Moss, S. (2000) *Human Communication* (8th edn) (Boston: McGraw-Hill).

Tubman, J. G., Wagner, E. F., Gil, A. G. and Pate, K. N. (2002) 'Brief motivational intervention for substance-abusing delinquent adolescents: guided self-change as a social work practice innovation', *Health and Social Work* **27**(3): 208–12.

Tully, J. B. (1976) 'Personal construct theory and psychological changes related to social work training', *British Journal of Social Work* **6**(4): 480–99.

Turner, F. J. (ed.) (1986) *Social Work Treatment: Interlocking Theoretical Approaches* (3rd edn) (New York: Free Press).

Turner, F. J. (ed.) (1995) *Differential Diagnosis and Treatment in Social Work* (4th edn) (New York: Free Press).

Turner, F. J. (ed.) (1996) *Social Work Treatment: Interlocking Theoretical Approaches* (4th edn) (New York: Free Press).

Ukpong, E. A. (1990) 'A quest for self-glory or self-reliance: upgrading the benefits of community development programmes', *Journal of Social Development in Africa* **5**(2): 73–85.

UNDP (United Nations Development Programme) (1994) *Human Development Report 1994* (New York: Oxford University Press).

Valentich, M. (1996) 'Feminist theory and social work practice', in Turner, F. J. (ed.) *Social Work Treatment: Interlocking Theoretical Approaches* (4th edn) (New York: Free Press): 282–318.

van den Bergh, N. (ed.) (1995a) *Feminist Practice in the 21st Century* (Washington, DC: NASW Press).

van den Bergh, N. (1995b) 'Feminist social work practice: where have we been…where are we going?' in Van den Bergh, N. (ed.) *Feminist Practice in the 21st Century* (Washington, DC: NASW Press): xi–xxxix.

van Elst, T. (1994) 'Gender-specific social work with men and boys', in Hesser, K.-E. and Koole, W. (eds) *Social Work in the Netherlands: Current Developments* (Utrecht: SWP): 24–34.

van Wormer, K. (1999) *Social Welfare: A World View* (Belmont, CA: Wadsworth).

Vickery, A. (1974) 'A systems approach to social work intervention: its uses for work with individuals and families', *British Journal of Social Work* 4(4): 389–404.

Videka-Sherman, L. (1988) 'Meta-analysis of research on social work practice in mental health', *Social Work* 33: 325–38.

von Bertalanffy, L. (1971) *General System Theory: Foundations, Development, Application* (London: Allen Lane).

Voss, R. W., Douville, V., Soldier, A. L. and Twiss, G. (1999) 'Tribal and shamanic-based social work practice: a Lakota perspective', *Social Work* 44(3): 228–241.

Wakefield, J. C. (1996) 'Does social work need the eco-systems perspective? Part 1: is the perspective clinically useful?' *Social Service Review* 70(1): 1–31.

Walker, B. G. (1994) 'Science: feminists' scapegoat?', *Research on Social Work Practice* 4(4): 510–14.

Wallen, J. (1982) 'Listening to the unconscious in case material: Robert Langs' theory applied', *Smith College Studies in Social Work* 52(3): 203–33.

Walter, J. L. and Peller, J. E. (1992) *Becoming Solution focused in Brief Therapy* (New York: Bruner/Mozel).

Walter, U. M. (2003) 'Toward a third space: improvisation and professionalism in social work', *Families in Society* 84(3): 317–22.

Walter, U. M. and Peterson, K. J. (2002) 'Gendered differences: postmodern feminist perspectives and young women identified as "emotionally disabled"', *Families in Society* 83(5/6): 596–603.

Walton, R. G. (ed.) (1986) 'Integrating formal and informal care – the utilization of social support networks', *British Journal of Social Work* 16 (supplement).

Walton, R. G. and el Nasr, M. M. A. (1988) 'Indigenization and authentization in terms of social work in Egypt', *International Social Work* 31(2): 135–44.

Wambach, K. G., Haynes, D. T. and White, B. W. (1999) 'Practice guidelines: rapprochement or estrangement between social work practitioners and researchers', *Research on Social Work Practice* 9(3): 322–30.

Ward, L. (1980) 'The social work task in residential care', in Walton, R. and Elliott, D. (eds) *Residential Care: a Reader in Contemporary Theory and Practice* (Oxford: Pergamon).

Watson, D. (1980) *Caring for Strangers* (London: Routledge & Kegan Paul).

Webb, D. (1981) 'Themes and continuities in radical and traditional social work', *British Journal of Social Work* 11(2): 143–58.

Webb, S. A. (2001) 'Some considerations on the validity of evidence-based practice in social work', *British Journal of Social Work* 31(1): 57–79.

Webb, S. (2002) 'Evidence-based practice and decision analysis in social work', *Journal of Social Work* 2(1): 45–63.

Weber, M. (1930) *The Protestant Ethic and the Spirit of Capitalism* (London: Allen & Unwin).

Weick, A. (1981) 'Reframing the person-in-environment perspective', *Social Work* 26(2): 140–3.

Werner, H. D. (1982) *Cognitive Therapy: A Humanistic Approach* (New York: Free Press).

Werner, H. D. (1986) 'Cognitive theory', in Turner, F. J. (ed.) *Social Work Treatment: Interlocking Theoretical Approaches* (3rd edn) (New York: Free Press): 91–130.

Westcott, H. L. (1992) 'The cognitive interview – a useful tool for social workers', *British Journal of Social Work* 22(5): 519–33.

Wetherall, M. and Maybin, J. (1996) 'The distributed self: a social constructionist perspective', in Stevens, R. (ed.) *Understanding the Self* (London: Sage): 219–79.

White, M. and Epston, D. (1990) *Narrative Means to Therapeutic Ends* (New York: Norton).

White, S. (1997) 'Beyond retroduction? Hermaneutics, reflexivity and social work practice', *British Journal of Social Work* 275: 739–53.

White, S. A., Nair, K. S. and Ashcroft, J. (eds) (1994) *Participatory Communication: Working for Change and Development* (New Delhi: Sage).

White, V. (1995) 'Commonality and diversity in feminist social work', *British Journal of Social Work* **25**(2): 143–56.

Whiteley, J. (1979) 'The psychiatric hospital as a therapeutic setting', in Righton, P. (ed.) *Studies in Environment Therapy*, vol. 3 (Teddington: Planned Environment Therapy Trust): 42–58.

Whittaker, J. K. and Tracy, E. M. (1989) *Social Treatment: an Introduction to Interpersonal Helping in Social Work Practice* (New York: Aldine de Gruyter).

Whittington, C. and Holland, R. (1985) 'A framework for theory in social work', *Issues in Social Work Education* **5**(1): 25–50.

Whyte, W. F. (ed.)(1991) *Participative Action Research* (Newbury Park, CA: Sage).

Wignaraja, P. (ed.) (1993) *New Social Movements in the South: Empowering the People* (London: Zed Books).

Wilkes, R. (1981) *Social Work with Undervalued Groups* (London: Tavistock).

Wills, D. (1973) 'Planned environment therapy – what is it', in Klare, H. and Wills, D. (eds) *Studies in Environment Therapy*, vol. 2 (London: Planned Environment Therapy Trust): 9–21.

Wills, W. D. (1964) *Homer Lane: a Biography* (London: Allen & Unwin).

Wilson, A. and Beresford, P. (2000) ' "Anti-oppressive practice": emancipation or appropriation?' *British Journal of Social Work* **30**(5): 553–73.

Wilson, J. (1995a) *How to Work with Self-help Groups: Guidelines for Professionals* (Aldershot: Arena).

Wilson, J. (1995b) 'Self-help groups as a route to empowerment', in Jack, R. (ed.) *Empowerment in Community Care* (London: Chapman & Hall): 77–95.

Wilson, M. G. and Whitmore, E. (1994) 'Gender and international development praxis', *Social Development Issues* **16**(1): 55–66.

Winkels, D. (1994) 'Social work and community development work', in Hesser, K.-E. and Koole, W. (eds) *Social Work in the Netherlands: Current Developments* (Utrecht: SWP): 105–11.

Winnicott, D. W. (1964) *The Child, the Family and the Outside World* (Harmondsworth: Penguin).

Wise, S. (1995) 'Feminist ethics in practice', in Hugman, R. and Smith, D. (eds) *Ethical Issues in Social Work* (London: Routledge): 104–19.

Wodarski, J. S. and Thyer, B. A. (1998) *Handbook of Empirical Social Work Practice*, two vols (Hoboken, NJ: Wiley).

Wolf, D. B. (2003) 'The Vedic theory of clinical social work', *Indian Journal of Social Work* **64**(3): 333–49.

Wolf, D. B. and Abell, N. (2003) 'Examining the effects of meditation techniques on psychosocial functioning', *Research on Social Work Practice* **13**(1): 27–42.

Wolfensberger, W. (1972) *The Principle of Normalisation in Human Services* (Toronto: National Institute on Mental Retardation).

Wolfensberger, W. (1984) 'A reconceptualization of normalisation as social role valorization', *Mental Retardation* **34**: 22–5.

Wong, S. E., Woolsey, J. E. and Gallegos, E. (1987) 'Behavioral treatment of chronic psychiatric patients', *Journal of Social Services Research* **10**(2/3/4): 7–36.

Wood, G. G. and Middleman, R. R. (1989) *The Structural Approach to Direct Social Work Practice in Social Work* (New York: Columbia University Press).

Wood, K. M. (1971) 'The contribution of psychoanalysis and ego psychology to social work', in Strean, H. S. (ed.) *Social Casework: Theories in Action* (Metuchen, NJ: Scarecrow Press): 45–122.

Wood, K. M. (1978) 'Casework effectiveness: a new look at the research evidence', *Social Work* **23**: 437–58.

Woods, M. E. and Hollis, F. (1999) *Casework: A Psychosocial Therapy* (5th edn) (New York: MrGraw-Hill).

Wright, N. A. (1995) 'Social skills training for conduct-disordered boys in residential treatment: a promising approach', *Residential Treatment for Children and Youth* **12**(4): 15–28.

Wright, O. L. and Anderson, J. P. (1998) 'Clinical social work practice with urban African American Families' *Families in Society* 79(2): 197–205.

Yasas, F. M. and Mehta, V. (eds) (1990) *Exploring Feminist Visions: Case Studies on Social Justice Issues* (Pune: Streevani/Ishvani Kendra).

Yelaja, S. A. (1970) 'Toward a conceptualization of the social work profession in India', *Applied Social Studies* 2(1): 21–6.

Yelloly, M. A. (1980) *Social Work Theory and Psychoanalysis* (Wokingham: Van Nostrand Reinhold).

Yip, K-S (2003) 'The Grow movement in mental health in Australia, *Administration and Policy in Mental Health* 30(2): 179–87.

York, A. S. (1984) 'Towards a conceptual model of community social work', *British Journal of Social Work* 14(3): 241–55.

Young, K. P. H. (1983) *Coping in Crisis* (Hong Kong: Hong Kong University Press).

Young-Eisendrath, P. and Muramoto, S. (eds) (2002) *Awakening and Insight: Zen Buddhism and Psychotherapy* (Hove: Brunner-Routledge).

Author Index

Subject Index